Drawing and Detailing with SOLIDWORKS 2022

A Step-by-Step Project Based Approach
Utilizing 3D Solid Modeling

D1105777

David C. Planchard
CSWP & SOLIDWORKS Accredited Educator

SDC
PUBLICATIONS

Chapter 11 provides a section on the Certified
SOLIDWORKS Professional - Advanced Drawing tools
(CSWPA-DT) exam with sample exam questions and
initial and final SOLIDWORKS models. Understand the
curriculum and categories of the exam and the required
model knowledge needed to successfully take and pass
the exam.

The author developed the industry scenarios by
combining his own industry experience with the
knowledge of engineers, department managers, vendors
and manufacturers. These professionals are directly
involved with SOLIDWORKS every day.

Download all needed model files from the SDC Publications website
(https://www.sdcpublications.com/Downloads/978-1-63057-485-7)

About the Author

David Planchard is the founder of D&M Education LLC. Before starting D&M
Education, he spent over 35 years in industry and academia holding various engineering,
marketing, and teaching positions. He holds five U.S. patents. He has published and
authored numerous papers on Machine Design, Product Design, Mechanics of Materials,
and Solid Modeling. He is an active member of the SOLIDWORKS Users Group and the
American Society of Engineering Education (ASEE). David holds a BSME, MSM with
the following professional certifications: CCAI, CCNP, CSWA-SD, CSWA-S, CSWA-
AM, CSWP, CSWP-DRWT and SOLIDWORKS Accredited Educator. David is a
SOLIDWORKS Solution Partner, an Adjunct Faculty member and the SAE advisor at
Worcester Polytechnic Institute in the Mechanical Engineering department. In 2012,
David's senior Major Qualifying Project team (senior capstone) won first place in the
Mechanical Engineering department at WPI. In 2014, 2015 and 2016, David's senior
Major Qualifying Project teams won the provost award in the Mechanical Engineering
department for design excellence. In 2018, David's senior Major Qualifying Project team
(Co-advisor) won the Provost award in the Electrical and Computer Engineering
department—subject area: Electrical System Implementation of Formula SAE Racing
Platform. In 2020, he was awarded Emeritus status at Worcester Polytechnic Institute
(WPI). His ME design class achieved world recognition, featured in *Compass* published
by Dassault Systèmes, in the technical article, "Open Innovation in a Pandemic."

David Planchard is the author of the following books:

- **SOLIDWORKS® 2021 Reference Guide**, 2020, 2019, 2018, 2016, 2015, and 2014

- **Engineering Design with SOLIDWORKS® 2022**, 2021, 2020, 2019, 2018, 2017, 2016, 2015, 2014, and 2013

- **Engineering Graphics with SOLIDWORKS® 2022**, 2021, 2020, 2019, 2018, 2016, 2015, 2014, and 2013

- **SOLIDWORKS® 2022 Quick Start**, 2021, 2020, 2019, and 2018

- **SOLIDWORKS® 2022 Tutorial**, 2021, 2020, 2019, 2018, 2017, 2016, and 2014

- **Drawing and Detailing with SOLIDWORKS® 2022**, 2014, 2012, 2010, 2009, 2008, 2007, and 2006

- **Official Certified SOLIDWORKS® Professional (CSWP) Certification Guide Version 5: 2019 - 2020**, Version 4: 2015 - 2017, Version 3: 2012 - 2014, Version 2: 2012 - 2013, and Version 1: 2010 - 2010

- **Official Guide to Certified SOLIDWORKS® Associate Exams: CSWA, CSWA-SD, CSWA-S, CSWA-AM Version 5: 2019 - 2021**, Version 4: 2017 - 2019, Version 3: 2015 - 2017, Version 2: 2012 - 2015, and Version 1: 2012 -2013

Acknowledgements

Writing this book was a substantial effort that would not have been possible without the help and support of my loving family and of my professional colleagues. I would like to thank Professor John M. Sullivan Jr., Professor Jack Hall and the community of scholars at Worcester Polytechnic Institute who have enhanced my life, my knowledge and helped to shape the approach and content to this text.

The author is greatly indebted to my colleagues from Dassault Systèmes SOLIDWORKS Corporation for their help and continuous support: Mike Puckett, Avelino Rochino, Yannick Chaigneau, Terry McCabe and the SOLIDWORKS Partner team.

Thanks also to Professor Richard L. Roberts of Wentworth Institute of Technology, Professor Dennis Hance of Wright State University, Professor Jason Durfess of Eastern Washington University and Professor Aaron Schellenberg of Brigham Young University - Idaho who provided vision and invaluable suggestions.

SOLIDWORKS certification has enhanced my skills and knowledge and that of my students. Thank you to Ian Matthew Jutras (CSWE) who is a technical contributor and Stephanie Planchard, technical procedure consultant.

Contact the Author

We realize that keeping software application books current is imperative to our customers. We value the hundreds of professors, students, designers, and engineers that have provided us input to enhance the book. Please contact me directly with any comments, questions or suggestions on this book or any of our other SOLIDWORKS books at dplanchard@msn.com.

Note to Instructors

Please contact the publisher **www.sdcpublications.com** for classroom support materials (.ppt presentations, labs and more) and the Instructor's Guide with model solutions and tips that support the usage of this text in a classroom environment.

Trademarks, Disclaimer and Copyrighted Material

SOLIDWORKS®, eDrawings®, SOLIDWORKS Simulation®, SOLIDWORKS Flow Simulation, and SOLIDWORKS Sustainability are a registered trademark of Dassault Systèmes SOLIDWORKS Corporation in the United States and other countries; certain images of the models in this publication courtesy of Dassault Systèmes SOLIDWORKS Corporation.

Microsoft Windows®, Microsoft Office® and its family of products are registered trademarks of the Microsoft Corporation. Other software applications and parts described in this book are trademarks or registered trademarks of their respective owners.

The publisher and the author make no representations or warranties with respect to the accuracy or completeness of the contents of this work and specifically disclaim all warranties, including without limitation warranties of fitness for a particular purpose. No warranty may be created or extended by sales or promotional materials. Dimensions of parts are modified for illustration purposes. Every effort is made to provide an accurate text. The author and the manufacturers shall not be held liable for any parts, components, assemblies or drawings developed or designed with this book or any responsibility for inaccuracies that appear in the book. Web and company information was valid at the time of this printing.

The Y14 ASME Engineering Drawing and Related Documentation Publications utilized in this text are as follows: ASME Y14.1, ASME Y14.2M (R1998), ASME Y14.3M (R1999), ASME Y14.41, ASME Y14.5, ASME Y14.5, and ASME B4.2. Note: By permission of The American Society of Mechanical Engineers, Codes and Standards, New York, NY, USA. All rights reserved.

Additional information references the American Welding Society, AWS 2.4:2019 Standard Symbols for Welding, Braising, and Non-Destructive Examinations, Miami, Florida, USA.

References

- SOLIDWORKS Help Topics and What's New, SOLIDWORKS Corporation, 2022.
- ASME B4.2 Dimensions Preferred Metric Limits and Fits, ASME, NY[1].
- AWS 2.4: 1997 Standard Symbols for Welding, Braising and Non-Destructive Examinations, American Weld Society, Miami, Florida[4].
- Betoline, Wiebe, Miller, Fundamentals of Graphics Communication, Irwin, 1995.
- Earle, James, Engineering Design Graphics, Addison Wesley, 1999.
- Giesecke et al. Modern Graphics Communication, Prentice Hall, 1998.
- Hoelscher, Springer, Dobrovolny, Graphics for Engineers, John Wiley, 1968.
- Jensel & Helsel, Engineering Drawing and Design, Glencoe, 1990.
- Jensen, Cecil, Interpreting Engineering Drawings, Delmar-Thomson Learning, 2002.
- Lockhart & Johnson, Engineering Design Communications, Addison Wesley, 1999.
- Madsen, David et al. Engineering Drawing and Design, Delmar Thomson Learning, 2002.
- SMC Corporation, Compact Guide Cylinder Product Manual, SMC Corporation.[2]
- Emerson-EPT Corporation, Shaft Mount Reducer Product Manual, Emerson-EPT Corporation, a division of Emerson[3].
- Walker, James, Machining Fundamentals, Goodheart Wilcox, 1999.

[1] An on-line catalog of ASME Codes and Standards is available on their web site www.asme.org.

[2.] An on-line catalog of SMC parts and documents is available on their web site www.smcusa.com. Instructions to download additional SMC components are available in the Appendix.

[3.] An on-line catalog of Emerson-EPT parts and documents is available on their web site www.emerson-ept.com.

[4.] An on-line catalog of AWS Standards is available on their web site www.aws.org.

During the initial SOLIDWORKS installation, you are requested to select either the ISO or ANSI drafting standard. ISO is typically a European drafting standard and uses First Angle Projection. The book is written using the ANSI (US) overall drafting standard and Third Angle Projection for drawings.

To obtain additional CSWA exam information and to take an exam, visit https://3dexperience.virtualtester.com/#home.

To obtain additional information on the Certified SOLIDWORKS Professional - Advanced Drawing tools (CSWPA-DT) exam visit https://www.solidworks.com/certifications/drawing-tools-cswpa-dt

TABLE OF CONTENTS

Overview of Chapters

Chapter 1: History of Engineering Graphics

Provides a broad discussion of the history of
Engineering Graphics and the evolution of manual
drawing/drafting.

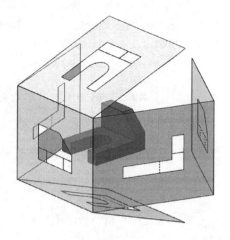

General understanding of the following: 2D hand
sketching techniques, Alphabet of lines, Precedence of
line types, Global and Local Coordinate system, 2D and
3D Cartesian Coordinate system, Terminology and
divisions of Projection, Orthographic Projection, Glass
Box, Principle views and First and Third Angle
Projection type.

Chapter 2: Isometric Projection and Multi View Drawings

Provides a general introduction into Isometric
Projection (six principle views) using Third
Angle projection and sketching along with
additional projections and arrangement of views.

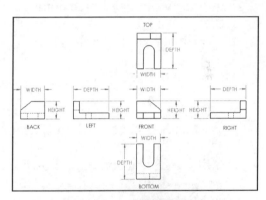

Covers freehand engineering sketching and
drawing techniques, the three main projection
divisions (Axonometric, Obliques and
Perspective), along with Boolean operation
(Union, Difference and Intersection), proper
design intent, advanced drawing views and an
introduction to the evolution from manual
drawing/drafting to early CAD systems and
finally to SOLIDWORKS.

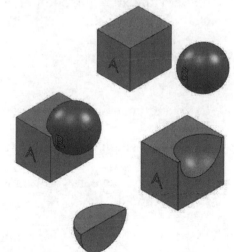

Chapter 3: Dimensioning Practices, Scales, Tolerancing and Fasteners

Provides an introduction into dimensioning systems, dimensioning units, and scales along with knowledge of the ASME Y14.5 standard.

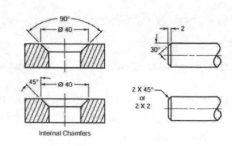

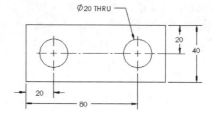

- Understand and apply the ASME Y14.5 dimensioning standard.

- Awareness of measurement units:

  o Metric system (MMGS).

  o English system (IPS).

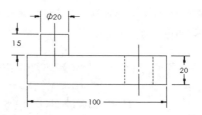

- Familiarity of dual dimensioning:

  o (Primary vs. Secondary).

- Understand Scale type:

  o Engineer's scale, Architect's scale, Linear scale, Vernier scale and Linear encoder.

- Ability to dimension the following features, objects and shapes: rectangle, Cone, Sphere, hole, cylinder, angle, point or center, arc, chamfer and more.

- Understand and apply part and drawing Tolerance.

- Read and understand Fastener notation.

- Recognize single, double and triple thread.

- Distinguish between Right-handed and Left-handed thread.

- Recognize annotations for a simple hole, Counterbore and Countersink in a drawing.

- Identify Fit type.

.

Chapter 4: Overview of SOLIDWORKS 2022 and the User Interface

SOLIDWORKS is a design software application used to create 2D and 3D sketches, 3D parts and assemblies and 2D drawings.

Introduces the user to the SOLIDWORKS Welcome dialog box, the User Interface (UI) and CommandManager: Menu bar toolbar, Menu bar menu, Drop-down menus, Context toolbars, Consolidated drop-down toolbars, System feedback icons, Confirmation Corner, Heads-up View toolbar, Document Properties and more.

Start a new SOLIDWORKS Session. Create a new part. Open an existing part and view the created features and sketches using the Rollback bar. Design the part using proper design intent.

Chapter 5: Structure of a Drawing

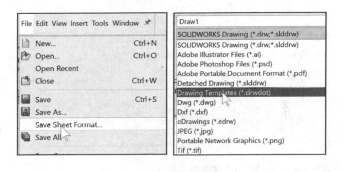

Provides an understanding of how SOLIDWORKS drawing documents and templates are created and used. It creates an awareness on the structure of a Drawing Document.

General knowledge of the ASME Y14 Engineering Drawing and Related Documentation is addressed.

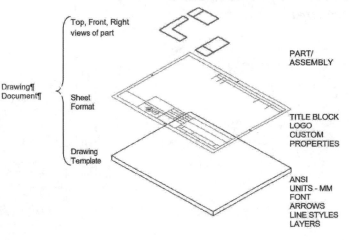

Drawing templates in this section are based on the American Society of Mechanical Engineers ASME Y14 American National Standard for Engineering Drawing and Related Documentation Practices.

Chapter 6: Drawings and Various Drawing Views

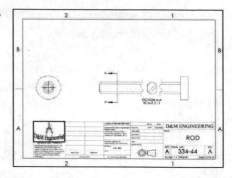

Create three drawings: ROD, TUBE, and COVERPLATE. The ROD drawing has three Sheets with Custom Properties and configurations. The ROD drawing contains: 3 Standard views, Projected view, Break view with a constant cross section, Broken view, and two Detail views. Two Detail views were combined to construct the Broken Isometric view. The Detail views were aligned with a Contruction line on a layer.

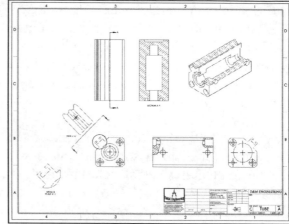

The TUBE drawing has a single Sheet with Custom Properties. The TUBE drawing contains: 3 Standard views, Projected Back view, Section view, Detail view, Auxiliary view, and a Half Section Isometric (Cut away) view.

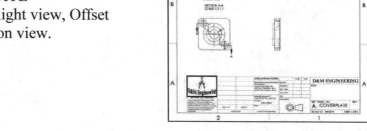

The COVERPLATE drawing has two Sheets with Custom Properties and configurations. The COVERPLATE drawing contains: Front view, Right view, Offset Section view and Aligned Section view.

Chapter 7: Fundamentals of Detailing

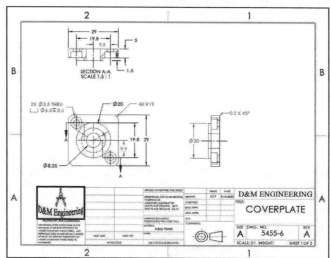

Insert and add views for the TUBE, ROD, and COVERPLATE drawings from Chapter 6.

Insert, add, and modify dimensions.

Details are the drawing
dimensions and annotations
required to document part
features. There are two types of
dimensions: Insert dimensions
and Add dimensions.

Add annotations such as: Notes,
Hole Callouts, Centerlines, and
Center Marks to the drawing
document from the Annotation
CommandManager.

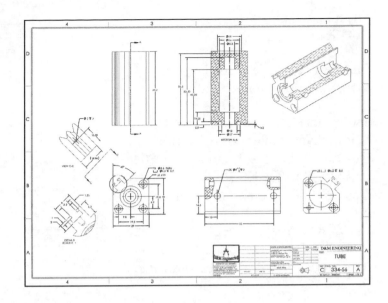

Chapter 8: Assembly Modeling - Bottom-up method

Create the CYLINDER assembly
with Custom and Linked
Properties and a Design Table.

The CYLINDER drawing
consists of multiple
configurations of the
CYLINDER assembly and a
Custom Bill of Materials.

Sheet1 contains an Exploded
Isometric view with a Bill of
Materials using equations.

Sheet2 contains two CYLINDER
configurations. The
COVERPLATE and CAP-
SCREWS are suppressed in the
Top Left Isometric view.

Custom Properties, Linked
Properties, SOLIDWORKS
Properties, and a Custom Sheet
format are used.

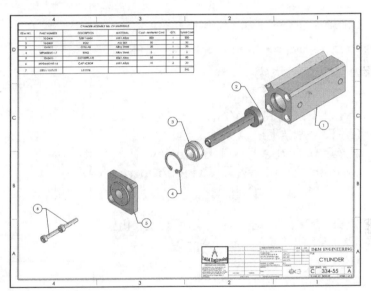

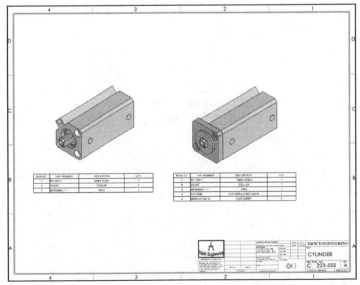

Sheet3 contains two Front views of the COVERPLATE part.

The Left Front view displays the WithNoseHoles configuration.

The Right Front view displays the WithoutNoseHoles configuration. Custom Properties, Linked Properties and SOLIDWORKS Properties and a Custom Sheet format are used.

COVERPLATE4-Sheet1 contains the Revision Table. Use a Custom Sheet format, Custom Properties and Linked Properties.

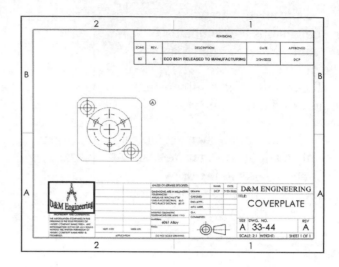

Chapter 9: Datums, Feature Control Frames, Geometric Tolerancing and other Drawing Symbols

Create four drawings: VALVEPLATE1, VALVEPLATE1-GDT, VALVEPLATE1-GDT eDrawing, PLATE-TUBE, using Custom Templates, Drawing Properties and Link Properties.

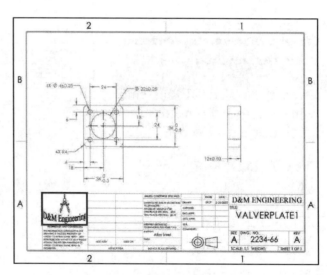

VALVEPLATE1 Drawing: Open the VALVEPLATE1 part. Apply DimXpert: Plus and Minus option. Insert dimensions and Geometric tolerances. Create the VALVEPLATE1 drawing with the View Palette tool. Insert three drawing views. Hide the Top view. Insert a Centerline and Hide Tangent Edges in the Right view. Display None and Bilateral tolerance. Use a Custom Drawing Template, Drawing Properties and Link Properties.

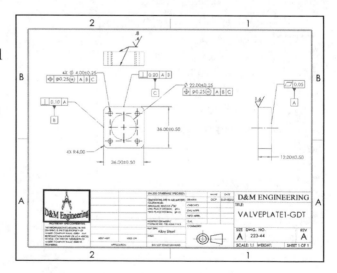

VALVEPLATE1-GDT Drawing:

Open the VALVEPLATE1-GDT part.
Apply DimXpert: Geometric option.
Apply DBM Dimensions
CommandManager tools. Insert Datums,
Feature Control Frames, and Geometric
Tolerances. Edit Feature Control Frames.
Create the VALVEPLATE1-GDT
drawing using the View Palette tool.
Insert three drawing views. Insert the
Surface Finish symbol on the Top and
Right view. Create multiple Leaders to
the Surface Finish symbol. Insert Hide
Tangent Edges in the Top and Right
view.

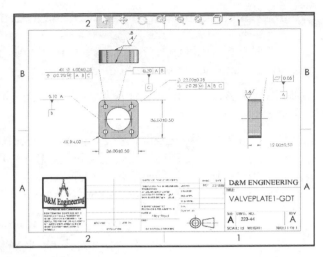

VALVEPLATE1-GDT eDrawing:

Create an eDrawing. In eDrawings®, you
can view and animate models and
drawings and create documents
convenient for sending to others. Send a
SOLIDWORKS eDrawing outside to a
machine shop for quotation. The
VALVEPLATE1-GDT eDrawing is a
compressed standalone document.

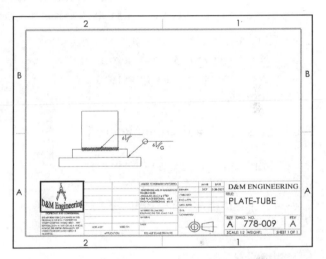

PLATE-TUBE Drawing:

Open the PLATE-TUBE assembly.
Create the PLATE-TUBE drawing. The
PLATE-TUBE drawing is a conceptual
customer drawing. The customer is
concerned about the cosmetic appearance
of a weld. Insert the Weld Bead assembly
feature between the TUBE and PLATE
parts in the PLATE-TUBE assembly. Use
a Custom Drawing Template. Insert
Custom Drawing
Properties and
Link Properties.

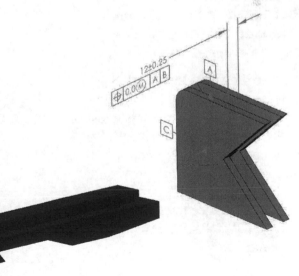

MBD: Apply
MBD (Model
Base Definition)
tools to two
parts.

Chapter 10: Introduction to the Certified SOLIDWORKS Associate (CSWA) Exam

The CSWA certification indicates a foundation in and apprentice knowledge of 3D CAD design and engineering practices and principles.

The CSWA Academic exam is provided either in a single 3 hour segment, or 2 - 90 minute segments.

Part 1 of the CSWA Academic exam is 90 minutes, minimum passing score is 80, with 6 questions. There are two questions in the Basic Part Creation and Modification category, two questions in the Intermediate Part Creation and Modification category and two questions in the Assembly Creation and Modification category.

Part 2 of the CSWA Academic exam is 90 minutes, minimum passing score is 80 with 8 questions. There are three questions on the CSWA Academic exam in the Drafting Competencies category, three questions in the Advanced Part Creation and Modification category and two questions in the Assembly Creation and Modification category.

The CSWA exam for industry is only provided in a single 3 hour segment. The exam consists of 14 questions, five categories.

All exams cover the same material.

To obtain additional CSWA exam information and to take an exam, visit https://3dexperience.virtualtester.com/#home.

Chapter 11: Certified SOLIDWORKS Professional - Advanced Drawing Tools (CSWPA-DT)

The Certified SOLIDWORKS Professional - Advanced Drawing tools (CSWPA-DT) exam is a test of one's knowledge of SOLIDWORKS Drawing functionality and tools. The completion of the exam proves that you have successfully demonstrated your ability to use the tools located in the SOLIDWORKS Drawing environment.

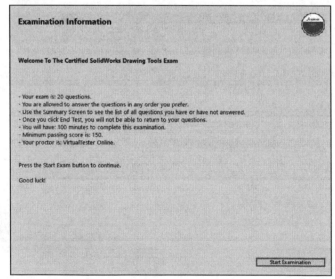

This is not a test on creating dimensioned drawings that adhere to any specific standard such as ANSI or ISO standards. There are no questions on actual dimensioning processes.

To obtain additional information on the Certified SOLIDWORKS Professional - Advanced Drawing tools (CSWPA-DT) exam visit https://www.solidworks.com/certifications/drawing-tools-cswpa-dt

About the Book

The following conventions are used throughout this book:

- The term document is used to refer to a SOLIDWORKS part, drawing, or assembly file.

- The list of items across the top of the SOLIDWORKS interface is the Menu bar menu or the Menu bar toolbar. Each item in the Menu bar has a pull-down menu. When you need to select a series of commands from these menus, the following format is used: Click **View**, **Hide/Show**, check **Origins** from the Menu bar. The Origins are displayed in the Graphics window.

- The ANSI overall drafting standard and Third Angle projection is used as the default setting in this text. IPS (inch, pound, second) and MMGS (millimeter, gram, second) unit systems are used.

- The book is organized into various chapters. Each chapter is focused on a specific subject or feature.

- Download all model files from the SDC Publications website (https://www.sdcpublications.com/Downloads/978-1-63057-485-7).

- Screen captures in the book were made using SOLIDWORKS 2022 SP1.

The book provides information on creating and storing special Part, Assembly and Drawing templates in the MY-TEMPLATES folder. The MY-TEMPLATES folder is added to the New SOLIDWORKS Document dialog box. Talk to your IT department *before you set* any new locations on a network system. The procedure in the book is designed for your personal computer.

If you do not create the MY-TEMPLATE tab or the special part, drawing, or assembly templates, use the standard SOLIDWORKS default template and apply all of the needed document properties and custom properties.

The following command syntax is used throughout the text. Commands that require you to perform an action are displayed in **Bold** text.

Format:	Convention:	Example:
Bold	• All commands actions. • Selected icon button. • Selected geometry: line, circle. • Value entries.	• Click **Options** ⚙ from the Menu bar toolbar. • Click **Corner Rectangle** ▱ from the Sketch toolbar. • Click **Sketch** ⌐ from the Context toolbar. • Select the **centerpoint**. • Enter **3.0** for Radius.
Capitalized	• Filenames. • First letter in a feature name.	• Save the **FLATBAR** assembly. • Click the **Fillet** ▱ feature.

Windows Terminology in SOLIDWORKS

The mouse buttons provide an integral role in executing SOLIDWORKS commands. The mouse buttons execute commands, select geometry, display Shortcut menus and provide information feedback.

Item:	Description:
Click	Press and release the left mouse button.
Double-click	Double press and release the left mouse button.
Click inside	Press the left mouse button. Wait a second, and then press the left mouse button inside the text box. Use this technique to modify Feature names in the FeatureManager design tree.
Drag	Point to an object, press and hold the left mouse button down. Move the mouse pointer to a new location. Release the left mouse button.
Right-click	Press and release the right mouse button. A Shortcut menu is displayed. Use the left mouse button to select a menu command.
Tool Tip	Position the mouse pointer over an Icon (button). The tool name is displayed below the mouse pointer.
Large Tool Tip	Position the mouse pointer over an Icon (button). The tool name and a description of its functionality are displayed below the mouse pointer.
Mouse pointer feedback	Position the mouse pointer over various areas of the sketch, part, assembly or drawing. The cursor provides feedback depending on the geometry.

A mouse with a center wheel provides additional functionality in SOLIDWORKS. Roll the center wheel downward to enlarge the model in the Graphics window. Hold the center wheel down. Drag the mouse in the Graphics window to rotate the model.

Visit SOLIDWORKS website: http://www.SOLIDWORKS.com/sw/support/hardware.html to view their supported operating systems and hardware requirements.

Hardware & System Requirements
Research graphics cards hardware, system requirements, and other related topics.

SolidWorks System Requirements
Hardware and system requirements for SolidWorks 3D CAD products.

Data Management System Requirements
Hardware and system requirements for SolidWorks Product Data Management (PDM) products.

SolidWorks Composer System Requirements
Hardware and system requirements for SolidWorks Composer and other 3DVIA related products.

SolidWorks Electrical System Requirements
Hardware and system requirements for SolidWorks Electrical products.

Graphics Card Drivers
Find graphics card drivers for your system to ensure system performance and stability.

Anti-Virus
The following Anti-Virus applications have been tested with SolidWorks 3D CAD products.

Hardware Benchmarks
Applications and references that can help determine hardware performance.

The book does not cover starting a SOLIDWORKS session in detail for the first time. A default SOLIDWORKS installation presents you with several options. For additional information for an Education Edition, visit the following site: http://www.SOLIDWORKS.com/sw/engineering-education-software.htm

Notes:

Notes:

Chapter 1

History of Engineering Graphics

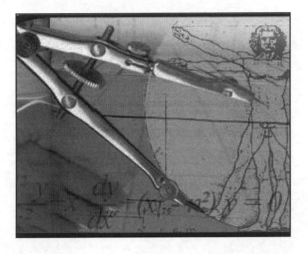
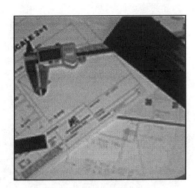

Below are the desired outcomes and usage competencies based on the completion of Chapter 1.

Desired Outcomes:	Usage Competencies:
• Appreciate the history of Engineering Graphics.	• Identify categories and disciplines related to Engineering Graphics.
• Knowledge of the Cartesian Coordinate system.	• Apply 2D and 3D Cartesian Coordinate system: Absolute, Relative, Polar, Cylindrical, and Spherical.
• Understand Geometric entities. • Comprehend Free Hand Sketches.	• Points, Circles, Arcs, Planes, etc. • Solid Primitives. • Generate basic 2D shapes and objects. • Create 2D and 3D freehand sketches.
• Recognize Alphabet of Lines and Precedence of Line types.	• Create and understand correct line precedence.
• Grasp the concept of Multi-view drawings. • Comprehend Orthographic Projection/Glass Box.	• Select the proper Front view. • Explain First and Third Angle projection type. • Identify the six Principal views.

Notes:

Chapter 1 - History of Engineering Graphics

Chapter Overview

Chapter 1 provides a broad discussion of the history of Engineering Graphics and the evolution from manual drawing/drafting along with an understanding of the Cartesian Coordinate system, Geometric entities, general sketching techniques, alphabet of lines, precedence of line types and Orthographic projection.

On the completion of this chapter, you will be able to:

- Appreciate the history of Engineering Graphics.
- Comprehend Global and Local Coordinate system.
- Understand 2D and 3D Cartesian Coordinate system:
  - o Right-handed vs. Left-handed.
  - o Absolute, Relative, Polar, Cylindrical, and Spherical.
- Understand Geometric entities:
  - o Point, Circle, Arc, Plane, etc.
- Recognize Alphabet of Lines and Precedence of Line types.
- Grasp the concept of multi-view drawings:
  - o Select the proper Front view.
- Understand the general terminology and divisions of Projection.
- Comprehend Orthographic Projection and the Glass Box method.
- Identify the six Principal views.
- Explain First and Third Angle Projection type.

History of Engineering Graphics

Engineering Graphics is the academic discipline of creating standardized technical drawings by architects, interior designers, drafters, design engineers and related professionals.

Standards and conventions for layout, sheet size, line thickness, text size, symbols, view projections, descriptive geometry, dimensioning, tolerancing, abbreviations and notation are used to create drawings that are ideally interpreted in only one way.

A technical drawing differs from a common drawing by how it is interpreted. A common drawing can hold many purposes and meanings, while a technical drawing is intended to concisely and clearly communicate all needed specifications to transform an idea into physical form for manufacturing, inspection or purchasing.

We are all aware of the amazing drawings and inventions of Leonardo da Vinci (1453-1528). It is assumed that he was the father of mechanical drafting. Leonardo was probably the greatest engineer the world has ever seen. Below are a few freehand sketches from his notebooks.

Example 1:

The first freehand sketch is of a crossbow. Note the detail and notes with the freehand sketch.

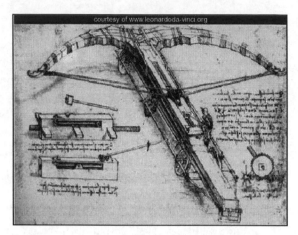

Example 2:

The second freehand sketch is of an early example of an exploded assembly view.

The only source for the detailed history of Leonardo's work is his own careful representations. His drawings were of an artist who was an inventor and a modern-day engineer. His drawings were three-dimensional (3D) and they generally were without dimensional notations.

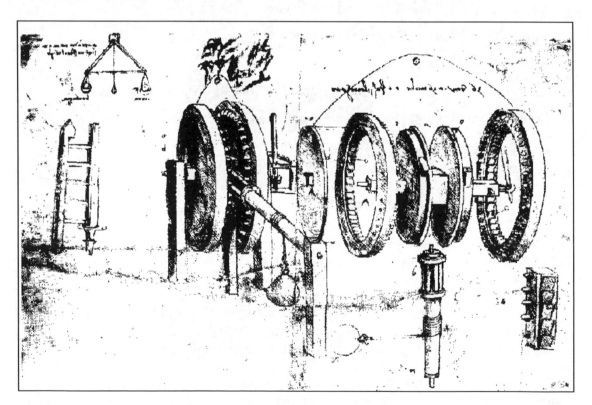

Craftsmen created objects from his drawings, and each machine or device was a one-of-a-kind creation. Assembly line manufacturing and interchangeable parts were not a concern.

Engineering graphics is a visual means to develop ideas and convey designs in a technical format for construction and manufacturing. Drafting is the systematic representation and dimensional specification and annotation of a design.

The basic mechanics of drafting is to place a piece of paper (or other material) on a smooth surface with right-angle corners and straight sides - typically a drafting table. A sliding straightedge known as a T-square is then placed on one of the sides, allowing it to be slid across the side of the table and over the surface of the paper.

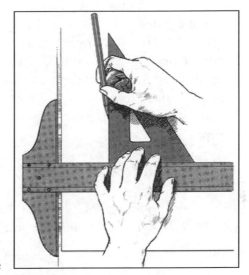

"Parallel lines" can be drawn simply by moving the T-square and running a pencil or technical pen along the T-square's edge, but more typically the T-square is used as a tool to hold other devices such as set squares or triangles. In this case, the drafter places one or more triangles of known angles on the T-square, which is itself at right angles to the edge of the table, and can then draw lines at any chosen angle to others on the page.

Modern drafting tables (which have by now largely been replaced by CAD workstations) come equipped with a parallel rule that is supported on both sides of the table to slide over a large piece of paper. Because it is secured on both sides, lines drawn along the edge are guaranteed to be parallel.

In addition, the drafter uses several tools to draw curves and circles. Primary among these are the compasses, used for drawing simple arcs and circles; the French curve, typically made out of plastic, metal, or wood composed of many different curves; and a spline, which is a rubber coated articulated metal that can be manually bent to most curves.

A drafting triangle always has one right angle 90°. This makes it possible to put a triangle against a T-square to draw vertical lines. A 30, 60, 90 triangle is used with a T-square or parallel straightedge to draw lines that are 30, 60, 90 degrees. A 45, 90 triangle is used to draw lines with a T-square or parallel straightedge that are 45 or 90 degrees.

Global and Local Coordinate System

Directional input refers by default to the Global coordinate system (X-, Y- and Z-), which is based on Plane1 with its origin located at the origin of the part or assembly.

The figure below illustrates the relationship between the Global coordinate system and Plane 1 (Front), Plane 2 (Top) and Plane 3 (Right).

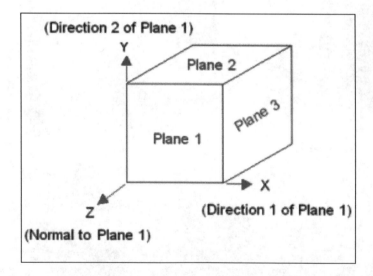

Where X- is Direction 1 of Plane 1, Y- is Direction 2 of Plane 1, and Z- is the Normal to Plane 1.

Local (Reference) coordinate systems are coordinate systems other than the Global coordinate system. You can specify restraints and loads in any desired direction. Example: Defining a force on a cylindrical face, you can apply it in the radial, circumferential, or axial directions. Similarly, if you choose a spherical face, you can choose the radial, longitude, or latitude directions. In addition, you can use reference planes and axes.

2-Dimensional Cartesian Coordinate System

A Cartesian coordinate system in two dimensions is commonly defined by two axes, at right angles to each other, forming a plane (an x,-y plane). The horizontal axis is normally labeled x, and the vertical axis is normally labeled y.

The axes are commonly defined as mutually orthogonal to each other (each at a right angle to the other). Early systems allowed "oblique" axes, that is, axes that did not meet at right angles, and such systems are occasionally used today, although mostly as theoretical exercises. All the points in a Cartesian coordinate system taken together form a so-called Cartesian plane. Equations that use the Cartesian coordinate system are called Cartesian equations.

The point of intersection, where the axes meet, is called the origin. The x and y axes define a plane that is referred to as the xy plane. Given each axis, choose a unit length, and mark off each unit along the axis, forming a grid. To specify a particular point on a two dimensional coordinate system, indicate the x unit first (abscissa), followed by the y unit (ordinate) in the form (x,-y), an ordered pair.

Example 1:

Example 1 displays an illustration of a Cartesian coordinate plane. Four points are marked and labeled with their coordinates: (2,3), (-3,1), (-1.5,-2.5) and the origin (0,0).

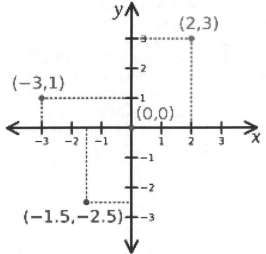

The intersection of the two axes creates four regions, called quadrants, indicated by the Roman numerals I, II, III and IV. Conventionally, the quadrants are labeled counterclockwise starting from the upper right ("northeast") quadrant.

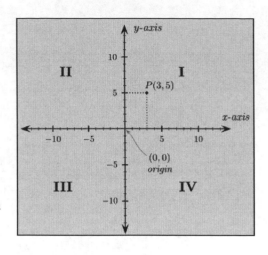

Example 2:

Example 2 displays an illustration of a Cartesian coordinate plane. Two points are marked and labeled with their coordinates: (3,5) and the origin (0,0) with four quadrants.

In the first quadrant, both coordinates are positive, in the second quadrant x-coordinates are negative and y-coordinates positive, in the third quadrant both coordinates are negative and in the fourth quadrant, x-coordinates are positive and y-coordinates negative.

3-Dimensional Cartesian Coordinate System

The three-dimensional coordinate system provides the three physical dimensions of space: height, width and length. The coordinates in a three dimensional system are of the form (x,y,z).

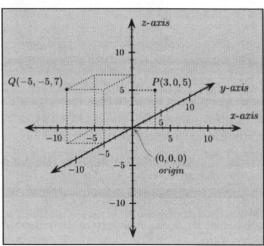

Once the x- and y-axes are specified, they determine the line along which the z-axis should lie, but there are two possible directions on this line. The two possible coordinate systems which result are called "Right-hand" and "Left-hand."

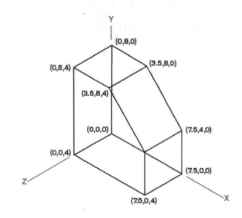

Cartesian coordinates are the foundation of analytic geometry, and provide enlightening geometric interpretations for many other branches of mathematics, such as linear algebra, complex analysis, differential geometry, multivariate calculus, group theory and more.

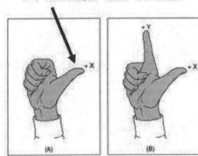

X- Always the thumb

Most CAD systems use the Right-hand rule for a coordinate system. To use the Right-hand rule - point the thumb of your right hand in the positive direction for the x axis and your index finger in the positive direction for the y axis; your remaining fingers curl in the positive direction for the z axis as illustrated.

When the x,-y plane is aligned with the screen in a CAD system, the z axis is oriented horizontally (pointing towards you). In machining and many other applications, the z-axis is considered to be the vertical axis. In all cases, the coordinate axes are mutually perpendicular and oriented according to the Right-hand or Left-hand rule.

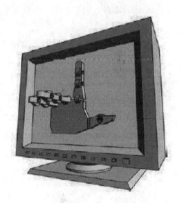

The Right-hand rule is also used to determine the direction of rotation. For rotation using the right-hand rule, point your thumb in the positive direction along the axis of rotation. Your fingers will curl in the positive direction for the rotation.

Some CAD systems use a Left-hand rule. In this case, the curl of the fingers on your left hand provides the positive direction for the z axis. In this case, when the face of your computer monitor is the x,-y plane, the positive direction for the z axis would extend into the computer monitor, not towards you.

Models and drawings created in SOLIDWORKS or a CAD system are defined and stored using sets of points in what is sometimes called World Space.

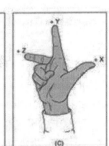

Each reference line is called a coordinate axis or just axis of the system, and the point where they meet is its origin. The coordinates can also be defined as the positions of the perpendicular projections of the point onto the two axes, expressed as a signed distance from the origin.

The origin in SOLIDWORKS is displayed in blue in the center of the Graphics window. The origin represents the intersection of the three default reference planes: *Front Plane, Top Plane,* and *Right Plane* illustrated in the FeatureManager. The positive x-axis is horizontal and points to the right of the origin in the Front view. The positive y-axis is vertical and points upward in the Front view. The FeatureManager contains a list of features, reference geometry, and settings utilized in the part.

Absolute Coordinates

Absolute coordinates are the coordinates used to store the location of points in your CAD system. These coordinates identify the location in terms of distance from the origin (0,0,0) in each of the three axis (x, y, z) directions of the Cartesian coordinate system.

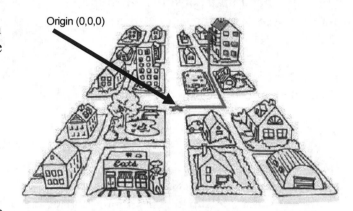

Origin (0,0,0)

As an example, someone provides directions to your house (or to a house in an area where the streets are laid out in nice rectangular blocks). A way to describe how to get to your house would be to inform the person how many blocks over and how many blocks up it is from two main streets (and how many floors up in the building, for 3D). The two main streets are like the x and y axes of the Cartesian coordinate system, with the intersection as the origin (0,0,0).

Relative Coordinates

Instead of having to specify each location from the origin (0,0,0), using relative coordinates allows you to specify a 3D location by providing the number of units from a previous location. In other words, the location is defined relative to your previous location. To understand relative coordinates, think about giving someone directions from his or her current position, not from two main streets. Use the same map as before but this time with the location of the house relative to the location of the person receiving directions.

Polar Coordinates

Polar coordinates are used to locate an object by providing an angle (from the x axis) and a distance. Polar coordinates can either be absolute, providing the angle and distance from the origin (0,0,0), or they can be relative, providing the angle and distance from the current location.

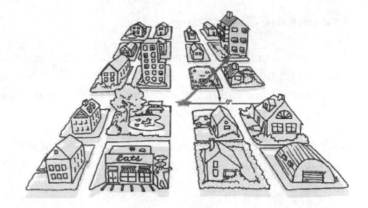

Picture the same situation of having to provide directions. You could inform the person to walk at a specified angle from the crossing of the two main streets, and how far to walk. In the illustration, it shows the angle and direction for the shortcut across the empty lot using absolute polar coordinates. Polar coordinates can also be used to provide an angle and distance relative to a starting point.

Cylindrical and Spherical Coordinates

Cylindrical and spherical coordinates are similar to polar coordinates except that you specify a 3D location instead of one on a single flat plane (such as a map). Cylindrical coordinates specify a 3D location based on a radius, angle, and distance (usually in the z axis direction). It may be helpful to think about this as giving a location as though it were on the edge of a cylinder. The radius tells how far the point is from the center (or origin); the angle is the angle from the x axis along which the point is located; and the distance gives you the height where the point is located on the cylinder. Cylindrical coordinates are similar to polar coordinates, but they add distance in the z direction.

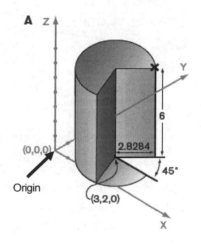

Spherical coordinates specify a 3D location by the radius, an angle from the X axis, and the angle from the x,y plane. It is helpful to think of locating a point on a sphere, where the origin of the coordinate system is at the center of the sphere. The radius gives the size of the sphere, and the first angle gives a location on the equator. The second angle gives the location from the plane of the equator to the point on the sphere in line with the location specified on the equator.

Freehand Sketching

Freehand sketching is a method of visualizing and conceptualizing your idea that allows you to communicate that idea with others. Sketches are not intended to be final engineering documents or drawings but are a step in the process from an idea or thought to final design or to production.

Two types of drawings are generally associated with the four key stages of the engineering process: (1) Freehand sketches and (2) Detailed Engineering Drawings.

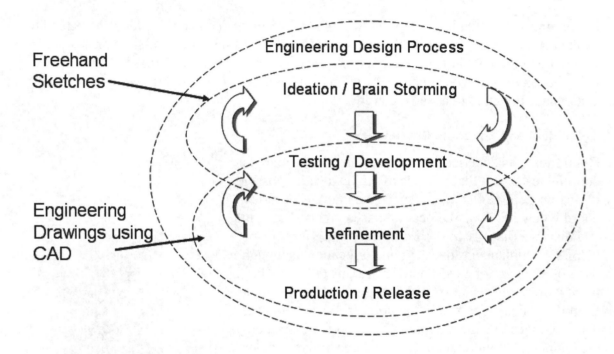

Freehand sketching is an important method to quickly document and to communicate your design ideas. Freehand sketching is a process of creating a rough, preliminary drawing to represent the main features of a design, whether it is a manufactured product, a chemical process or a structure.

Sketches take many forms and vary in level of detail. The designer or engineer determines the level of detail based on clarity and purpose of the sketch, as well as the intended audience. Sketches are important to record the fleeting thoughts associated with idea generation and brainstorming in a group.

Freehand sketching is considered one of the most powerful methods to help develop visualization skills. The ability to sketch is helpful, not only to communicate with others, but also to work out details in ideas and to identify any potential problems.

Freehand sketching requires simple tools, a pencil, piece of paper, straight edge and can be accomplished almost anywhere. Creating freehand sketches does not require artistic ability, as some may assume.

General Sketching Techniques

Understand that it takes practice to perfect your skills in any endeavor, including freehand sketching. When sketching, you need to coordinate your eyes, hands (wrist and arm), and your brain. Chances are you have had little opportunity in recent years to use these together, so your first experience with freehand sketching will be taxing. Some tips to ease the process include:

- Orient the paper in a comfortable position.

- Determine the most comfortable drawing direction, such as left to right, or drawing either toward or away from your body.

- Relax your hand, arm and body.

- Use the edge of the paper as a guide for straight lines.

- When using pencil, work from the top left to the lower right corner (if you are right-handed). This helps avoid smudging your work (your hand is resting on blank paper, rather than on your work).

- Remember that sketches are generally drawn without dimensions, since you are trying to represent the main features of your design concept.

- Use a wooden pencil with soft HB lead or a mechanical pencil in 5mm or 7mm.

Today, you may not have a T-square available, but you can still sketch in your notebook and use good sketching techniques. You should also be prepared to sketch anywhere, even on the back of a napkin.

Geometric Entities

Points

Points are geometrical constructs. Points are considered to have no width, height, or depth. Points are used to indicate locations in space. When you represent a point in a freehand sketch, the convention is to make a small cross or a bar if it is along a line, to indicate the location of the point.

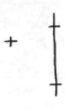

In CAD drawings, a point is located by its coordinates and usually shown with some sort of marker like a cross, circle, or other representation. Many CAD systems allow you to choose the style and size of the mark that is used to represent points. Most CAD systems offer three ways to specify a point:

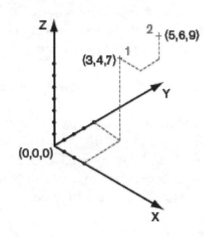

- End the coordinates for the point.

- Select a point in the Graphics window.

- Enter a point's location by its relationship to existing geometry. (Example: a centerpoint, an endpoint of a line, or an intersection of two lines).

Picking a point from the screen is a quick way to enter points when the exact location is not important, but the accuracy of the CAD database makes it impossible to enter a location accurately in this way.

Lines

A straight line is defined as the shortest distance between two points. Geometrically, a line has length, but no other dimension such as width or thickness. Lines are used in drawings to represent the edge view of a surface, the limiting element of a contoured surface, or the edge formed where two surfaces on an object join.

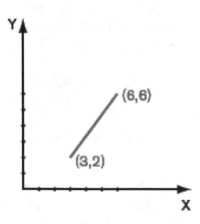

In CAD, 2D lines are typically stored by the coordinates (x,y) of their endpoints.

Planes

Planes are defined by:

- Two parallel lines.

- Three points not lying in a straight line.

- A point and a line.

- Two intersecting lines.

The last three ways to define a plane are all special cases of the more general case - three points not in a straight line. Knowing what can determine a plane can help you understand the geometry of solid objects - and use the geometry to work in CAD.

For example, a face on an object is a plane that extends between the vertices and edges of the surface. Most CAD programs allow you to align new entities with an existing plane. You can use any face on the object - whether it is normal, inclined, or oblique - to define a plane for aligning a new entity. The plane can be specified using existing geometry.

Defining planes on the object or in 3D space is an important tool for working in 3D CAD. You will learn more about specifying planes to orient a user coordinate system to make it easy to create CAD geometry later in this text.

Circles

A circle is a set of points that are equidistant from a center point. The distance from the center to one of the points is the radius. The distance across the center to any two points on opposite sides is the diameter. The circumference of a circle contains 360° of arc. In a CAD file, a circle is often stored as a center point and radius. Most CAD systems allow you to define circles by specifying:

- Center and a radius.

- Center and a diameter.

- Two points on the diameter.

- Three points on the circle.

- Radius and two entities to which the circle is tangent.

- Three entities to which the circle is tangent.

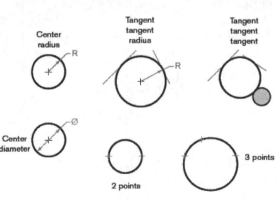

As with any points, the points defining a circle can be entered with absolute, relative, polar, cylindrical, or spherical coordinates; by picking points from the screen; or by specifying existing geometry.

Arcs

An arc is a portion of a circle. An arc can be defined by specifying:

- Center, radius, and angle measure (sometimes called the included angle or delta angle).

- Center, radius and arc length.

- Center, radius and chord length.

- Endpoints and arc length.

- Endpoints and a radius.

- Endpoints and one other point on the arc (3 points).

- Start point, Center point and a chord length.

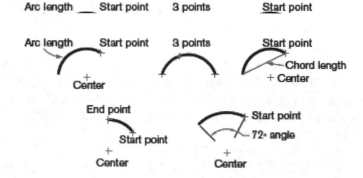

Solid Primitives

Many 3D objects can be visualized, sketched, and modeled in a CAD system by combining simple 3D shapes or primitives. Solid primitives are the building blocks for many solid objects. You should become familiar with these common primitive shapes and their geometry. The same primitives that helped you understand how to sketch objects can also help you create 3D models of them using your computer.

A common set of primitive solids that you can use to build more complex objects is illustrated: (a) box, (b) sphere, (c) cylinder, (d) cone, (e) torus, (f) wedge and (g) pyramid.

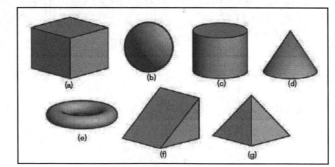

Look around and identify some solid primitives. The ability to identify primitive shapes can help you model features of the object.

Alphabet of Lines

The lines used in drafting (technical drawings) are referred to as the alphabet of lines.

Line types and conventions for technical drawings are covered in ASME Y14.2M-1992 standard. There are four distinct thicknesses of lines: *Very Thick*, *Thick*, *Medium* and *Thin*. Thick lines are drawn using soft lead, such as F or HB. Thin lines are drawn using a harder lead, such as an H or 2H.

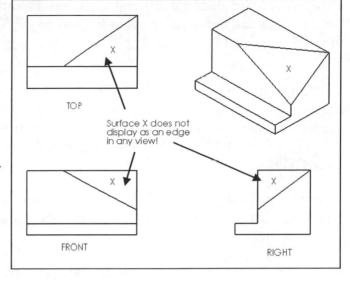

Every line on your drawing has a meaning. In other words, lines are symbols that mean a specific thing. The line type determines if the line is part of the object or conveys information about the object.

Below is a list of the most common line types and widths used in orthographic projection.

Visible lines: Visible lines (object or feature lines) are continuous lines used to represent the visible edges and contours (features) of an object. Since visible lines are the most important lines, they must stand out from all other secondary lines on the drawing. The line type is continuous and the line weight is thick (0.5 - 0.6mm).

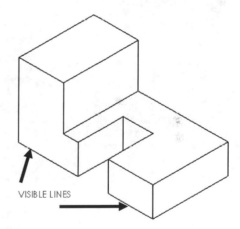

Hidden lines: Hidden lines are short-narrow dashed lines. They represent the hidden features of an object. Hidden lines should always begin and end with a dash, except when a dash would form a continuation of a visible line.

Dashes always meet at corners, and a hidden arc should start with dashes at the tangent points. When the arc is small, the length of the dash may be modified to maintain a uniform and neat appearance.

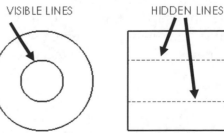

Excessive hidden lines are difficult to follow. Therefore, only lines or features that add to the clearness and the conciseness of the drawing should be displayed. Line weight is medium thick (0.35 - 0.45mm).

☀ Confusing and conflicting hidden lines should be eliminated. If hidden lines do not adequately define a part's configuration, a section should be taken that imaginarily cuts the part. Whenever possible, hidden lines are eliminated from the sectioned portion of a drawing. In SOLIDWORKS, to hide a line, right click the line in a drawing view, and click Hide.

Dimension lines: Dimension lines are thin lines used to show the extent and the direction of dimensions. Space for a single line of numerals is provided by a break in the dimension line.

If possible, dimension lines are aligned and grouped for uniform appearance and ease of reading. For example, parallel dimension lines should be spaced not less than (6mm) apart, and no dimension line should be closer than (10mm) to the outline of an object feature [(12mm) is the preferred distance].

All dimension lines terminate with an arrowhead on mechanical engineering drawings, a slash or a dot in architecture drawings. The preferred ending is the arrowhead to an edge or a dot to a face. Line weight is thin (0.3mm).

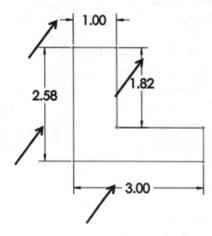

Extension lines: Extension lines are used to indicate the termination of a dimension. An extension line must not touch the feature from which it extends, but should start approximately (2 - 3mm) from the feature being dimensioned and extended the same amount beyond the arrow side of the last dimension line.

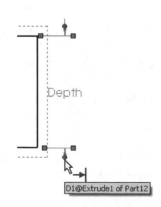

In SOLIDWORKS, use the control points to create the needed extension line gap of ~1.5 - 2.5mm.

In SOLIDWORKS, inserted dimensions in the drawing are displayed in gray. Imported dimensions from the part are displayed in black.

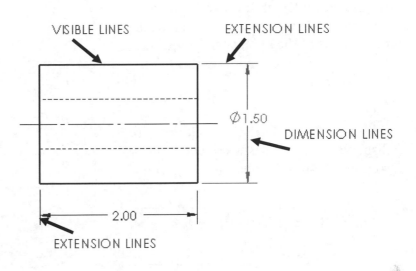

When extension lines cross other extension lines, dimension lines, leader lines, or object lines, they are usually not broken. When extension lines cross dimension lines close to an arrowhead, breaking the extension line is recommended for clarity. Line weight is thin (0.3mm).

Leader lines: A leader line is a continuous straight line that extends at an angle from a note, a dimension, or other reference to a feature. An arrowhead touches the feature at that end of the leader. At the note end, a horizontal bar (6mm) long terminates the leader approximately (3mm) away from mid-height of the note's lettering, either at the beginning or end of the first line.

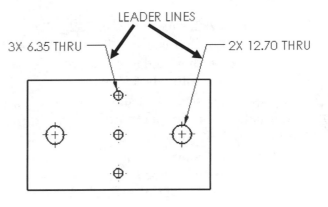

Leaders should not be bent to underline the note or dimension. Unless unavoidable, leaders should not be bent in any way except to form the horizontal terminating bar at the note end of the leader.

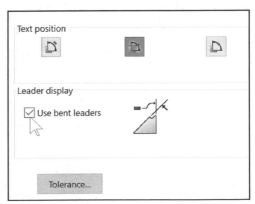

In SOLIDWORKS, use the dimension option to control Leader display.

Leaders usually do not cross. Leaders or extension lines may cross an outline of a part or extension lines if necessary, but they usually remain continuous and unbroken at the point of intersection. When a leader is directed to a circle or a circular arc, its direction should be radial. Line weight is thin (0.3mm).

Break lines: Break lines are applied to represent an imaginary cut in an object, so the interior of the object can be viewed or fitted to the sheet. Line weight is thick (0.5 - 0.6mm).

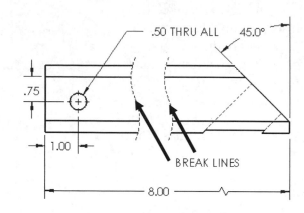

In SOLIDWORKS, Break lines are displayed as short dashes or continuous solid lines, straight, curved or zig zag.

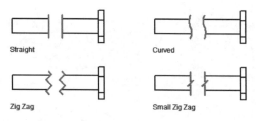

Centerlines: Centerlines are thin, long and short dashes, alternately and evenly spaced, with long dashes placed at each end of the line. The long dash is dependent on the size of the drawing and normally varies in length from (20mm to 50mm). Short dashes, depending on the length of the required centerline, should be approximately (1.5 to 3.0mm). Very short centerlines may be unbroken with dashes at both ends.

Centerlines are used to represent the axes of symmetrical parts of features, bolt circles, paths of motion, and pitch circles.

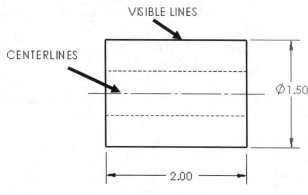

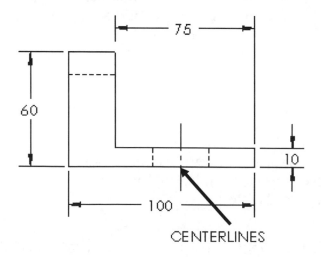

They should extend about (3mm) beyond the
outline of symmetry, unless they are used as
extension lines for dimensioning. Every circle,
and some arcs, should have two centerlines
that intersect at the center of the short dashes.
Line weight is thin (0.3mm).

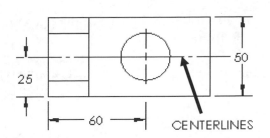

Phantom lines: Phantom lines consist of
medium - thin, long and short dashes.

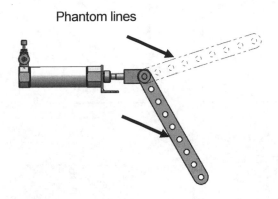

They are used to represent alternate positions of moving parts, adjacent positions of
related parts, and repeated details. They are also used to show the cast, or the rough
shape, of a part before machining. The line starts and ends with the long dash of (15mm)
with about (1.5mm) space between the long and short dashes. Line weight is usually
(0.45mm).

Section lines: Section lines are thin, uniformly spaced lines that indicate the exposed
cut surfaces of an object in a sectional view.

Spacing should be approximately (3mm) and at
an angle of 45°. The section pattern is
determined by the material being "cut" or
sectioned. Section lines are commonly referred
to as "cross-hatching." Line weight is thin
(0.3mm). Multiple parts in an assembly use
different section angles for clarity.

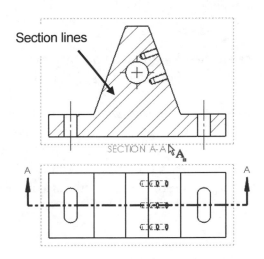

In this text, you will concentrate on creating 3D
models using SOLIDWORKS. Three-
dimensional modeling is an integral part of the
design, manufacturing and construction industry
and contributes to increased productivity in all
aspects of a project.

Section lines can serve the purpose of identifying the kind of material the part is made from.

Below are a few common section line types for various materials:

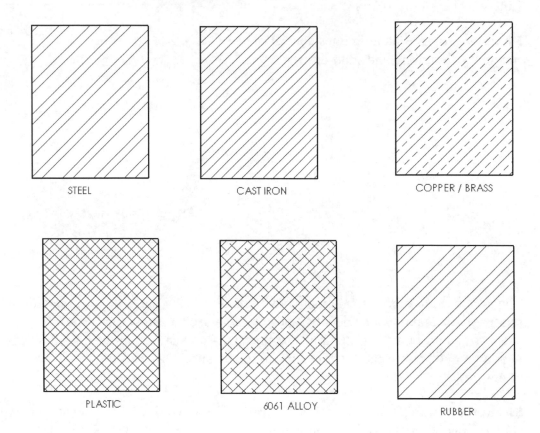

STEEL   CAST IRON   COPPER / BRASS

PLASTIC   6061 ALLOY   RUBBER

A Section lined area is always completely bounded by a visible outline.

Cutting Plane lines: Cutting Plane lines show where an imaginary cut has been made through an object in order to view and understand the interior features. Line type is phantom. Line weight is very thick (0.6 - 0.8mm).

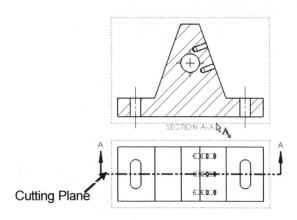

SECTION A-A

Cutting Plane

Arrows are located at the ends of the cutting plane line and the direction indicates the line of sight into the object.

Line weight (also called hierarchy) refers to thickness.

In hand drafting, the contrast in lines should be in the line weight and not in the density. All lines are of equal density except for Construction lines - Light Thin so they can be erased. Construction lines are drawn using 4H or 6H lead.

Precedence of Line Types

When creating Orthographic views, it is common for one line type to overlap another line type. When this occurs, drawing conventions have established an order of precedence. For example - perhaps a visible line type belongs in the same location as a hidden line type; since the visible features of a part (object lines) are represented by thick solid lines, they take precedence over all other lines.

If a centerline and cutting plane coincides, the more important one should take precedence. Normally the cutting plane line, drawn with a thicker weight, will take precedence.

The following list gives the preferred precedence of lines on your drawing:

1. **Visible (Object/Feature) Lines**.

2. **Hidden Lines**.

3. **Cutting Plane Lines**.

4. **Centerlines**.

5. **Phantom lines**.

6. **Break Lines**.

7. **Dimension Lines**.

8. **Extension Lines/Lead Lines**.

9. **Section Lines/Crosshatch Lines**.

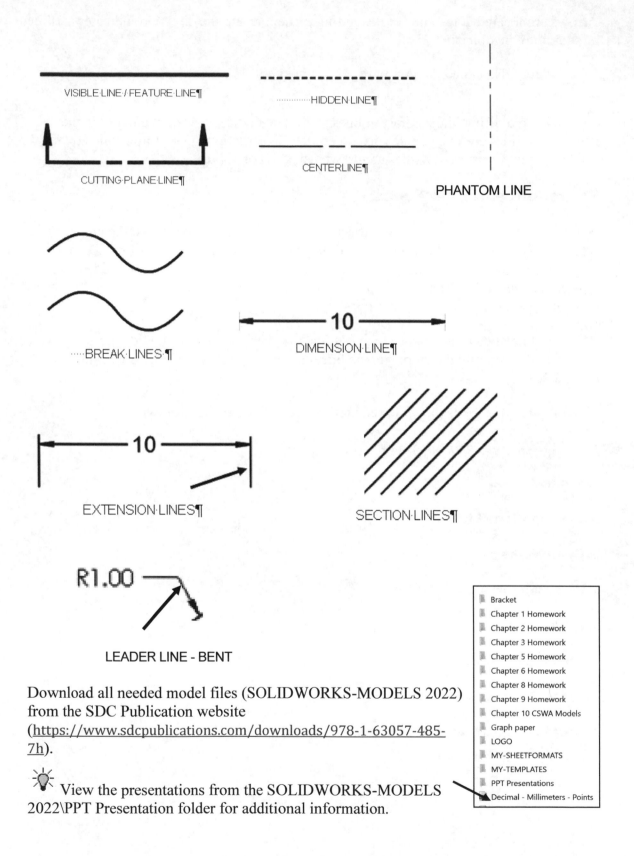

Download all needed model files (SOLIDWORKS-MODELS 2022) from the SDC Publication website (https://www.sdcpublications.com/downloads/978-1-63057-485-7h).

View the presentations from the SOLIDWORKS-MODELS 2022\PPT Presentation folder for additional information.

Alphabet of Lines Exercises:

Identify the correct line types:

Exercise 1:

Identify the number of line types and the type of lines in the below view.

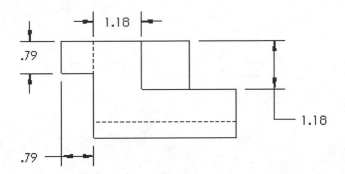

Number of Line Types:_____

Types of Lines: _____

_____

Exercise 2:

Identify the number of line types and the type of lines in the below view.

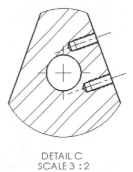

DETAIL C
SCALE 3 : 2

Number of Line Types:_____

Types of Lines: _____

_____

Exercise 3:

Identify the number of line types and the type of lines in the below view.

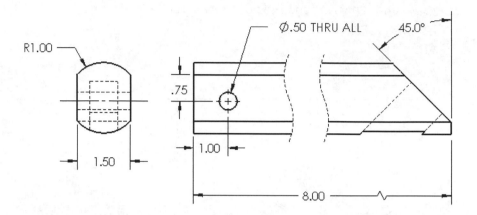

Number of Line Types:_____

Types of Lines: _____

_____

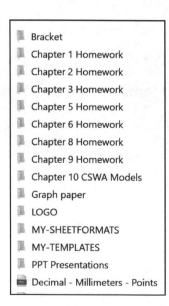 View the presentations from the SOLIDWORKS-MODELS 2022\PPT Presentation folder for additional information.

Projections in General

To better understand the theory of projection, one must first become familiar with the general terminology and divisions of Projections as illustrated in the below figure.

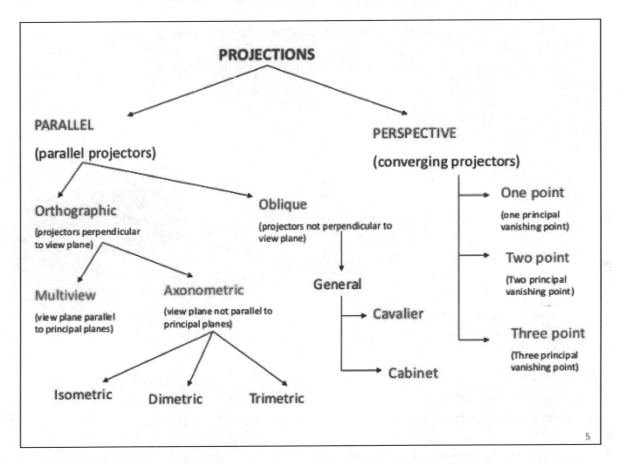

Projection from 3D to 2D is defined by straight Projection rays (projectors) emanating from the center of projection, passing through each point of the object and intersecting the projection plane to form a projection.

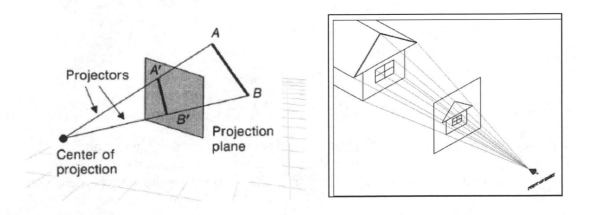

To better understand the theory of projection, you need to become familiar with the elements that are common to the principles of projection.

The point of sight is the position of the observer in relation to the object and the plane of projection. It's from this point that the view of the object is taken.

The observer views the features of the object through an imaginary plane of projection. Imagine yourself standing in front of a glass window (Projection plane) looking outward; the image of a house at a distance is sketched onto the glass which is a 2D view of a 3D house.

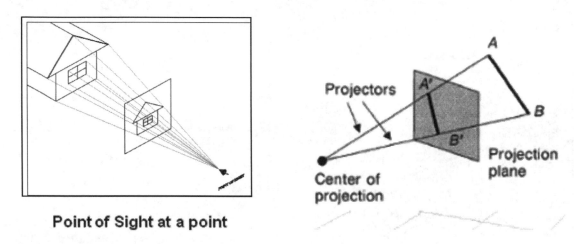

Point of Sight at a point

The lines connecting from the point of sight to the 3D object are called the projection lines or projectors. The projectors are connected at the point of sight, and the projected 2D image is smaller than the actual size (foreshortening) of the 3D object.

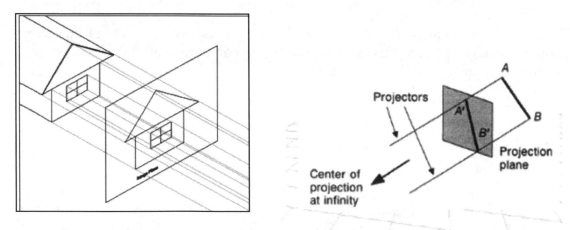

If the projectors are parallel to each other (no foreshortening) and the image plane is also perpendicular (normal) to the projectors, the result is what is known as an orthographic projection. The term orthographic is derived from the word *orthos* meaning perpendicular or 90°.

Projection Types

Parallel Projection

- It preserves relative proportion of object.

- Less realistic view because of not foreshortening.

- However, parallel lines remain parallel.

Perspective Projection

- Visual effect is similar to human visual system.

- Has perspective foreshortening.

- Projectors are rays (non-parallel).

- Vanishing points.

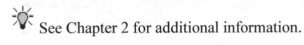 See Chapter 2 for additional information.

There are two types of Parallel projections: Orthographic and Oblique.

Orthographic Projection

- When the projection is perpendicular to the view.

- Direction of projection = normal to the project plane.

- Projection is perpendicular to the view plane.

Oblique Projection

- When the projection is not perpendicular to the view plane.

- Direction of projection is not normal to the Projection plane.

- Not perpendicular.

Multi-view Projections

Multi-view drawings are based on parallel projection techniques and are used when there is a need to represent the features of an object more accurately than is possible with a single view. A multi-view drawing is a collection of flat 2D drawings that work together to provide an accurate representation of the overall model.

With a pictorial drawing, all three dimensions (**height**, **width**, and **depth**) of the object are represented in a single view. The disadvantage of this approach is that not all the features in all three dimensions can be illustrated with optimal clarity.

In a multi-view projection, however, each view concentrates on only two dimensions of the object, so particular features can be shown with a minimum of distortion. Enough views should be created to capture all the important features of the model.

A multi-view drawing should have the minimum number of views necessary to describe an object completely. Normally, three views are all that are needed; however, the three views chosen must be the most descriptive ones. The most descriptive views are those that reveal the most information about the features, with the fewest features hidden from view.

Orient and Select the Front View

When creating a multi-view drawing of a design, the selection and orientation of the front view is an important first step. The front view is chosen as the *most descriptive* of the object or model. It should be *positioned in a natural orientation* based on its function. For example, for an automobile, the normal or operation position is on its wheels rather than on its roof or bumper.

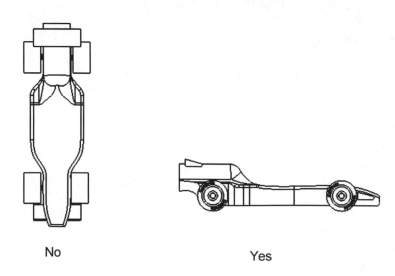

No   Yes

Orthographic Projection (Third Angle)

Before an object is drawn or created, it is examined to determine which views will best furnish the information required to manufacture the object. The surface, which is to be displayed as the observer looks at the object, is called the Front view.

To obtain the front view of an object, turn the object (either physically or mentally) so that the front of the object is all you see. The top and right-side views can be obtained in a similar fashion.

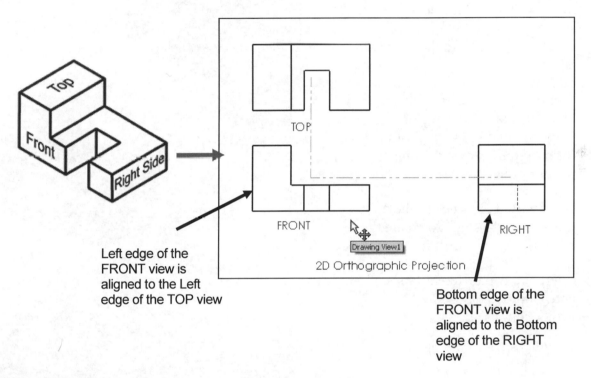

Left edge of the FRONT view is aligned to the Left edge of the TOP view

Bottom edge of the FRONT view is aligned to the Bottom edge of the RIGHT view

Orthographic projection is a common method of representing three-dimensional objects, usually by three two-dimensional drawings, in which each of the objects is viewed along parallel lines that are perpendicular to the plane of the drawing as illustrated. These lines remain parallel to the projection plane and are not convergent.

Orthographic projection provides the ability to represent the shape of an object using two or more views. These views together with dimensions and annotations are sufficient to manufacture the part.

The six principal views of an orthographic projection are illustrated. Each view is created by looking directly at the object in the indicated direction.

Glass Box and Six Principal Orthographic Views

The Glass box method is a traditional method of placing an object in an imaginary glass box to view the six principal views.

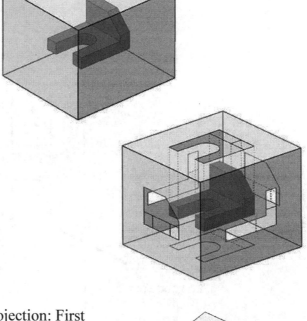

Imagine that the object you are going to draw is placed inside a glass box, so that the large flat surfaces of the object are parallel to the walls of the box.

From each point on the object, imagine a ray, or projector, perpendicular to the wall of the box forming the view of the object on that wall or projection plane.

Then unfold the sides of the imaginary glass box to create the orthographic projection of the object.

There are two different types of Angle Projection: First and Third Angle Projection.

- First Angle Projection is used in Europe and Asia.

- Third Angle Projection is used in the United States.

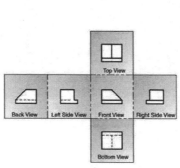

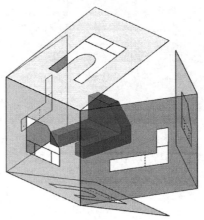

These six views are known as the **six principal views**. In performing orthographic projection, each of 2D views shows only two of the three dimensions (**height**, **width**, and **depth**) of the 3D object.

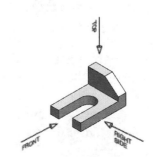

Third Angle Projection is used in the book. Imagine that the walls of the box are hinged and unfold the views outward around the front view. This will provide you with the standard arrangement of views.

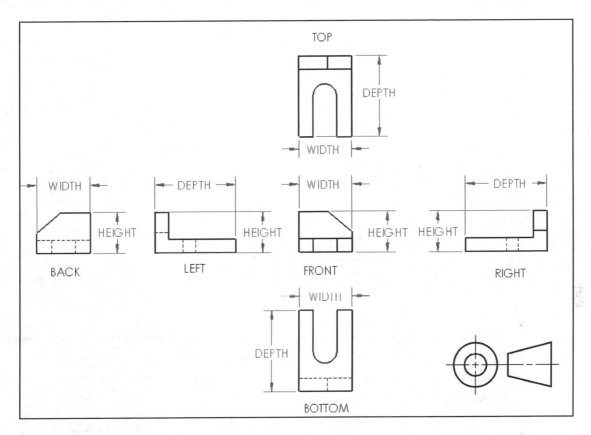

SOLIDWORKS uses BACK view vs. REAR view.

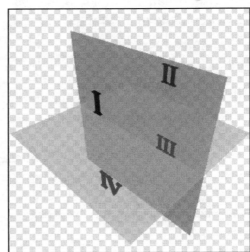

Modern orthographic projection is derived from Gaspard Monge's descriptive geometry. Monge defined a reference system of two viewing planes, horizontal H ("ground") and vertical V ("backdrop"). These two planes intersect to partition 3D space into four quadrants. In Third-Angle projection, the object is conceptually located in quadrant III.

Both First Angle and Third Angle projections result in the same six views; the difference between them is the arrangement of these views around the box.

Below is an illustration of First Angle Projection.

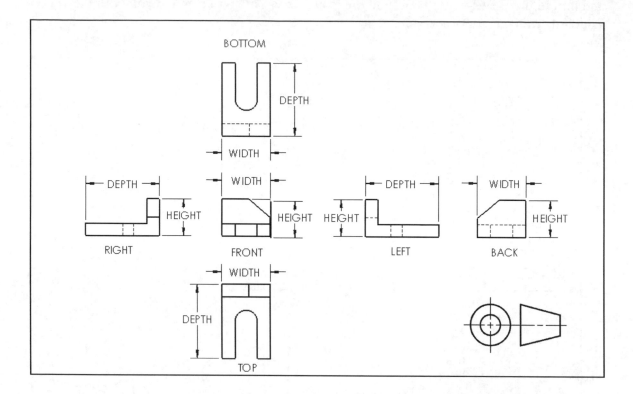

In First Angle projection, the object is conceptually located in quadrant I; i.e., it floats above and before the viewing planes, the planes are opaque, and each view is pushed through the object onto the plane furthest from it.

Both First Angle and Third Angle projections result in the same six principal views; the difference between them is the arrangement of the principal views around the box.

💡 In SOLIDWORKS, when you create a new part or assembly, the three default Planes (Front, Right and Top) are aligned with specific views. The Plane you select for the Base sketch determines the orientation of the part or assembly.

💡 https://www.youtube.com/watch?v=yGjVnXgUpQM. Great link for First vs Third angle project.

Height, Width, and Depth Dimensions

The terms height, width and depth refer to specific dimensions or part sizes. ANSI designations for these dimensions are illustrated above. Height is the vertical distance between two or more lines or surfaces (features) which are in horizontal planes. Width refers to the horizontal distance between surfaces in profile planes. In the machine shop, the terms length and width are used interchangeably. Depth is the horizontal (front to back) distance between two features in frontal planes. Depth is often identified in the shop as the thickness of a part or feature.

No orthographic view can show height, width and depth in the same view. Each view only depicts two dimensions. Therefore, a minimum of two projections or views are required to display all three dimensions of an object. Typically, most orthographic drawings use three standard views to accurately depict the object unless additional views are needed for clarity.

The Top and Front views are aligned vertically and share the same width dimension. The Front and Right side views are aligned horizontally and share the same height dimension.

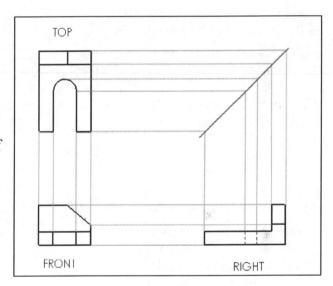

When drawing orthographic projections, spacing is usually equal between each of the views. The Front, Top and Right views are most frequently used to depict orthographic projection.

The Front view should show the **most features** or characteristics of the object. It usually contains the least number of hidden lines. All other views are based (projected) on the orientation chosen for the front view.

Transferring Dimensions

In SOLIDWORKS, you can view the projection lines from the Front view placement.

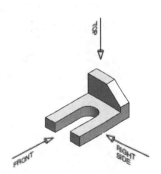

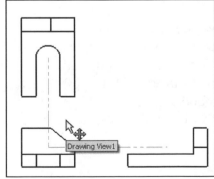

When transferring measurements between views, the width dimension can be projected from the Front view upward to the Top view or vice versa and the height dimension can be projected directly across from the Front view to the Right view.

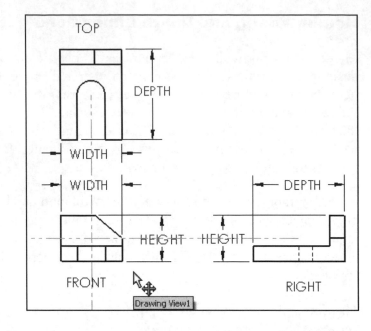

Depth dimensions are transferred from the Top view to the Right view or vice versa.

Height dimensions can be easily projected between two views using the grid-on-grid paper. Note: the grid is not displayed in the illustration to provide improved line and picture quality.

The miter line drawn at 45° is used to transfer depth dimensions between the Top and Right view.

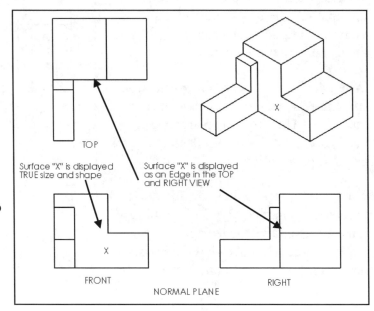

When constructing an Orthographic projection, you need to include enough views to completely describe the true shape of the part. You will address this later in the book.

Sheet Media

Media are the surfaces upon which an engineer communicates graphical information. The American National Standards Institute (ANSI) has established standard sheet sizes and title blocks for the media used for technical drawings.

ANSI Standard Sheet Sizes:

Metric (mm)	US Standard	Architectural
A4 210 x 297	A-Size 8.5" x 11"	9" x 12"
A3 297 x 420	B-Size 11" x 17"	12" x 18"
A2 420 x 594	C-Size 17" x 22"	18" x 24"
A1 594 x 841	D-Size 22" x 34"	24" x 36"
A0 841 x 1189	E-Size 34" x 44"	36" x 48"

Orthographic Projection Exercises:
Exercise 1:

Label the four remaining Principal views with the appropriate view name. Identify the Angle of Projection type.

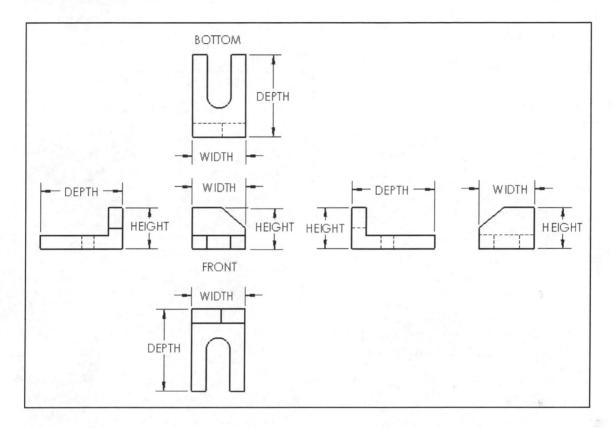

Angle of Projection type:_____

Describe the difference between the BOTTOM view and the TOP view._____

Describe the difference between the RIGHT view and the LEFT view._____

Which view should have the least amount of Hidden Lines?_____

🔆 https://www.youtube.com/watch?v=Zptb2epQoEc. Great link for going from Isometric projecting to a three-view drawing.

Exercise 2:

Identify the number of views required to completely describe the illustrated box.

1.) One view

2.) Two views

3.) Three views

4.) Four views

5.) More than four views

Explain
Why._____

_____

_____

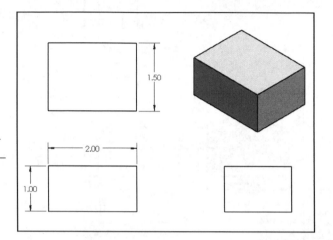

Exercise 3:

Identify the number of views required to completely describe the illustrated sphere.

1.) One view

2.) Two views

3.) Three views

4.) Four views

5.) More than four views

Explain
Why._____

_____

_____

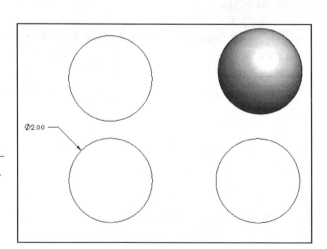

Exercise 4:

In Third Angle Projection, identify the view that **should** display the most information about the illustrated model.

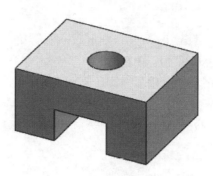

1.) FRONT view

2.) TOP view

3.) BOTTOM view

4.) RIGHT view

Explain
Why._____

_____

Exercise 5:

Third Angle Projection is displayed. Draw the Visible Feature Lines of the TOP view for the model. Fill in the missing lines in the FRONT view, RIGHT view and TOP view.

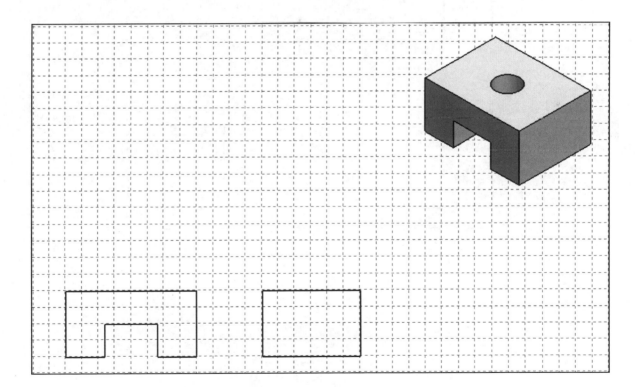

Exercise 6:

Third Angle Projection is displayed. Fill in the
missing lines in the FRONT view, RIGHT view, and
TOP view.

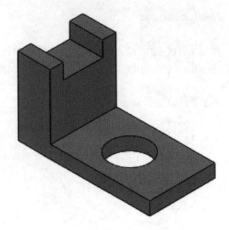

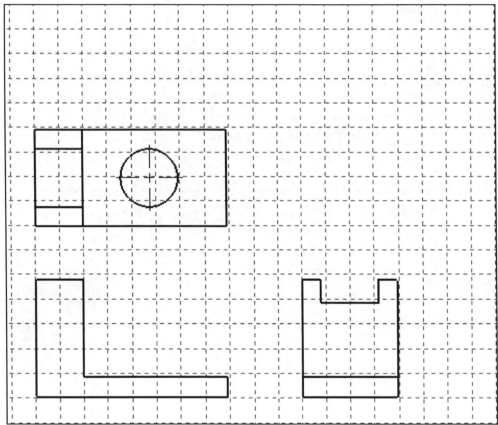

Exercise 7:

Third Angle Projection is displayed. Fill in the missing lines in the FRONT view, RIGHT view, and TOP view.

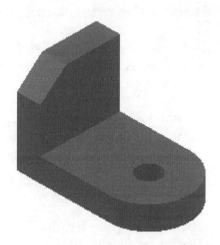

Tangent Edges are displayed for educational purposes.

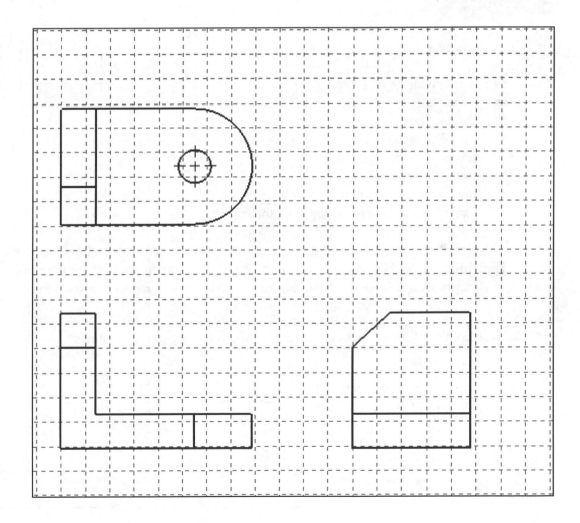

Planes (Normal, Inclined and Oblique)

Each type of plane (Normal, Inclined and Oblique) has unique characteristics when viewed in orthographic projection. To understand the three basic planes, each is illustrated.

Normal planes appear as an edge in two views and true sized in the remaining view when using three views such as the Front, Top, and Right side views.

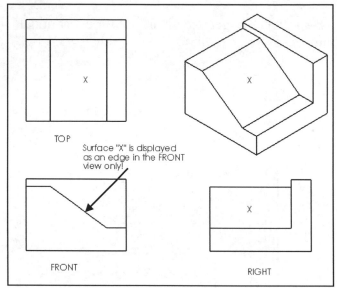

When viewing the six possible views in an orthographic projection, a normal plane appears as an edge in four views and a true sized plane in the other two views.

Inclined Planes appear as an edge view in one of the three views as illustrated. The inclined plane is displayed as a rectangular surface in the other two views. Note: The two rectangular surfaces appear "normal"; they are foreshortened and do not display the true size or shape of the object.

Oblique Planes do not display as an edge view in any of the six principal orthographic views. They are not parallel or perpendicular to the projection planes. Oblique planes are displayed as a plane and have the same number of corners in each of the six views.

In SOLIDWORKS, you can create a 2D sketch on any plane or face.

When you create a new part or assembly, the three default Planes (Front, Right and Top) are aligned with specific views. The Plane you select for the Base sketch determines the orientation of the part or assembly in the document.

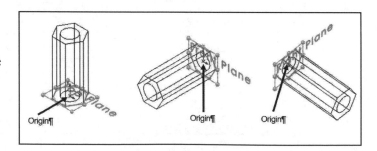

Plane Exercises:
Exercise 1:

Identify the surfaces with the appropriate letter that
will appear in the FRONT view, TOP view and
RIGHT view.

FRONT view surfaces:_____

TOP view surfaces:_____

RIGHT view surfaces:_____

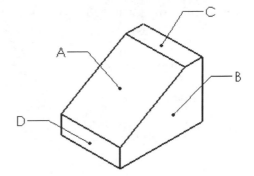

Exercise 2:

Estimate the size; draw the FRONT view, TOP view, and RIGHT view of the illustrated
part in Exercise 1 on graph paper.

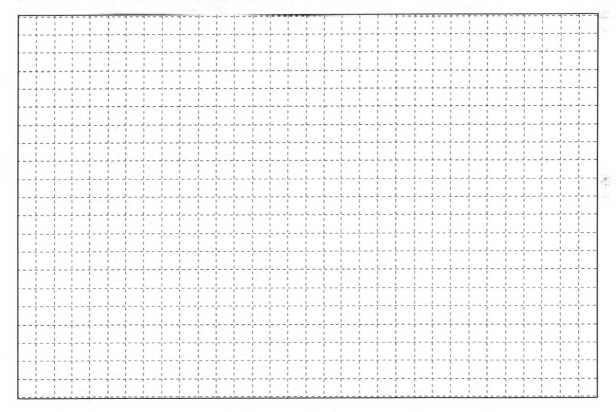

Exercise 3:

Identify the surfaces with the appropriate letter
that would appear in the FRONT view, TOP view,
and RIGHT view.

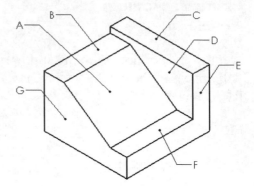

FRONT view surfaces:_____

TOP view surfaces:_____

RIGHT view surfaces:_____

Exercise 4:

Estimate the size; draw the FRONT view, TOP view, and RIGHT view of the illustrated
part in Exercise 3 on graph paper.

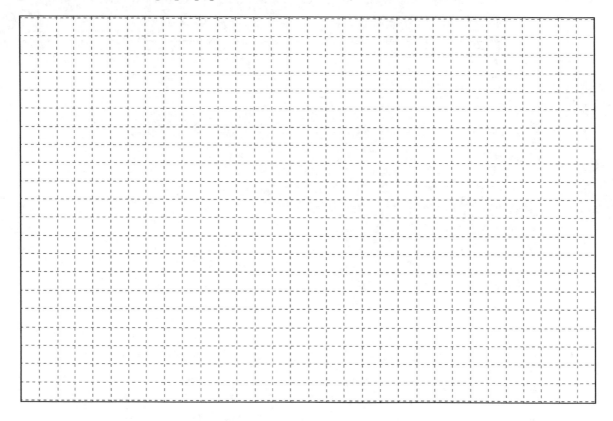

Exercise 5:

Identify the surfaces with the appropriate letter that would appear in the FRONT view, TOP view, and RIGHT view.

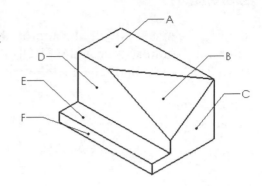

FRONT view surfaces:_____

TOP view surfaces:_____

RIGHT view surfaces:_____

Exercise 6:

Estimate the size; draw the FRONT view, TOP view, and RIGHT view of the illustrated part in Exercise 5 on graph paper.

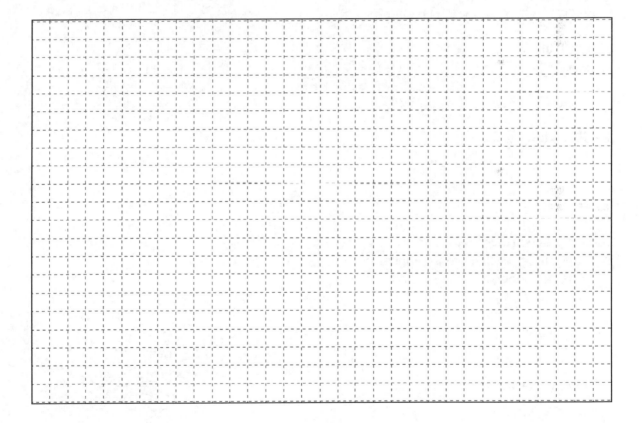

Exercise 7:

Identify the surfaces with the appropriate letter that would appear in the FRONT view, TOP view, and RIGHT view.

FRONT view
surfaces:_____

TOP view surfaces:_____

RIGHT view surfaces:_____

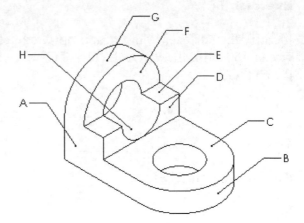

Exercise 8:

Identify the surfaces with the appropriate letter that would appear in the FRONT view, TOP view, and RIGHT view.

FRONT view
surfaces:_____

TOP view surfaces:_____

RIGHT view surfaces:_____

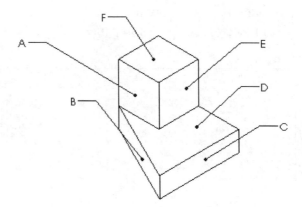

Exercise 9:

Identify the surfaces with the appropriate letter that would appear in the FRONT view, TOP view, and RIGHT view.

FRONT view
surfaces:_____

TOP view surfaces:_____

RIGHT view
surfaces:_____

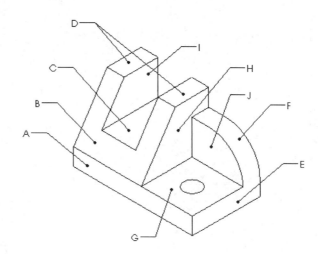

Exercise 10:

Fill in the following table for the below object.

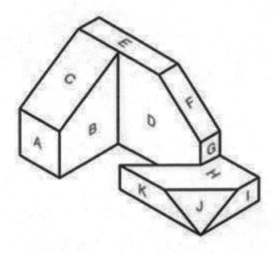

SURFACE	TOP	FRONT	RIGHT
A			
B			
C			
D			
E			
F			
G			
H			
I			
J			
K			

Exercise 11:

Fill in the following table for the below object.

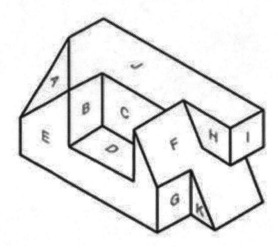

SURFACE	TOP	FRONT	RIGHT
A			
B			
C			
D			
E			
F			
G			
H			
I			
J			
K			

Chapter Summary

Chapter 1 provided a short discussion on the history of Engineering Graphics and the evolution of manual drawing/drafting. You were introduced to general sketching techniques and the 2D and 3D Cartesian Coordinate system. In engineering graphics there is a specific alphabet of lines that represent different types of geometry.

Freehand sketching is an important method to quickly document and to communicate your design ideas. Freehand sketching is a process of creating a rough, preliminary drawing to represent the main features of a design, whether it is a manufactured product, a chemical process, or a structure.

All orthographic views must be looked at together to comprehend the shape of the three-dimensional object. The arrangement and relationship between the views are therefore very important in multi-view drawings.

In creating multi-view orthographic projection, different systems of projection can be used to create the necessary views to fully describe the 3D object. In the figure below, two perpendicular planes are established to form the image planes for a multi-view orthographic projection.

The angles formed between the horizontal and the vertical planes are called the **first**, **second**, **third**, and **fourth angles** as indicated in the figure.

For engineering drawings, both **First angle projection** and **Third angle projection** are commonly used.

In first-angle projection, the object is placed in **front** of the image planes and the views are formed by projecting to the image plane located at the back.

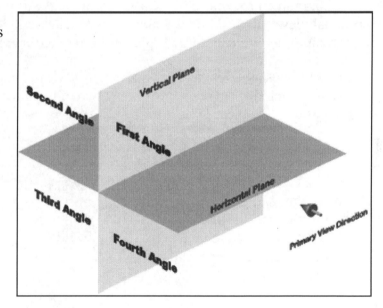

Great link for going from Isometric projecting to a three view drawing: https://www.youtube.com/watch?v=Zptb2epQoEc

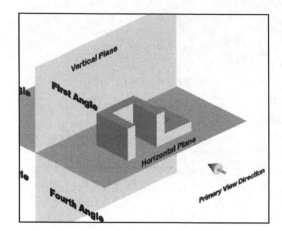

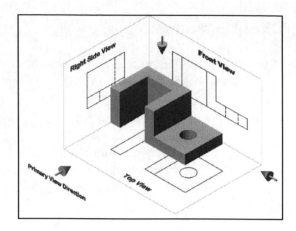

In order to draw all three views of the object on the same plane, the horizontal (Top view) and profile (Right Side view) are rotated into the same plane as the primary image plane (Front view).

In third-angle projection, the image planes are placed in between the object and the observer. And the views are formed by projecting to the image plane located in front of the object.

In Orthographic projection, the Glass Box method was used to distinguish the six principal views. In the United States, you use Third Angle Projection. However, it is important to know First Angle Projection and other international standards.

These six views are known as the six principal views. In performing orthographic projection, each of 2D views shows only two of the three dimensions (**height**, **width**, and **depth**) of the 3D object.

When you create a new part or assembly, the three default Planes (Front, Right, and Top) are aligned with specific views. The Plane you select for the Base sketch determines the orientation of the part or assembly.

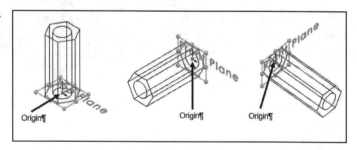

Questions

1. Describe the Cartesian coordinate system.

2. Name the point of intersection, where the axes meet _____.

3. Explain the Right-hand rule in drafting.

4. Why is freehand sketching important to understand?

5. Describe the difference between First and Third Angle Projection type.

6. True or False. First Angle Projection type is used in the United States.

7. Explain the Precedent of Line types. Provide a few examples.

8. True or False. A Hidden Line has precedence over a Visible/Feature line.

9. True or False. The intersection of the two axes creates four regions, called quadrants, indicated by the Roman numerals I, II, III, and IV.

10. Explain the Glass Box method in Standard Orthographic Projection.

11. True or False. Both First Angle and Third Angle Projection type result in the same six views; the difference between them is the arrangement of these views.

12. True or False. Section lines can serve the purpose of identifying the kind of material the part is made from.

13. True or False. All dimension lines terminate with an arrowhead on mechanical engineering drawings.

14. True or False. Break lines are applied to represent an imaginary cut in an object, so the interior of the object can be viewed or fitted to the sheet. Provide an example.

15. True or False. The Front view should show the most features or characteristics of the object. It usually contains the least number of hidden lines. All other views are based (projected) on the orientation chosen for the front view. Explain your answer.

Exercises

Exercise 1.1: Third Angle Projection type is displayed. Name the six illustrated views in the below document.

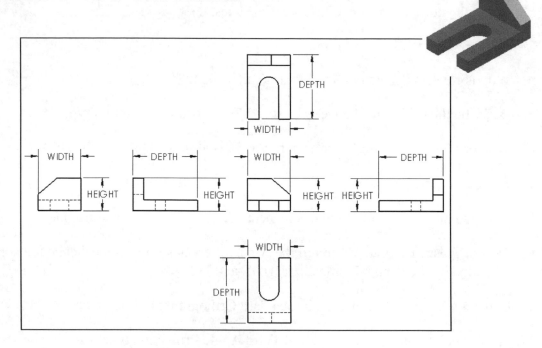

Exercise 1.2: First Angle Projection type is displayed. Name the six illustrated views in the below document.

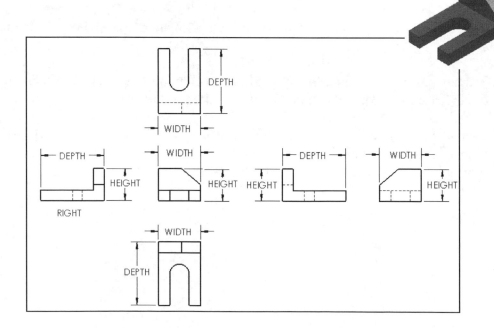

Exercise 1.3: Identify the various Line types in the below model.

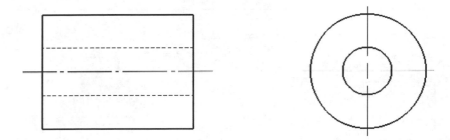

Exercise 1.4: Third Angle Projection type is displayed. Estimate the size using graph paper. Draw the Visible Feature Lines of the Top view for the model. Draw any Hidden lines or Centerlines if needed. Identify the view that should display the most information about the illustrated model.

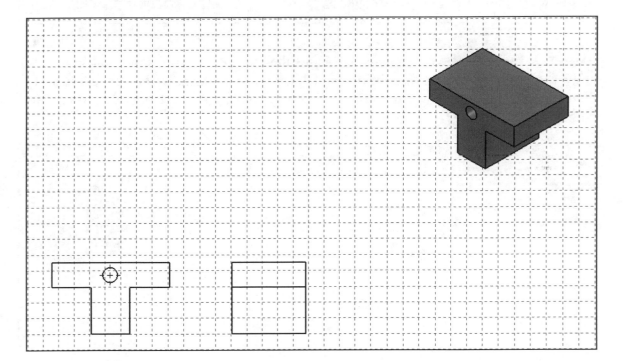

Exercise 1.5: Third Angle Projection type is displayed. Estimate the dimensions. Draw the Visible Feature Lines of the Right view for the model. Draw any Hidden lines if needed. Identify the view that should display the most information about the illustrated model.

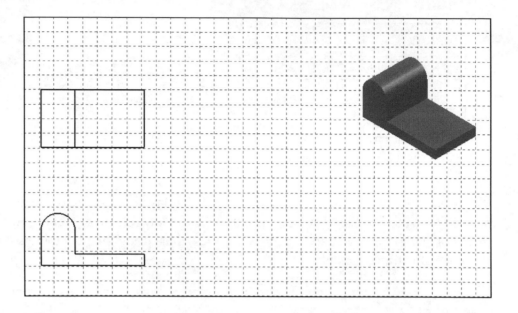

Exercise 1.6: Estimate the dimensions. Draw the Front view, Top view and Right view. Draw the Visible Feature Lines for the model. Draw any Hidden lines if needed. Identify the view that should display the most information about the illustrated model. Note: Third Angle Projection.

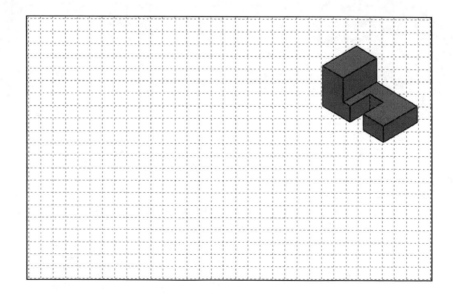

Exercise 1.7: Estimate the dimensions. Draw the Front view, Top view and Right view. Draw the Visible Feature Lines for the model. Draw any Hidden lines or Centerlines if needed. Which view displays the most information about the illustrated model? Note: Third Angle Projection type.

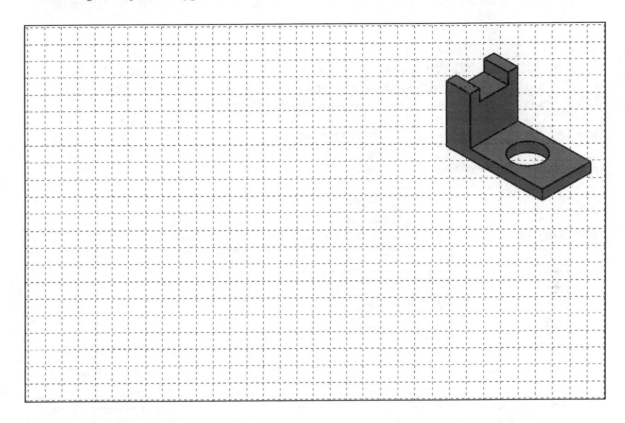

Exercise 1.8: Draw the Isometric view from the provided views (Front, Top, Right). Note: Third Angle Projection.

Isometric Rule #1: Measurement can only be made on or parallel to the isometric axis.

Isometric Rule #2: When drawing ellipses on normal isometric planes, the minor axis of the ellipse is perpendicular to the plane containing the ellipse. The minor axis is perpendicular to the corresponding normal isometric plane.

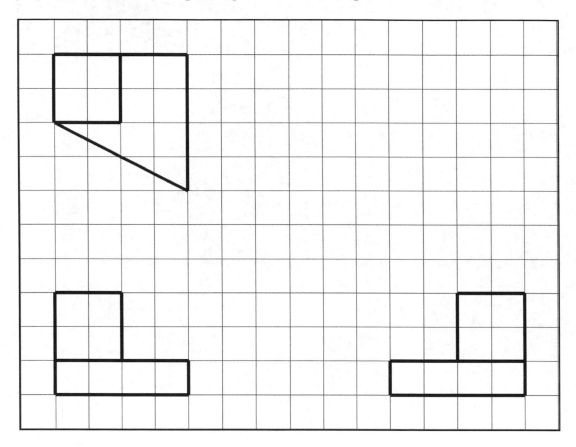

Exercise 1.9: Draw the Isometric view from the provided views (Front, Top, Right). Note: Third Angle Projection.

Isometric Rule #1: Measurement can only be made on or parallel to the isometric axis.

Isometric Rule #2: When drawing ellipses on normal isometric planes, the minor axis of the ellipse is perpendicular to the plane containing the ellipse. The minor axis is perpendicular to the corresponding normal isometric plane.

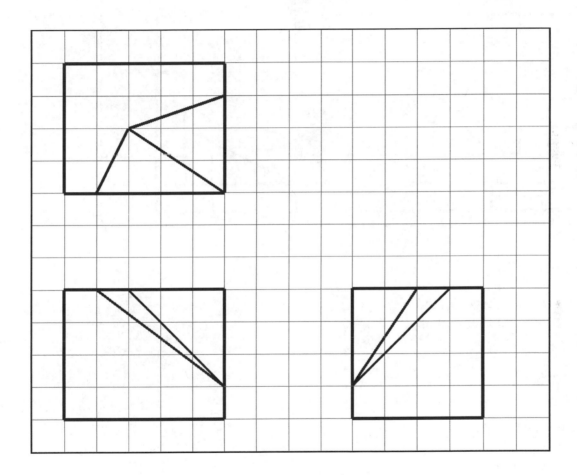

Exercise 1.10: Draw the Isometric view from the provided views (Front, Top, Right).
Note: Third Angle Projection.

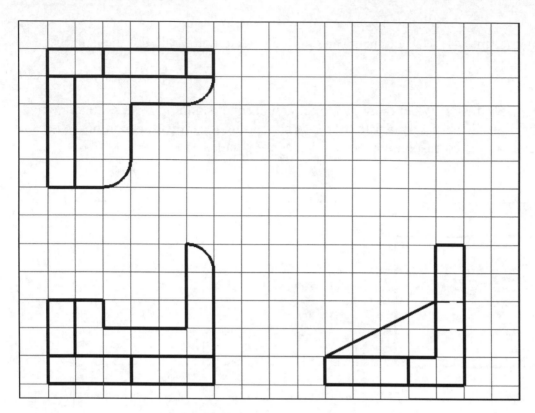

Exercise 1.11:

Identify the surfaces with the
appropriate letter that will appear in the
Front view, Top view and Right view.

Front view
surfaces:_____

Top view surfaces:_____

Right view surfaces:_____

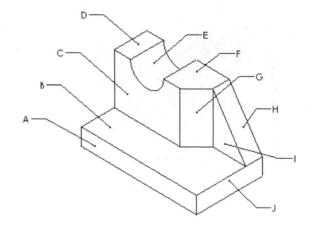

Chapter 2

Isometric Projection and Multi View Drawings

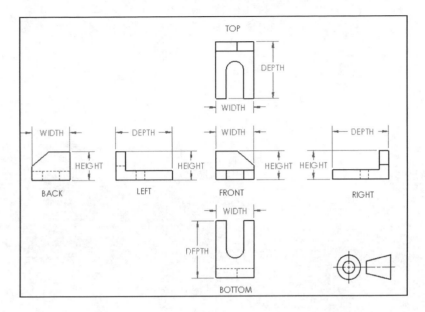

Below are the desired outcomes and usage competencies based on the completion of Chapter 2.

Desired Outcomes:	Usage Competencies:
• Understand Isometric Projection and 2D sketching.	• Identify the three main projection divisions in freehand engineering sketches and drawings: o Axonometric, Oblique, and Perspective
• Knowledge of additional Projection views and arrangement of drawing views.	• Create one and two view drawings.
• Comprehend the history and evolution of CAD and the development of SOLIDWORKS. • Recognize Boolean operations and feature based modeling.	• Identify the development of historic CAD systems and SOLIDWORKS features, parameters and design intent of a sketch, part, assembly, and drawing. • Apply the Boolean operation: Union, Difference, and Intersection.

Notes:

Chapter 2 - Isometric Projection and Multi View Drawings

Chapter Overview

Chapter 2 provides a general introduction into Isometric Projection and Sketching along with Additional Projections and arrangement of views. It also covers advanced drawing views and an introduction from manual drafting to CAD.

On the completion of this chapter, you will be able to:

- Understand and explain Isometric Projection.

- Create an Isometric sketch.

- Identify the three main projection divisions in freehand engineering sketches and drawings:

  o Axonometric.

  o Oblique.

  o Perspective.

- Comprehend the history and evolution of CAD.

- Recognize the following Boolean operations: Union, Difference, and Intersection.

- Understand the development of SOLIDWORKS features, parameters, and design intent of a sketch, part, assembly, and drawing.

Isometric Projections

There are three main projection divisions commonly used in freehand engineering sketches and detailed engineering drawings; they are 1.) Axonometric, with its divisions in Isometric, Dimetric and Trimetric, 2.) Oblique and 3.) Perspective. Let's review the three main divisions.

Axonometric is a type of parallel projection, more specifically a type of Orthographic projection, used to create a pictorial drawing of an object, where the object is rotated along one or more of its axes relative to the plane of projection.

There are three main types of axonometric projection: *Isometric*, *Dimetric*, and *Trimetric* projection depending on the exact angle at which the view deviates from the Orthogonal.

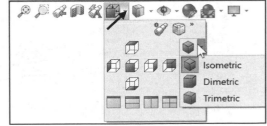

To display Isometric, Dimetric, or Trimetric of a 3D SOLIDWORKS model, select the drop-down arrow from the View Orientation 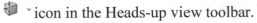 icon in the Heads-up view toolbar.

Axonometric drawings often appear distorted because they ignore the foreshortening effects of perspective (foreshortening means the way things appear to get smaller in both height and depth as they recede into the distance). Typically, Axonometric drawings use vertical lines for those lines representing height and sloping parallel edges for all other sides.

- *Isometric Projection.* Isometric projection is a method of visually representing three-dimensional objects in two dimensions, in which the three coordinate axes appear equally foreshortened and the angles between them are 120°.

The term "Isometric" comes from the Greek for "equal measure" reflecting that the scale along each axis of the projection is the same (this is not true of some other forms of graphical projection).

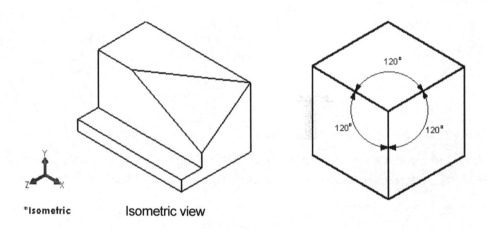

*Isometric   Isometric view

- *Dimetric Projection.* A Dimetric projection is created using 3 axes, but only two of the three axes have equal angles. The smaller these angles are, the less we see of the top surface. The angle is usually around 105°.

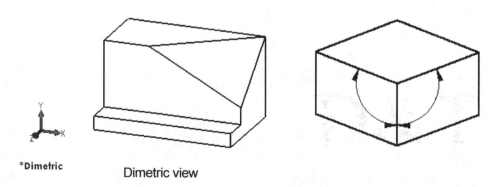

*Dimetric   Dimetric view

- *Trimetric Projection.* A Trimetric projection is created using 3 axes where each of the angles between them is different (there are no equal angles). The scale along each of the three axes and the angles among them are determined separately as dictated by the angle of viewing. Approximations in trimetric drawings are common.

Isometric Sketching

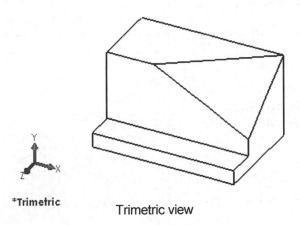

*Trimetric

Trimetric view

Isometric sketches provide a 3D dimensional pictorial representation of an object. Isometric sketches help in the visualization of an object.

The surface features or the axes of the object are drawn around three axes from a horizontal line: a vertical axis, a 30° axis to the right, and a 30° axis to the left. All three axes intersect at a single point on the horizontal line.

All horizontal lines in an Isometric sketch are always drawn at 30° and parallel to each other and are either to the left or to the right of the vertical.

For this reason, all shapes in an Isometric sketch are not true shapes; they are distorted shapes.

All vertical lines in an Isometric sketch are always drawn vertically, and they are always parallel to each other as illustrated in the following example.

Example 1:

Exercise: Draw an Isometric sketch of a cube.

1. Draw a light horizontal axis (construction line) as illustrated on graph paper. Draw a light vertical axis. Draw a light 30° axis to the right. Draw a light 30° axis to the left.

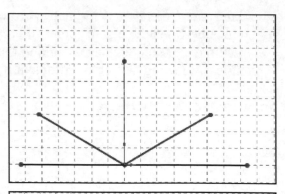

2. Measure the length along the left 30° axis, make a mark and draw a light vertical line.

3. Measure the height along the vertical axis, make a mark and draw a light 30° line to the left to intersect the vertical line drawn in step 2.

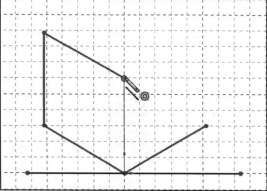

4. Measure the length along the right 30° axis, make a mark and draw a light vertical line.

5. From the height along the vertical axis, make a mark and draw a light 30° line to the right to intersect the vertical line drawn in step 4.

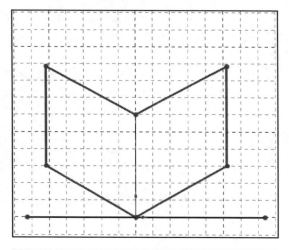

6. Draw a light 30° line to the right and a light 30° line to the left to complete the cube. Once the sketch is complete, darken the shape.

🔆 In an Isometric drawing, the object is viewed at an angle, which makes circles appear as ellipses.

🔆 Isometric Rule #1: Measurement can only be made on or parallel to the isometric axis.

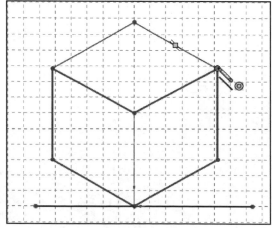

Circles drawn in Axonometric view

A circle drawn on a sloping surface in Axonometric projection will be drawn as an ellipse. An ellipse is a circle turned through an angle. All the examples shown above were box shapes without any curved surfaces. In order to draw curved surfaces we need to know how to draw an ellipse.

If you draw a circle and rotate it slowly, it will become an ellipse. As it is turned through 90° - it will eventually become a straight line. Rotate it 90° again, and it will eventually be back to a circle.

Example 1:

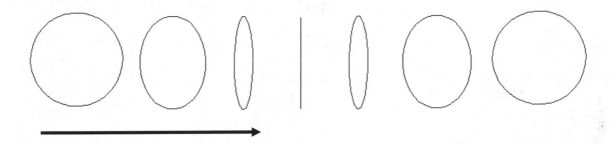

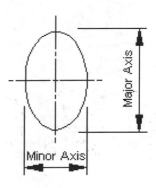

An ellipse has a major axis and a minor axis. The major axis is the axis about which the ellipse is being turned. The minor axis becomes smaller as the angle through which the ellipse is turned approaches 90°.

You can draw a cylinder using the technique shown below. The ellipses can either be sketched freehand or drawn using an ellipse template.

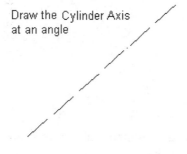

Draw the Cylinder Axis
at an angle

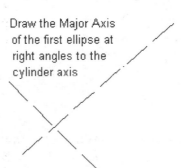

Draw the Major Axis
of the first ellipse at
right angles to the
cylinder axis

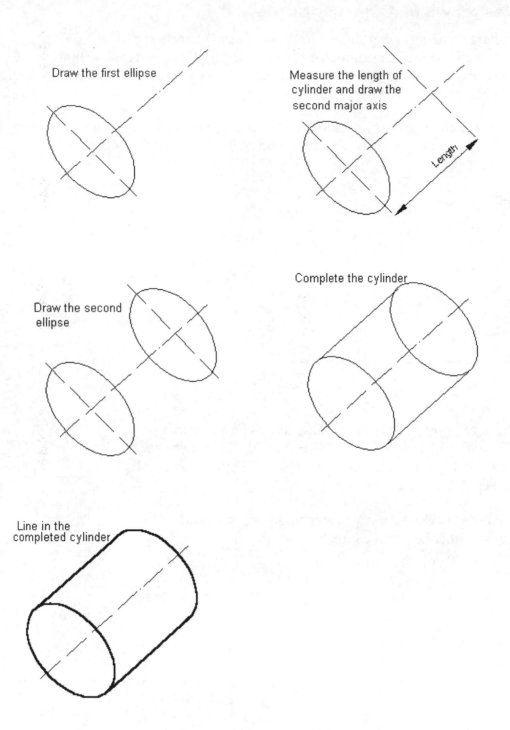

Isometric Rule #2: When drawing ellipses on normal isometric planes, the minor axis of the ellipse is perpendicular to the plane containing the ellipse. The minor axis is perpendicular to the corresponding normal isometric plane.

Additional Projections

Oblique Projection: In Oblique projections, the front view is drawn true size, and the receding surfaces are drawn on an angle to give it a pictorial appearance. This form of projection has the advantage of showing one face (the front face) of the object without distortion. Generally, the face with the greatest detail faces the front.

There are two types of Oblique projection used in engineering design.

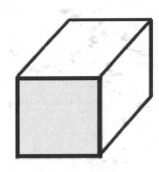

- *Cavalier*: In Cavalier Oblique drawings, all lines (including receding lines) are created to their true length or scale (1:1).

- *Cabinet*: In Cabinet Oblique drawings, the receding lines are shortened by one-half their true length or scale to compensate for distortion and to approximate more closely what the human eye would see. It is for this reason that Cabinet Oblique drawings are the most used form of Oblique drawings.

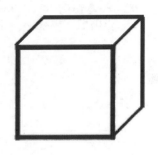

In Oblique drawings, the three axes of projection are vertical, horizontal, and receding. The front view (vertical & horizontal axis) is parallel to the frontal plane and the other two faces are oblique (receding). The direction of projection can be top-left, top-right, bottom-left, or bottom-right. The receding axis is typically drawn at 60°, 45° or 30°.

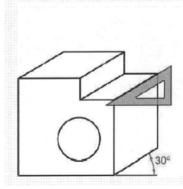
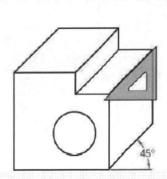
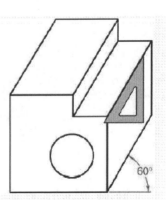

In the oblique pictorials coordinate system, only one axis is at an angle. The most commonly used angle is 45°.

Isometric Rule #1: A measurement can only be made on or parallel to the isometric axis. Therefore, you cannot measure an isometric inclined or oblique line in an isometric drawing because they are not parallel to an isometric axis.

Example: Drawing cylinders in Oblique projection is quite simple if the stages outlined below are followed. In comparison with other ways of drawing cylinders (for example, perspective and isometric) using Oblique projection is relatively easy.

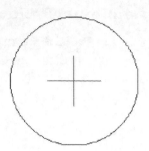

Step One: Draw vertical and horizontal centerlines to indicate the center of a circle, then use a compass to draw the circle itself.

Step Two: Draw a 45° line to match the length on the cylinder. At the end of this line, draw vertical and horizontal centerlines.

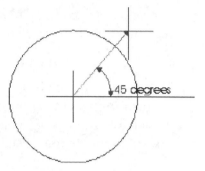

Remember the general rule for Oblique is to half all distances projected backwards. If the cylinder is 100mm in length the distance back must be drawn to 50mm.

Step Three: Draw the second circle with a compass as illustrated.

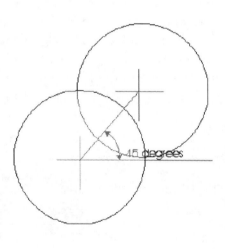

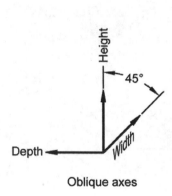

Oblique axes

Step Four: Draw two 45° lines to join the front and back circles.

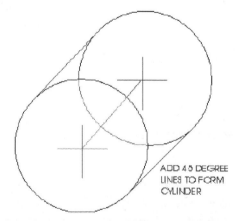

Step Five: Go over the outline of the cylinder with a fine
pen or sharp pencil. Add shading if required.

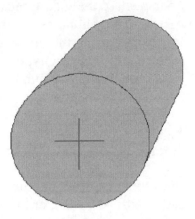

Perspective Projection: If you look along a straight road, the parallel sides of the road
appear to meet at a point in the distance. This point is called the vanishing point and has
been used to add realism. Suppose you want to draw a road that vanishes into the
distance. The rays from the points a given distance from the eye along the lines of the
road are projected to the eye. The angle formed by the rays decreases with increasing
distance from the eye.

To display a Perspective view in SOLIDWORKS of
a 3D model, click View, Display, Perspective from the
Main toolbar.

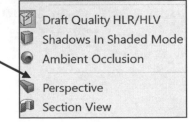

A perspective drawing typically aims to reproduce how humans see the world: objects that are farther away seem smaller, etc. Depending on the type of perspective (1-pt, 2-pt, 3-pt), vanishing points are established in the drawing towards which lines recede, mimicking the effect of objects diminishing in size with distance from the viewer.

One vanishing point is typically used for roads, railroad tracks, or buildings viewed so that the front is directly facing the viewer as illustrated above.

Any objects that are made up of lines either directly parallel with the viewer's line of sight or directly perpendicular (the railroad slats) can be represented with one-point perspective.

The selection of the locations of the vanishing points, which is the first step in creating a perspective sketch, will affect the looks of the resulting images.

Two-point perspective can be used to draw the same objects as one-point perspective, rotated: looking at the corner of a house, or looking at two forked roads shrink into the distance, for example. One point represents one set of parallel lines, the other point represents the other. Looking at a house from the corner, one wall would recede towards one vanishing point; the other wall would recede towards the opposite vanishing point as illustrated.

Two Point
Perspective

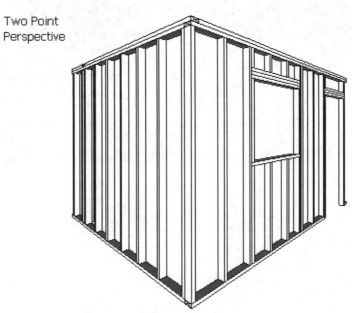

Three-point perspective is usually used for buildings seen from above (or below). In addition to the two vanishing points from before, one for each wall, there is now one for how those walls recede into the ground. This third vanishing point will be below the ground. Looking up at a tall building is another common example of the third vanishing point. This time the third vanishing point is high in space.

One-point, two-point and three-point perspectives appear to embody different forms of calculated perspective. Despite conventional perspective drawing wisdom, perspective basically just means "position" or "viewpoint" of the viewer relative to the object.

Arrangement of Views

The main purpose of an engineering drawing is to provide the manufacturer with sufficient information needed to build, inspect or assemble the part or assembly according to the specifications of the designer. Since the selection and arrangement of views depends on the complexity of a part, only those views that are needed should be drawn.

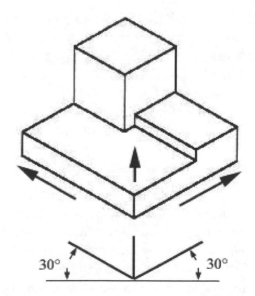

The average part drawing which includes the Front view, Top view and Right view are known as a three-view drawing. However, the designation of the views is not as important as the fact that the combination of views must give all the details of construction in a clear, correct and concise way.

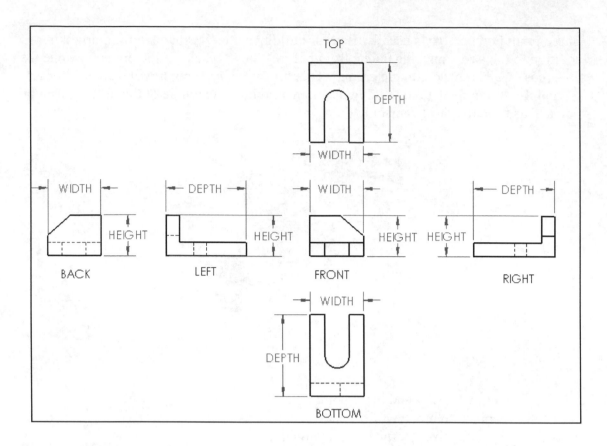

Third "3rd" Angle Projection is displayed and used in the book.

In SOLIDWORKS, when you create a new part or assembly, the three default Planes (Front, Right and Top) are aligned with specific views. The Plane you select for the Base sketch determines the orientation of the part, the drawing views and the assembly.

Two-view drawing

Simple symmetrical flat objects and cylindrical parts such as sleeves, shafts, rods and studs most of the time only require two views to provide the full details of construction and or inspection. Always use annotations when needed.

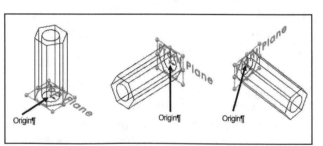

In the Front view below, a centerline runs through the axis of the part as a horizontal centerline.

The second view (Right view) of the two-view drawing contains a center mark at the center of the cylinders.

The selection of views for a two-view drawing rests largely with the designer/engineer.

Example 1:

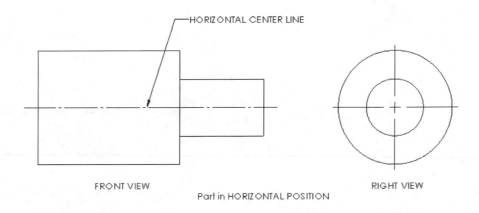

Example 2:

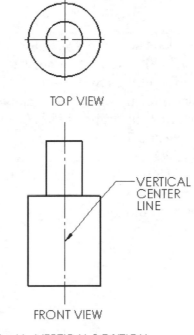

One-view drawing

Parts that are uniform in shape often require only one view to describe them adequately. This is particularly true of cylindrical objects where a one-view drawing saves time and simplifies the drawing.

When a one-view drawing of a cylindrical part is used, the dimension for the diameter (according to ANSI standards) must be preceded by the symbol Ø, as illustrated.

Example 1:

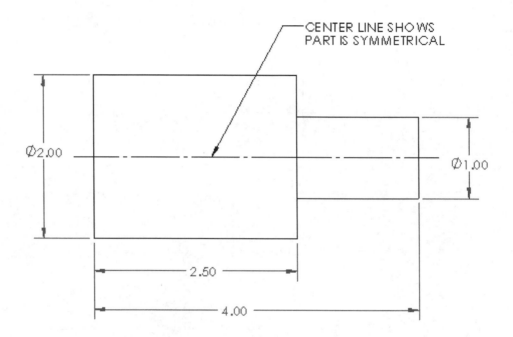

The one-view drawing is also used extensively for flat (Sheet metal) parts. With the addition of notes to supplement the dimensions on the view, the one view furnishes all the necessary information for accurately describing the part. In the first illustration below, you have two views: Front view and Top view. In the section illustration below, you replace the Top view with a Note: MATERIAL THICKNESS .125 INCH. Utilize Smart Notes when using a 3D software package. The note is linked to the dimension/s of the model.

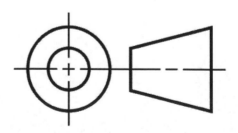

Third Angle Projection type symbol is illustrated.

Example 1: No Note Annotation

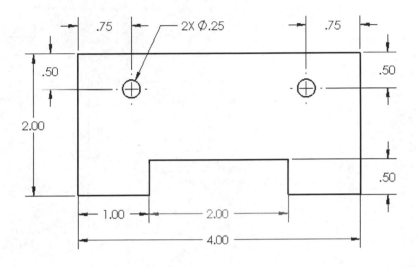

Example 2: Note Annotation to replace the Top view

MATERIAL THICKNESS .125 INCH

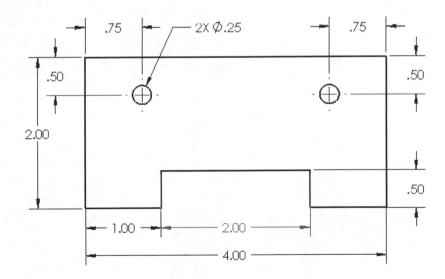

Example 3: Note Fastener Annotation

A multi-view drawing should have the minimum number of views necessary to describe an object completely. The most descriptive views are those that reveal the most information about the features, with the fewest features hidden from view.

English – IPS Unit system

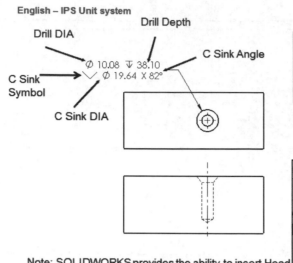

Drill DIA

Drill Depth

Ø 10.08 ⬇ 38.10

C Sink Symbol

∨ Ø 19.64 X 82°

C Sink DIA

C Sink Angle

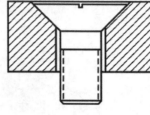

Note: SOLIDWORKS provides the ability to insert Head clearance for the Counter Sink hole.

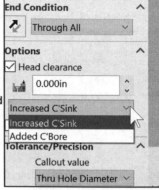

When you create a new part or assembly, the three default Planes (Front, Right and Top) are aligned with specific views. The Plane you select for the Base sketch determines the orientation of the part, the orientation of the Front drawing view and the orientation of the first component in the assembly.

Exercises:
Exercise 1:

Draw freehand the Isometric view of the illustrated model on graph paper. Approximate the size of the model.

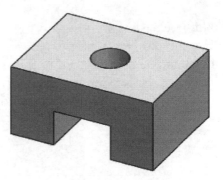

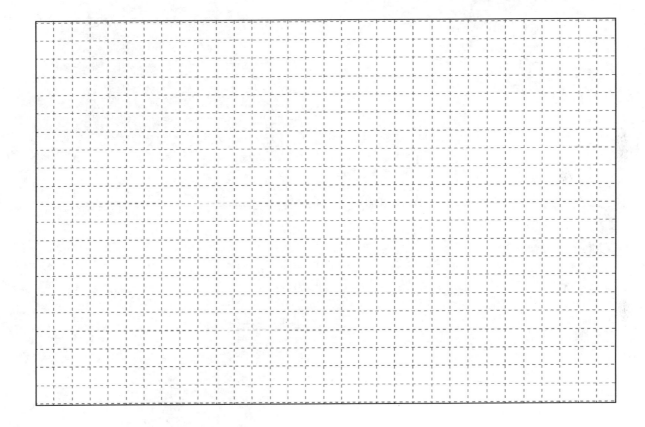

Exercise 2:

Name each view and insert the Width, Height and Depth name. No dimensions are required in this exercise. Note: Centerlines are not displayed. Third Angle Projection is used.

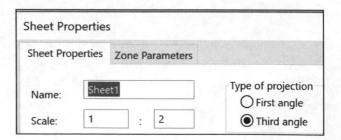

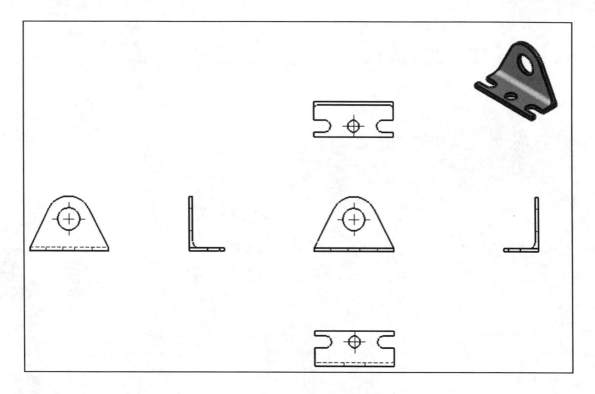

Drawing Views - Advanced

The standard views used in an orthographic projection are Front view, Top view, Right view and Isometric view. Non-standard orthographic drawing views are used when the six principal views do not fully describe the part for manufacturing or inspection. Below are a few non-standard orthographic drawing views.

Section view

Section views are used to clarify the interior of a part that can't clearly be seen by hidden lines in a view.

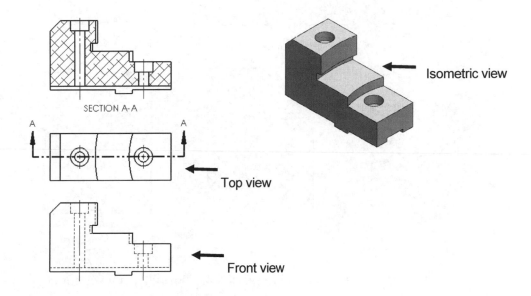

SECTION A-A

Top view

Front view

Isometric view

Think of an **imaginary** cutting (Plane) through the object and removing a portion. Imaginary is the key word.

A Section view is a child of the parent view. The Cutting Plane arrows used to create a Section view indicate the direction of sight. Section lines in the Section view are bounded by visible lines.

Section lines in the Section view can serve the purpose of identifying the kind of material the part is made from. Below are a few examples:

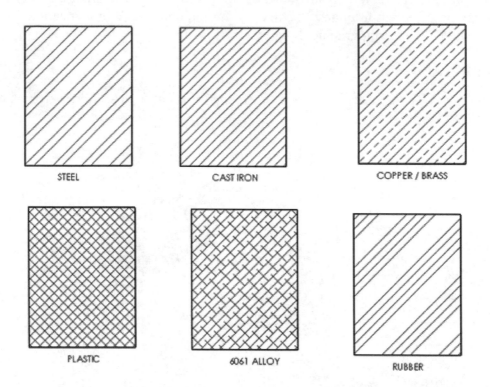

To avoid a false impression of thickness, ribs are normally not sectioned.

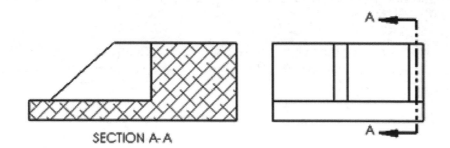

Detail View

The Detail view provides the ability to add a portion of a view, usually at an enlarged scale. A Detail view is a child of the parent view. Create a detail view in a drawing to display or highlight a portion of a view.

A Detail view may be of an Orthographic view, a non-planar (isometric) view, a Section view, a Crop view, an Exploded assembly view or another detail view.

Example 1:

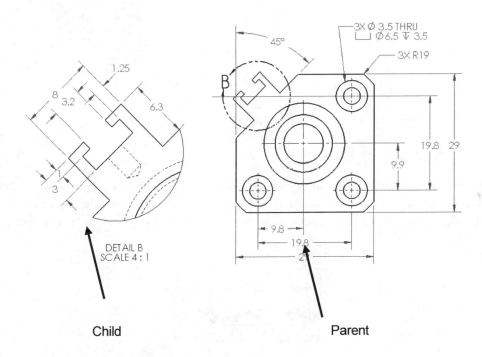

Child   Parent

If the Detail view has a different scale than the sheet, the scale needs to be supplied as an annotation as illustrated.

Example 2:

Below is a Detail view of a Section view. The Detail view is a child view of the parent view (Detail view). The Section view cannot exist without the Detail view.

Parent   Child

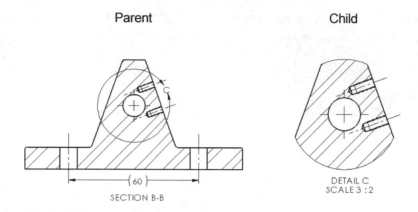

SECTION B-B

DETAIL C
SCALE 3 : 2

Broken out View

A Broken-out section is part of an existing drawing view, not a separate view. Material is removed to a specified depth to expose inner details. Hidden lines are displayed in the non-sectioned area of a broken section. View two examples of a Broken out View below.

Example 1:

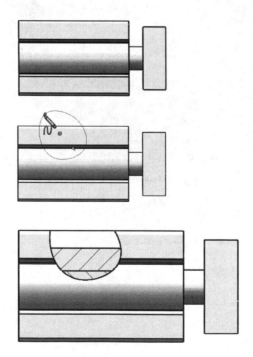

Example 2:

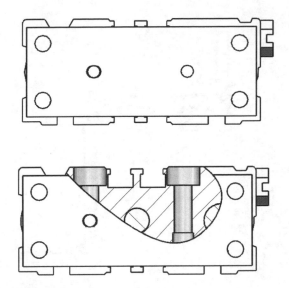

Break or Broken View

A Break view is part of an existing drawing view, not a separate view. A Break view provides the ability to add a break line to a selected view. Create a Broken view to display the drawing view in a larger scale on a smaller drawing sheet size. Reference dimensions and model dimensions associated with the broken area reflect the actual model values.

Example 1:

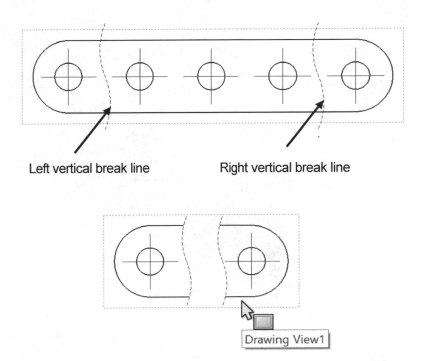

Left vertical break line   Right vertical break line

Drawing View1

Example 2:

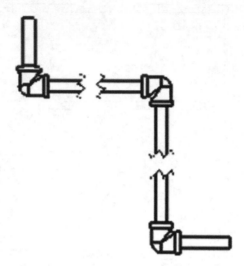

Crop View

A Crop view is a Child of the Parent view. A Crop view provides the ability to crop an existing drawing view. You cannot create a Crop view on a Detail view, a view from which a Detail view has been created or an Exploded view.

Create a Crop view to save time. Example: instead of creating a Section view and then a Detail view, then hiding the unnecessary Section view, create a Crop view to crop the Section view directly.

Example 1:

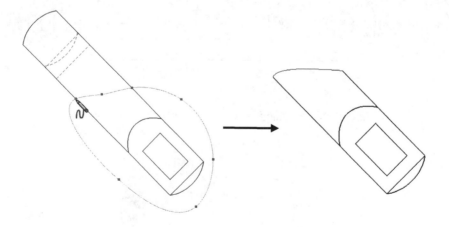

Auxiliary View

An Auxiliary view is a Child of the Parent view. An Auxiliary view provides the ability to display a plane parallel to an angled plane with true dimensions. A primary Auxiliary view is hinged to one of the six principle orthographic views.

Example 1:

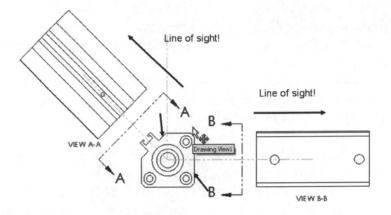

Exercises:

Exercise 1:

Label all of the name views below. Note: Third Angle projection.

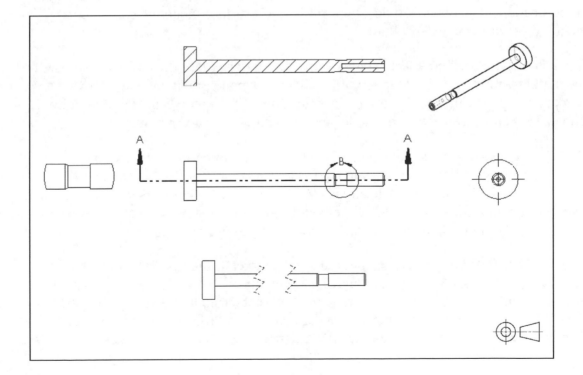

History of Computer Aided Design (CAD)

In 1963, Ivan Sutherland of MIT developed "Sketchpad," a graphical communication system, where with a light pen, Sutherland was able to select and modify geometry on a Cathode Ray System (CRT) and input values through a key pad. Geometric relationships were made between lines and arc and geometry could be moved and copied.

With aerospace and automotive technologies becoming more complex and IBM mainframe computers commercially available in the late 1960s and early 1970s, companies such as MacDonald-Douglas, Lockheed, General Motors, and Ford were utilizing their own internal CAD systems to design, manipulate and store models and drawings. Digital Equipment Corporation (DEC) and Prime Computer introduced computer hardware platforms that made CAD data storage and development more affordable. Ford's Product Design Graphics System (PDGS) developed into one of the largest integrated CAD systems in the 1980s.

By 1980, Cambridge Interact Systems (UK) introduced CIS Medusa, that was bought and distributed by Prime Computer and ran on a proprietary workstation and used Prime mini computers for data storage. Mid size companies, such as AMP and Carrier, were now using CAD in their engineering departments. Other CAD software companies also introduced new technology. Computervision utilized both proprietary hardware and SUN workstations and became a leader in 2D drafting technology.

But in the early 80s, 3D CAD used Boolean algorithms for solid geometry that were a challenge for engineers to manipulate. Other major CAD players were Integraph, GE Calma, SDRC, and IBM (Dassault Systèmes). Dassault Systèmes, with its roots in the aerospace industry, expanded development in CAD surface modeling software technology with Boeing and Ford.

In the late 80s, Parametric Technology Corporation (PTC) introduced CAD software to the market with the ability to manipulate a 3D solid model, running on a UNIX workstation platform. By changing dimensions directly on the 3D model, driven by dimensions and parameters, the model updated and was termed parametric.

By the early 90s, the Personal Computer (PC) was becoming incorporated in the engineer's daily activities for writing reports and generating spreadsheets. In 1993, SOLIDWORKS founder Jon Hirschtick recruited a team of engineers to build a company and develop an affordable, 3D CAD software application that was easy to use and ran on an intuitive Windows platform, without expensive hardware and software to operate.

In 1995, SOLIDWORKS was introduced to the market as the first 3D feature based, parametric solid modeler running on a PC. The company's rapidly growing customer base and continuous product innovation quickly established it as a strong competitor in the CAD market. The market noticed, and global product lifecycle technology giant Dassault Systèmes S.A. acquired SOLIDWORKS for $310 million in stock in June of 1997.

SOLIDWORKS went on to run as an independent company, incorporating finite element analysis (FEA) which has advanced dynamics, nonlinear, fatigue, thermal, steady state and turbulent fluid flow (CFD) and electromagnetic analysis capabilities, as well as design optimization. SOLIDWORKS open software architecture has resulted in over 1500 partner applications such as Computer Aided Manufacturing (CAM), robot simulation software, and process management. Today, SOLIDWORKS software has the most worldwide users in production - more than 8,500,000 users at over 600,000 locations in more than 300 countries.

Note: There are many university researchers and commercial companies that have contributed to the history of computer aided design. We developed this section on the history of CAD based on the institutions and companies that we worked for and worked with over our careers and as it relates to the founders of SOLIDWORKS.

Boolean operations

To understand the difference between parametric solid modeling and Boolean based solid modeling you will first review Boolean operations. In the 1980s, one of the key advancements in CAD was the development of the Constructive Solid Geometry (CSG) method. Constructive Solid Geometry describes the solid model as combinations of basic three-dimensional shapes or better known as primitives. Primitives are typically simple shapes: cuboids, cylinders, prisms, pyramids, spheres and cones.

Two primitive solid objects can be combined into one using a procedure known as the Boolean operations. There are three basic Boolean operations:

- Boolean Union

- Boolean Difference

- Boolean Intersection

Boolean Operation:	Result:
Boolean Union - The merger of two separate objects into one. A + B	
Boolean Difference - The subtraction of one object from another. A - B	
Boolean Intersection - The portion common to both objects. A ∩ B	

Even today, Boolean operations assist the SOLIDWORKS designer in creating a model with more complex geometry by combining two bodies together with a Boolean intersection.

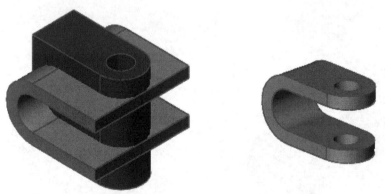

Use the SOLIDWORKS Tutorial to view Multi-body Parts, Boolean model examples.

What is SOLIDWORKS?

SOLIDWORKS® is a mechanical design automation software package used to build parts, assemblies and drawings that takes advantage of the familiar Microsoft® Windows graphical user interface.

SOLIDWORKS is an easy to learn design and analysis tool (SOLIDWORKS Simulations, SOLIDWORKS Motion, SOLIDWORKS Flow Simulation etc.), which makes it possible for designers to quickly sketch 2D and 3D concepts, create 3D parts and assemblies and detail 2D drawings.

In SOLIDWORKS, you create 2D and 3D sketches, 3D parts, 3D assemblies and 2D drawings. The part, assembly and drawing documents are related. Additional information on SOLIDWORKS and its family of products can be obtained at their URL, www.SOLIDWORKS.com.

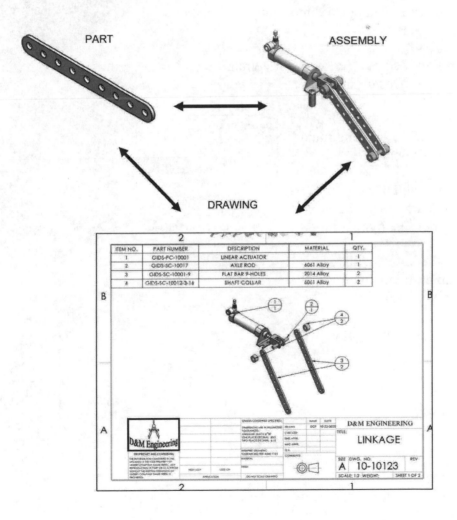

Features are the building blocks of parts. Use features to create parts, such as Extruded Boss/Base and Extruded Cut. Extruded features begin with a 2D sketch created on a Sketch plane.

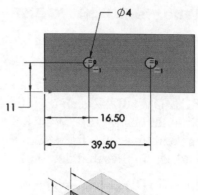

The 2D sketch is a profile or cross section. Sketch tools such as lines, arcs and circles are used to create the 2D sketch. Sketch the general shape of the profile. Add Geometric relationships and dimensions to control the exact size of the geometry.

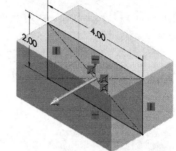

Create features by selecting edges or faces of existing features, such as a Fillet. The Fillet feature rounds sharp corners.

Dimensions drive features. Change a dimension, and you change the size of the part.

Apply Geometric relationships: Vertical, Horizontal, Parallel, etc. to maintain Design intent.

Create a hole that penetrates through a part (Through All). SOLIDWORKS maintains relationships through the change.

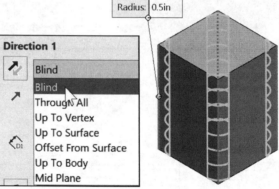

The step-by-step approach used in this text allows you to create parts, assemblies and drawings by doing, not just by reading.

The book provides the knowledge to modify all parts and components in a document.

Change is an integral part of design.

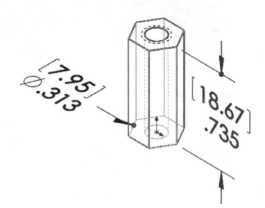

Design Intent

What is design intent? All designs are created for a purpose. Design intent is the intellectual arrangements of features and dimensions of a design. Design intent governs the relationship between sketches in a feature, features in a part and parts in an assembly.

The SOLIDWORKS definition of design intent is the process in which the model is developed to accept future modifications. Models behave differently when design changes occur.

Design for change. Utilize geometry for symmetry, reuse common features, and reuse common parts. Build change into the following areas that you create:

- Sketch

- Feature

- Part

- Assembly

- Drawing

When editing or repairing geometric relations, it is considered best practice to edit the relation vs. deleting it.

Design Intent in a sketch

Build design intent in a sketch as the profile is created. A profile is determined from the Sketch Entities. Example: Rectangle, Circle, Arc, Point, Slot, etc. Apply symmetry into a profile through a sketch centerline, mirror entity and position about the reference planes and Origin.

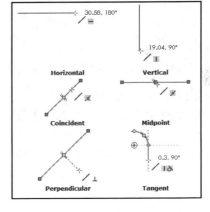

Build design intent as you sketch with automatic Geometric relations. Document the decisions made during the up-front design process. This is very valuable when you modify the design later.

A rectangle (Center Rectangle Sketch tool) contains Horizontal, Vertical and Perpendicular automatic Geometric relations.

Apply design intent using added Geometric relations if needed. Example: Horizontal, Vertical, Collinear, Perpendicular, Parallel, Equal, etc.

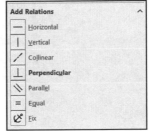

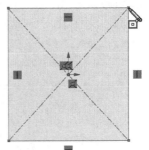

Example A: Apply design intent to create a square profile. Sketch a rectangle. Apply the Center Rectangle Sketch tool. Note: No construction reference centerline or Midpoint relation is required with the Center Rectangle tool. Insert dimensions to fully define the sketch.

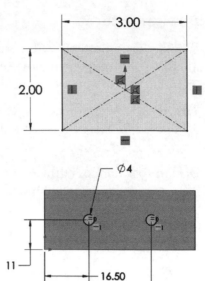

Example B: Develop a rectangular profile. Apply the Corner Rectangle Sketch tool. The bottom horizontal midpoint of the rectangular profile is located at the Origin. Add a Midpoint relation between the horizontal edge of the rectangle and the Origin. Insert two dimensions to fully define the rectangle as illustrated.

Design intent in a feature

Build design intent into a feature by addressing symmetry, feature selection, and the order of feature creation.

Example A: The Extruded Base feature remains symmetric about the Front Plane. Utilize the Mid Plane End Condition option in Direction 1. Modify the depth, and the feature remains symmetric about the Front Plane.

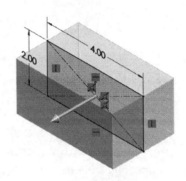

Example B: Create 34 teeth in the model. Do you create each tooth separately using the Extruded Cut feature? No.

Create a single tooth and then apply the Circular Pattern feature. Modify the Circular Pattern from 32 to 24 teeth.

Design intent in a part

Utilize symmetry, feature order and reusing common features to build design intent into a part. Example A: Feature order. Is the entire part symmetric? Feature order affects the part.

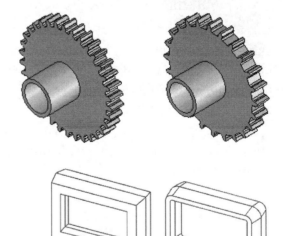

Apply the Shell feature before the Fillet feature and the inside corners remain perpendicular.

Design intent in an assembly

Utilizing symmetry, reusing common parts and using the Mate relation between parts builds the design intent into an assembly.

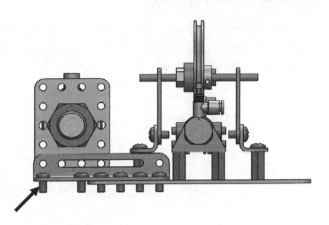

Example A: Reuse geometry in an assembly. The assembly contains a linear pattern of holes. Insert one screw into the first hole. Utilize the Component Pattern feature to copy the machine screw to the other holes.

Design intent in a drawing

Utilize dimensions, tolerance and notes in parts and assemblies to build the design intent into a drawing.

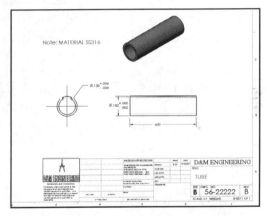

Example A: Tolerance and material in the drawing. Insert an outside diameter tolerance +.000/-.002 into the TUBE part. The tolerance propagates to the drawing.

Define the Custom Property Material in the Part. The Material Custom Property propagates to your drawing.

Create a sketch on any of the default planes: Front, Top, Right or a created plane.

Additional information on design process and design intent is available in SOLIDWORKS Help.

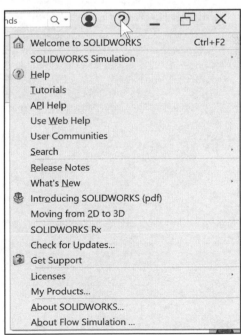

The book is designed to expose the new user to many tools, techniques and procedures. It does not always use the most direct tool or process.

Chapter Summary

Chapter 2 provided a general introduction into isometric projection and sketching along with additional projections and the arrangement of standard views and advanced views. You explored the three main projection divisions in freehand engineering sketches and drawings: Axonometric, Oblique and Perspective.

This chapter also introduced you to the history of CAD and the development of DS SOLIDWORKS Corp. From early Boolean CAD software, you explored Union, Difference, and Intersection operations which are modeling techniques still used today. You were also introduced to the fundamentals of SOLIDWORKS, its feature based modeling, driven by parameters that incorporates your design intent into a sketch, part, assembly and drawing.

Isometric Rule #1: A measurement can only be made on or parallel to the isometric axis. Therefore, you cannot measure an isometric inclined or oblique line in an isometric drawing because they are not parallel to an isometric axis.

Isometric Rule #2: When drawing ellipses on normal isometric planes, the minor axis of the ellipse is perpendicular to the plane containing the ellipse. The minor axis is perpendicular to the corresponding normal isometric plane.

Questions

1. Name the three main projection divisions commonly used in freehand engineering sketches and detailed engineering drawings: _____ , _____ and _____

2. Name the projection divisions within Axonometric projection: _____ , _____ , and _____ .

3. True or False: In oblique projections the front view is drawn true size, and the receding surfaces are drawn on an angle to give it a pictorial appearance.

4. Name the two types of Oblique projection used in engineering design: _____ , _____ .

5. Describe Perspective Projection. Provide an example.

6. True or False: Parts that are uniform in shape often require only one view to describe them adequately.

7. True or False: The designer usually selects as a Front view of the object that view which best describes the general shape of the part. This Front view may have no relationship to the actual front position of the part as it fits into an assembly.

8. True or False: When a one-view drawing of a cylindrical part is used, the dimension for the diameter (according to ANSI standards) must be preceded by the symbol Ø.

9. Draw a Third Angle Projection Symbol.

10. Draw a First Angle Projection Symbol.

11. Describe the difference between First and Third Angle Projection.

12. True or False. First Angle Projection is used in the United States.

13. True or False. Section lines can serve the purpose of identifying the kind of material the part is made from.

14. True or False. All dimension lines terminate with an arrowhead on mechanical engineering drawings.

15. True or False. Break lines are applied to represent an imaginary cut in an object, so the interior of the object can be viewed or fitted to the sheet. Provide an example.

Exercises

Exercise 2.1: Hand draw the Isometric view from the illustrated model below.

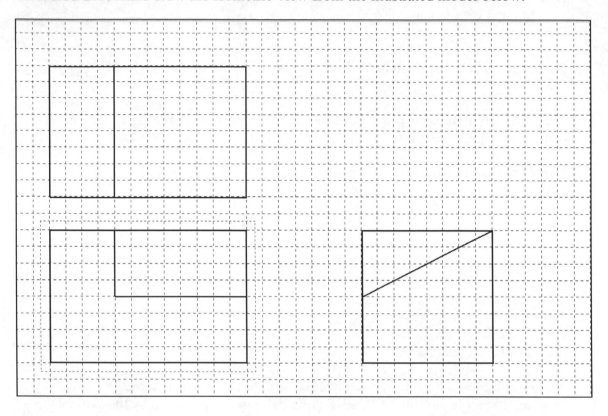

Exercise 2.2: Hand draw the Isometric view for the following models. Approximate the size of the model.

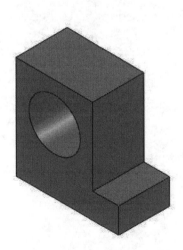

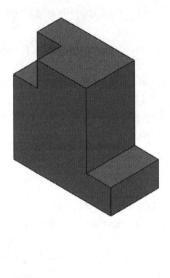

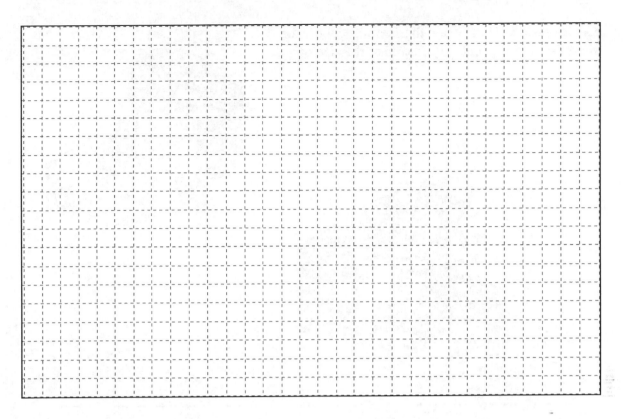

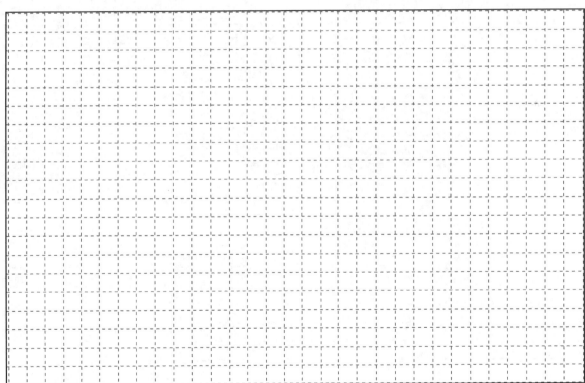

Exercise 2.3: Hand draw the Isometric view for the following models. Approximate the size of the model.

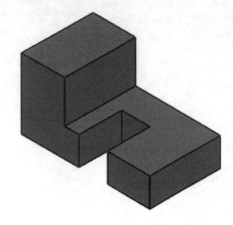

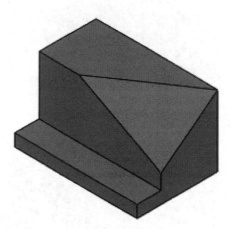

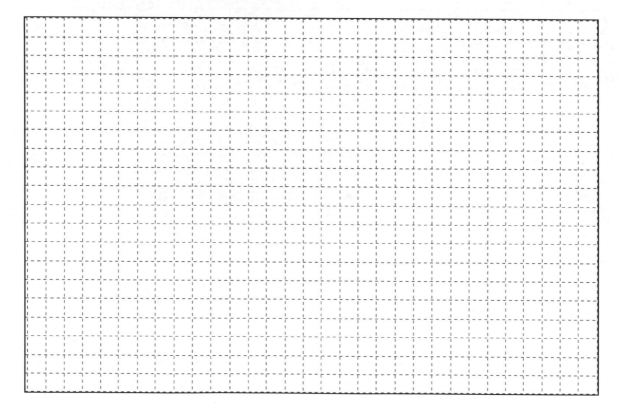

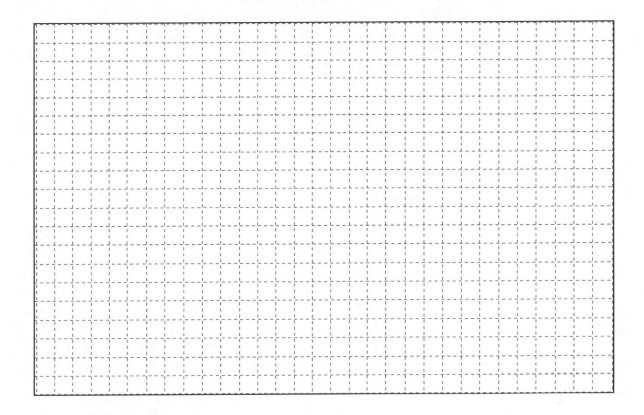

Exercise 2.4: Identify the number of vanishing points for each picture.

1. Number of vanishing points for the first picture._____

2. Number of vanishing points for the second picture._____

3. Number of vanishing points for the third picture. _____

Notes:

Chapter 3

Dimensioning Practices, Scales, Tolerancing and Fasteners

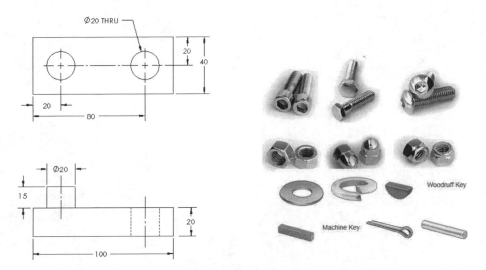

Below are the desired outcomes and usage competencies based on the completion of Chapter 3.

Desired Outcomes:	Usage Competencies:
• Knowledge of dimensioning and the ASME Y14.5-2009 standard.	• Ability to correctly dimension the following features, objects and shapes: rectangle, cone, sphere, hole, cylinder, angle, point or center, arc, chamfer and more.

• Awareness of measurement units.
• Understand Scale type.
	• Apply the following measurement system:
	  o Metric system (MMGS).
	  o English system (IPS).
	• Engineer's scale, Architect's scale, Linear scale, Vernier scale, and Linear encoder.

• Understand Tolerancing for a drawing. • Comprehend Fasteners and hole dimensioning. • Recognize Fit type.	• Apply dimension and drawing Tolerances. • Read and understand general Fastener and hole annotation. • Apply Fit type.

Notes:

Chapter 3 - Dimensioning Practices, Tolerancing and Fasteners

Chapter Overview

Chapter 3 provides a general introduction into dimensioning systems and the ANSI Y14.5 2009 standards along with fasteners, fits, and general tolerancing practices.

On the completion of this chapter, you will be able to:

- Understand and apply the ASME Y14.5-2009 dimensioning standard.

- Awareness of measurement units:

  o Metric system (MMGS).

  o English system (IPS).

- Familiarity of dual dimensioning:

  o (Primary vs. Secondary).

- Understand Scale type:

  o Engineer's scale, Architect's scale, Linear scale, Vernier scale and Linear encoder.

- Ability to correctly dimension the following features, objects and shapes: rectangle, Cone, Sphere, hole, cylinder, angle, point or center, arc, chamfer and more.

- Understand and apply part and drawing Tolerance.

- Read and understand Fastener notation.

- Recognize single, double and triple thread.

- Distinguish between Right-handed and Left-handed thread.

- Recognize annotations for a simple hole, Counterbore and Countersink in a drawing.

- Identify Fit type.

American National Standards Institute (ANSI)

To ensure some measure of uniformity in industrial drawings, the American National Standards Institute (ANSI) has established drafting standards; these standards are called the language of drafting and are in general use throughout the United States.

ANSI was originally formed in 1918, when five engineering societies and three government agencies founded the American Engineering Standards Committee (AESC). In 1928, the AESC became the American Standards Association (ASA). In 1966, the ASA was reorganized and became the United States of America Standards Institute (USASI). The present name was adopted in 1969 and the standards are published by the American Society of Mechanical Engineers (ASME).

While these drafting standards or practices may vary in some respects between industries, the principles are basically the same. The practices recommended by ANSI for dimensioning and for marking notes are followed in this book.

Dimensioning

Dimensioning is the process of defining the size, form and location of geometric features and components on an engineering drawing. The principle for dimensioning a drawing is clarity and accuracy. To promote clarity and accuracy, ANSI developed standard practices.

There are two key types of dimensions:

- **Location dimension** - locates a horizontal position, vertical position, center of a hole, slot, chamfer or other model features.

- **Size dimension** - provides a horizontal position, vertical position, angle, diameter, radius etc.

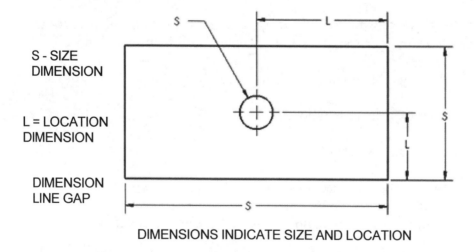

DIMENSIONS INDICATE SIZE AND LOCATION

Dimensions should not be duplicated or the same information given in two different ways. If a reference dimension is used, the size value is placed within parentheses (X).

Measurement

Measurement is the process or the result of determining the ratio of a physical quantity, such as a length, time, temperature etc., to a unit of measurement, such as the meter, second or degree Celsius.

The metric system is a decimal system of measurement based on its units for length, the meter and for mass, the kilogram.

Other names for the Metric system include:

- International System of Units SI.

- International Organization for Standardization ISO units.

The Metric system is the most commonly used system of measurement in the world.

The Metric system is based on the meter as the standard unit of reference. A meter (approximately 39.37 inches in length) is subdivided into 10 equal parts called decimeters. Each decimeter is divided into 10 parts called centimeters and each centimeter is divided into 10 parts called millimeters.

The Metric system is a very coherent system because it is exclusively a decimal system and therefore has a common multiplier and divisor of 10. Regular fractions are not used in the metric system. Instead the metric system uses only decimal fractions.

The default SOLIDWORKS (SI) metric unit system is millimeter, gram, second (MMGS).

The United States Customary units are a system of measurements commonly used in the United States.

Many U.S. units are virtually identical to their imperial counterparts, but the U.S. customary system developed from English units used in the British Empire before the system of imperial units was standardized in 1824.

The U.S system is a system of measurement based on its units for length, the inch and for mass, the pound.

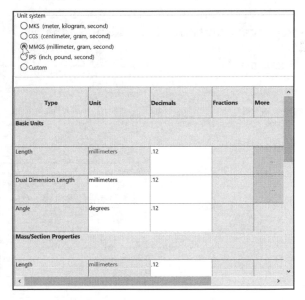

The Inch system is based on the foot as the standard unit of reference. A foot is divided into 12 equal parts called inches. Each inch is subdivided into a variety of fractions and decimals.

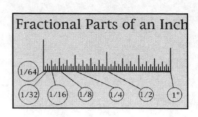

Parts of a foot cannot be easily expressed as decimal inches. For example, in the metric system 7 millimeters is 0.7 centimeters which is 0.07 decimeters which is 0.007 meters. But 7 inches is 0.583333 feet which is 0.19444 yards and so on. This is a clear advantage for the metric system.

The default SOLIDWORKS English system is inch, pound, second (IPS).

Architectural drawings using Metric units are based on the meter. Architectural drawings using English units are based on feet.

Dual dimensioning

Working drawings are usually drawn with all U.S. or all metric dimensions. Sometimes the object manufactured requires using both the U.S. and metric measuring system. In the illustration, the primary units are in inches and the secondary units (mm) are displayed in parentheses.

Example 1:

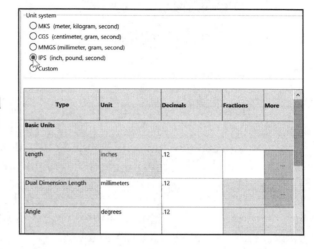

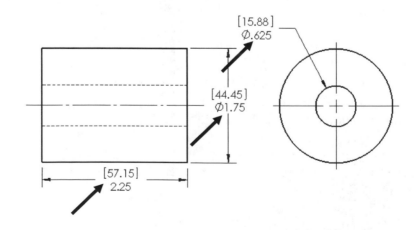

Scale

An engineer's scale is a tool for measuring distances and transferring measurements at a fixed ratio of length. A few of the common scale types are:

- **Architect's scale**: A ruler-like device which facilitates the production of technical drawings.

- **Engineer's scale**: A ruler-like device similar to the Architect's scale, helpful when drawing rooms.

- **Linear encoder**: A kind of linear scale used in precision manufacturing for positioning.

- **Linear scale**: A means of showing the scale of a map, chart, or drawing.

- **Vernier scale**: A scale that allows for higher precision than a uniformly-divided straight or circular measurement scale.

Never measure a drawing directly. Its dimensions can be printed at any scale or the drawing may be drawn one way and dimensioned another.

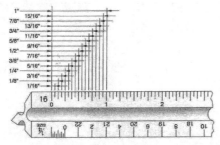

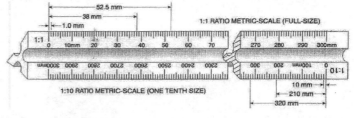

Engineering Scale - English
Full inches are measured to the right while fractions of an inch are measured to the left.

Engineering Scale - Metric
Note the Scale - Full Size: (1:1)

Visit the following sites for additional information on scales: http://www.usfa.dhs.gov/downloads/pdf/nfa/engineer-architect-scales.pdf

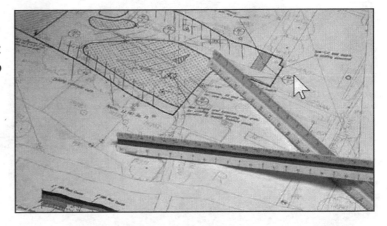

Standards for Dimensioning

All drawings should be dimensioned completely so that a minimum of computation is necessary, and the part can be built without scaling the drawing. However, there should not be a duplication of dimensions unless such dimensions make the drawing clearer and easier to read. These dimensions are called reference dimensions and are enclosed in parentheses.

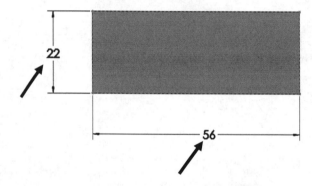

Linear dimension

A Linear dimension is a dimension that is either horizontal or vertical to the dimensioning plane. Read a drawing from left to right.

Example 1:

Stagger dimension

The general practice is to stagger the dimension text on <u>parallel dimensions</u> (small to large) as illustrated.

Example 1:

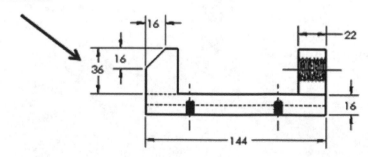

Aligned dimension

Aligned dimension is a style of dimensioning in which text is placed parallel to the dimension line. The aligned method of dimensioning is **not** approved by the current ANSI standards but may be seen on older drawings.

Example 1:

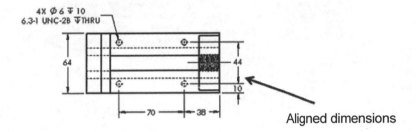

Aligned dimensions

Angular dimension

The design of a part may require some lines to be drawn at an angle. The amount of the divergence (the amount the lines move away from each other) is indicated by an angle measured in degrees or fractional parts of a degree. The degree is indicated by a symbol ° placed after the numerical value of the angle.

Example 1:

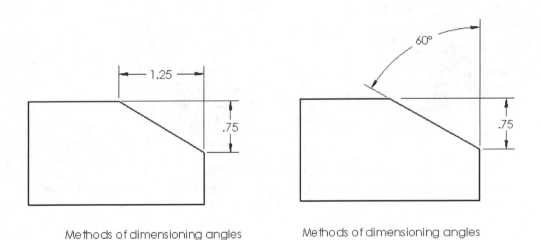

Methods of dimensioning angles   Methods of dimensioning angles

The dimension line for an angle should be an arc whose ends terminate in arrowheads.

The numeral indication, the number of degrees in the angle, is read in a horizontal position, except where the angle is large enough to permit the numerals to be placed along the arc.

Example 2:

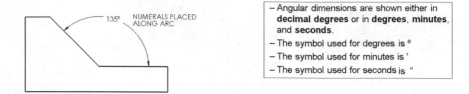

Chamfer dimension

A chamfer connects two objects to meet in a flattened or beveled corner.
In SOLIDWORKS, the chamfer tool creates a beveled feature on selected edges, faces or a vertex.

Example 1:

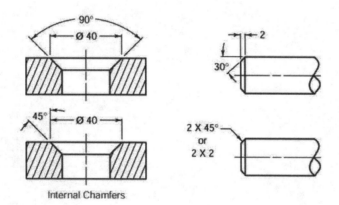

Slot dimension

Create a slot dimension with a combination of radii, linear dimensions and annotations. SOLIDWORKS has a Slot Sketch tool with various options.

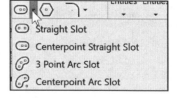

Example 1:

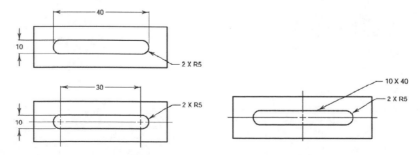

Radius dimension (Leader line)

The Radius leader line is a continuous straight line that extends at an angle from a note, a dimension, or other reference to a feature. A leader line for a diameter or radius should be radial. A radial line is one that passes through the center of the circle or arc if extended.

If an arc is less than half a circle, the radius is specified, preceded by an R. The leader dimension line for a radius shall have a single arrowhead touching the arc as illustrated.

Example 1:

Simple Hole dimension (Leader line)

The simple hole dimension leader line is a continuous straight line that extends at an angle from a note, a dimension, or other reference to a feature.

Example 1:

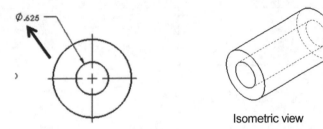

Isometric view

ANSI standard requires that full cylinders (holes and bosses) must always be measured by their diameter. The diameter symbol must precede the numerical value to indicate that the dimension shows the diameter of a circle or cylinder. The symbol used is the Greek letter phi (Ø).

A feature should be dimensioned only once. Each feature should be dimensioned or identified with a note. Dimension features or surfaces should be done to a logical reference point.

Enough space should be provided to avoid crowding and misinterpretation. Extension lines and object lines should not overlap.

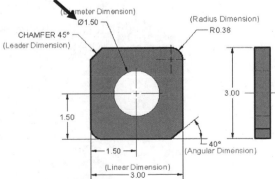

The standard size ratio for all arrowheads on mechanical drawings is ~2.5:1 (Length to width).

Simple Hole dimension

A simple hole is created by drilling, reaming or punching. A simple hole must be measured by its diameter. The diameter symbol must precede the numerical value followed by a note (annotation) indicating the operation to be performed and the number of holes to be produced, as illustrated.

Example 1:

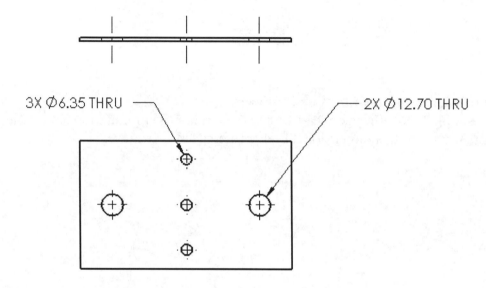

DIMENSIONING A SIMPLE HOLE

Repetitive features or dimensions can be specified by using the symbol "X" along with the number of times the feature is repeated as illustrated above. There is no space between the number of times the feature is repeated and the "X" symbol; however, there is a space between the symbol "X" and the dimension.

If a hole goes completely through the feature and it is not clearly shown on the drawing, the abbreviation "THRU" in all upper case follows the dimension. All notes should be in UPPER CASE LETTERS.

Fastener Hole dimension (Annotations)

Denote drilled hole information by a bent leader line as illustrated.

Example 1:

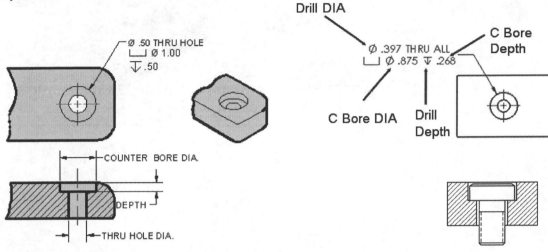

If a hole goes completely through the feature and it is not clearly shown on the drawing, the abbreviation **"THRU"** or **"THRU ALL"** in all upper case follows the dimension. Additional information is presented later in the chapter on Fasteners.

Cylindrical dimension

Full cylinders (holes and bosses) must always be measured by their diameter. The diameter symbol must precede the numerical value to indicate that the dimension shows the diameter of a circle or cylinder. The symbol used is the Greek letter phi (ø).

The length and diameter of the cylinder are usually placed in the view which shows the cylinder as a rectangle as illustrated below.

Example 1:

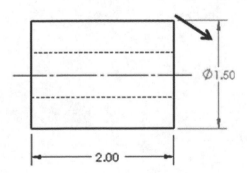

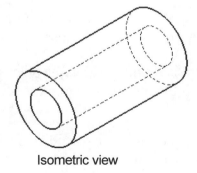

Isometric view

Example 2:

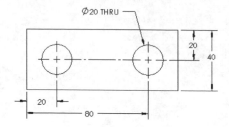

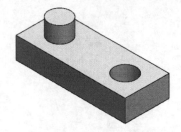

Isometric view

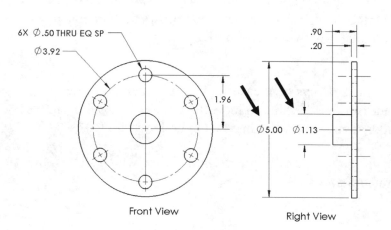

Example 3:

Isometric view

Front View

Right View

Your choice of dimensions will directly influence the method used to manufacture the part.

If there is room, position the diameter dimension up and to the left, off the model in a circular view.

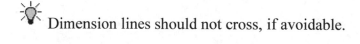 The Front view should be the most descriptive view if appropriate.

Dimension lines should not cross, if avoidable.

Equally spaced hole dimension

Dimension equally spaced holes on a cylinder. The exact location of the first hole is given by a location dimension. To locate the remaining holes, the location dimension is followed by 1.) Diameter of the holes, 2.) Number of holes, 3.) Notation EQUALLY SPACED or "EQ SP" as illustrated.

Example 1:

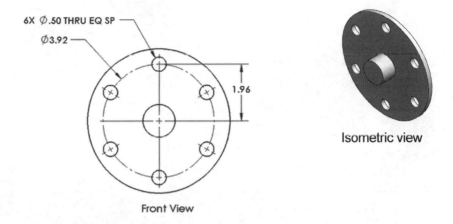

Front View

Isometric view

Hole dimension location

Holes are often dimensioned in relation to one another and to a finished surface. Dimensions are usually given, in such cases, in the view in which the shape of the hole is, that is, square, round or elongated. The preferred method of placing these dimensions is illustrated below.

Example 1:

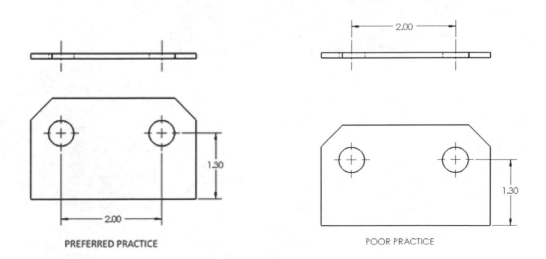

PREFERRED PRACTICE   POOR PRACTICE

Point/center of a circle dimension

Center of an arc or circle can be found by creating vertical and horizontal center lines from the machined surfaces.

Example 1:

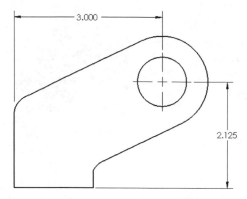

Dimensioning the center of a circle

Arc dimension

Arc dimensions measure the distance along an arc or polyline arc segment. Apply Foreshortened leader lines for large arcs as illustrated. Typical uses of arc length dimensions include measuring the travel distance around a cam or indicating the length of a cable.

Example 1:

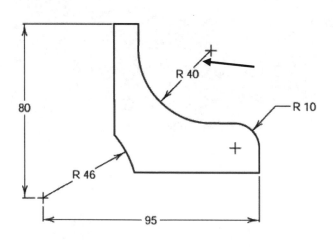

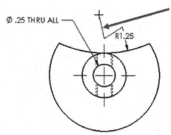

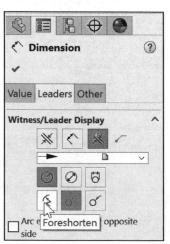

Order of Preference - Linear Dimension line

There is an order and style of preference for a linear dimension line using arrowheads. The first order of preference is that the dimension and arrowheads are drawn between the extension line if space is available. If space is limited, see the below order of preference.

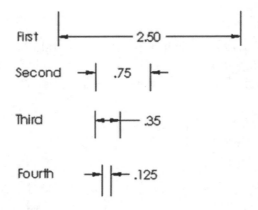

1.	Arrows in / dimension in
2.	Arrows out / dimension in
3.	Arrows in / dimension out
4.	Arrows out / dimension out

Precision

In the fields of science and engineering the accuracy of a measurement system is the degree of closeness of measurements of a quantity to that quantity's actual (true) value.

The precision of a measurement system, also called reproducibility or repeatability, is the degree to which repeated measurements under unchanged conditions show the same results. Although the two words precision and accuracy can be synonymous in colloquial use, they are deliberately contrasted in the context of the scientific method.

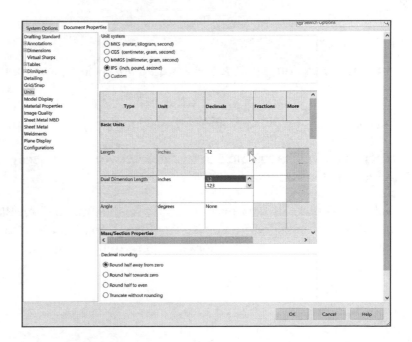

Precision of a dimension on an engineering drawing is the number of digits located after the decimal point. Dimensions may appear on drawings as a one-place decimal, two-place decimal or more. SOLIDWORKS provides the ability to set both primary and secondary precision.

Three and four place decimal dimensions continue to be used for more precise dimensions requiring machining accuracies in thousandths or ten-thousandths of an inch.

Size Dimension

Every solid or part has three size dimensions: width or length, height and depth. In the case of the Glass box method, two of the dimensions are usually placed on the Principal view and the third dimension is located on one of the other (Top, Right) views.

Example 1:

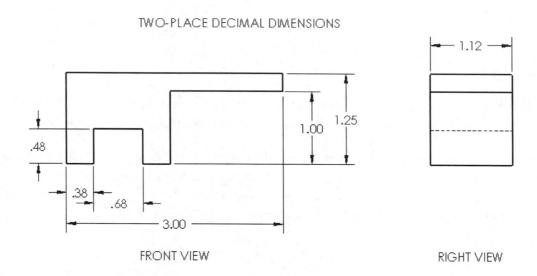

Do not dimension inside a view and do not over dimension the model in a drawing.

Always locate the dimension off of the view if possible. Only place dimensions on the inside of the view if they add clarity, simplicity, and ease of reading.

There should be a visible gap ~1.5mm between the object (feature) line and the beginning of each extension line.

When you create a new part or assembly, the three default Planes (Front, Right and Top) are aligned with specific views. The Plane you select for the Base sketch determines the orientation of the part, the drawing views and the assembly.

Continuous Dimensions

Sets of dimension lines and dimensions should be located on drawings close enough so they may be read easily without any possibility of confusing one dimension with another. If a series of dimensions is required, the dimensions should be placed in a line as continuous dimensions (chain dimensioning or point-to-point dimensioning) as illustrated below. This method is preferred over the staggering of dimensions, because of ease in reading, appearance, and simplified dimensioning. Note: Tolerance stack-up can be an issue with this method.

Example 1:

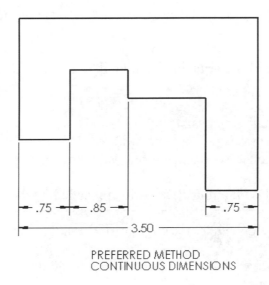

PREFERRED METHOD
CONTINUOUS DIMENSIONS

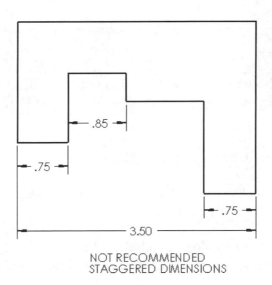

NOT RECOMMENDED
STAGGERED DIMENSIONS

 Spacing between dimension lines should be uniform throughout the drawing.

Principles of good dimensioning

The overriding principle of dimension is clarity. Below are a few key rules that you should know when applying dimensions:

- A dimension is a numerical value shown on a drawing to define the size of an object or a part of an object.

- Each feature of an object is dimensioned once and only once.

- Dimensions should be selected to suit the function of the model or feature.

- Dimensions should be placed in the most descriptive view of the feature being dimensioned.

- Dimensions should be located outside the boundaries (view) of the object whenever possible.

- Group dimensions whenever possible.

- Diameters are dimensioned with a numerical value preceded by the diameter symbol.

- Radii are dimensioned with a numerical value preceded by the radius symbol.

- Dimension a slot in a view where the contour of the slot is visible.

- When a dimension is given to the center of an arc or radius, a small cross (center mark) should be displayed.

- Place a smaller dimension inside a larger dimension on a drawing view to avoid dimension line crossing.

- The depth of a blind hole may be specified in a note. The depth is measured from the surface of the object to the deepest point where the hole still measures a full diameter in width.

- Counter bored, spotfaced, or countersunk holes should be specified in a note.

- A leader line for a diameter or radius should be radial. A radial line is one that passes through the center of the circle or arc if extended.

- ANSI standard states, "Dimensioning to hidden lines should be avoided wherever possible." However, sometimes it is necessary if additional views are needed to fully define the model.

Example 1:

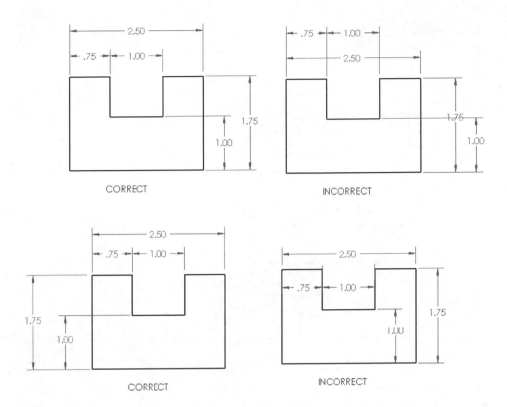

There is an order and style of preference for a linear dimension line using arrowheads. The first order of preference is that the dimension and arrowheads are drawn between the extension line if space is available. If space is limited, see the below order of preference.

Example 1:

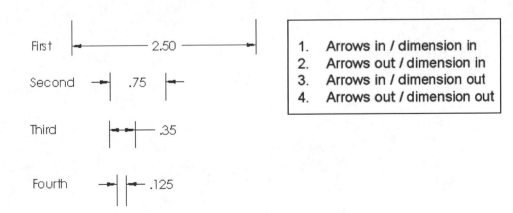

1.	Arrows in / dimension in
2.	Arrows out / dimension in
3.	Arrows in / dimension out
4.	Arrows out / dimension out

Dimension Exercises:
Exercise 1:

Identify the dimension errors in the below illustration. Circle and list the errors.

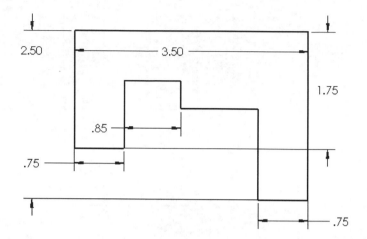

Errors:_____

_____

Exercise 2:

Identify the dimension errors in the below illustration. Circle and list the errors.

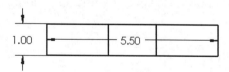

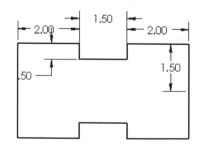

Errors:_____

_____

Exercise 3:

Identify the duplicate dimensions and cross out the ones that you feel should be omitted. Explain why. Are there any dimensioning mistakes in this drawing? Explain.

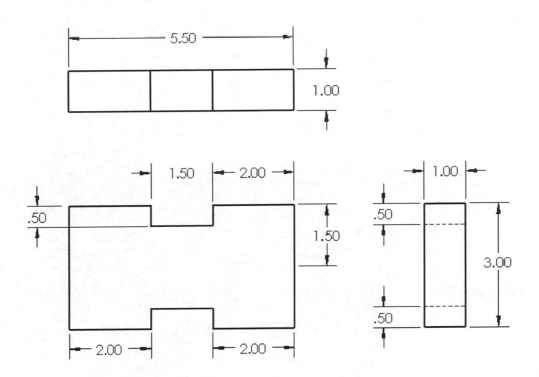

Explain:

_____

_____

_____

Dimension Exercises:

Exercise 1:

Identify the dimension errors in the below illustration. Circle and list the errors.

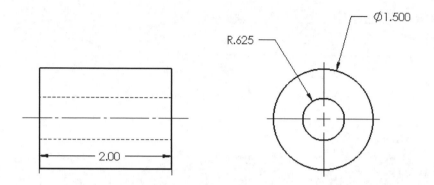

Errors:_____

_____

Exercise 2:

Identify the dimension errors in the below illustration. Circle and list the errors.

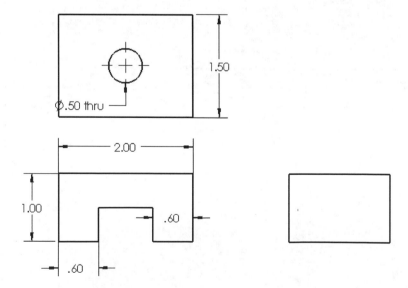

Errors:_____

_____

Exercise 3:

Identify the dimension errors in the below illustration. Circle and list the errors.

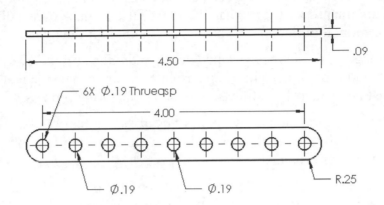

Explain:

_____

_____

Exercise 4:

Identify the dimension errors in the below illustration. Circle and list the errors.

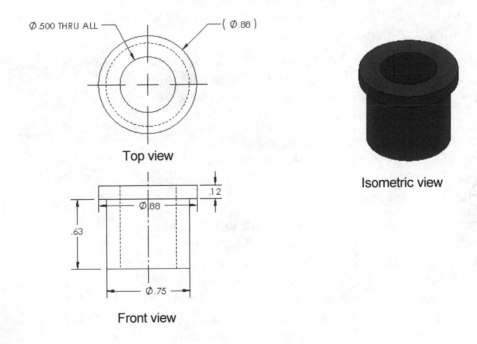

Explain:

_____

_____

Precision and Tolerance

In a manufacturing environment, quality and cost are two of the main considerations for an engineer or designer. Engineering drawings with local and general notes and dimensions often serve as purchasing documents, construction, inspection, and legal contracts to ensure the proper function and design of the product. When dimensioning a drawing, it is essential to reflect on the precision required for the model.

Precision is the degree of accuracy required during manufacturing. However, it is unfeasible to produce any dimension to an absolute, accurate measurement. Some discrepancy must be provided or allowed in the manufacturing process.

Specifying higher precision on a drawing may ensure better quality of a product, but doing so can increase the cost of the part and make it cost prohibitive in being competitive with similar products.

For example, consider a design that contains cast components. A cast part usually has two types of surfaces: 1.) mating surfaces, and 2.) non-mating surfaces.

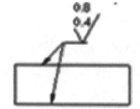

Mating surfaces work together with other surfaces, typically machined to a specified finish. Mating surfaces typically require higher precision on all corresponding dimensions.

Non-mating surfaces are usually left in the original rough-cast form. They have no significant connection with other surfaces. The dimensions on a drawing must clearly indicate which surfaces are to be finished and provide the degree of precision needed for the finishing.

The method of specifying the degree of precision is called Tolerancing. Tolerance in simple terms is the amount of size variation permitted and provides a useful means to achieve the precision necessary in a design.

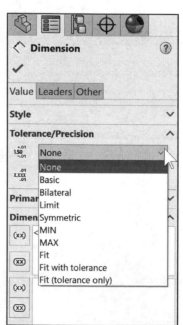

Tolerancing makes certain interchangeability in manufacturing. Parts can be manufactured by different companies in various locations while maintaining the proper functionality of the intended design.

In tolerancing, each dimension is permitted to vary within a specified amount. By assigning as large a tolerance as possible, without interfering with the functionality or intended design of a part, the production costs can be reduced and the product can be competitive in the real world. The smaller the tolerance range specified, the more expensive it is to manufacture. There is always a trade off in design.

Tolerance for a drawing

The two most common Tolerance Standard agencies are American National Standards Institute (ANSI)/(ASME) and the International Standards Organization (ISO). This book covers the ANSI (US) standards.

In this section we will discuss Dimensional Tolerances vs. Geometric Tolerances.

General Tolerance - Title Block

General tolerances are typically provided in the Title Block. General tolerances are applied to the dimensions in which tolerances are not given in the drawing.

As a part is designed, the engineer should consider: 1.) function either as a separate unit or as a component relation to other components in an assembly, 2.) manufacturing operations, 3.) material, 4.) quantity (run size), 5.) sustainability and 6.) cost.

The dimensions displayed on a drawing (obtained from the part) indicate the accuracy limits for manufacturing. The limits are called tolerances and are normally displayed in decimal notation. Tolerances can be specified in various unit systems. ANSI specifications are normally specified either in English (IPS) or Metric (MMGS).

Tolerances on decimal dimensions are expressed in terms of one, two, three, or more decimal places. This information can be documented on a drawing in several ways. One of the common methods of specifying a tolerance that applies to all dimensions is to use a general note in the Title block as illustrated.

Example 1 & 2:

UNLESS OTHERWISE SPECIFIED:	UNLESS OTHERWISE SPECIFIED:
DIMENSIONS ARE IN INCHES TOLERANCES: ANGULAR: ± 1° ONE PLANE DECIMAL ± .1 TWO PLACE DECIMAL ± .01 THREE PLACE DECIMAL ± .005	DIMENSIONS ARE IN MILLIMETERS TOLERANCES: ANGULAR: MACH± 0°30' ONE PLACE DECIMAL ±0.5 TWO PLACE DECIMAL ±0.15

Local Tolerance - Dimension

A Local Tolerance note indicates a special situation which is not covered by the General Title box. A Local Tolerance is located on the drawing (Not in the Title box) with the dimension.

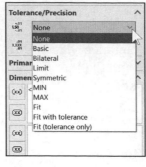

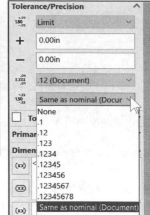

The three most common Tolerance types are *Limit, Bilateral and Unilateral*.

Limit Tolerance is when a dimension has high (upper) and low (Lower) limits stated. In a limit tolerance, the higher value is placed on top, and the lower value is placed on the bottom as illustrated.

Limits are the maximum and minimum size that a part can obtain and still pass

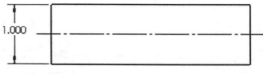

$$\varnothing^{1.001}_{.999} \quad \text{or} \quad \varnothing.999 - 1.001$$

inspection and function in the intended assembly. When both limits are placed on a single line, the lower limit precedes the higher limit. The tolerance for the dimension illustrated above is the total amount of variation permitted or .002.

In the angle example the dimension may vary between 60°and 59°45'.

Note: Each degree is one three hundred and sixtieth of a circle (1/360). The degree (°) may be divided into smaller units called minutes ('). There are 60 minutes in each degree. Each minute may be divided into smaller units called seconds ("). There are 60 seconds in each minute. To simplify the dimensioning of angles, symbols are used to indicate degrees, minutes and seconds as illustrated below.

Name	Symbol
Degrees	°
Minutes	'
Seconds	"

Unilateral Tolerance is the variation of size in a single direction - either (+) or (-). The examples of Unilateral tolerances shown below indicate that the first part meets standards of accuracy when the nominal or target dimension varies in one direction only and is between 3.000" and 3.025".

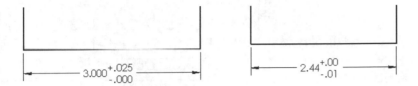

Bilateral Tolerance is the variation of size in both directions. The dimensions may vary from a larger size (+) to a smaller size (-) than the basic dimension (nominal size). The basic 2.44" dimension as illustrated with a bilateral tolerance of +-.01" is acceptable within a range of 2.45" and 2.43".

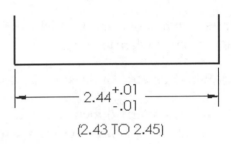

(2.43 TO 2.45)

💡 Specify a tolerance with the degree of accuracy that is required for the design to work properly and is cost effective.

💡 You can also create a note on the drawing referring to a specific dimension or specifying general tolerances in the Title block.

Formatting Inch Tolerances

The basic dimension and the plus and minus values should have the same number of decimal places. Below are examples of *Unilateral* and *Bilateral* tolerances.

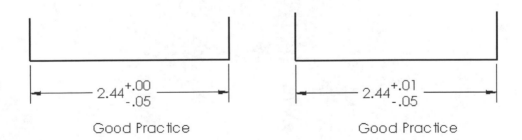

Good Practice   Good Practice

Metric Dimension Specifications

For Metric dimension specification, the book uses the Metric International System of Units (SI). The millimeter is the common unit of measurement used on engineering drawings made to the metric system.

In industry, a general note would be displayed in the Title block section of the drawing to invoke the metric system. A general note is "UNLESS OTHERWISE SPECIFIED: DIMENSIONS ARE IN MILLIMETERS."

UNLESS OTHERWISE SPECIFIED:

DIMENSIONS ARE IN MILLIMETERS
TOLERANCES:
ANGULAR: MACH± 0°30'
ONE PLACE DECIMAL   ±0.5
TWO PLACE DECIMAL ±0.15

Three conventions are used when specifying dimensions in metric units:

1.) When a metric dimension is a whole number, the decimal point and zero are omitted.

2.) When a metric dimension is less than 1 millimeter, a zero precedes the decimal point. Example - 0.2 has a zero to the left of the decimal point.

3.) When a metric dimension is not a whole number, a decimal point with the portion of a millimeter (10ths or 100ths) is specified.

Tolerance Parts and Important Terms

The illustration below shows a system of two parts with tolerance dimensions. The two parts are an example of ASME Y14.5 2009 important terms.

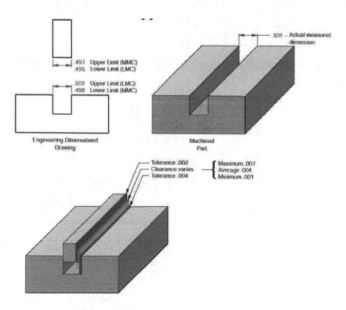

- **Nominal size** - a dimension used to describe the general size, usually expressed in common fractions. The slot in the above illustration has a nominal size of ½".

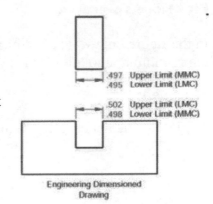

- **Basic size** - the theoretical size used as a starting point for the application of tolerances. The basic size of the slot is .500".

- **Actual size** - the measured size of the finished part after machining is .501".

- **Limits** - the maximum and minimum sizes shown by the tolerance dimension. The slot has limits of .502" and .498", and the mating part has limits of .495" and .497". The larger value for each part is the upper limit, and the smaller value is the lower limit.

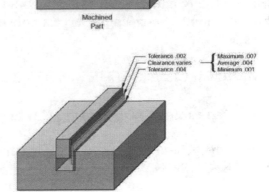

- **Allowance** - the minimum clearance or maximum interference between parts, or the tightest fit between two mating parts. In the illustration, the allowance is .001", meaning that the tightest fit occurs when the slot is machined to its smallest allowable size of .498" and the mating part is machined to its largest allowable size of .497". The difference between .498" and .497" or 001" is the allowance.

- **Tolerance** - the total allowable variance in a dimension; the difference between the upper and lower limits. The tolerance of the slot is .004". (.502" - .498" = .004") and the tolerance of the mating parts is .002" (.497" - .495" = .002").

- **Maximum material condition (MMC)** - the condition of a part when it contains the greatest amount of material. The MMC of an external feature, such as a shaft, is the upper limit. The MMC of an internal feature, such as a hole, is the lower limit.

- **Least material condition (LMC)** - the condition of a part when it contains the least amount of material possible. The LMC of an external feature is the lower limit. The LMC of an internal feature is the upper limit.

- **Piece tolerance** - the difference between the upper and lower limits of a single part.

- **System tolerance** - the sum of all the piece tolerances.

Fit - Hole Tolerance

In the figure below, what is the minimum clearance (Allowance)? Minimum clearance is the minimum amount of space which exists between the hole and the shaft.

Example 1:

Minimum Clearance (Allowance) = $(0.49d_{hole})$ - $(0.51D_{shaft})$ = -0.02in.

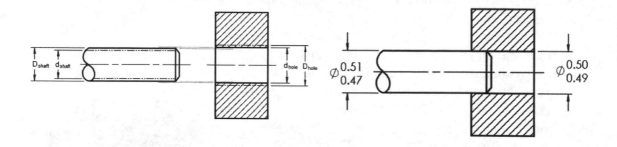

In the figure above, what is the maximum clearance (Allowance)? Maximum clearance is the difference between the largest hole diameter D_{hole} and the smallest shaft diameter d_{shaft}.

Maximum Clearance (Allowance) = $(0.50D_{hole})$ - $(0.47d_{shaft})$ = 0.03in.

Fit Types between Mating Parts

Fit is the general term used to signify the range of tightness in the design of mating parts. In ANSI/ASME Y 14.5M, three general types of fits are designated for mating parts:

1. Clearance Fit

2. Interference Fit

3. Transition Fit

A basic hole and shaft system will be used to apply English unit tolerances to parts in the following examples.

Clearance Fit: The difference between the hole and shaft sizes before assembly is positive. Clearance fits have limits of size prearranged such that a clearance always results when the mating parts are assembled. Clearance fits are intended for accurate assembly of parts and bearings. The parts can be assembled by hand because the hole is always larger than the shaft. Min. Clearance > 0. Two examples: Lock and Key, Door and Door frame.

Interference Fit: (also referred to as Force fit or Shrink fit) - interference fit has limits of size that always result in interference between mating parts. The hole is always smaller than the shaft. Interference fits are for permanent assemblies of parts which require rigidity and alignment, such as dowel pins and bearings in casting, hinge pin or a pin in a bicycle chain. Max. Clearance ≤ 0.

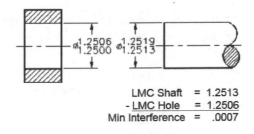

LMC Shaft	= 1.2513
- LMC Hole	= 1.2506
Min Interference	= .0007

MMC Shaft	= 1.2519
- MMC Hole	= 1.2500
Max Interference	= .0019

Transition Fit: May provide either clearance or interference, depending on the actual value of the tolerance of individual parts. Transition fits are a compromise between the clearance and Interference fits. They are used for applications where accurate location is important, but either a small amount of clearance or interference is permissible. Max. Clearance > 0, Min. Clearance < 0.

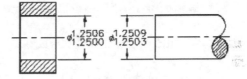

LMC Hole	= 1.2506
- LMC Shaft	= 1.2503
Positive Clearance	= .0003
MMC Shaft	= 1.2509
- MMC Hole	= 1.2500
Negative Allowance (Interference)	= .0003

Why is this information important? By specifying the correct allowances and tolerances, mating components in an assembly can be completely interchangeable.

Sometimes the desired fit may require very small allowances and tolerances, and the production cost may become too high and cost prohibitive. In these cases, either manual or computer-controlled selective assembly is often used. The manufactured parts are then graded as small, medium and large based on the actual sizes. In this way, very satisfactory fits are achieved at a much lower cost than manufacturing all parts to very accurate dimensions.

Fasteners in General

Fasteners include Bolts and Nuts (threaded), Set screws (threaded), Washers, Keys, and Pins to name a few. Fasteners are not a permanent means of assembly such as welding or adhesives.

Fasteners and threaded features should be specified on your engineering drawing.

- Threaded features: Threads are specified in a thread note. In SOLIDWORKS, apply the Hole Wizard feature.

- General Fasteners: Purchasing information must be given to allow the fastener to be ordered correctly.

Woodruff Key

Machine Key

A few commonly used Fasteners

What is the difference between a bolt and a screw?

- A bolt is designed to be inserted through a hole and secured with a nut.

- A screw is designed to be used in a threaded hole - sometimes with a nut.

Fully Threaded

Partially Threaded

See American Society of Mechanical Engineers (ASME) standard B18.2.1 (1996) for additional information.

Hex Bolt:

A bolt is a fastener having a head on one end and a thread on the other end. A bolt is used to hold two parts together by means of passing through aligned clearance holes with a nut screwed on the threaded end.

Carriage Bolt:

A carriage bolt is mostly used in wood with a domed shape top and a square under the head, which is pulled into the wood as the nut is tightened.

Studs:

A stud is a rod with threaded ends.

Cap Screws:

A hexagon cap screw is similar to a bolt except it is used without a nut and generally has a longer thread. Cap screws are available in a variety of head styles and materials.

Machine Screws:

A machine screw is similar to the slot-head cap screw but smaller, available in many styles and materials. A machine screw is also commonly referred to as a stove bolt. From left to right: Slotted, Phillips and Square.

Wood Screws:

A tapered shank screw is for use exclusively in wood. Wood screws are available in a variety of head styles and materials. From left to right: Slotted, Phillips and Hex.

Sheet Metal Screws:

Highly versatile fasteners designed for thin materials. Sheet metal screws can be used in wood, fiberglass and metal, also called self-tapping screws, available in steel and stainless steel. From left to right: Slotted, Square and Phillips.

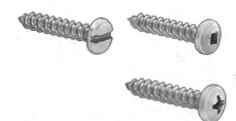

Socket Screws:

Socket screws, also known as Allen head, are fastened with a hexagonal Allen wrench, available in several head styles and materials.

Allen wrench

Set Screws:

Set screws are used to prevent relative motion between two parts. A set screw is screwed into one part so that its point is pushed firmly against the other part, available in a variety of point styles and materials.

Nuts:

Nuts are used to attach machine thread fasteners. From left to right there is a Hex nut, Locked nut, Slotted nut and a Wing nut.

Washers:

Washers provide a greater contact surface under the fastener. This helps prevent a nut, bolt or screw from breaking through the material. Shown is a Flat vs. Split Lock washer.

Keys:

Keys are used to prevent relative motion between shafts and wheels, couplings and similar parts attached to shafts.

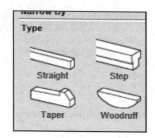

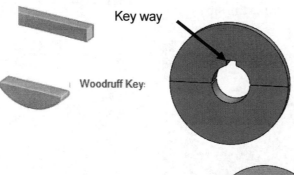

Key way

Woodruff Key

Step Key

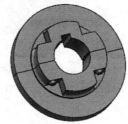

Rivets:

Rivets are generally used to hold sheet metal
parts together. Rivets are generally
considered as permanent fasteners and are
available in a variety of head styles and
materials.

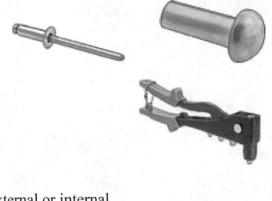

🔅 Threads are only symbolically
represented on drawings; therefore, thread
notes are needed to provide the required
information. A thread note must be included
on all threaded parts, with a leader line to the external or internal
in a circular view.

Representing External (Male) Threads

Screw threads are used widely (1) to fasten two or more parts together in position, (2) to
transmit power such as a feed screw on a machine, and (3) to move a scale on an
instrument used for precision measurements.

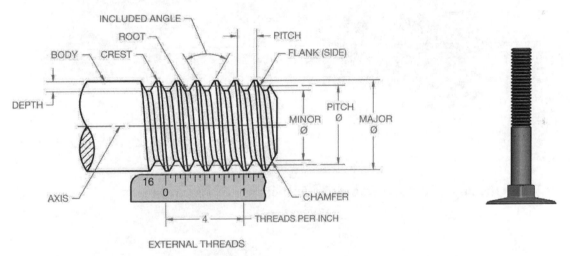

EXTERNAL THREADS

*Profile of UNIFIED and the American National Threads.

🔅 An edge of a uniform section in the form of a helix on the **external** surface of a
cylinder or cone. **"A"** suffix.

Cutting External (Male) Threads

Start with a shaft the same size as the major diameter. An external thread is cut using a die or a lathe as illustrated below.

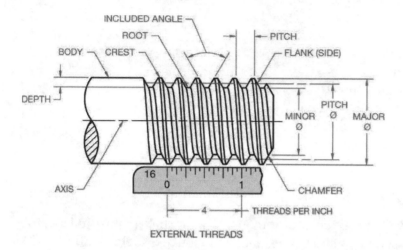

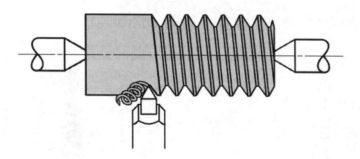

A chamfer on the end of the screw thread makes it easier to engage the nut.

Representing Internal (Female) Threads

An internal thread is a ridge of a uniform section in the form of a helix on the **internal** surface of a cylinder or cone. **"B"** suffix.

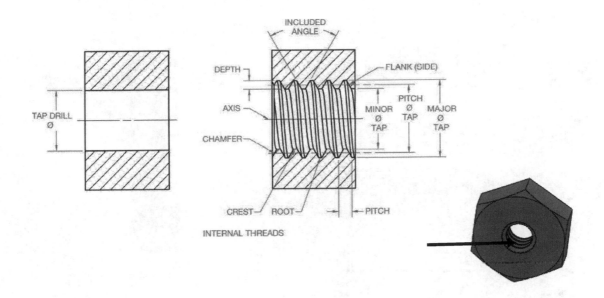

Cutting Internal (Female) Threads

In general, a tap drill hole is cut with a twist drill. The tap drill hole is a little larger than the minor diameter. Start with a shaft the same size as the major diameter as illustrated below.

Minor Diameter: The smallest diameter (fractional diameter or number) of a screw thread.

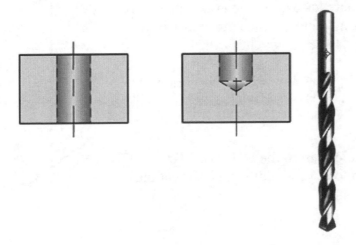

Then the threads are cut using a tap. Major tap types:

- **Taper** tap.

- **Plug** tap.

- **Bottoming** tap.

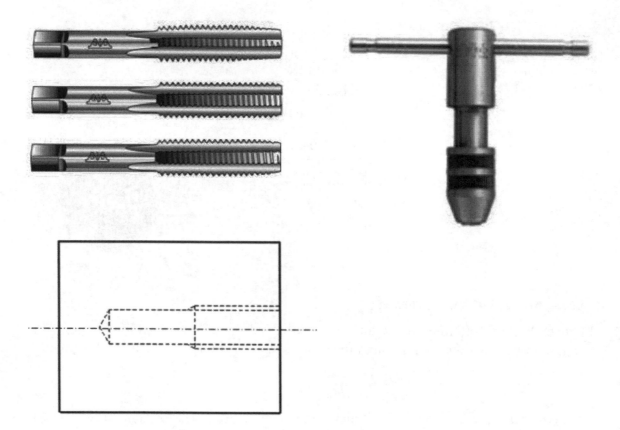

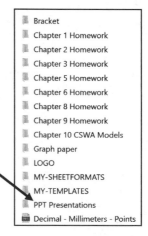

The process of cutting threads using a tap is called tapping, whereas the process using a die is called threading. Both tools can be used to clean up a thread, which is called chasing.

Download all model files from the SDC Publication website (https://www.sdcpublications.com/downloads/978-1-63057-485-7).

View the presentations from the SOLIDWORKS-MODELS 2022\PPT Presentation folder for additional information.

American National Standard and Unified Screw threads

The basic profile is the theoretical profile of the thread. An essential principle is that the actual profiles of both the nut and bolt threads must never cross or transgress the theoretical profile. So bolt threads will always be equal to, or smaller than, the dimensions of the basic profile. Nut threads will always be equal to, or greater than, the basic profile. To ensure this in practice, tolerances and allowances are applied to the basic profile.

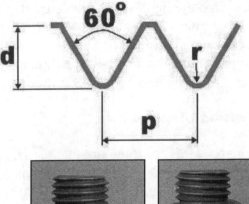

The most common screw thread form is the symmetrical V-Profile with an included angle of 60 degrees. This form is prevalent in the Unified National Screw Thread Series (UN, UNC, UNF, UNRC, UNRF) form as well as the ISO/Metric.

A thread may be either right-hand or left-hand. A right-hand thread on an external member advances into an internal thread when turned clockwise. Threads are always considered to be Right-handed unless otherwise specified.

A left-hand thread advances when turned counterclockwise (bike pedals, older propane tanks, etc.). All left-hand threads are labeled LH.

RIGHT HANDED   LEFT HANDED

Single vs. Double or Triple Threads

If a single helical groove is cut or formed on a cylinder, it is called a single-thread screw. Should the helix angle be increased sufficiently for a second thread to be cut between the grooves of the first thread, a double thread will be formed on the screw. Double, triple, and even quadruple threads are used whenever a rapid advance is desired, as on valves.

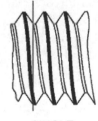

SINGLE   DOUBLE

To designate a multiple thread the word "DOUBLE" (or "TRIPLE," and so on) is placed after the class of fit, like this: 3/8x1-16 UNC 2B DOUBLE.

Pitch and Major Diameter

Pitch and major diameter designates a thread. Lead is the distance advanced parallel to the axis when the screw is turned one revolution.

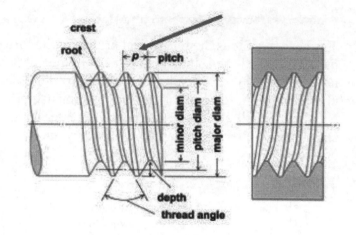

For a single thread, *lead is equal to the pitch*; for a double thread, lead is twice the pitch. For a straight thread, the pitch diameter is the diameter of an imaginary coaxial cylinder that would cut the thread forms at a height where the width of the thread and groove would be equal.

Thread Class of Fit

Classes of fit are tolerance standards; they set a plus or minus figure that is applied to the pitch diameter of bolts or nuts. The classes of fit used with almost all bolts sized in inches are specified by the ANSI/ASME Unified Screw Thread standards (which differ from the previous American National standards). There are three major Thread classes of fits:

Class 1: The loosest fit. Used on parts which require assembly with a minimum of binding. Only found on bolts ¼ inch in diameter and larger.

Class 2: By far the most common class of fit. General purpose threads for bolts, nuts, and screws used in mass production.

Class 3: The closest fit. Used in precision assemblies where a close fit is desired to withstand stress and vibration.

Thread class identifies a range of thread tightness or looseness.

Classes for **External (male)** threads have an "A" suffix, for example, "2A," and classes for **Internal threads** have a "B" suffix.

General Thread Notes

The Thread note is usually applied to a drawing with a leader in the view where the thread is displayed as a circle for internal threads as illustrated below. External threads can be dimensioned with a leader with the thread length given as a dimension or at the end of the note. Below is the English – IPS unit system.

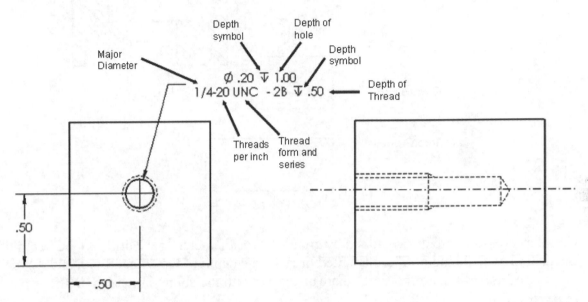

Per the illustration to the right: Major Diameter - .25in, 20 threads per inch or a Pitch - 1/20, threads 2 inches long, Unified National Series Course, Thread Class 2, A - male. Note: If not stated, the thread is always Right-handed, Single.

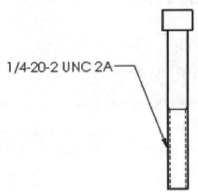

Threads are only symbolically represented on drawings; therefore, thread notes are needed to provide the required information. A thread note must be included on all threaded parts, with a leader line to the external or internal in a circular view.

Dimensioning a Counterbore Hole

A Counterbore hole is a cylindrical flat bottom hole that has been machined to a larger diameter for a specified depth, so that a bolt or pin will fit into the recessed hole. The Counterbore provides a flat surface for the bolt or pin to seat against. In SOLIDWORKS, use the Hole Wizard to insert the hole callout for a Counterbore.

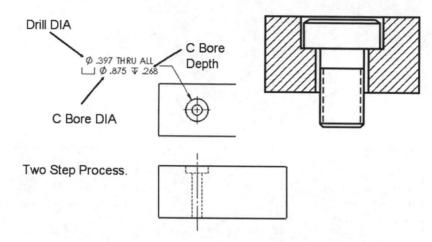

Counterbore holes are dimensioned by giving 1.) the diameter of the drill, 2.) the depth of the drill, 3.) the diameter of the counterbore , 4.) the depth of the counterbore, and 4.) the number of holes. Counterbore holes are displaced with the abbreviation C'BORE, C BORE or the symbol ⊔.

The difference between a C'BORE and a SPOTFACE is that the machining operation occurs on a curved surface.

Dimensioning a Countersunk Hole

The Countersunk hole, as illustrated below, is a cone-shaped recess machined in a part to receive a cone-shaped flat head screw or bolt.

A Countersunk hole is dimensioned by giving 1.) the diameter of the hole, 2.) the depth of the hole 3.) the diameter of the Countersunk, 4.) the angle at which the hole is to be Countersunk, 5.) the Counterbore diameter, 6.) the depth of the Counterbore, and 7.) the number of holes to be Countersunk.

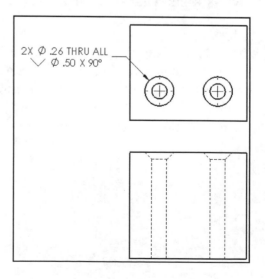

Adding a Counterbore for head clearance to a
Countersink is optional. In SOLIDWORKS, the
Head Clearance option is located in the Hole
Wizard Property Manager. The symbol for a
Countersunk hole on a drawing annotation is
CSK or $\vee$.

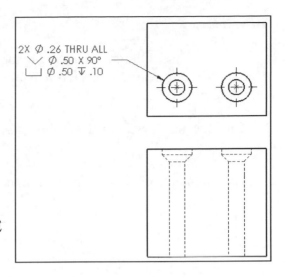

Chapter Summary

In Chapter 3 you reviewed basic dimensioning
practices and were introduced to general
tolerancing terminology according to the ASME
Y14.5-2009 standard. You reviewed various
dimensioning systems and fits and were
presented with the right and wrong way to
dimension simple shapes, lines, angles, circles
and arcs.

Dimensioning a drawing is a means to communicate the requirements to manufacture a
part. It requires special annotations for fasteners, threads, countersunk holes,
counterbored holes and other types of holes.

Tolerances determine the maximum and minimum variation that a dimension on a part is
manufactured to. By understanding the required tolerance, you can save both time and
money to create a part from your drawing.

Although SOLIDWORKS automatically generates most annotations for a part, it is up to
the designer to determine if all the required information is available to manufacture the
part. The annotations must be presented according to a dimensioning standard. There is
no partial credit in the machine shop.

Questions

1. True or False: Dimensions should not be duplicated or the same information given in two different ways. If a reference dimension is used, the size value is placed within parentheses (X).

2. The U.S. unit system is also known as the (IPS) unit system. What does IPS stand for?

3. The diameter of a hole is placed in the view in which the hole is shown as a _____.

4. The length and diameter of cylinder are usually placed in the view which shows the cylinder as a _____.

5. Dimension a hole by its _____.

6. True or False: Dimensioning to hidden lines should be avoided wherever possible.

7. If a hole goes completely through the feature and it is not clearly shown on the drawing, the abbreviation _____ follows the dimension.

8. True or False: A dimension is said to have a *Unilateral* (single) tolerance when the total tolerance is in one direction only, either (+) or (-).

9. The degree (°) may be divided into smaller units called _____. There are 60 _____ in each degree. Each minute may be divided into smaller units called _____.

10. Classes for an **External (male thread)** have a _____ suffix.

11. Classes for an **Internal (female thread)** have a _____ suffix.

12. There are three major Thread classes of fits; they are: _____, _____, _____. Explain the differences.

13. Identify the pitch of the following Thread note: 3/8-16 UNC 2B DOUBLE_____.

14. Identify the symbol of a Counterbore and Countersunk:_____, _____.

Exercises

Exercise 3.1: Estimate the dimensions in a whole number. Dimension the below illustration. Note: There is more than one way to dimension an angle.

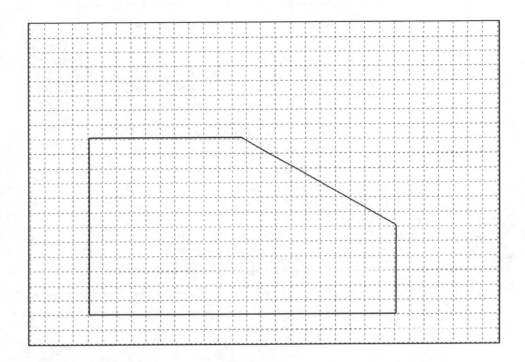

Exercise 3.2:
Estimate the dimensions in a whole number. Dimension the illustration. Note: There is more than one way to dimension an angle.

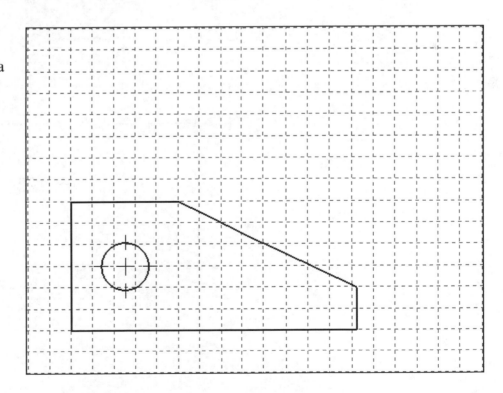

Exercise 3.3: Identify the dimension errors in the below illustration. Circle and list the errors.

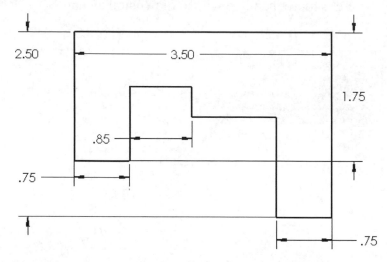

Errors:_____

_____

Exercise 3.4: Arrowheads are drawn between extension lines if space is available. If space is limited, what is the preferred Arrowhead and dimension location order? List the preferred order.

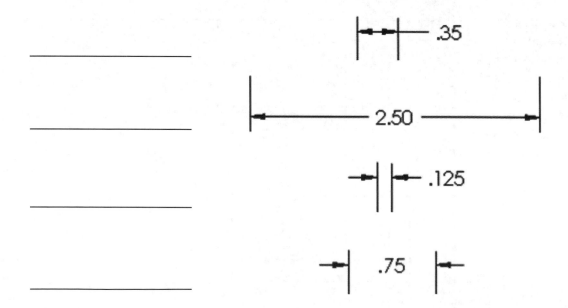

Exercise 3.5: Identify the dimension errors in the below illustration. Circle and list the errors.

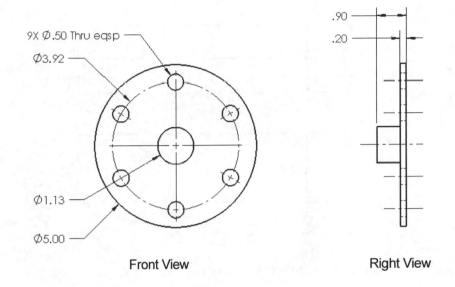

Front View   Right View

Errors:_____

_____

Exercise 3.6: Identify the dimension errors in the below illustration. Circle and list the errors.

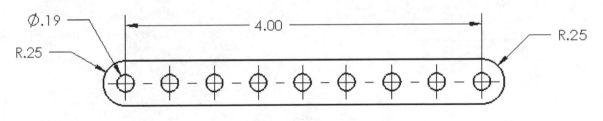

Front View

Errors:_____

_____

Exercise 3.7: Place a *limit* tolerance of 002 on the below model.

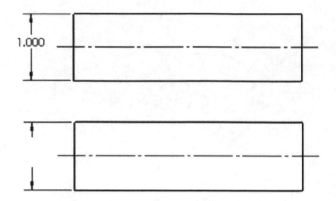

Exercise 3.8: Name three of the most common Tolerance Types.

1._____

2._____

3._____

Exercise 3.9: Identify the following symbols.

_____	∨
_____	⊔
_____	∅
_____	⟱

Exercise 3.10: Describe the following hole callouts (symbols and meanings) in detail.

⌀ .2500 THRU ALL
⌴ ⌀ .5000 ▽ .1250

⌀ .3970 THRU ALL
∨ ⌀ .7731 X 82°
⌴ ⌀ .7731 ▽ .0402

Exercise 3.11: True/False - The loosest fit is a Class 1 fit. A Class 1 fit is used on parts which require assembly with a minimum of binding.

Exercise 3.12: The two most common Tolerance Standard agencies are American National Standards Institute (ANSI)/(ASME) and the International Standards Organization (ISO). In the ANSI (US) standard: This is a two part question.

True or False:

T   F   The higher limit is placed below the lower limit.

T   F   When both limits are placed on one line, the lower limit precedes the higher limit.

Exercise 3.13: There are basically two types of dimensioning systems used in creating parts and drawings - **U.S.** and **Metric**.

True or False: The U.S. system uses the decimal inch value. When the decimal inch system is used, a zero is not used to the left of the decimal point for values less than one inch and trailing zeros are not used.

True or False: The Metric system normally is expressed in millimeters. When the millimeter system is used, the number is rounded to the nearest whole number. Trailing zeros are used.

Exercise 3.14: Identify the illustrated Thread Note.
Remember units.

1/4-20-2 UNC 2A

1.) Pitch of the Thread:_____

2.) Major Thread Diameter:_____

3.) Internal or External Threads:_____

4.) Left Handed or Right Handed Threads:_____

5.) Number of Threads per inch:_____

6.) Identify the Thread class:_____

7.) Length of the Thread:_____

Exercise 3.15: In the figure below, the **tightest fit** between the two parts will be when the **largest shaft** is fit inside the **smallest hole**. Calculate the Allowance (MMC).

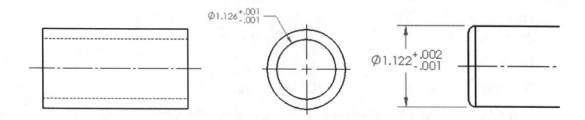

Exercise 3.16: In the figure below, the **loosest fit** between the two parts below will be when the **smallest shaft** is fit inside the **largest hole**. Calculate the maximum clearance between the two parts.

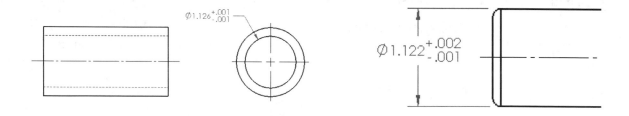

Chapter 4

Overview of SOLIDWORKS® 2022 and the User Interface

Below are the desired outcomes and usage competencies based on the completion of Chapter 1.

Desired Outcomes:	Usage Competencies:
• A comprehensive understanding of the SOLIDWORKS® User Interface (UI) and CommandManager.	• Ability to establish a SOLIDWORKS session. • Aptitude to utilize the following items: Menu bar toolbar, Menu bar menu, Drop-down menus, Context toolbars, Consolidated drop-down toolbars, System feedback icons, Task Pane, Confirmation Corner, Heads-up View toolbar, Document Properties and more. • Open a new and existing SOLIDWORKS part. • Knowledge to zoom, rotate and maneuver a three-button mouse in the SOLIDWORKS Graphics window.

Notes:

Chapter 1 - Overview of SOLIDWORKS® 2022 and the User Interface

Chapter Objective

Provide a comprehensive understanding of the SOLIDWORKS® default User Interface and CommandManager: Menu bar toolbar, Menu bar menu, Drop-down menu, Right-click Pop-up menus, Context toolbars/menus, Fly-out tool button, System feedback icons, Confirmation Corner, Heads-up View toolbar and more.

On the completion of this chapter, you will be able to:

- Utilize the Welcome - SOLIDWORKS dialog box.

- Establish a SOLIDWORKS session.

- Comprehend the SOLIDWORKS User Interface.

- Recognize the default Reference Planes in the FeatureManager.

- Open a new and existing SOLIDWORKS part.

- Utilize Help and SOLIDWORKS Tutorials.

- Zoom, rotate and maneuver a three-button mouse in the SOLIDWORKS Graphics window.

What is SOLIDWORKS®?

- SOLIDWORKS® is a mechanical design automation software package used to build parts, assemblies and drawings that takes advantage of the familiar Microsoft® Windows graphical user interface.

- SOLIDWORKS is an easy to learn design and analysis tool (SOLIDWORKS Simulation, SOLIDWORKS Motion, SOLIDWORKS Flow Simulation, Sustainability, etc.), which makes it possible for designers to quickly sketch 2D and 3D concepts, create 3D parts and assemblies and detail 2D drawings.

- Model dimensions in SOLIDWORKS are associative between parts, assemblies and drawings. Reference dimensions are one-way associative from the part to the drawing or from the part to the assembly.

- This book is written for the beginner to intermediate user.

Start a SOLIDWORKS Session

Start a SOLIDWORKS session and familiarize yourself with the SOLIDWORKS User Interface. As you read and perform the tasks in this chapter, you will obtain a sense of how to use the book and the structure. Actual input commands or required actions in the chapter are displayed in bold.

The book does not cover starting a SOLIDWORKS session in detail for the first time. A default SOLIDWORKS installation presents you with several options. For additional information, visit http://www.SOLIDWORKS.com.

Activity: Start a SOLIDWORKS Session.

Start a SOLIDWORKS session.

1) Type **SOLIDWORKS 2022** in the Search window.

2) Click the **SOLIDWORKS 2022** application (or if available, **double-click** the SOLIDWORKS icon on the desktop). The Welcome - SOLIDWORKS dialog box is displayed by default.

The Welcome - SOLIDWORKS box provides a convenient way to open recent documents (Parts, Assemblies and Drawings), view recent folders, access SOLIDWORKS resources, and stay updated on SOLIDWORKS news.

3) **View** your options. Do not open a document at this time.

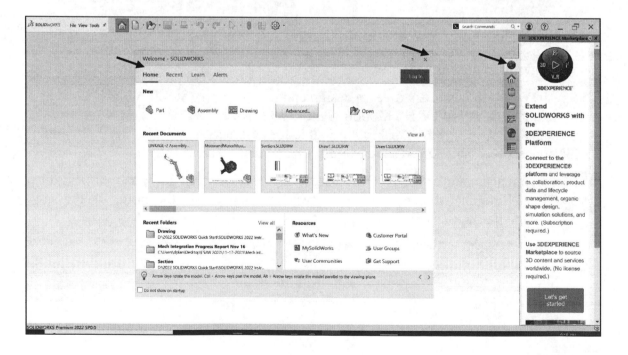

Home Tab

The Home tab lets you open new and existing documents, view recent documents and folders, and access SOLIDWORKS resources (*Part, Assembly, Drawing, Advanced mode, Open*).

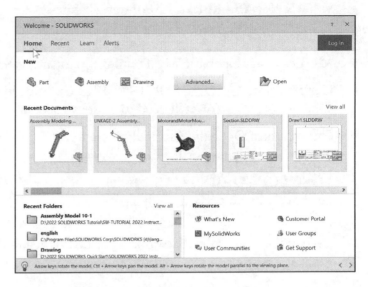

Recent Tab

The Recent tab lets you view a longer list of recent documents and folders. Sections in the Recent tab include *Documents* and *Folders*.

The Documents section includes thumbnails of documents that you have opened recently.

Click a thumbnail to open the document, or hover over a thumbnail to see the document location and access additional information about the document. When you hover over a thumbnail, the full path and last saved date of the document appears.

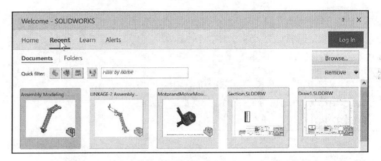

Learn Tab

The Learn tab lets you access instructional resources to help you learn more about the SOLIDWORKS software.

Sections in the Learn tab include:

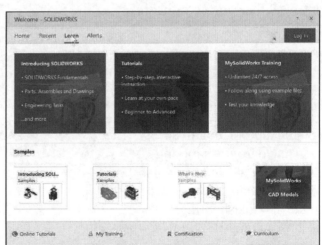

- **Introducing SOLIDWORKS**. Open the Introducing SOLIDWORKS book.

- **Tutorials**. Open the step-by-step tutorials in the SOLIDWORKS software.

- **MySolidWorks Training**. Open the Training section at MySolidWorks.com.

- **Introducing SOLIDWORKS (Samples)**. Open local folders containing sample models.

- **Tutorials (Samples)**. Open the SOLIDWORKS Tutorials (videos) section at solidworks.com.

- **What's New (Samples)**. List of new changes.

- **Online Tutorials**.

- **My Training**. Open the My Training section at MySolidWorks.com.

- **Certification**. Open the SOLIDWORKS Certification Program section at solidworks.com. You will need to create an account with a password.

- **Curriculum**. Open the Curriculum section at solidworks.com. You will need to create an account with a password.

- **MySOLIDWORKS - CAD Models**. Open models in the Community Library. You will need to create an account with a password.

When you install the software, if you do not install the Help Files or Example Files, the Tutorials and Samples links are unavailable.

Alerts Tab

The Alerts tab keeps you updated with SOLIDWORKS news.

Sections in the Alerts tab include Critical, Troubleshooting, and Technical.

The Critical section does not appear if there are no critical alerts to display.

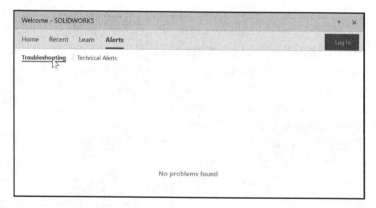

- **Troubleshooting**. Includes troubleshooting messages and recovered documents that used to be on the SOLIDWORKS Recovery tab in the Task Pane.

If the software has a technical problem and an associated troubleshooting message exists, the Welcome dialog box opens to the Troubleshooting section automatically on startup, even if you selected **Do not show at startup** in the dialog box.

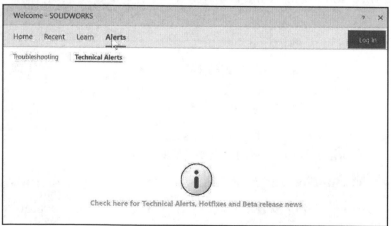

- **Technical Alerts**. Open the contents of the SOLIDWORKS Support Bulletins RSS feed (Hotfixes, release news) at solidworks.com.

Close the Welcome - SOLIDWORKS dialog box.

4) Click **Close** ☒ from the Welcome - SOLIDWORKS dialog box. The SOLIDWORKS Graphics window is displayed. You can also click outside the Welcome - SOLIDWORKS dialog box, in the Graphics window.

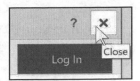

View the SOLIDWORKS Graphics window.

Menu Bar toolbar

The SOLIDWORKS (UI) is designed to make maximum use of the Graphics window. The Menu Bar toolbar contains a set of the most frequently used tool buttons from the Standard toolbar.

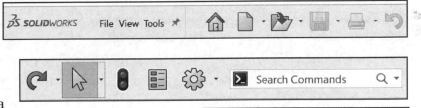

The following default tools are available:

- **Welcome to SOLIDWORKS** 🏠 - Open the Welcome dialog box, **New** 🗋 - Create a new document; **Open** 📂 - Open an existing document; **Save** 💾 - Save an active document; **Print** 🖶 - Print an active document; **Undo** ↩ - Reverse the last action; **Redo** ↪ - Redoes the last action that you reverse; **Select** ▷ - Select Sketch entities, components and more; **Rebuild** 🔴 - Rebuild the active part, assembly or drawing; **File Properties** 📋 - Summary information on the active document;

Options 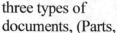 ▾ - Change system options and Add-Ins for SOLIDWORKS; **Login** 🔵 - Login to SOLIDWORKS. You will need to create an account with a password; **Help** ⑦ - access to help, tutorials, updates and more.

Menu Bar menu (No model open)

SOLIDWORKS provides a context-sensitive menu structure. The menu titles remain the same for all three types of documents, (Parts, Assemblies and

Drawings) but the menu items change depending on which type of document is active.

Menu Bar menu (Model open)

The Pin ✗ option displays the Menu bar toolbar and the Menu bar menu as illustrated. Throughout the book, the Menu bar menu and the Menu bar toolbar are referred to as the Menu bar.

Drop-down menu (Open part document)

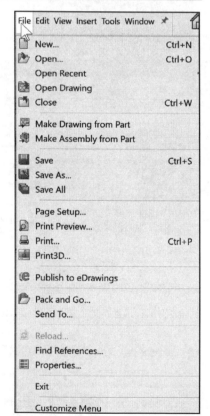

SOLIDWORKS takes advantage of the familiar Microsoft® Windows user interface. Communicate with SOLIDWORKS through drop-down menus, Context sensitive toolbars, Consolidated toolbars or the CommandManager tabs.

To close a SOLIDWORKS drop-down menu, press the Esc key. You can also click any other part of the SOLIDWORKS Graphics window or click another drop-down menu.

Create a New Part Document

Activity: Create a new Part Document.

A part is a 3D model, which consists of features. What are features? Features are geometry building blocks. Most features either add or remove material. Some features do not affect material (Cosmetic Thread).

Features are created either from 2D or 3D sketched profiles or from edges and faces of existing geometry.

Features are individual shapes that combined with other features make up a part or assembly. Some features, such as bosses and cuts, originate as sketches. Other features, such as shells and fillets, modify a feature's geometry.

Features are displayed in the FeatureManager.

☀ The first sketch of a part is called the Base Sketch. The Base sketch is the foundation for the 3D model. The book focuses on 2D sketches and 3D features.

☀ FeatureManager, CommandManager, and tree folders will vary depending on system setup, version, and Add-ins.

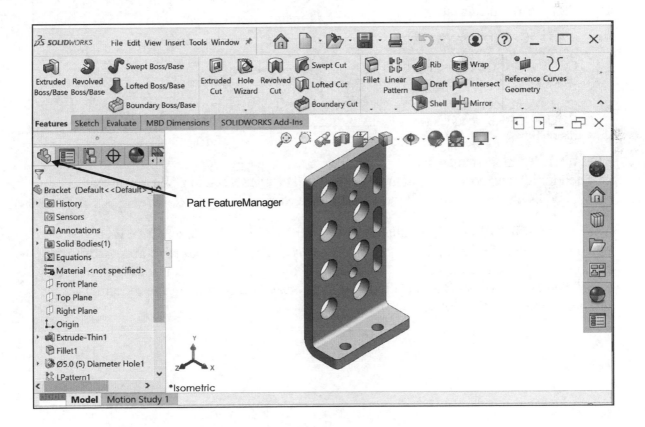

There are two modes in the New SOLIDWORKS Document dialog box: Novice and Advanced. The Novice option is the default option with three templates. The Advanced mode contains access to additional templates and tabs that you create in system options. Use the Advanced mode in this book.

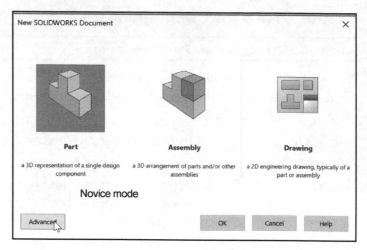

Novice mode

Create a new part.

5) Click **New** from the Menu bar. The New SOLIDWORKS Document dialog box is displayed.

Select the Advanced mode.

6) If needed, click the **Advanced** tab. The below New SOLIDWORKS Document box is displayed.

7) Click the **Templates** tab.

8) Click **Part**. Part is the default template from the New SOLIDWORKS Document dialog box.

9) Click **OK** from the New SOLIDWORKS Document dialog box.

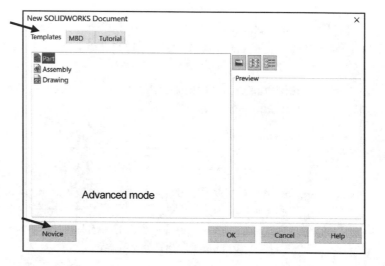

Advanced mode

The Advanced mode remains selected for all new documents in the current SOLIDWORKS session. When you exit SOLIDWORKS, the Advanced mode setting is saved.

The default SOLIDWORKS installation contains three tabs in the New SOLIDWORKS Document dialog box: *Templates, MBD, and Tutorial*. The *Templates* tab corresponds to the default SOLIDWORKS templates. The *MBD* tab corresponds to the templates utilized in the SOLIDWORKS (Model Based Definition). The *Tutorial* tab corresponds to the templates utilized in the SOLIDWORKS Tutorials.

Part1 is displayed in the FeatureManager and is the name of the document. Part1 is the default part window name.

The Part Origin ↳ is displayed in blue in the center of the Graphics window. The Origin represents the intersection of the three default reference planes: *Front Plane*, *Top Plane* and *Right Plane*. The positive X-axis is horizontal and points to the right of the Origin in the Front view. The positive Y-axis is vertical and points upward in the Front view. The FeatureManager contains a list of features, reference geometry, and settings utilized in the part.

Edit the document units directly from the Graphics window as illustrated.

CommandManager, FeatureManager tabs will vary depending on system setup, version, and Add-ins.

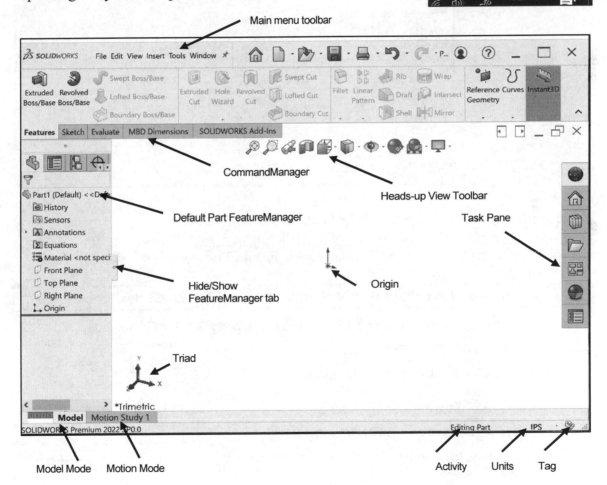

View the Default Sketch Planes.

10)   Click the **Front Plane** from the FeatureManager.

11)   Click the **Top Plane** from the FeatureManager.

12)   Click the **Right Plane** from the FeatureManager.

13)   Click the **Origin** from the FeatureManager. The Origin is the intersection of the Front, Top, and Right Planes. The Origin point is displayed.

14)   Click **inside** the Graphics window.

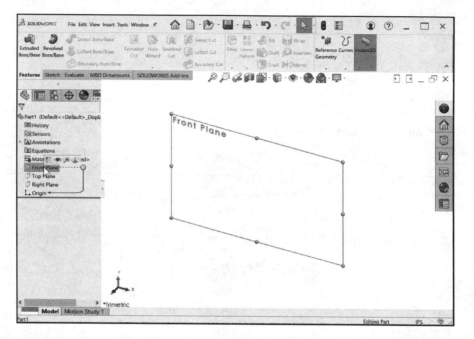

Download all model files from the SDC Publication website (https://www.sdcpublications.com/Downloads/978-1-63057-485-7). Open the Bracket part. Review the features and sketches in the Bracket FeatureManager. Work directly from a local hard drive.

Activity: Download the SOLIDWORKS 2022 Model folder. Open the Bracket Part.

Download the SOLIDWORKS 2022 model folder. Open an existing SOLIDWORKS part.

15)   **Download** the SOLIDWORKS 2022 folder.

16)   **Unzip** the folder. **Work** from the unzip folder.

17)   Click **Open** 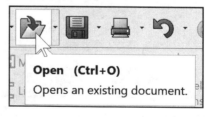 from the Menu bar menu.

18)   Browse to the **SOLIDWORKS 2022\Bracket** folder.

19)   Double-click the **Bracket** part. The Bracket part is displayed in the Graphics window.

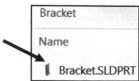

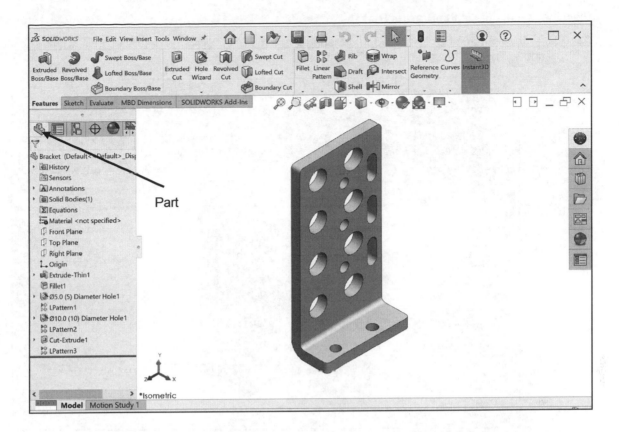

The FeatureManager design tree is located on the left side of the SOLIDWORKS Graphics window. The FeatureManager provides a summarized view of the active part, assembly, or drawing document. The tree displays the details on how the part, assembly or drawing document was created.

Use the FeatureManager rollback bar to temporarily roll back to an earlier state, to absorbed features, roll forward, roll to previous, or roll to the end of the FeatureManager design tree. You can add new features or edit existing features while the model is in the rolled-back state. You can save models with the rollback bar placed anywhere.

In the next section, review the features in the Bracket FeatureManager using the Rollback bar.

Activity: Use the FeatureManager Rollback Bar option.

Apply the FeatureManager Rollback Bar. Revert to an earlier state in the model.

20) Place the **mouse pointer** over the rollback bar in the FeatureManager design tree as illustrated. The pointer changes to a hand 🖑. Note the provided information on the feature. This is called Dynamic Reference Visualization.

21) Drag the **rollback bar** up the FeatureManager design tree until it is above the features you want rolled back, in this case 10.0 (10) Diameter Hole1.

22) **Release** the mouse button.

View the first feature in the Bracket Part.

23) Drag the **rollback bar** up the FeatureManager above Fillet1. View the results in the Graphics window. This is a great feature to re-engineer a part.

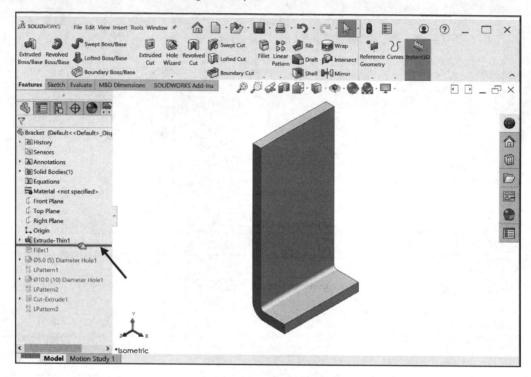

Return to the original Bracket Part FeatureManager.

24) Right-click **Extrude-Thin1** in the FeatureManager. The Pop-up Context toolbar is displayed.

25) Click **Roll to End**. View the results in the Graphics window.

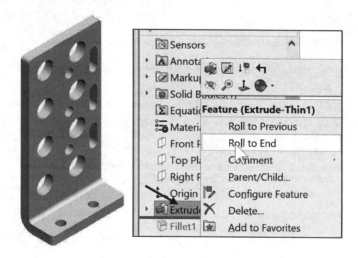

Heads-up View toolbar

SOLIDWORKS provides the user with numerous view options. One of the most useful tools is the Heads-up View toolbar displayed in the Graphics window when a document is active.

💡 *Dynamic Annotation Views* 🖈 : Only available with SOLIDWORKS MBD (Model Based Definition). Provides the ability to control how annotations are displayed when you rotate models.

In the next section, apply the following tools: Zoom to Fit, Zoom to Area, Zoom out, Rotate and select various view orientations from the Heads-up View toolbar.

Activity: Utilize the Heads-up View toolbar.

Zoom to Fit the model in the Graphics window.

26) Click the **Zoom to Fit** 🔍 icon. The tool fits the model to the Graphics window.

Zoom to Area on the model in the Graphics window.

27) Click the **Zoom to Area** 🔍 icon. The Zoom to Area 🔍 icon is displayed.

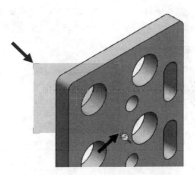

Zoom in on the top left hole.

28) **Window-select** the top left corner as illustrated. View the results.

De-select the Zoom to Area tool.

29) Click the **Zoom to Area** 🔍 icon.

Fit the model to the Graphics window.

30) Press the **f** key.

Rotate the model.

31) Hold the **middle mouse button** down.

    Drag **upward** ↻,

    downward ↻, to the

    left ↻ and to the **right**

    ↻ to rotate the model in the Graphics window.

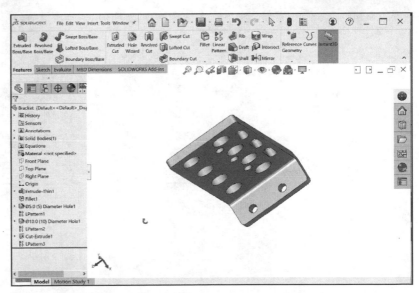

Display a few Standard Views.

32) Click **inside** the Graphics window.

33) Click **Front** from the drop-down Heads-up view toolbar. The model is displayed in the Front view.

34) Click **Right** from the drop-down Heads-up view toolbar. The model is displayed in the Right view.

35) Click **Top** from the drop-down Heads-up view toolbar. The model is displayed in the Top view.

Display a Trimetric view of the Bracket model.

36) Click **Trimetric** from the drop-down Heads-up view toolbar as illustrated. Note your options. View the results in the Graphics window.

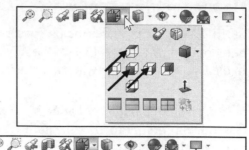

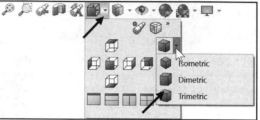

SOLIDWORKS Help

Help in SOLIDWORKS is context-sensitive and in HTML format. Help is accessed in many ways, including Help buttons in all dialog boxes and PropertyManager and Help ⑦ on the Standard toolbar for SOLIDWORKS Help.

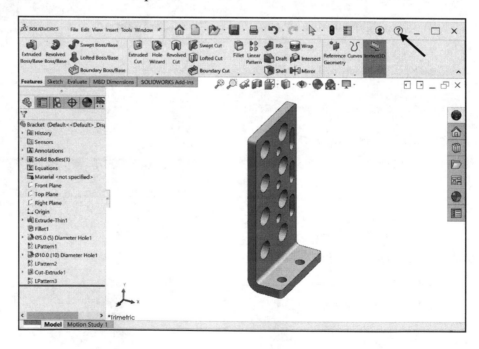

37)   Click ⑦ from the Standard toolbar.

38)   Click ⑦ **Help** from the drop-down menu. The SOLIDWORKS Home Page is displayed by default. View your options.

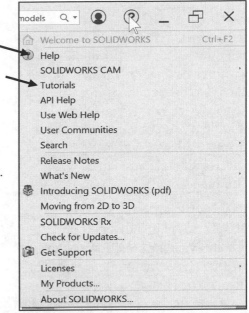

🔆 SOLIDWORKS Web Help is active by default under Help in the Main menu.

Close Help. Return to the SOLIDWORKS Graphics window.

39)   **Close** ☒ SOLIDWORKS Home.

SOLIDWORKS Tutorials

Display and explore the SOLIDWORKS tutorials.

40)   Click ⑦ from the Standard toolbar.

41)   Click **Tutorials**. The SOLIDWORKS Tutorials are displayed. The SOLIDWORKS Tutorials are presented by category.

42)   Click the **Getting Started** category. The Getting Started category provides lessons on parts, assemblies, and drawings.

In the next section, close all models, tutorials and view the additional User Interface tools.

Activity: Close all Tutorials and Models.

Close SOLIDWORKS Tutorials and models.

43)   **Close** ☒ SOLIDWORKS Tutorials.

44)   Click **Window, Close All** from the Menu bar menu.

User Interface Tools

The book utilizes additional areas of the SOLIDWORKS User Interface. Explore an overview of these tools in the next section.

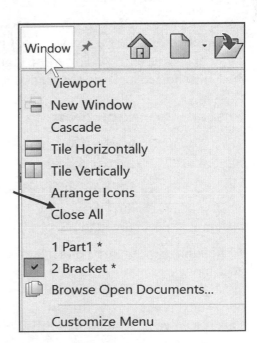

Right-click

Right-click in the Graphics window on a model, or in the FeatureManager on a feature or sketch to display the Context-sensitive toolbar. If you are in the middle of a command, this toolbar displays a list of options specifically related to that command.

Right-click an empty space in the Graphics window of a part or assembly, and a selection context toolbar above the shortcut menu is displayed. This provides easy access to the most commonly used selection tools.

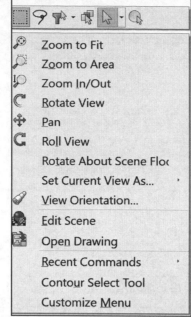

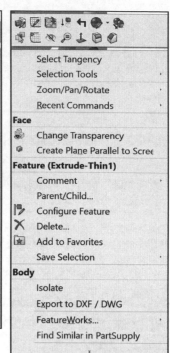

Consolidated toolbar

Similar commands are grouped together in the CommandManager. For example, variations of the Rectangle sketch tool are grouped in a single fly-out button as illustrated.

If you select the Consolidated toolbar button without expanding:

For some commands such as Sketch, the most commonly used command is performed. This command is the first listed and the command shown on the button.

For commands such as rectangle, where you may want to repeatedly create the same variant of the rectangle, the last used command is performed. This is the highlighted command when the Consolidated toolbar is expanded.

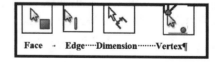

System feedback icon

SOLIDWORKS provides system feedback by attaching a symbol to the mouse pointer cursor.

The system feedback symbol indicates what you are selecting or what the system is expecting you to select.

As you move the mouse pointer across your model, system feedback is displayed in the form of a symbol, riding next to the cursor as illustrated. This is a valuable feature in SOLIDWORKS.

Confirmation Corner

When numerous SOLIDWORKS commands are active, a symbol or a set of symbols is displayed in the upper right hand corner of the Graphics window. This area is called the Confirmation Corner.

When a sketch is active, the confirmation corner box displays two symbols. The first symbol is the sketch tool icon. The second symbol is a large red X. These two symbols supply a visual reminder that you are in an active sketch. Click the sketch symbol icon to exit the sketch and to save any changes that you made.

When other commands are active, the confirmation corner box provides a green check mark and a large red X. Use the green check mark to execute the current command. Use the large red X to cancel the command.

Confirm changes you make in sketches and tools by using the D keyboard shortcut to move the OK and Cancel buttons to the pointer location in the Graphics window.

Heads-up View toolbar

SOLIDWORKS provides the user with numerous view options from the Standard Views, View and Heads-up View toolbar.

The Heads-up View toolbar is a transparent toolbar that is displayed in the Graphics window when a document is active.

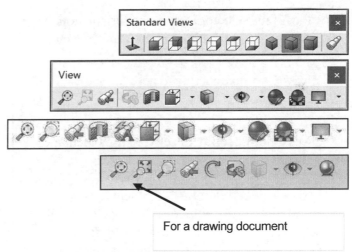

For a drawing document

You can hide, move or modify the Heads-up View toolbar. To modify the Heads-up View toolbar, right-click on a tool and select or deselect the tools that you want to display.

The following views are available.
Note: available views are document dependent.

*   *Zoom to Fit*: Fit the model to the Graphics window.

*   *Zoom to Area*: Zoom to the areas you select with a bounding box.

*   *Previous View*: Display the previous view.

- *Section View* 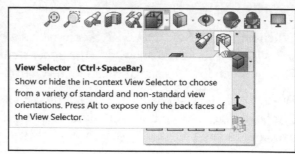 : Display a cutaway of a part or assembly, using one or more cross section planes.

- *Dynamic Annotation Views* : Only available with SOLIDWORKS MBD. Control how annotations are displayed when you rotate a model.

The Orientation dialog has an option to display a view cube (in-context View Selector) with a live model preview. This helps the user to understand how each standard view orientates the model. With the view cube, you can access additional standard views. The views are easy to understand and they can be accessed simply by selecting a face on the cube.

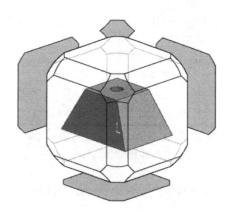

To activate the Orientation dialog box, press (Ctrl + spacebar) or click the View Orientation icon from the Heads-up View toolbar. The active model is displayed in the View Selector in an Isometric orientation (default view).

Click the View Selector icon in the Orientation dialog box to show or hide the in-context View Selector.

Press **Ctrl + spacebar** to activate the View Selector.

Press the **spacebar** to activate the Orientation dialog box.

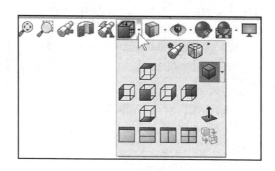

- *View Orientation box* : Select a view orientation or the number of viewports. The options are: *Top, Left, Front, Right, Back, Bottom, Single view, Two view - Horizontal, Two view - Vertical, Four view*. Click the drop-down arrow to access Axonometric views: *Isometric, Dimetric* and *Trimetric*.

- *Display Style* : Display the style for the active view. The options are: *Wireframe, Hidden Lines Visible, Hidden Lines Removed, Shaded, Shaded With Edges*.

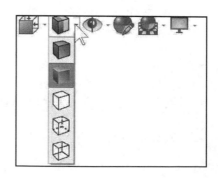

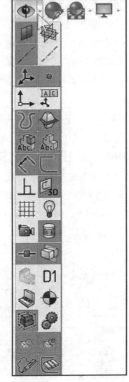

- *Hide/Show Items* : Select items to hide or show in the Graphics window. The available items are document dependent. Note the View Center of Mass ✛ icon.

- *Edit Appearance* : Edit the appearance of entities of the model.

- *Apply Scene* : Apply a scene to an active part or assembly document. View the available options.

- *View Setting* : Select the following settings: *RealView Graphics, Shadows In Shaded Mode, Ambient Occlusion, Perspective* and *Cartoon*.

- *Rotate view* ↻ : Rotate a drawing view. Input Drawing view angle and select the ability to update and rotate center marks with view.

- *3D Drawing View* : Dynamically manipulate the drawing view in 3D to make a selection.

To display a grid for a part, click Options ⚙ ▾ , Document Properties tab. Click Grid/Snaps, check the Display grid box.

🔆 Add a custom view to the Heads-up View toolbar. Press the space key. The Orientation dialog box is displayed. Click the New View tool. The Name View dialog box is displayed. Enter a new named view. Click OK.

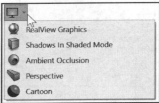

Use commands to display information about the triad or to change the position and orientation of the triad. Available commands depend on the triad's context.

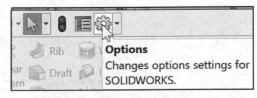

🔆 Save space in the CommandManager, limit your CommandManager tabs. **Right-click** on a CommandManager tab. Click **Tabs**. View your options to display CommandManager tabs.

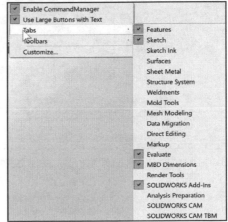

SOLIDWORKS CommandManager

The SOLIDWORKS CommandManager is a Context-sensitive toolbar. By default, it has toolbars embedded in it based on your active document type. When you click a tab below the CommandManager, it updates to display that toolbar. For example, if you click the Sketch tab, the Sketch toolbar is displayed.

For commercial users, SOLIDWORKS Model Based Definition (MBD) and SOLIDWORKS CAM is a separate application. For education users, SOLIDWORKS MBD and SOLIDWORKS CAM is included in the SOLIDWORKS Education Edition.

Below is an illustrated CommandManager for a **Part** document. Tabs will vary depending on system setup and Add-ins.

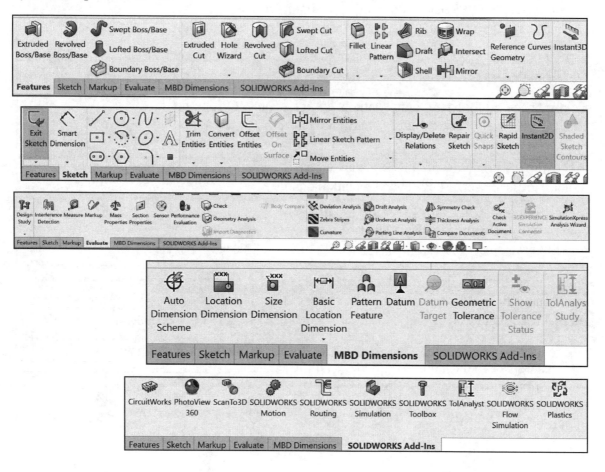

Set button size from the Toolbars tab of the Customize dialog box. To facilitate element selection on touch interfaces such as tablets, you can set up the larger Size buttons and text from the Options menu (Standard toolbar).

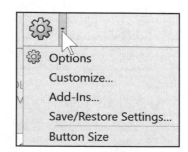

The SOLIDWORKS CommandManager is a Context-sensitive toolbar that automatically updates based on the toolbar you want to access. By default, it has toolbars embedded in it based on your active document type. The available tools are feature and document dependent.

Below is an illustrated CommandManager for a **Drawing** document. Tabs will vary depending on system setup and Add-ins.

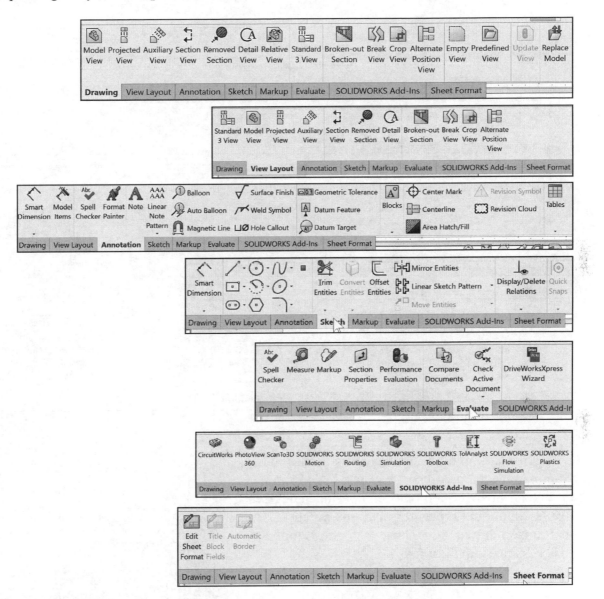

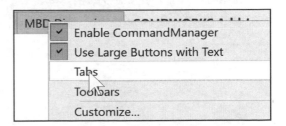 To add a custom tab, right-click on a tab and click Customize. You can also select to add a blank tab and populate it with custom tools from the Customize dialog box.

The SOLIDWORKS CommandManager is a Context-sensitive toolbar that automatically updates based on the toolbar you want to access. By default, it has toolbars embedded in it based on your active document type. The available tools are feature and document dependent.

Below is an illustrated CommandManager for an **Assembly** document. Tabs will vary depending on system setup and Add-ins.

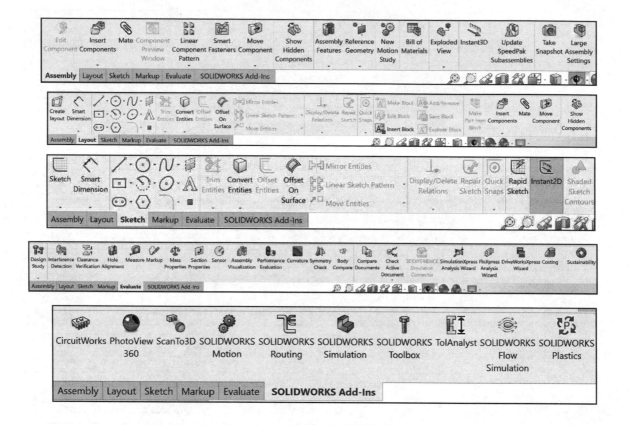

 The Markup tab is displayed by default in the CommandManager on some systems. You can draw markups with a mouse on non-touch devices, display bounding boxes for markups, create markups in drawings, and use the context toolbar to access markup options.

The Markup toolbar displays different options depending on the device. **Draw** Draw and **Touch** Touch are **not** available for non-touch devices.

Float the CommandManager. Drag the Features, Sketch or any CommandManager tab. Drag the CommandManager anywhere on or outside the SOLIDWORKS window.

To dock the CommandManager, perform one of the following:

While dragging the CommandManager in the SOLIDWORKS

window, move the pointer over a docking icon - Dock above , Dock left , Dock right and click the needed command.

Double-click the floating CommandManager to revert the CommandManager to the last docking position.

Collapse the CommandManager

Collapse the CommandManager to only display the available tabs. No tools are shown.

Click the Collapsed CommandManager arrow to the right of the active CommandManager tab as illustrated. Only the tabs are displayed.

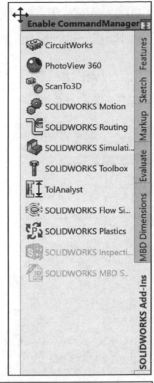

To display the CommandManager tools back, click on a CommandManager tab. Click the Pin CommandManager as illustrated.

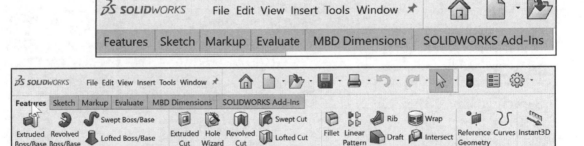

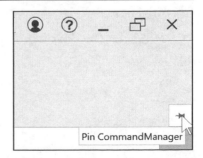

Part FeatureManager Design Tree

The Part FeatureManager consists of various tabs:

- *FeatureManager design tree* 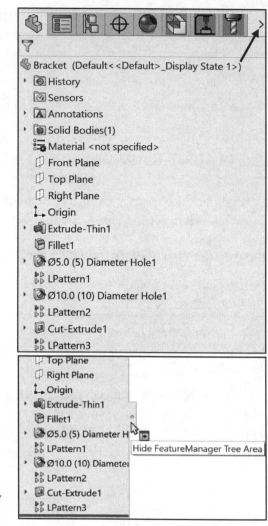 tab.

- *PropertyManager* tab.

- *ConfigurationManager* tab.

- *DimXpertManager* tab.

- *DisplayManager* tab.

- *CAM FeatureManager tree* tab.

- *CAM Operation tree* tab.

- *CAM Tools tree* tab.

Click the direction arrows to expand or collapse the FeatureManager design tree.

CommandManager and FeatureManager tabs and folder files will vary depending on your SOLIDWORKS applications and Add-ins.

Select the Hide/Show FeatureManager Area tab

as illustrated to enlarge the Graphics window for modeling.

The Sensors tool located in the FeatureManager monitors selected properties in a part or assembly and alerts you when values deviate from the specified limits. There are five sensor types: Simulation Data, Mass properties, Dimensions, Measurement and Costing Data.

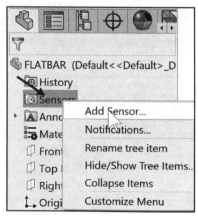

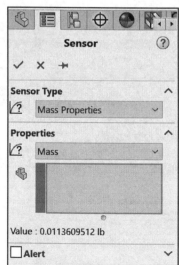

Various commands provide the ability to control what is displayed in the FeatureManager design tree.

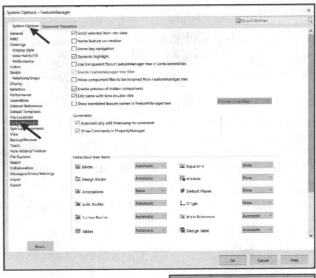

1. Show or Hide FeatureManager items.

Click **Options** ⚙ ˙ from the Menu bar. Click **FeatureManager** from the System Options tab. Customize your FeatureManager from the Hide/Show tree Items dialog box.

2. Filter the FeatureManager design tree. Enter information in the filter field. You can filter by *Type of features, Feature names, Sketches, Folders, Mates, User-defined tags* and *Custom properties*.

Tags are keywords you can add to a SOLIDWORKS document to make them easier to filter and to search. The Tags ⊘ icon is located in the bottom right corner of the Graphics window.

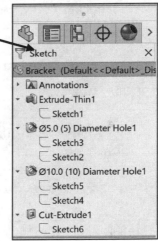

Collapse all items in the FeatureManager, **right-click** and select **Collapse items**, or press the **Shift** + **C** keys.

The FeatureManager design tree and the Graphics window are dynamically linked. Select sketches, features, drawing views, and construction geometry in either pane.

Split the FeatureManager design tree and either display two FeatureManager instances, or combine the FeatureManager design tree with the ConfigurationManager or PropertyManager.

Move between the FeatureManager design tree, PropertyManager, ConfigurationManager, DimXpertManager, DisplayManager and others by selecting the tab at the top of the menu.

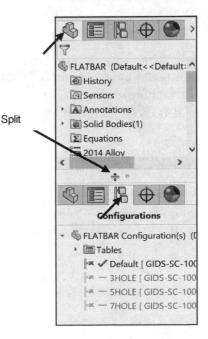

The ConfigurationManager 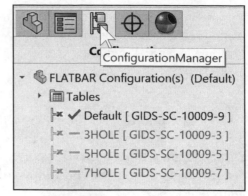 tab is located to the right of the PropertyManager 📋 tab. Use the ConfigurationManager to create, select and view multiple configurations of parts and assemblies.

The icons in the ConfigurationManager denote whether the configuration was created manually or with a design table.

The DimXpertManager ⊕ tab provides the ability to insert dimensions and tolerances manually or automatically. The options are: **Auto Dimension Scheme** 🖾, **Auto Pair Tolerance** 🖾, **Basic, Location Dimension** ⊩⊶, **Basic Size Dimension** ⬎, **General Profile Tolerance** 🖾, **Show Tolerance Status** ⬆⊚, **Copy Scheme** ⬦, **Import Scheme** ⊕, **TolAnalyst Study** ·🖾 and **Datum Target** 🗿.

💡 TolAnalyst is available in SOLIDWORKS Premium.

Fly-out FeatureManager

The fly-out FeatureManager design tree provides the ability to view and select items in the PropertyManager and the FeatureManager design tree at the same time.

Throughout the book, you will select commands and command options from the drop-down menu, fly-out FeatureManager, Context toolbar, or from a SOLIDWORKS toolbar.

💡 Another method for accessing a command is to use the accelerator key. Accelerator keys are special keystrokes, which activate the drop-down menu options. Some commands in the menu bar and items in the drop-down menus have an underlined character.

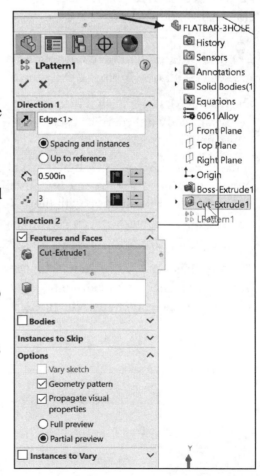

Task Pane

The Task Pane is displayed when a SOLIDWORKS session starts. You can show, hide, and reorder tabs in the Task Pane. You can also set a tab as the default so it appears when you open the Task Pane, pin or unpin to the default location.

The Task Pane contains the following default tabs:

- *3DEXPERIENCE Marketplace*

- *SOLIDWORKS Resources* .

- *Design Library* .

- *File Explorer* .

- *View Palette* .

- *Appearances, Scenes and Decals* .

- *Custom Properties* .

Additional tabs are displayed with Add-Ins.

Use the **Back** and **Forward** buttons in the Design Library tab and the Appearances, Scenes, and Decals tab of the Task Pane to navigate in folders.

3DEXPERIENCE MARKETPLACE

Click the 3DEXPERIENCE MARKETPLACE icon to connect to the 3DEXPERIENCE platform and leverage its collaboration, product data and lifecycle management, organic shape design, simulation solutions, and more. (Subscription required.)

Use 3DEXPERIENCE MARKETPLACE to source 3D content and services worldwide. (No license required.)

SOLIDWORKS Resources

The SOLIDWORKS Resources 🏠 icon displays the following default selections:

- *Welcome to SOLIDWORKS.*

- *SOLIDWORKS Tools.*

- *Online Resources.*

- *Subscription Services.*

Other user interfaces are available during the initial software installation selection: *Machine Design, Mold Design, Consumer Products Design, etc.*

Design Library

The Design Library 📚 contains reusable parts, assemblies, and other elements including library features.

The Design Library tab contains default selections. Each default selection contains additional subcategories.

The default selections are:

- *Design Library.*

- *SOLIDWORKS Content (Internet access required).*

- *Toolbox.*

🔆 Activate the SOLIDWORKS Toolbox. Click Tools, Add-Ins.., from the Main menu. Check the SOLIDWORKS Toolbox Library and SOLIDWORKS Toolbox Utilities box from the Add-ins dialog box or click SOLIDWORKS Toolbox from the SOLIDWORKS Add-Ins tab.

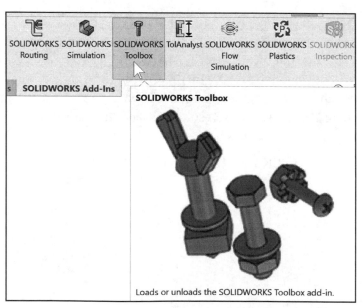

To access the Design Library folders in a non-network environment, click Add File Location
and browse to the needed path. Paths may vary depending on your SOLIDWORKS
version and window setup. In a network environment, contact your IT department for system
details.

File Explorer

File Explorer ⌐ duplicates Windows Explorer from your local
computer and displays:

- *Recent Documents.*

- *Samples.*

- *Open in SOLIDWORKS*

- *Desktop.*

View Palette

The View Palette tool located in the Task Pane provides the
ability to insert drawing views of an active document, or click the
Browse button to locate the desired document.

Click and drag the view from the View Palette into an active
drawing sheet to create a drawing view.

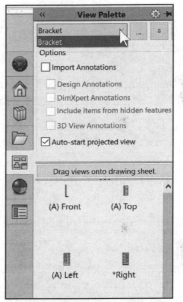

The selected model is Bracket.

Appearances, Scenes, and Decals

Appearances, Scenes, and Decals ● provide a simplified way
to display models in a photo-realistic setting using a library of
Appearances, Scenes, and Decals.

An appearance defines the visual properties of a model, including
color and texture. Appearances do not affect physical properties,
which are defined by materials.

Scenes provide a visual backdrop behind a model. In
SOLIDWORKS they provide reflections on the model.
PhotoView 360 is an Add-in. Drag and drop a selected
appearance, scene or decal on a feature, surface, part or assembly.

Custom Properties

The Custom Properties ▦ tool provides the ability to enter custom and configuration specific properties directly into SOLIDWORKS files.

Motion Study tab

Motion Studies are graphical simulations of motion for an assembly. Access the MotionManager from the Motion Study tab. The Motion Study tab is located in the bottom left corner of the Graphics window.

Incorporate visual properties such as lighting and camera perspective. Click the Motion Study tab to view the MotionManager. Click the Model tab to return to the FeatureManager design tree.

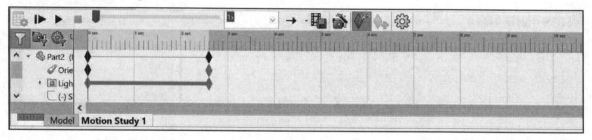

The MotionManager displays a timeline-based interface and provides the following selections from the drop-down menu as illustrated:

- *Animation:* Apply Animation to animate the motion of an assembly. Add a motor and insert positions of assembly components at various times using set key points. Use the Animation option to create animations for motion that do **not** require accounting for mass or gravity.

- *Basic Motion:* Apply Basic Motion for approximating the effects of motors, springs, collisions and gravity on assemblies. Basic Motion takes mass into account in calculating motion. Basic Motion computation is relatively fast, so you can use this for creating presentation animations using physics-based simulations. Use the Basic Motion option to create simulations of motion that account for mass, collisions or gravity.

If the Motion Study tab is not displayed in the Graphics window, click **View** ➤ **Toolbars** ➤ **MotionManager** from the Menu bar.

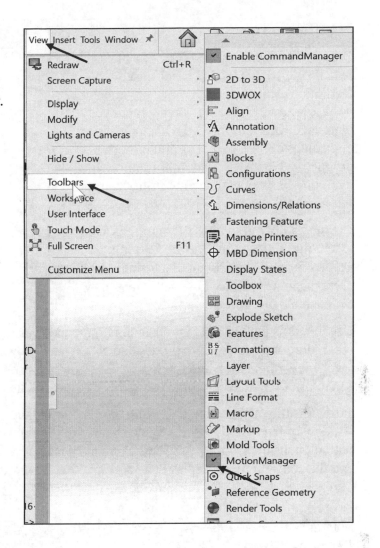

3D Views tab

Only available in SOLIDWORKS MBD. SOLIDWORKS MBD (Model Based Definition) lets you create models without the need for drawings giving you an integrated manufacturing solution. MBD helps companies define, organize, and publish 3D product and manufacturing information (PMI), including 3D model data in industry standard file formats.

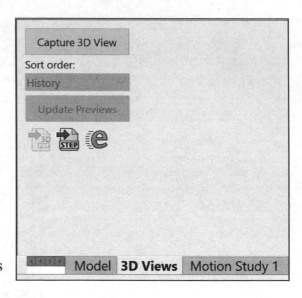

Create 3D drawing views of your parts and assemblies that contain the model settings needed for review and manufacturing. This lets users navigate back to those settings as they evaluate the design.

Use the tools in the MBD Dimensions CommandManager to set up your model with selected configurations, including explodes and abbreviated views, annotations, display states, zoom level, view orientation and section views. Capture those settings so that you and other users can return to them at any time using the 3D view palette.

To access the 3D View palette, click the 3D Views tab at the bottom of the SOLIDWORKS window or the SOLIDWORKS MBD tab in the CommandManager. The Capture 3D View button opens the Capture 3D View PropertyManager, where you specify the 3D view name, and the configuration, display state and annotation view to capture. See help for additional information.

Dynamic Reference Visualization (Parent/Child)

Dynamic Reference Visualization provides the ability to view the parent/child relationships between items in the FeatureManager design tree. When you hover over a feature with references in the FeatureManager design tree, arrows display showing the relationships. If a reference cannot be shown because a feature is not expanded, the arrow points to the feature that contains the reference and the actual reference appears in a text box to the right of the arrow.

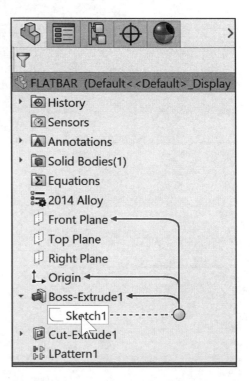

Use Dynamic reference visualization for a part, assembly and mates.

To display the Dynamic Reference Visualization, click **View ➤ User Interface ➤ Dynamic Reference Visualization Parent/Child)** from the Main menu bar.

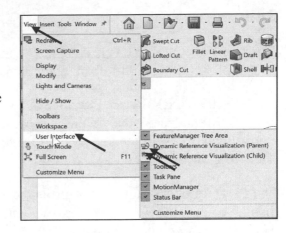

Mouse Movements

A mouse typically has two buttons: a primary button (usually the left button) and a secondary button (usually the right button). Most mice also include a scroll wheel between the buttons to help you scroll through documents and to Zoom in, Zoom out and rotate models in SOLIDWORKS. It is highly recommended that you use a mouse with at least a Primary, Scroll and Secondary button.

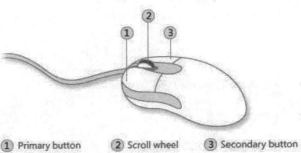

Single-click

To click an item, point to the item on the screen, and then press and release the primary button (usually the left button). Clicking is most often used to select (mark) an item or open a menu. This is sometimes called single-clicking or left-clicking.

Double-click

To double-click an item, point to the item on the screen, and then click twice quickly. If the two clicks are spaced too far apart, they might be interpreted as two individual clicks rather than as one double-click. Double-clicking is most often used to open items on your desktop. For example, you can start a program or open a folder by double-clicking its icon on the desktop.

Right-click

To right-click an item, point to the item on the screen, and then press and release the secondary button (usually the right button). Right-clicking an item usually displays a list of things you can do with the item. Right-click in the open Graphics window or on a command in SOLIDWORKS, and additional pop-up context is displayed.

Scroll wheel

Use the scroll wheel to zoom-in or to zoom-out of the Graphics window in SOLIDWORKS. To zoom-in, roll the wheel backward (toward you). To zoom-out, roll the wheel forward (away from you).

Summary

The SOLIDWORKS (UI) is designed to make maximum use of the Graphics window for your model. Displayed toolbars and commands are kept to a minimum.

The SOLIDWORKS User Interface and CommandManager consist of the following main options: Menu bar toolbar, Menu bar menu, Drop-down menus, Context toolbars, Consolidated fly-out menus, System feedback icons, Confirmation Corner and Heads-up View toolbar.

The Part CommandManager controls the display of tabs: *Features*, *Sketch*, *Evaluate*, *MBD Dimensions* and various *SOLIDWORKS Add-Ins*.

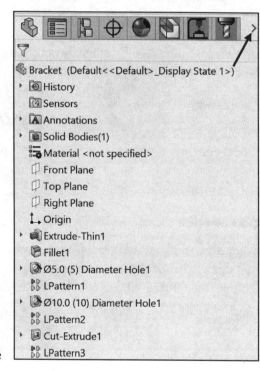

The FeatureManager consists of various tabs:

- *FeatureManager design tree* tab.

- *PropertyManager* tab.

- *ConfigurationManager* tab.

- *DimXpertManager* tab.

- *DisplayManager* tab.

- *CAM FeatureManager tree* tab.

- *CAM Operation tree* tab.

- *CAM Tools tree* tab.

Click the direction arrows to expand or collapse the FeatureManager design tree.

CommandManager, FeatureManager, and file folders will vary depending on system set-up and Add-ins.

You learned about creating a new SOLIDWORKS part and opening an existing SOLIDWORKS part along with using the Rollback bar to view the sketches and features.

If you modify a document property from an Overall drafting standard, a modify message is displayed as illustrated.

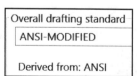

Use the Search box, in the upper left corner of the Materials dialog box, to search through the entire materials library.

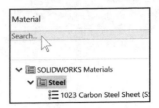

Templates are part, drawing and assembly documents which include user-defined parameters. Open a new part, drawing or assembly. Select a template for the new document.

The book provides information on creating and storing special Part templates, Assembly templates and Drawing templates in the MY-TEMPLATES folder. The MY-TEMPLATES folder is added to the New SOLIDWORKS Document dialog box. Talk to your IT department *before you set* any new locations on a network system. The procedure in the book is designed for your personal computer.

If you do not create the MY-TEMPLATE tab or the special part, drawing, or assembly templates, use the standard SOLIDWORKS default template and apply all of the needed document properties and custom properties.

Notes:

Chapter 5

Structure of a Drawing Document

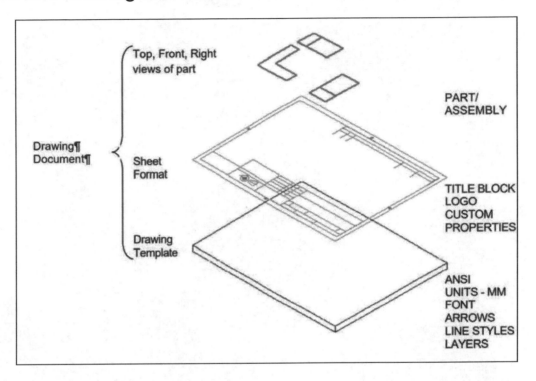

Below are the desired outcomes and usage competencies based on the completion of Chapter 5.

Desired Outcomes:	Usage Competencies:
<ul><li>Drawing Templates:<ul><li>C-(ANSI)-MM Landscape.</li><li>A-(ANSI)-MM Landscape.</li><li>C-(ANSI)-MM Landscape with Pre-defined views.</li></ul></li></ul>	<ul><li>Understand the structure of a drawing document.</li><li>Work with System Options and Document Properties, which influence the drawing, Drawing template, and Sheet format.</li></ul>
<ul><li>C-CUSTOM.</li><li>A-CUSTOM.</li></ul>	<ul><li>Insert SOLIDWORKS System Properties and Custom Properties.</li></ul>
<ul><li>New file location for drawing templates and Sheet format.</li></ul>	<ul><li>Design a Drawing template without a Sheet format file.</li><li>Define the file location for custom document templates.</li></ul>

Notes:

Chapter 5 - Structure of a Drawing Document

Chapter Objective

The purpose of this chapter is to provide an understanding of how SOLIDWORKS Drawing documents and templates are created and used. Create an awareness on the structure of a Drawing document. Provide a general knowledge of the ASME Y14 2009 Engineering Drawing and Related Documentation Practices. On the completion of this chapter, you will be able to:

- Identify elements which construct a Drawing document.

- Successfully develop a Drawing document.

- Distinguish between System Options and Document Properties as they relate to Drawings and Templates.

- Create a new SOLIDWORKS File Location for a Drawing Template.

- Set Reference Document Properties in a Drawing Template.

- Create a C-size (ANSI) Landscape Drawing Template and Sheet format.

- Create a A-size (ANSI) Landscape Drawing Template and Sheet format.

- Propagate the settings to the Drawing sizes.

- Develop Linked Notes to SOLIDWORKS Properties and Custom Properties in the Sheet format.

- Insert a company logo and Third Angle icon with a relation in the Title block.

- Understand an Annotation Links Error.

- Create a Drawing Template without a Sheet format file and define it File Location in System Options.

- Create a sample model and drawing document with Custom Properties.

- Understand where the property information is being populated from: SOLIDWORKS Special Properties, Model Custom Properties, and Drawing Custom Properties.

- Save the Sheet format and define the File location in System Options.

During the initial SOLIDWORKS installation, you are requested to select either the ISO or ANSI drafting standard. ISO is typically a European drafting standard and uses First Angle Projection. The book is written using the ANSI (US) overall drafting standard and Third Angle Projection for drawings.

Download all needed model files from the SDC Publication website (https://www.sdcpublications.com/Downloads/978-1-63057-485-7).

Engineering Drawing and Related Documentation Practices

Drawing Templates in this section are based on the American Society of Mechanical Engineers ASME Y14 2009 American National Standard for Engineering Drawing and Related Documentation Practices.

These standards represent the drawing practices used by U.S. industry. The ASME Y14 practices supersede the American National Standards Institute ANSI standards.

The ASME Y14 2009 Engineering Drawing and Related Documentation Practices are published by The American Society of Mechanical Engineers, New York, NY. References to the current ASME Y14 standards are used with permission.

ASME Y14 Standard Name:	American National Standard Engineering Drawing and Related Documentation:	Revision of the Standard:
ASME Y14.100M-1998	Engineering Drawing Practices	DOD-STD-100
ASME Y14.1-2009	Decimal Inch Drawing Sheet Size and Format	ANSI Y14.1
ASME Y14.1M-2009	Metric Drawing Sheet Size and Format	ANSI Y14.1M
ASME Y14.24M	Types and Applications of Engineering Drawings	ANSI Y14.24M
ASME Y14.2M(Reaffirmed 1998)	Line Conventions and Lettering	ANSI Y14.2M
ASME Y14.3M-2009	Multi-view and Sectional View Drawings	ANSI Y14.3
ASME Y14.41-2003	Digital Product Definition Data Practices	N/A
ASME Y14.5M -1994 (Reaffirmed 1999)	Dimensioning and Tolerancing	ANSI Y14.5-1982 (R1988)

The book presents a portion of the ASME Y14 American National Standard for Engineering Drawing and Related Documentation Practices. Information presented in Chapters 5 - 9 represents sample illustrations of drawings, various drawing views, and or dimension types.

The ASME Y14 standards committee develops and maintains additional Drawing Standards. Members of these committees are from Industry, Department of Defense, and Academia.

Companies create their own drawing standards based on one or more of the following:

- ASME Y14 2009.

- ISO or other International drawing standards.

- Older ANSI standards.

- Military standards.

There is also the "We've always done it this way" drawing standard or "Go ask the Drafting supervisor" drawing standard.

Structure of a Drawing Document

There are 2 primary pieces to a new Drawing document. These elements work together to produce the paper sheet, title block and border for drawings.

The Drawing document, Drawing Sheet and Sheet format each contain different properties and pieces of information.

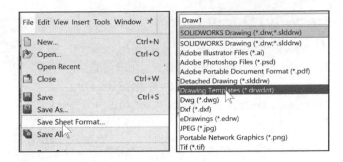

- **Drawing Document**: Is the entire Drawing file. Drawing Templates are the files use to begin a new Drawing document. Drawing Templates can include both a Drawing sheet and a Sheet format file.

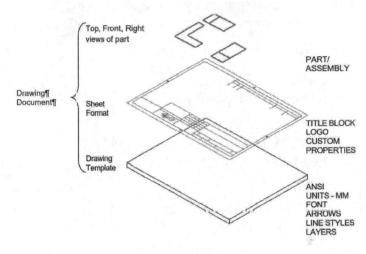

- **Drawing Sheet**: Drawing views and Annotations, Sheet Format/Size, Sheet Scale, Type of Projection, Datum Label, etc.

- **Sheet Format File**: The Sheet format file is incorporated into the Drawing Template. The Sheet format contains the border, Title block information, revision block information, company name, and or company logo information, Table Anchors, Custom Properties, and SOLIDWORKS Properties. Custom Properties and SOLIDWORKS Properties are shared values between documents.

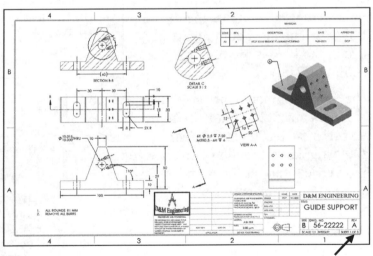

Drawing Document

The Drawing document contains Document Properties. These include important settings such as units, drafting standard, dimensions, annotations, line font, etc.

The default Documents Properties of a drawing are determined by the settings saved with the drawing template.

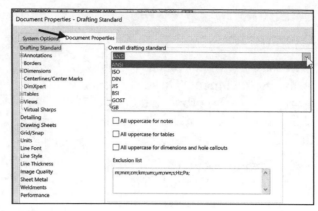

Drawing Sheet and Format

There are two ASME standards that define sheet size and format. They are:

1. ASME Y14.1-2009 Decimal Inch Drawing Sheet Size and Format.

2. ASME Y14.1M-2009 Metric Drawing Sheet size.

Drawing size refers to the physical paper size used to create the drawing. The most common paper size in the U.S. is the A-size: (8.5in. x 11in.).

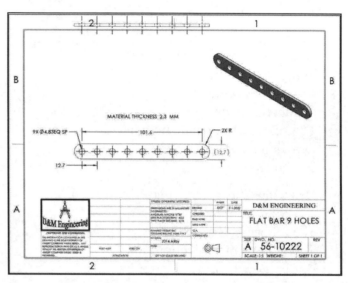

The most common paper size internationally is the A4 size: (210mm x 297mm). The ASME Y14.1-2009 and ASME Y14.1M-2009 standards contain both a horizontal and vertical format for A and A4 size respectively. The corresponding SOLIDWORKS Sheet format is Landscape for horizontal and Portrait for vertical.

SOLIDWORKS predefines U.S. drawing sizes A through E. Drawing sizes F, G, H, J, & K utilize the Custom sheet size option. Enter values for width and height. SOLIDWORKS predefines metric drawing sizes A4 through A0. Metric roll paper sizes utilize the Custom sheet size option.

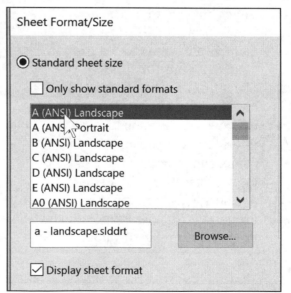

The ASME Y14.1-2009 Decimal Inch Drawing and ASME Y14.1-2009 Metric Sheet size standard are as follows:

Drawing Size: "Physical Paper"	Size in inches: Vertical Horizontal	
A horizontal (landscape)	8.5	11.0
A vertical (portrait)	11.0	8.5
B	11.0	17.0
C	17.0	22.0
D	22.0	34.0
E	34.0	44.0
F	28.0	40.0
G, H, J and K apply to roll sizes, User Defined		

Drawing Size: "Physical Paper" Metric	Size in Millimeters: Vertical Horizontal	
A0	841	1189
A1	594	841
A2	420	594
A3	297	420
A4 horizontal (landscape)	210	297
A4 vertical (portrait)	297	210

Drawing Sheet

The drawing sheet represents the paper size and is the active area of the drawing when performing detailing tasks (views, dimensions, annotations, tables, display modes, centerlines, centermarks, etc.). Each drawing sheet includes properties that can be modified through the Sheet Properties dialog box.

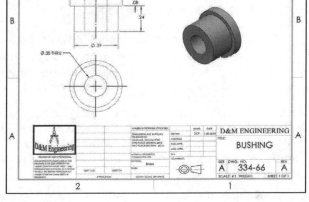

During the initial SOLIDWORKS installation, you are requested to select either the ISO or ANSI drafting standard. ISO is typically a European drafting standard and uses First Angle Projection.

The book is written using the ANSI (US) overall drafting standard and Third Angle Projection for all chapter drawings.

Third Angle Projection icon

In the next section create a new drawing with the default SW Drawing Template. Utilize C size (ANSI) Landscape paper.

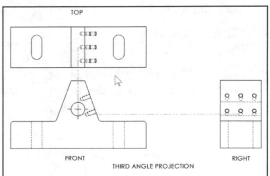

THIRD ANGLE PROJECTION

💡 Landscape indicates that the larger dimension is along the horizontal. A-Portrait and A4-Portrait indicate that the larger dimension is along the vertical.

> **Activity: Create a Drawing Document. Set a few Document Properties. Explore Sheet Properties.**

Create a new SOLIDWORKS Drawing. Set Overall drafting standard, Units, and Precision.

1. Click **New** ⬜ from the Menu bar toolbar.

2. Double-click **Drawing** from the Templates tab.

Create a C (ANSI) Landscape Sheet Format/Size drawing.

3. Select **C (ANSI) Landscape** from the Standard sheet size drop-down menu. View your options. A C (ANSI) Landscape drawing is either 22"x 17" or 279.40mm x 215.90mm depending on units. Use the default SW Sheet format (c - landscape.slddt).

4. Click **OK** from the Sheet Format/Size dialog box.

Exit the Model View PropertyManager.

5. Click **Cancel** ✖ from the Model View PropertyManager. Draw1 is the default drawing name. Sheet1 is the default first Sheet name. CommandManager, FeatureManager and Task Pane tabs will vary depending on system setup and Add-ins.

Set Document Properties for the Drawing Document. Set Overall drafting standard, Units, and Precision. Remember, Drawing Templates are the files used to begin a new Drawing Document. Drawing Templates can include both a drawing sheet and a sheet format file.

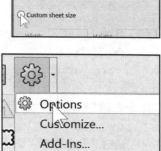

6. Click **Options** ⚙ ⌄ from the Main menu.

7. Click the **Document Properties** tab.

8. Select **ANSI** from the Overall drafting standard drop-down menu.

9. **View** your options.

10. **Explore** the various folders.

💡 The Drafting standard options are: **ANSI**: American National Standards Institute, **ISO**: International Standards Organization, **DIN**: Deutsche Institute für Normumg (German), **JIS**: Japanese Industry Standard, **BSI**: British Standards Institution, **GOST**: Gosndarstuennye State Standard (Russian), **GB**: Guo Biao (Chinese).

11. Click the **Units** folder.

12. **View** your options.

13. Click **MMGS** (millimeter, gram, second) Unit system.

14. Select **two places** for Length precision.

15. Select **None** for Angle precision.

16. Click the **Drafting Standard** folder.

17. **View** the options.

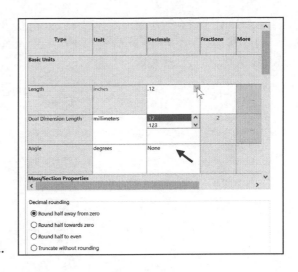

If you modify a document property from an Overall drafting standard, a modify message (ANSI-MODIFIED) is displayed as illustrated.

The Uppercase section controls the following options.

- **All uppercase for notes**: Set the default case as all uppercase for all new notes and balloons in a document.

- **All uppercase for tables:** Set the default as all uppercase for all new tables in a document.

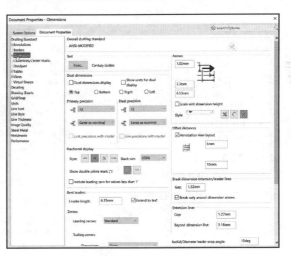

- **All uppercase for dimensions and hole callouts:** Set the default as all uppercase for all new dimensions and hole callouts in a document.

- **Exclusion list:** List strings that you specify to exclude from automatic capitalization. To exclude strings such as units of measurement from capitalization, enter them in the box, separated by semicolons.

18. Click the **Dimension** folder.

19. **View** the options. Location to display Dual dimensions, set arrow head size, Leading zeroes, Trailing zeroes and more.

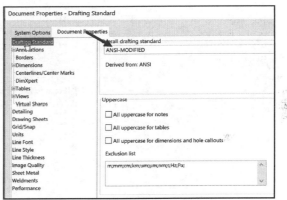

Secondary units are displayed in parenthesis. Drawing dimensions are associated with the model. Use custom properties in the model and drawing to keep the association between documents.

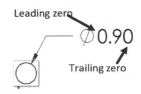

The ASME Y14.2M-1992(R1998) standard lists the following: *lettering, arrowhead, line conventions* and *lettering conventions* for engineering drawings and related documentation practices.

Minimum Drawing Letter Height based on ASME Y14.2.				
Annotation	Inch drawing sizes: A, B, C Metric drawing sizes: A2, A3, A4		Inch drawing sizes: D, E Metric drawing sizes: A0, A1	
	Inch	Millimeter	Inch	Millimeter
Drawing Title, Drawing Size, Cage Code, Drawing Number and Revision letter positioned inside the Title block.	.12in	3mm	.24in	6mm
Section views, Zone letter and numerals.	.24in	6mm	.24in	6mm
Drawing block headings in Title block.	.10in	2.5mm	.10mm	2.5mm
All other characters inside the Sheet boundary. Corresponds to the SW Dimension and Note font.	.12in.	3mm	.12in	3mm

The ASME Y14.2M-1992 (R1998) standard recommends *two line widths* with a 2:1 ratio. The minimum width of a thin line is 0.3mm. The minimum width of a thick, "normal" line is 0.6mm.

SolidWorks Line Style	Thin: (0.3mm)	Normal: (0.6mm)
Solid		
Dashed		
Phantom		
Chain		
Center		
Stitch		
Thin/Thick Chain		

The ASME Y14.2M-1992(R1998) standard addresses the type and style of lines used in engineering drawings. Combine different Line Styles and use drawing layers to achieve the following types of ASME lines as illustrated.

Return to Sheet1.

20. Click **OK**.

ASME Y14.2-1992(R1998) TYPE of LINE & example:	SolidWorks Line Font Type of Edge:	Style:	Thickness:
Visible line displays the visible edges or contours of a part.	Visible Edge	Solid	Thick "Normal"
Hidden line displays the hidden edges or contours of a part.	Hidden Edge	Dashed	Thin
Section lining displays the cut surface of a part assembly in a section view.	Crosshatch	Solid	Thin Different Hatch patterns relate to different materials
Center line displays the axes of center planes of symmetrical parts/features.	Construction Curves	Center	Thin
Symmetry line displays an axis of symmetry for a partial view.			Sketch Thin Center Line and Thick Visible lines on drawing layer.
Dimension lines/Extension lines/Leader lines combine to dimension drawings.	DIMENSION LINE Extension Line Leader Line Dimensions	Solid	Thin
Cutting plane line or Viewing plane line display the location of a cutting plane for sectional views and the viewing position for removed views.	Section Line View Arrows D D	Phantom Solid	Thick Thick, "Normal"

Draw1 is the default drawing name. Sheet1 is the default first Sheet name. CommandManager, FeatureManager and Task Pane tabs will vary depending on system setup and Add-ins.

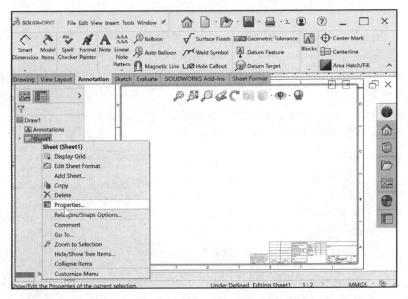

The Standard Sheet formats are located in the C:\ProgramData\SOLIDWORKS\ SOLIDWORKS 2022\lang\english\sheetformat in a non-network system.

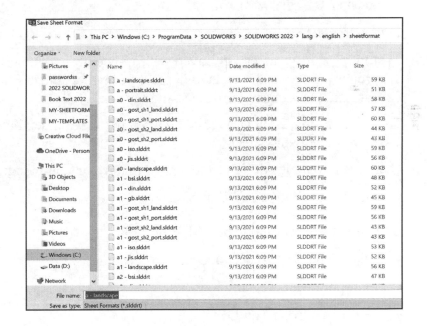

Utilize the Save As option to save a custom Drawing Template. Always select the Save as type option first, then select the Save in folder to avoid saving in default SOLIDWORKS installation directories.

Drawing Templates include at least one drawing sheet. Each drawing sheet has properties that are stored with the document template. These properties include a name for the sheet, default sheet scale, type of projection, and whether or not a sheet format is applied to the sheet.

Explore Sheet Properties. Set Third angle projection, C (ANSI) Landscape, and Sheet Scale.

21. Right click **Sheet1**.

22. Click **Properties**. The Sheet Properties dialog box is displayed. The default tab is Sheet Properties. The Zone Parameters tab provides the ability to set Zone Size and Margins.

23. Click **C (ANSI) Landscape** for Sheet Format/Size.

24. Click **Third angle** for Type of projection

25. Set Scale: **1:2**.

26. Click **Apply Changes** to close the dialog box. Apply Changes is active if you changed any of the default settings. Drawing1 is displayed.

Sheet Format

Custom property data can be saved with a Sheet format to ensure the proper properties are created in the drawing document. Sheet formats exist as a separate files (*.slddrt).

The Sheet format is NOT accessible when performing detailing tasks on the drawing sheet.

There are two major design modes used to develop a drawing:

- Edit Sheet Format and Edit Sheet.

Edit Sheet Format mode provides the ability to:

- Change the Title block size and text headings.
- Incorporate a Company logo.
- Define the Zone Tag Editor.
- Add Custom Properties, text and more.

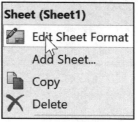

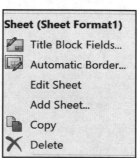

Edit Sheet mode provides the ability to:

- Add or modify views.

- Add or modify dimensions.

- Add or modify notes and more.

In the next section apply the Edit Sheet Format and Edit Sheet command.

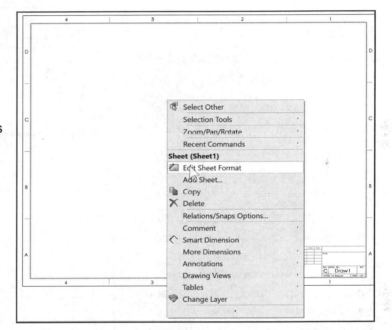

Activity: Apply the Edit Sheet Format and Edit Sheet Command

Access Sheet Format1. Enter a Custom Property "$PRP."DrawnBy". Use the Edit Sheet Format and Edit Sheet command.

27. **Right-click** in the empty Sheet1 document.

28. Click **Edit Sheet Format**.

29. View **Sheet Format1** and the links.

30. **Zoom in** on the Title block.

31. Hover over an **empty block** as illustrated. In this case the DRAWNBy box.

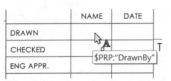

This displays the Custom Notes Linked to Properties for Sheet Format1.

 The format of notes linked to properties can be explored by hovering the cursor over the center of the title block. When editing a Sheet format, notes with links are displayed in blue. Notes that are static are displayed in black. You will address them later in the chapter.

Enter a Custom Note Linked to Properties, "DrawnBy".

32. Click **File**, **Properties** from the Main menu. The Summary Information dialog box is displayed.

33. Click the **Custom** tab.

34. Click **DrawnBy** from the drop-down menu as illustrated.

35. View the options.

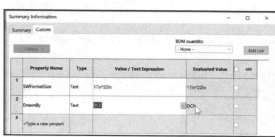

36. Click inside the **Value / Text Expression** box.

Enter your initials.

37. Example: **DCP**.

38. Click inside the **Evaluated Value** box.

39. View the results.

Return to Sheet Format1.

40. Click **OK** return to Sheet Format1.

Return to Sheet1.

41. Right-click **Edit Sheet**.

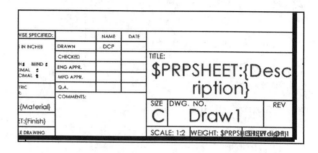

🔆 The Automatic Border tool lets you control every aspect of a sheet format's border, including zone layout and border size. Using the Automatic Border tool, borders and zones automatically update to match changes in the Zone Parameters tab of the Sheet Properties dialog box without having to manually edit the sheet format. You can also include Margin Mask areas where formatting elements such as labels and dividers are not shown. This is helpful when you want to mask an area on a sheet for notes.

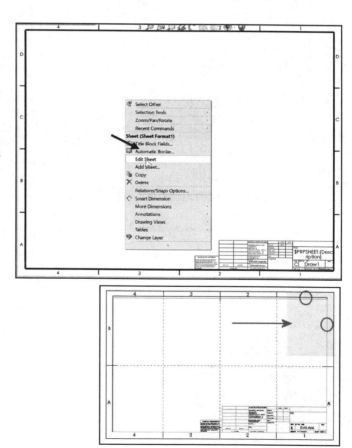

Understand Drawing Templates

Drawing Templates are the files used to begin a new drawing document. They have a file extension of (*.drwdot).

SOLIDWORKS starts with a default Drawing Template. The default Drawing Template is located in the C:\ProgramData\SOLIDWORKS\SOLIDWORKS 2022\templates folder on a non-network system. Note: the option "Prompt user to select document template".

The Drawing Template can be displayed with or without the Sheet format. Combine the Sheet format with the Drawing Template to create a custom Drawing Template.

Utilize the Save As option to save a custom Drawing Template. Always select the Save as type option first, then select the Save in folder to avoid saving in the default SOLIDWORKS installation directories.

Specify folders to search for different types of documents. Folders are searched in the order in which they are listed. The illustration displays a new MY-TEMPLATES tab which was created and is displayed in the Advanced New SOLIDWORKS Document dialog box.

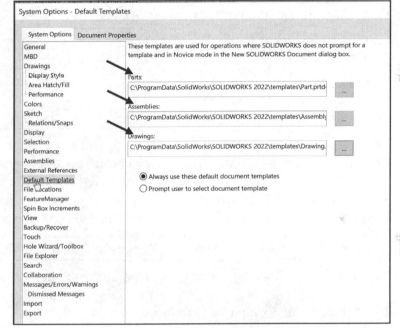

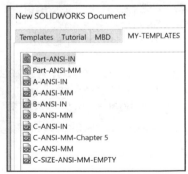

The MY-TEMPLATES tab will not be displayed in the Advanced New SOLIDWORKS Document dialog box if the folder is empty. The MY-TEMPLATES tab will not be displayed if you do not address System Options - File Locations for the folder.

In the next section, save the Sheet format for Sheet1 to the SOLIDWORKS 2022/MY-SHEETFORMATS folder.

Activity: Save Sheet Format. Create a Custom Sheet format.

Save the Sheet Format. Use the SOLIDWORKS 2022/MY SHEETFORMATS folder.

42. Click **File**, **Save Sheet Format** from the Menu bar. The Save Sheet Format dialog box is displayed. The default SW location folder is displayed.

43. Select **SOLIDWORKS 2022/MY-SHEETFORMATS** for the Save in folder.

44. Enter **CUSTOM-C-CHAPTER 5** for File name.

45. Click **Save** from the Save Sheet Format dialog box.

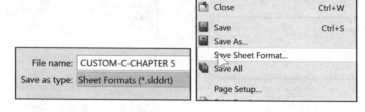

In the next section, save the Drawing Template to the MY-TEMPLATES folder. Utilize the

Save As 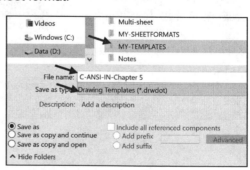 option to save a custom Drawing Template. Always select the Save As type option first, then select the Save in folder to avoid saving in the default SOLIDWORKS installation directories. The MY-TEMPLATES tab will not be displayed if you do not address System Options - File Locations for the folder. We will address this later in the book.

Activity: Save a Custom Drawing Template with a Custom Sheet Format.

Save the Custom Drawing Template with the Custom Sheet format.

46. Click **Save As** from the Main menu.

47. Click **Drawing Templates (*.drwdot)** from the Save as type box. The default SW location templates folder is displayed.

48. Select **SOLIDWORKS 2022/MY-TEMPLATES** for the Save in folder. Note: These folders were downloaded in Chapter 4.

49. Enter **C-ANSI-MM-Chapter 5** for File name.

50. Click **Save**.

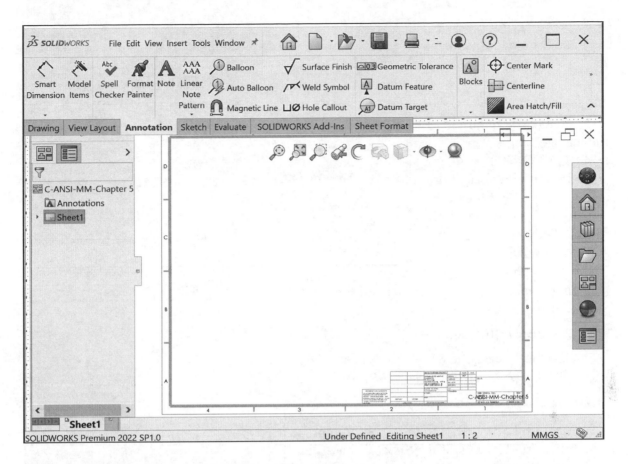

Why are Drawings Structured this way?

Sheet formats exist as separate, external files so that the Sheet size, title block and border information can easily be changed. For instance, if you begin a detailing project on an C-size sheet, but later decide A-size would be a better fit, you can simply modify the sheet properties to select a new format. If the Sheet format was a fixed entity in a Drawing Template you would have to copy your views to a new template to make this change.

In the next section, modify the Sheet format to A (ANSI) Portrait.

> **Activity: Modify the Sheet Format size.**

Access Sheet Properties. Modify the Sheet format from C (ANSI) Landscape to A (ANSI) Portrait.

51. Right-Click **Sheet1** from the Drawing PropertyManager.

52. Click **Properties**. The Sheet Properties dialog box is displayed.

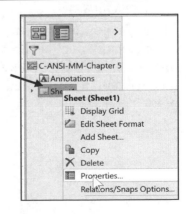

53. Click **A (ANSI) Portrait** as illustrated. Note the Sheet size: 8.50in x 11.00in.

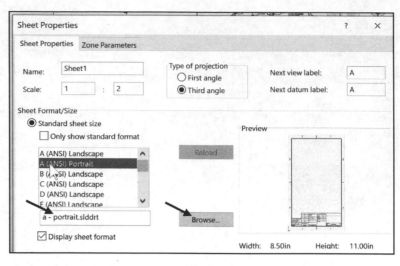

Select a standard sheet size, (SOLIDWORKS installation directories) or click Browse and locate a Custom Sheet format file. Select Only show standard formats to display Sheet formats for the current drafting standard only. Otherwise, all formats from all standards are listed.

54. Click **Apply Changes**.

55. **View** the results. The Sheet size is updated and the new Sheet format is displayed.

Sheet Format Features.

When editing or modifying the Sheet format, the following features of the Sheet format file are available:

Title Block Sketch: The Title block area is made up of sketch lines. They can be modified and constrained in the same way as sketch lines within a model. Standard formats contain Title blocks. The Title block in the A (ANSI) Portrait Sheet format contains the following lines and text as illustrated.

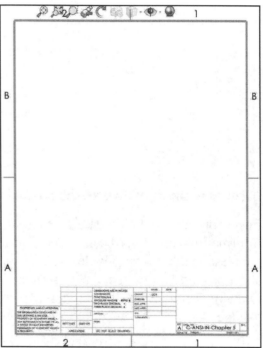

Notes: Sheet formats often contain static text notes as well as notes Linked to Properties. Linking notes to properties allows them to be automatically populated with information relevant to the current drawing. We will cover this in detail in the Linked to Properties section of the book.

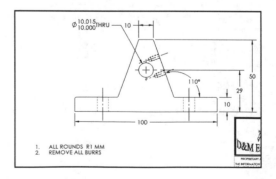

Border: The Sheet format border includes the border surrounding the sheet as well as the zone lines and labels. We will use the zone lines and labels in various tables. The borders included in the SOLIDWORKS default Sheet formats are generated using the Automatic Border tool.

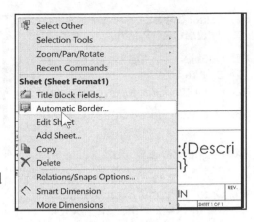

Inserted Picture: Although the SOLIDWORKS default Sheet format does not include pictures, it is common practice to add a Company logo or a Third Angle projection icon in the Comments box as illustrated.

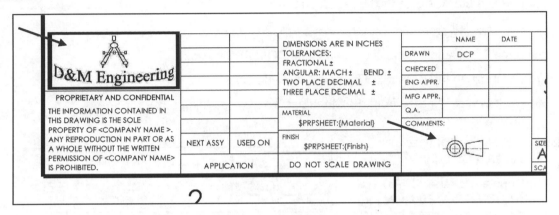

Insert a company logo and the Third Angle Projection icon in the Title block.

Activity: Insert a company logo. Insert the Third Angle Projection icon.

Edit Sheet Format1. Insert two pictures in the Title bock. Insert them in the Edit Sheet Format mode.

56. Right-click **Edit Sheet Format** in Sheet1.

57. Click the **Zoom to Area** 🔍 tool from the Heads-up View toolbar.

58. **Zoom in** on the Title block.

59. Click the **Zoom to Area** 🔍 tool to deactivate.

A Company logo is normally located in the Title block of the drawing. Create your own Company logo or copy and paste an existing picture. The Logo.jpeg file is provided in the SOLIDWORKS 2022/LOGOS folder.

60. Click **Insert**, **Picture** from the Main menu bar. The Open dialog box is displayed.

61. Select the **SOLIDWORKS 2022/LOGOS** folder.

62. Double-click the **Logo.jpg**. The Sketch Picture PropertyManager is displayed.

63. Uncheck the **Lock aspect ratio** box.

64. Uncheck the **Enable scale tool** box.

65. Drag the picture handles to size the **picture** to the left side of the Title block. Note: Text was added to the picture.

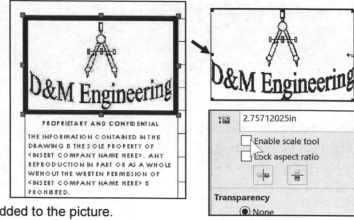

66. Click **OK** ✔ from the Sketch Picture PropertyManager.

Insert the Third Angle Projection icon in the COMMENTS box.

67. **Zoom in** on the COMMENTS box in the Title block.

68. Click **Insert**, **Picture** from the Menu bar. The Open dialog box is displayed.

69. Select the **SOLIDWORKS 2022/LOGOS** folder.

70. Double-click the **THIRD ANGLE PROJECTION.jpg**. The Sketch Picture PropertyManager is displayed.

71. Uncheck the **Lock aspect ratio** box.

72. Uncheck the **Enable scale tool** box.

73. Drag the picture handles to size the **picture** to fit inside the COMMENTS box.

74. Click **OK** ✔ from the Sketch Picture PropertyManager.

75. **View** the results.

Anchors: Anchors position tables with respect to a drawing sheet format. Each type of annotation table has its own anchor point in a drawing sheet format.

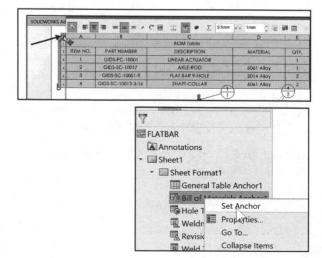

Note Linked to Properties.

Links can be created to custom properties of the current document, Custom Properties from a referenced model, or to existing file information such as file or folder names. The different property links seen in a drawing title block are formatted as follows:

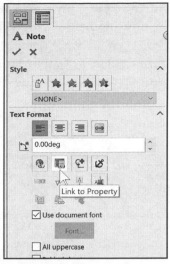

$PRP: "property name". Property links with this format are linked to Custom Properties of the current document - the drawing document. These are properties that are accessed from the File Properties  dialog in the drawing.

$PRPSHEET: "property name". Property links with this format are linked to Custom Properties that are accessible

from the File Properties dialog in the part or assembly document used in the drawing views on the sheet.

For drawings that reference more than one model, Sheet Properties can be used to choose the proper model to populate these properties links.

$PRP: "SW - property name" or $PRPSHEET: "SW-property name". Properties names that begin with SW are referred to as SOLIDWORKS Special Properties. SOLIDWORKS Special Properties are properties that exist in the SOLIDWORKS file by default. They do not require creation or input from the user; example: include properties such as the sheet scale, (SW-Sheet Scale) or the file Name (SW-File Name).

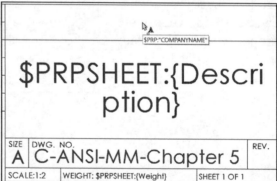

Return to Sheet1.

76. Right-click **Edit Sheet**.

Save the Drawing. Close all documents.

77. Click **File**, **Save As** from the Main
menu.

78. Enter File name: **A-ANSI-MM Chapter5**.

79. Select the **SOLIDWORKS 2022/Chapter 5 Drawings** folder for Save As.

80. Click **Save**.

Close all open documents.

81. Click **File**, **Close** from the Main menu.

In the next section, display the MY-TEMPLATES tab in the New SOLIDWORKS
Document dialog box. Set System Options - File Locations. Only perform this procedure
if you are working on a non-network system.

Activity: Add the MY-TEMPLATES tab to the New SOLIDWORKS dialog box.

Display the MY-TEMPLATES tab in the New SOLIDWORKS
Document dialog box.

82. Click **Options**  from the Main menu. The System Options
General dialog box is displayed.

83. Click **File Locations** under the System Options tab.

84. Select **Document Templates** from Show folders for.

85. Click the **Add** button.

86. Select the **SOLIDWORKS 2022/MY-TEMPLATES** folder.
Note: Folders were downloaded in Chapter 4.

87. Click **Select Folder**.

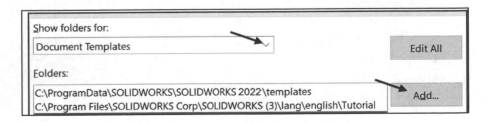

88. If needed click **Move down** to have the MY-TEMPLATES folder as the last folder.

89. Click **OK** from the System Options dialog box.

90. Click **OK** from the SOLIDWORKS dialog box.

91. Click **Yes** to the SOLIDWORKS user account dialog box.

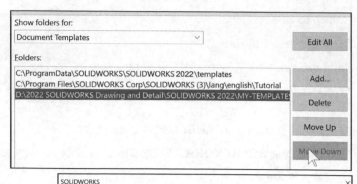

92. Click **Yes** again. An empty SOLIDWORKS window is displayed.

Display the MY-TEMPLATES folder in the Advance New SOLIDWORKS Document dialog box.

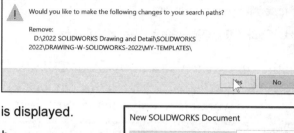

93. Click **File**, **New** from the Main menu. The New SOLIDWORKS Document dialog is displayed.

94. Double-click the **MY-TEMPLATES** folder tab.

95. **View** the existing templates. Save new Custom Drawing Templates in this location. Create new Drawing with Custom Templates using the MY-TEMPLATES tab.

96. Click **OK**. Note: Additional Templates are displayed.

97. **Close** all SOLIDWORKS documents.

Annotation Link Errors.

When a note is linked to property that does not exist, it is considered to be an error. By default, Annotation Links Errors are hidden from view. In the next section view annotation link errors.

Activity: View Link Errors in a drawing.

Open the Link Error drawing from the SOLIDWORKS 2022/Annotation Link Errors folder. View the Link Errors.

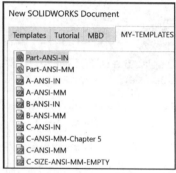

1. Select the **SOLIDWORKS 2022/Annotation Link Errors** folder.

2. Double-click the **Link Error** drawing from the Annotation Link Errors folder.

3. Click **View**, **Hide/Show**, **Annotation Link Errors** from the Main menu.

4. **View** the results.

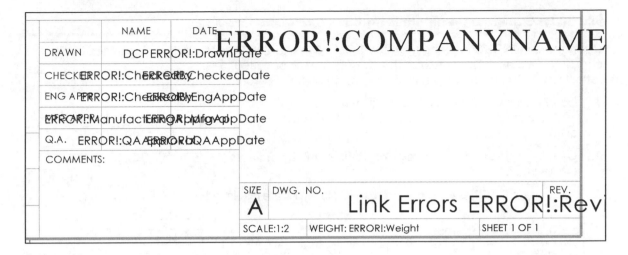

Turn off the Annotation Link Errors.

5. Click **View**, **Hide/Show**, **Annotation Link Errors** from the Main menu. View the results.

Close the Link Error drawing.

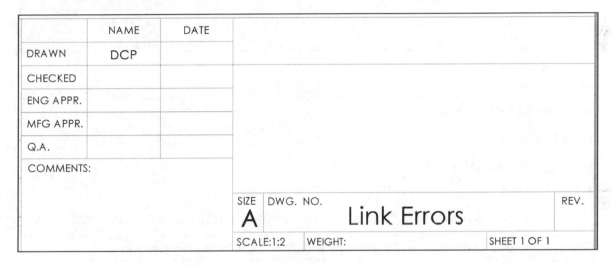

6. Click **File**, **Close** from the Main menu.

In the next section, explore a completed Title box.

Activity: Explore a Complete Title Box - CYLINDER drawing.

Open the CYLINDER drawing from the SOLIDWORKS 2022/Complete Drawing folder. View a complete Title box. The notes on this drawing are color coded to reflect where the property information is being populated from.

1. Double-click **CYLINDER drawing** from the SOLIDWORKS 2022/Complete Drawing folder. The CYLINDER drawing is displayed.

2. Click **View**, **Hide/Show**, check **Annotation Link Errors** from the Main menu.

3. Click inside the **Sheet1**. **View** the results. No errors are displayed.

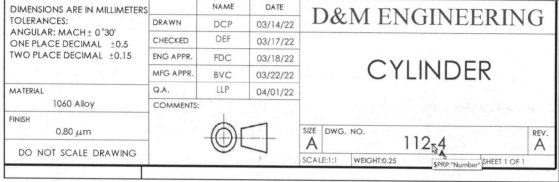

The notes in the drawing have been color coded to reflect where the property information is being populated from:

GREEN: SOLIDWORKS Special Properties.

BLUE: Model Custom Properties.

RED: Drawing Custom Properties.

In the next section, explore the custom properties of this drawing and model document.

Activity: Explore Additional Custom Properties of the Drawing and Part.

View the Custom Properties of this drawing. Deactivate the Annotation Link Errors option.

1. Click **View**, **Hide/Show**, uncheck **Annotation Link Errors** from the Main menu.

2. Click **File**, **Properties** from the Main menu. The Summary Information dialog box is displayed.

3. Click the **Custom** tab. These entries are displayed in red in the title box above..

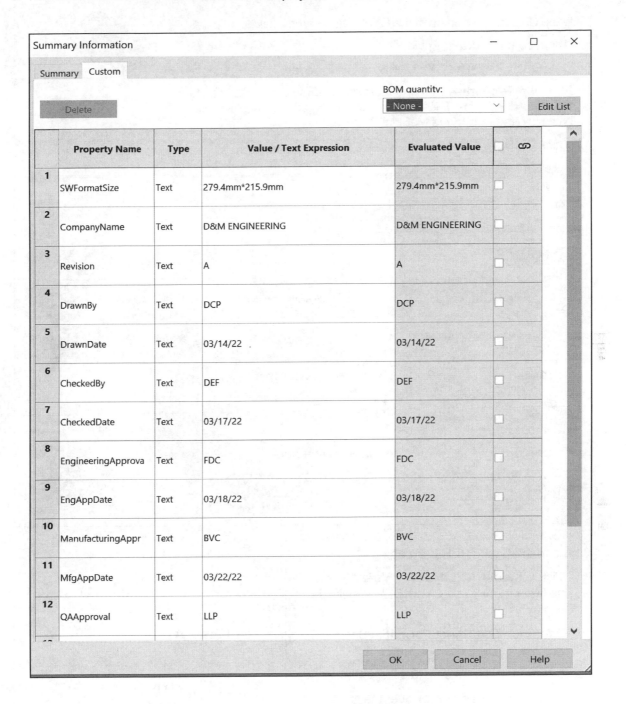

	Property Name	Type	Value / Text Expression	Evaluated Value		⚭
1	SWFormatSize	Text	279.4mm*215.9mm	279.4mm*215.9mm	☐	
2	CompanyName	Text	D&M ENGINEERING	D&M ENGINEERING	☐	
3	Revision	Text	A	A	☐	
4	DrawnBy	Text	DCP	DCP	☐	
5	DrawnDate	Text	03/14/22	03/14/22	☐	
6	CheckedBy	Text	DEF	DEF	☐	
7	CheckedDate	Text	03/17/22	03/17/22	☐	
8	EngineeringApprova	Text	FDC	FDC	☐	
9	EngAppDate	Text	03/18/22	03/18/22	☐	
10	ManufacturingAppr	Text	BVC	BVC	☐	
11	MfgAppDate	Text	03/22/22	03/22/22	☐	
12	QAApproval	Text	LLP	LLP	☐	

4. Click **Close**.

View the Custom Properties of the CYLINDER Part model.

5. Right-click in a **drawing view**.

6. Click **Open Part**. The CYLINDER part is displayed.

7. Click **File**, **Properties** from the Main menu. **View** the Properties of the CYLINDER part. These entries are displayed in blue in the Title box. Note the Finish and Material Properties Name.

8. Click **OK** from the Properties dialog box.

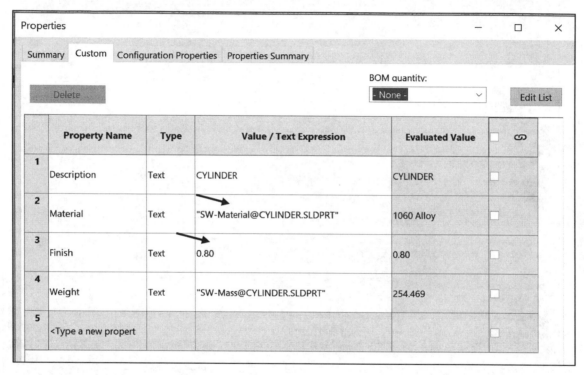

Return to the CYLINDER drawing.

9. Click **Window**, **CYLINDER - Sheet1** from the Main menu. The CYLINDER drawing is displayed.

10. Right-click **Edit Sheet Format** in Sheet1. Do not click inside a drawing view.

11. **Zoom in** on the Title box as illustrated.

12. Hover the **mouse curser** over the MATERIAL box as illustrated.

13. **View** the Part link $PRPSHEET. "Material".

14. **Double-click** inside the Tolerance block. The box turns black. The Note PropertyManager is displayed along with the Formatting toolbar. Use the Formatting toolbar to address Title box font text.

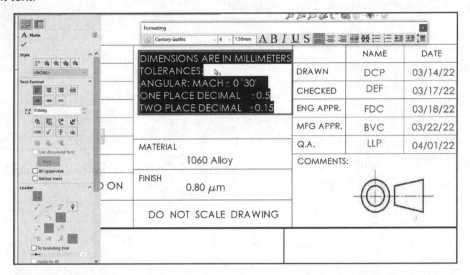

The Tolerance block provides information to the manufacturer on the minimum and maximum variation for each dimension on the drawing. If a specific tolerance or note is provided on the drawing, the specific tolerance or note will override the information in the Tolerance block.

General tolerance values are based on the design requirements and the manufacturing process.

Create Sheet formats for different part types; examples: sheet metal parts, plastic parts and high precision machined parts. Create Sheet formats for each category of parts that are manufactured with unique sets of Title block notes.

Modify the Tolerance block in the Sheet format for ASME Y14.5 machined millimeter parts. Delete unnecessary text. The FRACTIONAL text refers to inches. The BEND text refers to sheet metal parts. The Three Decimal Place text is not required for this millimeter part in the chapter.

15. Delete the **following items** as above in the Title box.

16. Click **inside the box** after ANGULAR: MACH ± as illustrated.

> DIMENSIONS ARE IN MILLIMETERS
> TOLERANCES:
> ANGULAR: MACH ±
> ONE PLACE DECIMAL ±
> TWO PLACE DECIMAL ±

17. Enter **0**.

18. Click the **Add Symbol** ⊄⁺ button from the Text Format box. The Symbols dialog box is displayed.

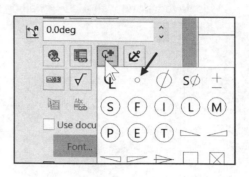

💡 The **Link to Property** 🔲 icon provides access to drawing properties and component properties from any model in the drawing so you can add them to the text string.

💡 The **Lock/Unlock Notes** ✍ icon provides the ability to fix the note in place. When you edit the note, you can adjust the bounding box, but you cannot move the note itself.

19. Select **Degree** ° from the Symbols dialog box.

20. Enter **30'** for minutes of a degree.

21. Enter **0.5** after ONE PLACE DECIMAL: ±.

22. Enter **0.15** after TWO PLACE DECIMAL±.

23. Click **OK** from the Note PropertyManager.

Note: Finish is 0.80 μm. To display a micrometer symbol in the CYLINDER drawing title box, Click **Edit Sheet format** in the CYLINDER drawing. Double-click inside the **FINISH** box. The Formatting

DIMENSIONS ARE IN MILLIMETERS
TOLERANCES:
ANGULAR: MACH ± 0 °30'
ONE PLACE DECIMAL   ±0.5
TWO PLACE DECIMAL ±0.15

MATERIAL
   1060 Alloy
FINISH
   0.80 μm

toolbar is displayed. Click **SWGrekc** from the Formatting toolbox Font. Press the **m** key to display the Greek letter μ. μ is the Greek letter for micro. Click **Century Gothic** for Font. Enter **m** for meter. The text reads μm for micrometer 0.80 μm

Various symbols are available through the Symbol dialog box. The ± symbol is located in the Modify Symbols list. The ± symbol is sometimes displayed as <MOD-PM>. The degree symbol ° is sometimes displayed as <MOD-DEG>.

Interpretation of tolerances is as follows:

• The angular dimension 110° is machined between 109.5° and 110.5°.

• The dimension 2.5 is machined between 2.0 and 3.0.

• The dimension 2.05 is machined between 1.90 and 2.20.

Return to Sheet1. Save the CYLINDER drawing.

24. Right-click **Edit Sheet**.

25. Click **Save** 💾.

General Notes

General notes are annotations that describe additional information on a drawing.
Conserve drawing time. Place common general notes in the Sheet format. The
Engineering department stores general notes in a Notepad file, GENERALNOTES.TXT.
General notes are usually located in a corner of a drawing.

> **Activity: Insert General Notes using a text file.**

Insert general notes from a text file. Copy and paste them in the drawing.

1. Double-click on the Notepad file, **SOLIDWORKS 2022/MY-SHEETFORMATS/GENERALNOTES.TXT**.

2. Click **Edit, Copy**.

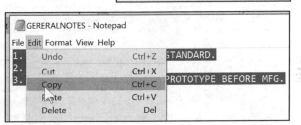

Return to Sheet1 in the drawing.

3. Click **Note** 𝐀 from the Annotation toolbar.

4. Click a **point** in the lower left-hand corner of Sheet1.

5. Click **inside** the Note text box.

6. Right click **Paste**. The three text lines are in the note box.

7. Click **6 for Font size** from the Formatting dialog box.

8. Click **OK** ✔ from the Note PropertyManager.

9. Click **Save** 💾.

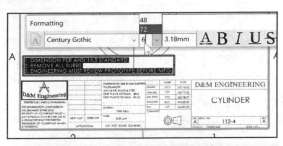

Display Styles / Modes

Most display modes for a Drawing
view are similar to a part except with
the addition of the 3D Drawing view
tool. This tool provides the ability to
rotate the model in an existing view.

Wireframe and Shaded Display
modes provide the best Graphic
performance. Mechanical details
require Hidden Lines Visible display
and Hidden Lines Removed display.
Select Shaded/Hidden Lines
Removed to display Auxiliary Views
to avoid confusion.

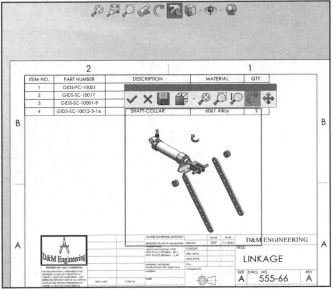

Tangent Edges Visible provides clarity for the start of a Fillet edge. Tangent Edges Removed provides the best graphic performance.

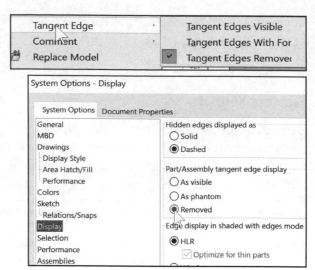

ANSI standards prefers no Tangent Edges display; however, individual company standards may display Tangents Edges for clarity.

Tangent Edges are displayed for educational purposes.

In the next section, explore the Custom properties of this drawing and model document.

Activity: Explore the 3D Drawing tool and various Display modes.

Open the LINKAGE drawing from the SOLIDWORKS 2022/Chapter 5 Drawing folder. Explore the 3D drawing tool.

1. Double-click the **LINKAGE drawing** from the SOLIDWORKS 2022/Chapter 5 Drawing. The LINKAGE drawing is displayed. The LINKAGE drawing has two Sheets. Sheet1 is selected by default.

2. Click inside **Drawing view1**.

3. Click the **3D Drawing View** icon as illustrated in the Heads-up View toolbar.

4. **Rotate** the view as illustrated.

5. **View** the results. Return to the original Isometric view.

6. Click **Exit** ✕.

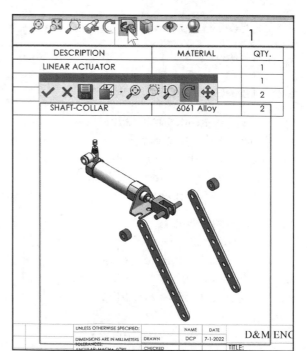

Explore the LINKAGE Drawing.

7.   Click the **Sheet2** tab in the lower left bottom section of the drawing as illustrated. View Sheet2.

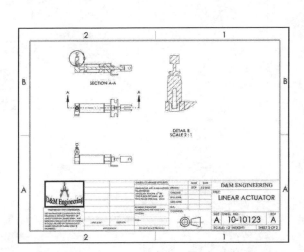

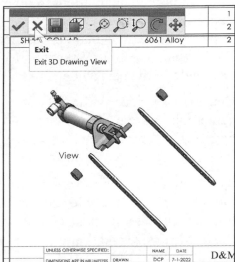

8.   Click inside **Drawing View2**.

9.   Click **Hidden Lines Visible** from the drop-down Heads-up View toolbar.

10. **View** the drawing view change.

Return to Hidden Lines Removed.

11. Click **Hidden Lines Removed** from the drop-down Heads-up View toolbar.

Close all drawings and open documents. Do not save.

12. Click **File**, **Close** from the Main menu.

13. Click **Don't Save** from the SOLIDWORKS dialog box.

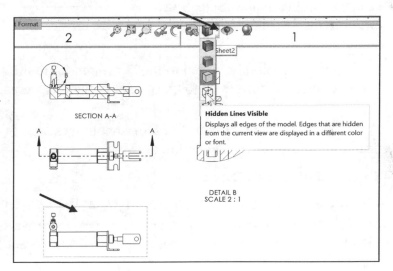

Centerlines and Center Marks

Centerlines should be added to the drawing prior to the addition of dimensions and annotations. You can resize them or modify their appearance. Resize their appearance by dragging the control points on each side of the centerline.

Center marks specify the default center mark size used with arcs and circles. Center marks are displayed with or without Center mark lines.

The Center mark lines extend past the circumference of the selected circle. Select the Center mark size based on the drawing size and scale.

The Center mark command creates a center mark, or a center point on selected circular edges. Selecting a circle creates a center mark. Selecting an arc creates a center point.

Center marks should be added to the drawing prior to the addition of dimensions and annotations. You can resize them or modify their appearance.

Center marks and Centerlines are annotations used to mark circle centers and describe the geometry size on the drawing.

Extension Lines Option

The ASME Y14.2M-1992(R1998) and ASME Y14.5M-1994(R1999) standard defines extension line length and gap. A visible gap exists between the extension line and the visible line. The extension line extends 3mm - 4mm past the dimension line.

The values 1.5mm and 3mm are a guide. Base the gap and extension line on the drawing size and scale.

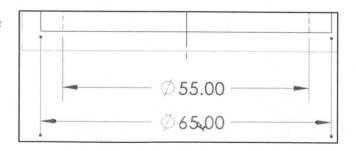

Predefined and Projected Views

In Orthographic Projection - the six principle views are *Top*, *Front*, *Right*, *Back*, *Bottom* and *Left*. Drawings commonly display the Top, Front, Right, and an Isometric view. You can define a view in a drawing sheet and then populate the view. You can save a drawing document with Predefined views as a Drawing Template.

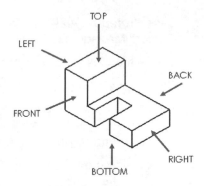

Insert the Top, Front, Right, and Isometric views into the Drawing. Utilize the Predefined command to create the Front and Isometric view. Utilize the Projected view command to create the Right and Top view.

The Drawing Template contains a Sheet format. Leave space when positioning views.

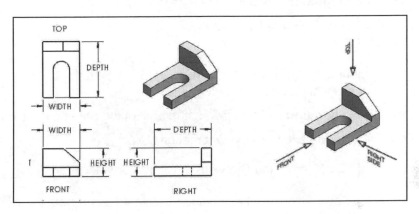

Save Predefined views with the Drawing Template. Save the Drawing Template in the next section, before you insert a part into the Predefined views.

Activity: Insert Predefined and Projected Views

Insert a Front Predefined view.

1. Create an **A-ANSI Landscape - MMGS, Third Angle** drawing.

2. Scale **1:2**. Precision .**12**.

3. Click **Insert, Drawing View, Predefined** ⬚ from the Main menu.

4. Click the **lower left corner** of the drawing. The Drawing View1 PropertyManager is displayed.

 *Front view is the default view in the Orientation dialog box.

5. Click **Hidden Lines Removed** from the Display Style box.

6. Click **OK** ✔ from the Drawing View1 PropertyManager.

Insert a Top Projected view.
7. Click the **View Layout** tab from the CommandManager.

8. Click **Projected view** ⊡ from the View Layout toolbar. The Projected View PropertyManager is displayed.

9. Check the **Use parent style** box to display Hidden Lines Removed.

10. Click a **position** directly above the Front view.

Insert the Right Projected view.

11. Click **Projected View** ⊡ from the View Layout toolbar.

12. Click inside the **Front** view.

13. Click a **position** directly to the right of the Front view.

Insert an Isometric Predefined view.
14. Click inside the **Front** view.

15. Click **Insert**, **Drawing View**, **Predefined** ⊡ from the Main menu. The Drawing View PropertyManager is displayed.

16. Click a **position** in the upper right corner of the Sheet as illustrated.

17. Click ***Isometric** from the Orientation box.

18. Click **OK** ✔ from the Drawing View4 PropertyManager.

19. Click **Save** 💾. View the drawing FeatureManager. Note the view icons for the Predefined and Projected views.

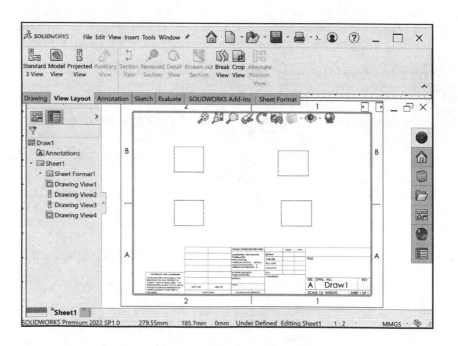

Save As

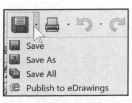

The Save As 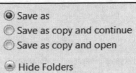 option provides the ability to save documents with various file types. The current document is a drawing named Draw1.slddrw. Save the document as a Drawing Template (*.drwdot).

Select the Drawing Templates (*.drwdot) option for Save as type before you browse to the MY-TEMPLATES folder. SOLIDWORKS selects the SOLIDWORKS\data\templates folder by default when you select Drawing Templates (*.drwdot).

Test the Drawing Template located in the MY-TEMPLATES folder. Create a new Drawing document.

Activity: Save As and Test New Drawing Template

Save the empty Drawing Template.

1. Click **Save As** from the Main menu.

2. Select **Drawing Templates (*.drwdot)** from the Save as type.

3. **Browse** and select the **SOLIDWORKS-2022\MY-TEMPLATES** for the Save in file folder.

4. Enter **C-SIZE-ANSI-MM-EMPTY** for the File name. The file extension for the Template is .drwdot.

5. Click **Save** from the Save As dialog box.

6. Click **Windows**, **Close All** from the Main menu.

Create a new drawing.

7. Click **New** from the Menu bar toolbar.

8. Select **MY-TEMPLATES** tab from the New SOLIDWORKS Document dialog box.

9. Double-click **C-SIZE-ANSI-MM-EMPTY**.

10. Click **Cancel** from the Model View PropertyManager. Draw2 is the current drawing document. Note the drawing view icons in the FeatureManager. Drag and drop the views if needed onto the sheet.

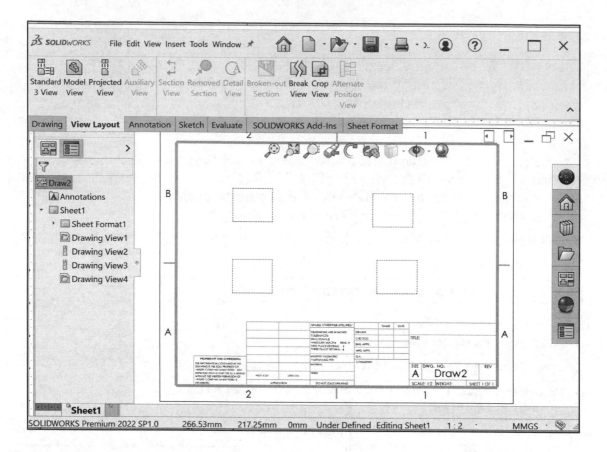

Save the drawing. Rename Draw2 to Link Note.

11. Rename Draw2 to Link Note.

12. Save the Link Note drawing to the SOLIDWORKS 2022/Chapter 5 Drawing folder. We will use this drawing in the next section.

You created a C (ANSI) size drawing with no Sheet format when you selected the C-SIZE-ANSI-MM-EMPTY template from the New SOLIDWORKS Document box. The Drawing Template controls sheet size and Document Properties. The Sheet format controls the Title block, company logo, and Custom Properties.

Conserve design time. Utilize the C-SIZE-ANSI-MM-EMPTY template to create empty templates for A and B size drawings. Modify the Sheet Properties size option and utilize the Save As options for the Drawing template.

Sheet Format

Customize drawing Sheet formats to create and match your company drawing standards.

A customer requests a new product. The engineer designs the product in one location, the company produces the product in a second location and the field engineer supports the customer in a third location.

The ASME Y14.24 standard describes various types of drawings. Example: The Engineering department produces detail and assembly drawings. The drawings for machined, plastic and sheet metal parts contain specific tolerances and notes used in fabrication.

Manufacturing adds vendor item drawings with tables and notes. Field Service requires installation drawings that are provided to the customer.

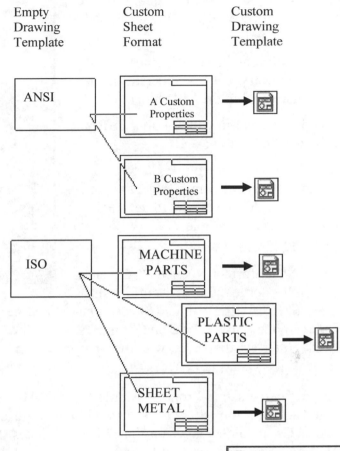

User Defined Properties

There are two types of User defined Properties: Custom Properties and Configuration Specific Properties. Custom Properties link all of the configurations of a part or an assembly. Configuration Specific Properties link only a single configuration of a part or an assembly.

Assign User defined Property values to named variables in the document. The default variables are listed in the text file C:\ProgramData\SOLIDWORKS\SOLIDWORKS 2022\lang\english, properties.txt.

Create your own User defined Property named variables. The properties.txt file is a hidden file. Insert the file path into your search bar to locate a hidden file.

Linked Notes

Insert Notes into the Title block. Link the Notes to SOLIDWORKS Properties and Custom Properties.

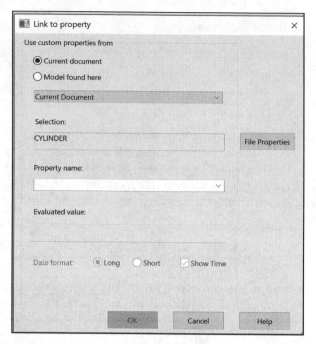

Review your company's Engineering documentation practices to determine the Notes displayed in the Title block.

Linked Notes begin with the four different prefixes listed below:

Linked Notes that reference Custom Properties in the drawing utilize the prefix: $PRP: Enter double quotes to define the property name: Example: $PRP:"Description"

Linked Sheet format Notes that reference Custom Properties in the part utilize the prefix: $PRPSHEET. Linked Sheet format Notes are displayed blank in the Edit Sheet mode. Linked Sheet format Notes are displayed with their property Name in the Edit Sheet Format mode. Example: $PRPSHEET:"Material".

User-defined Custom Property Names CONTRACT NUMBER and TREATMENT are displayed in capital letters for clarity. Utilize Large and small letters for Custom Property Names. Create a new layer for the Title block notes. The large yellow arrow in the Name column indicates the current layer.

Activity: Title Block and SW-File Name

Create a Linked Note for the DWG NO System Property.

1. Click **File**, **Properties** from the Drawing Main menu. The Summary Information dialog box is displayed.

2. Select **Number** from the drop-down menu in the Property Name box as illustrated.

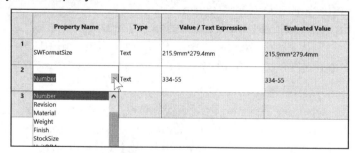

3. Click inside the **Value / Text Expression** box.

4. Enter **334-55**.

5. Click inside the **Evaluated Value** box.

6. Click **OK** from the Summary Information dialog box.

7. Right-click **Edit Sheet Format** in Sheet1.

8. **Zoom in** on the DWG. NO. box.

9. Hover over the box until you see **$PRP:"SW-File Name"**.

10. Double-click **$PRP:"SW-File Name"**.

11. **Delete** $PRP:"SW-File Name". The Note PropertyManager is displayed.

12. Click the **Link to Property** icon as illustrated. The Link to Property dialog box is displayed.

13. Select **Number** from the drop-down menu as illustrated.

14. Click **OK** from the Link to Property dialog box. Note the Formatting dialog box and the options. Use the same procedure above to address the other Link and Custom Properties in a drawing.

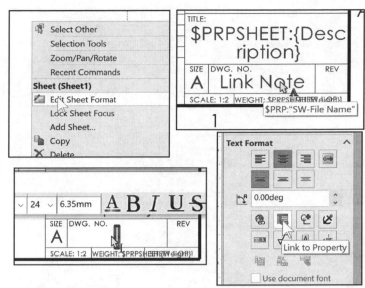

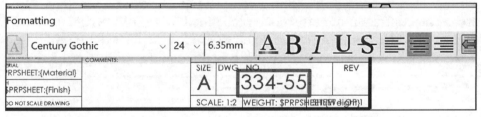

15. Click **OK** ✔ from the Note PropertyManager.

16. Right-click **Edit Sheet** in the graphic area.

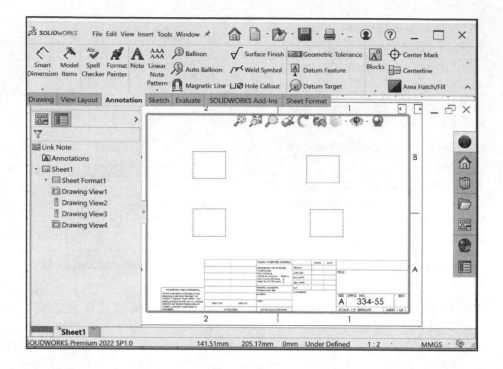

Save the Drawing. View the results.

17. Click **Save** 💾 .

User Defined Custom Property

Your company has a policy that a contract number must be contained in the Title block area. The contract number is not a predefined SOLIDWORKS Custom Property. Create a user defined Custom Property named CONTRACT NUMBER. Add it to the drawing Title block. The Custom Property is contained in the Sheet format.

Activity: User Defined Custom Property

Create a User defined Custom Property.

1. Right-click **Edit Sheet Format** in Sheet1.

2. Click **Note** A from the Annotation toolbar.

3. Click a **point** in the left-hand corner as illustrated.

4. Enter **CONTRACT NUMBER**.

5. Press the **space bar**.

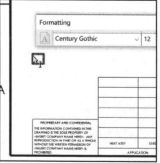

6. Click the **Link to Property** 🔲 icon from the Text Format box.

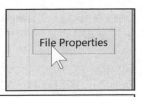

7. Click the **File Properties** button.

8. Click the **Custom** tab.

9. Click inside the **Property Name** box.

10. Enter **CONTRACT NUMBER** for Name.

11. Click inside the **Value / Text Expression** box.

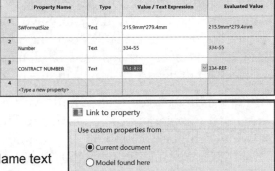

12. Enter **334-REF** for Value.

13. Click inside the **Evaluated Value** box.

14. Click **OK** from the Summary Information box.

15. Select **CONTRACT NUMBER** in the Property Name text box.

16. Click **OK** from the Link to Property box. **View** the results.

17. Click **OK** ✔ from the Note PropertyManager.

18. Right-click **Edit Sheet**.

Save the drawing. Close all documents.

19. Click **Save** 🔲.

20. **Close** all open documents.

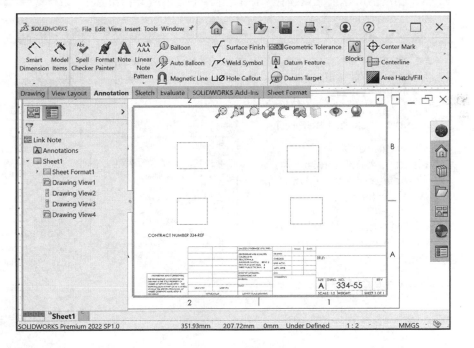

Save Sheet Format and Drawing Template

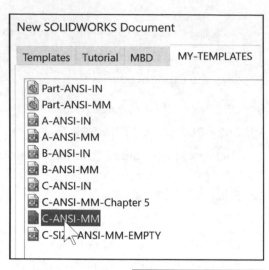

A Custom Sheet format (*.slddrt) and Custom Drawing Template (*.drwdot) utilize two different commands to save the current drawing document (.drw). Utilize the File, Save Sheet Format option to create a Custom Sheet format. The Custom Sheet formats are stored in the MY-SHEETFORMATS folder in this book.

Utilize the Save As command and select the Drawing Template option to create the Custom Drawing Template. Combine the Custom Sheet format with the Custom Drawing Template.

You created the Custom C-ANSI-MM-Chapter 5 and C-SIZE-ANSI-MM-EMPTY template with the standard SOLIDWORKS Sheet.

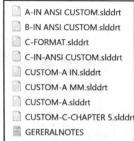

Note: There are additional Custom Sheets and Formats shown in the illustration.

Save the Sheet format and Drawing Templates in the Edit Sheet mode. Insert Drawing views into the drawing in Edit Sheet mode. Views can't be displayed in the Edit Sheet Format mode.

Activity: Open a Custom Template with a Custom Sheet Format

Create a new drawing using the Custom A-ANSI-MM Template.

1. Click **File**, **New** from the Main menu.

2. Click the **MY-TEMPLATES** tab.

3. Double-click **A-ANSI-MM**.

4. **View** the results. The Custom A-ANSI-MM Template use the CUSTOM-A Sheet format.

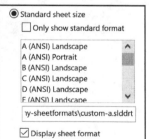

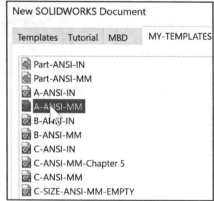

5. Click **Cancel** ✕ from the Model View PropertyManager.

6. **View** the results.

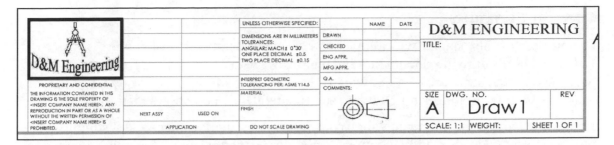

The Custom Title box was incorporated in the Custom Sheet (CUSTOM-A). The logos, Dimensions are in MILLIMETERS and the TOLERANCES are set per ASME Y14.5 alone with the Company Name (D&M ENGINEERING).

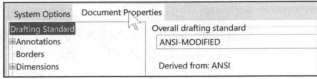

The Custom Template incorporated the Sheet Scale, Units, Precision, Drafting Standard and Angle of Projection for the drawing views.

View the Custom Drawing Properties.

7. Click **Options** ⚙, **Document Properties** from the Main menu.

8. **View** the Overall drafting standard.

9. Click the **Unit** folder.

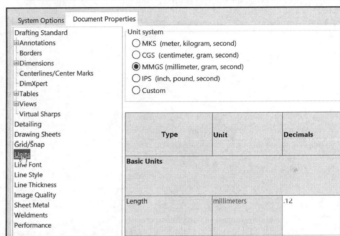

10. **View** units (MMGS) and precision (.12).

11. Click **OK** from the Document Properties dialog box.

12. Right-click **Sheet1** in the Drawing PropertyManager.

13. Click **Properties**. View Scale, Type of Projection and Sheet location.

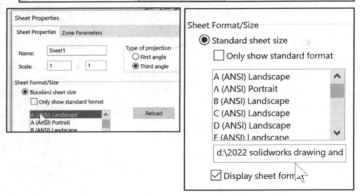

14. Click **OK** from the Sheet Properties dialog box.

15. **Close** the drawing.

Chapter Summary

The purpose of this chapter was to provide a deeper understanding of how SOLIDWORKS drawing documents and templates are created and used. Create an awareness on the structure of a Drawing Document. Provide a general knowledge of the ASME Y14 2009 Engineering Drawing and Related Documentation Practices.

You learned about the elements which construct a drawing document and distinguished between System Options and Document Properties as they relate to drawings, drawing templates and sheets.

You created a new SOLIDWORKS File Location for a drawing template and developed Linked Notes to SOLIDWORKS Properties and Custom Properties in the Sheet format.

You also worked with Annotation Links Error.

Questions

1. Explain the Structure of a Drawing Document.

2. Name four items that are contained in the Sheet format file.

3. Identify the paper dimensions (inches) required for an A (ANSI) Landscape size Sheet.

4. Identify the paper dimensions (inches) required for an A4 (ANSI) Landscape Sheet.

5. Name the three Drafting Standards.

6. Identify the primary type of projection utilized in a drawing in the United States.

7. Identify the primary type of projection utilized in a drawing in Europe.

8. Identify the location of the SW default Templates.

9. Name four Display Modes for a drawing view.

10. Identify two Unit Systems supported by SOLIDWORKS.

11. Identify 4 Custom Properties which are contained in a Title block.

12. The Drawing template ends with the SOLIDWORKS file extension _____.

13. A Sheet format ends with the SOLIDWORKS file extension _____.

14. Describe the procedure to insert a picture into the Sheet format.

15. True or False. You need to create a Custom Drawing Template before you create a Custom Sheet format.

Exercises

Exercise 5.1:

Create an A-ANSI-IN Landscape drawing template. Third Angle, Scale 1:2. Set Precision as illustrated.

Name Custom Drawing Template: A-ANSI-IN.

Create a Custom Sheet format. Name the Custom Sheet format: A-IN ANSI CUSTOM.

Incorporate all of the illustrated Title block information and logos. Note: Create and insert your school or company name and logo.

Use the Custom Template and Custom Sheet format to create a new drawing.

Name the new drawing Exercise 5.1.

Add a second sheet using the Custom Sheet format: A-IN-CUSTOM FORMAT.

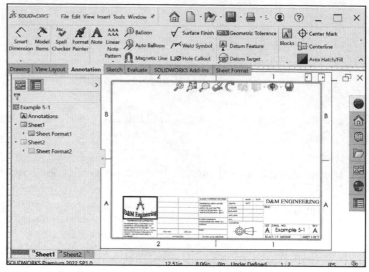

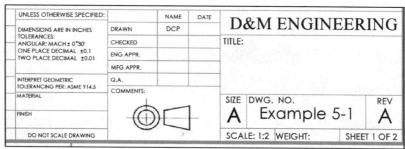

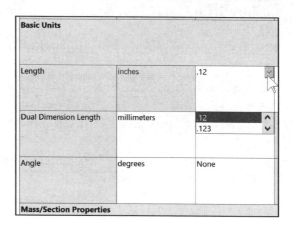

Exercise 5.2:

Create a C-ANSI-IN Landscape drawing template. Third Angle, Scale 1:2.

Set Precision as illustrated.

Name Custom Drawing Template: C-ANSI-IN.

Create a Custom Sheet format. Name the Custom Sheet format: C-IN-ANSI CUSTOM.

Incorporate all of the illustrated Title block information and logos. Note: Create and insert your school or company name and logo.

Use the Custom Template and Custom Sheet format to create a new drawing.

Name the new drawing Exercise 5.2.

Add a second sheet using the Custom Sheet format: C-IN-CUSTOM FORMAT.

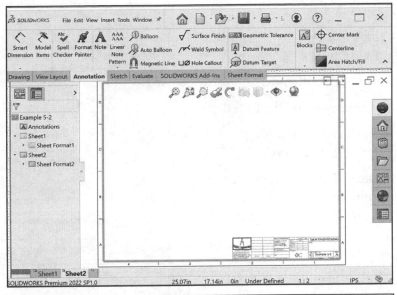

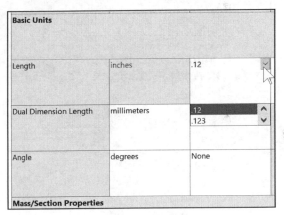

Exercise 5.3:

Create a B-ANSI-IN Landscape drawing template.

Third Angle, Scale 1:2.

Set Precision as illustrated.

Name Custom Drawing Template: B-ANSI-IN.

Create a Custom Sheet format. Name the Custom Sheet format: B-IN ANSI CUSTOM.

Incorporate all of the illustrated Title Block information and logos. Note: Create and insert your school or company name and logo.

Use the Custom Template and Custom Sheet format to create a new drawing.

Name the new drawing Exercise 5.3.

Add a second sheet using the Custom Sheet format: B-IN-CUSTOM FORMAT.

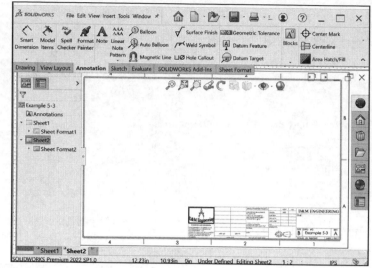

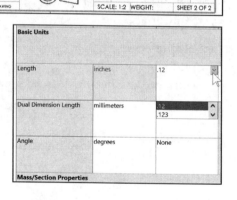

Chapter 6

Drawings and Various Drawing Views

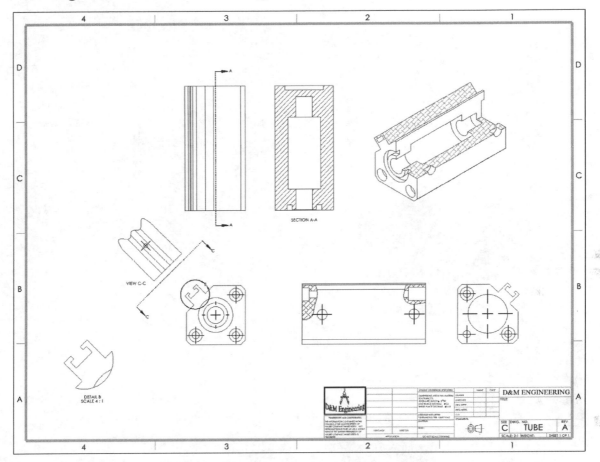

Below are the desired outcomes and usage competencies based on the completion of Chapter 6.

Desired Outcomes:	Usage Competencies:
Three Drawings: • ROD • TUBE • COVERPLATE	• Ability to create the following drawing views: Standard, Isometric, Auxiliary, Section, Broken Section, Detail, Half Section (Cut-away), Crop, Projected Back, and more.
	• Ability to create multi-sheet drawings from various part configurations.

Notes:

Chapter 6 - Drawings and Various Drawing Views

Chapter Objective

Create three drawings: ROD, TUBE, and COVERPLATE. The ROD drawing has three Sheets with Custom Properties and configurations. The ROD drawing contains: 3 Standard views, Projected view, Break view with a constant cross section, Broken view, Revolved Section view, Auxliary view, and two Detail views.

The TUBE drawing has a single Sheet with Custom Properties. The TUBE drawing contains: 3 Standard views, Projected Back view, Section view, Detail view, Auxiliary view, and a Half Section Isometric (Cut away) view.

The COVERPLATE drawing has two Sheets with Custom Properties and configurations. The COVERPLATE drawing contains: Front view, Right view, Offset Section view and Aligned Section view.

On the completion of this chapter, you will be able to:

- Create a single and multi Sheet drawing.

- Rename a standard Sheet tab.

- Comprehend Orthographic projection: First angle vs. Third angle.

- Use Custom Drawing Templetes and Sheet formats.

- Work between part configurations.

- Insert over 13 different drawing views.

- Combine two Detail views to construct an Broken Isometric view.

- Add a configuration to a part.

- Create and apply a Design Table.

- Suppress / UnSuppress Design Table configurations.

- Insert an Area Hatch.

- Insert and import dimensions and annotations.

- Create a Contstruction layer to lock a view.

Chapter Overview

A customer approaches the Engineering department to address an Air Cylinder for a new product application. In the new application, there is an interference concern with the positions of the current Air Cylinder switches.

The engineering team proposes a new design that would re-position the switches in a 45° grooved track.

The design incorporates three individual parts:

- **TUBE**

- **ROD**

- **COVERPLATE**

The parts are mated to create the CYLINDER in the Air Cylinder assembly.

The Marketing manager for the Air Cylinder product line reviews the new proposed assembly in SOLIDWORKS.

The design team decides to incorporate the new design in its standard product line. The original designer that developed the Air Cylinder was transferred to a different company division.

You are part of the CYLINDER project development team. All design drawings must meet the company's drawing standards.

What is the next step? Create drawings for various internal departments, namely: production, purchasing, engineering, inspection, and manufacturing.

First, review and discuss the features used to create the three parts.

Second, create three drawings with various drawing views using Custom Sheet formats and Custom Drawing Templates:

- ROD

- TUBE

- COVERPLATE

A SOLIDWORKS drawing document consists of a single sheet or multiple sheets.

The ROD drawing consists of three sheets.

Use three drawing sheets to display the required information for the ROD drawing.

The first drawing sheet utilizes the Short Rod configuration. ROD Sheet1 contains three Standard views, (Principle views) and an Isometric view. The Top view is hidden.

The three Standard views are:

- Top view

- Front view

- Right view

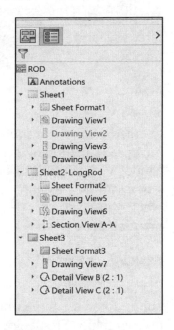

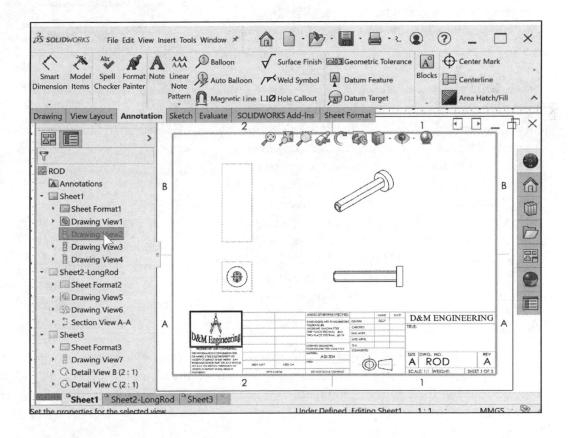

There are various ways to create the three Principle drawing views on Sheet1.

Model View:

Model View tool provides the ability to create a single or multi views based on a predefined view orientation. The Model View PropertyManager appears when you create a new drawing, or when you insert a model view into a drawing document.

Standard 3 View:

Standard 3 View tool provides the ability to create three related default orthographic (Front, Top, Right) views of a part or assembly displayed at the same time. The alignment of the Top and Right view is fixed in relation to the Front view (Third Angle Projection). The Top and Right side views are linked to the Front view. Right-click a Top view or Right side view and select Jump to Parent View.

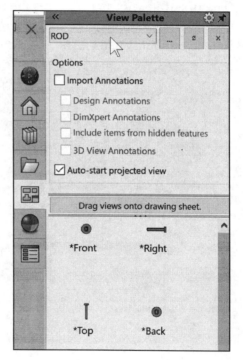

View Palette:

The Task Pane provides a quick way to insert one or more predefined views into the drawing using the View Palette tab. It contains images of standard views, annotation views, section views, and flat patterns (sheet metal parts) of the selected model. Drag views onto the drawing sheet to create a drawing view. Each view is created as a model view. The palette view orientations are based on the eight standard orientations (*Front, *Right, *Top, *Back, *Left, *Bottom, *Current, and *Isometric) and any custom views in the part or assembly.

Predefined Views:

Predefined views provide the ability to preselect an orientation, position, and scale for views on a drawing template. You can add the model or assembly reference later using Insert Model in the PropertyManager. You can save a drawing document with predefined views as a document template.

The second sheet of the ROD drawing is Sheet2.

Rename the Sheet2 tab to Sheet2-LongRod.

The Sheet2-LongRod contains the Long Rod configuration.

Copy the Front view from Sheet1 to Sheet2-LongRod.

Select the Long Rod configuration.

Insert a Projected Right view. Use a Sheet scale of 2:1 to display the Front view.

The Right view is too long for the sheet using the scale of 2:1.

Insert a Break Vertical Zig Zag. Modify the Zig Zag style and gap size.

The Break Vertical Zig Zag view represents the Long Rod with a constant cross section.

Dimensions associated with the Broken view reflect the actual model values.

A Revolved Section represents the cross section of the Rod. Utilize a Section view to create the Revolved Section between the two Break lines.

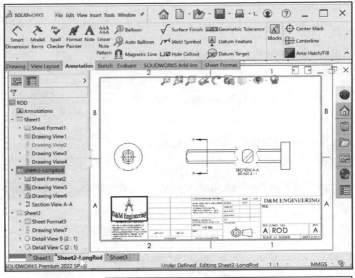

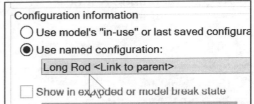

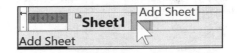

The third sheet of the ROD drawing is named Sheet3.

Copy the Isometric view from Sheet1.

Modify the configuration to Long Rod.

Create two Detail views using a Sketch spline.

Combine the two Detail views to construct the Broken Isometric view.

The Detail views were aligned with a Contruction line on a layer.

Move the Annotation off the sheet.

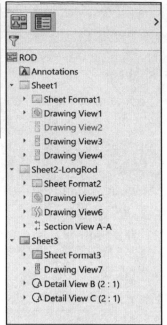

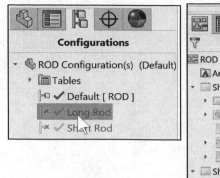

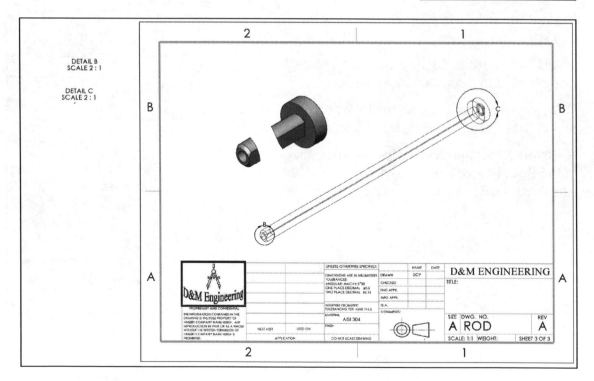

The second drawing is the TUBE drawing. The TUBE drawing is a single Sheet with eight views. The TUBE drawing contains:

Three Standard views and:

1.) Projected Back view

2.) Section view

3.) Detail view

4.) Auxiliary view

5.) Half Section Isometric view

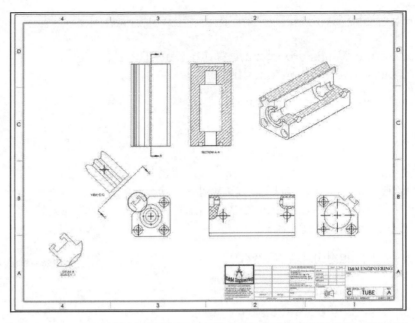

The Third drawing is the COVERPLATE drawing. The COVERPLATE drawing consists of two Sheets. There are two part configurations:

- Without Nose Holes

- With Nose Holes

Sheet1 utilizes the Without Nose Holes configuration.

COVERPLATE Sheet1 contains the following views: Front view, Right view, and an Offset Section view.

Sheet2 utilizes the With Nose Holes configuration.

COVERPLATE Sheet2 contains the Front view, and Aligned Section view.

Note: In the next chapter, address Custom Part Properties, Custom Drawing Properties, Custom Link Properties and SOLIDWORKS Properties for the TUBE and COVERPLATE.

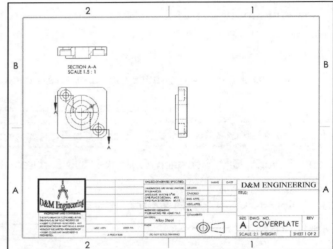

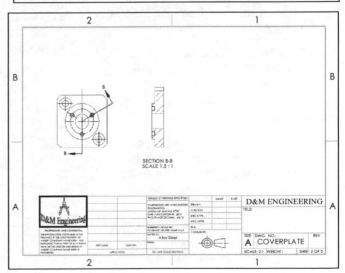

Review the ROD Part and Configurations

Configurations are variations of a part. The ROD part consists of two configurations:

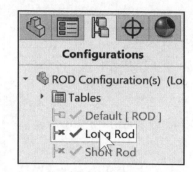

- Short Rod configuration

- Long Rod configuration

Material was added to the Configuration Specific Part Custom Property. This is linked to the Material Properties section in the Drawing document.

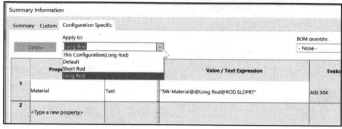

A drawing utilizes views, dimensioning, tolerances, notes, and other related design information from the part.

When you modify a feature dimension in a part, the drawing automatically updates.

The part and the drawing share the same file structure. Do not delete or move the part document.

Activity: Review the ROD Part and Configurations

Start a SOLIDWORKS session. Open the ROD part from the SOLIDWORKS 2022/Chapter 6 Models folder.

1) Start a **SOLIDWORKS 2022** session.

Open the ROD part.

2) Click **Open** from the Menu bar toolbar.

3) Double-click **ROD part** from the SOLIDWORKS 2022/Chapter 6 Models folder. The ROD PropertyManager is displayed in the part default configuration.

Review the ROD part features. Use the Rollback bar tool to better understand how a model was created with features and sketches.

4) Place the **mouse pointer** over the blue Rollback bar at the bottom of the FeatureManager design tree. The mouse pointer displays a symbol of a hand.

5)　　Drag the **Rollback** bar upward below the Base-Extrude feature.

Display the Base-Extrude dimensions.

6)　　Double-click **Base-Extrude** from the FeatureManager.

7)　　**View** the results.

8)　　Click **inside** the graphics area.

Return to the bottom of the ROD model.

9)　　Right-click **Base-Extrude**.

10)　　Click **Roll to End**.

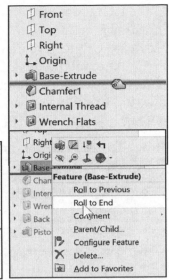

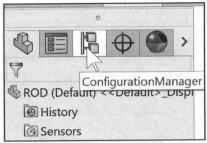

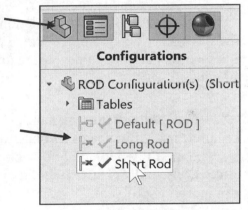

Display the ROD part configurations.

11)　　Click the **ConfigurationManager**

tab at the top of the FeatureManager.

12)　　Double-click the **Long Rod** configuration.

13)　　**View** the Long Rod configuration in the graphics area.

Fit the ROD to the Graphics window.

14)　　Press the **f** key.

15)　　Double-click the **Short Rod** configuration.

16)　　**View** the Short Rod configuration.

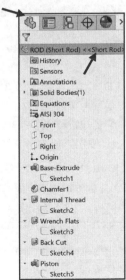

Press the z key to Zoom out or the middle mouse button. Press the f key to fit the model to the Graphics window.

Return to the ROD FeatureManager. View the Configuration Specific Part Custom Properies.

17)　　Click the **FeatureManager** tab. The Short Rod is the current configuration.

18)　　Click **File**, **Properties** from the Main menu.

19)　　Click the **Configuration Specific** tab.

20)　　**View** the results.

21)　　Click **OK**.

Fit the ROD to the graphics area.

22)　　Press the **f** key.

In the ROD part, the simulated internal thread was created with a simple Extruded Cut feature on the Front Plane. Internal threads require specific notes. Use a Hole Callout in the drawing to annotate the internal thread note.

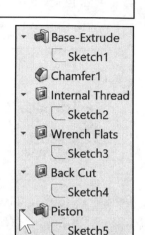

Note: To create a real thread, use the Thread tool under the Hole Wizard.

Locate the profile for the Wrench Flats on the Back Plane. The design engineer uses a Symmetric relation with the Right Plane. Add a centerline in the drawing to represent the Wrench Flat symmetry.

Utilize symmetry in the part whenever possible. This conserves rebuild time. Use Symmetric relations in the sketch. Use Mirror All and the Mirror Feature in the part. Symmetric dimension schemes and relations defined in the part require added dimensions in the drawing.

Create fully defined sketches. A minus sign (-) displayed in the FeatureManager indicates an under defined Sketch. Sketch1 through Sketch5 are fully defined. Fully defined sketches provide marked dimensions, address faster rebuild times, and create fewer configuration problems.

ROD Drawing: Sheet1-Short Rod Configuration

The ROD drawing contains three drawing sheets. Sheet1 contains the Short Rod configuration, three Standard views, (Principle views) and an Isometric view. Use the Task Pane View Palette procedure. Use the Custom A-ANSI-MM drawing template created in Chapter 5. The FeatureManager displays the Drawing view name.

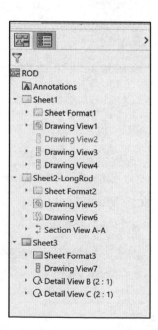

Detail views and Section views are labeled with their view name followed by a letter or number. Example: Section view A-A. Reposition the drawing views. Drag the drawing view by its green view boundary or a drawing entity inside the view.

Provide approximately 1in. - 2in., (25mm - 50mm) between each view for dimension placement. The Right and Top views align to the Front view position. The Isometric view is free to move and contains no alignment. The Sheet, View, Edge, and Component contain specific properties. Select the right mouse button on an entity to review the Properties.

Activity: Create ROD Drawing-Sheet1. Use the A-ANSI-MM Template.

Create Sheet1 of the ROD Drawing. Use the custom A-ANSI-MM Drawing Template. The ROD part (Short configuration) is open.

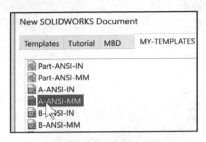

23) Click **New** ⬚ from the Main menu.

24) Click the **MY-TEMPLATES** tab.

25) Double-click **A-ANSI-MM**.

26) Click **Cancel** ✖ in the Model View PropertyManager.

Create the Front, Top, Right and Isometric views. Use the View Palette.

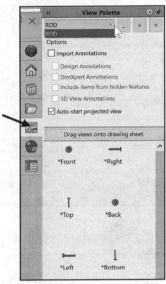

27) Click the **View Palette** icon in the Task Pane.

28) Click the **drop down arrow** menu in the Task Pane as illustrated. This will display all open models.

29) Click **ROD. View** the available views.

30) Click and drag the ***Front** view in the Front view location as illustrated.

31) Click directly **upward** for the Top view.

32) Click directly **downward** and to the **right** to create the Right view.

33) Click a location **approximately 45 degrees** to the upper right of the Front view. This is the Isometric view.

34) Click **OK** ✔ from the Projected View PropertyManager. **View** the four views.

35) Click and drag the **drawing views** to space them for dimensions and annotations. The Top and Right view are directly projected from the Front view.

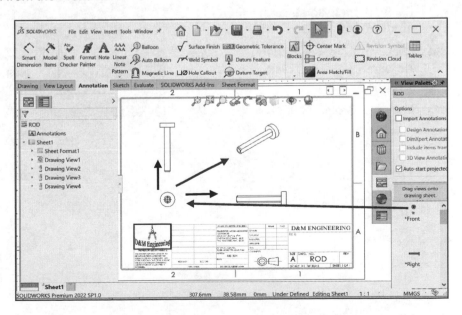

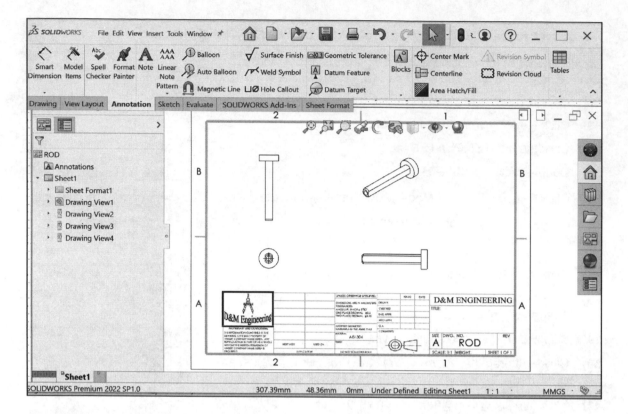

Save the Drawing with the ROD part in the same folder.

36) Click **Save As**  from the Main menu drop-down bar.

37) Select **SOLIDWORKS 2022/Chapter 6 Drawings/ROD** folder for Save in.

38) Enter **ROD** for File name.

39) Enter **ROD 2A** for Description.

40) Click the **Include all referenced components** box.

41) Click the **Advanced** button. The Save As with References dialog box is displayed.

42) Click the **Browse** button.

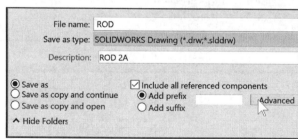

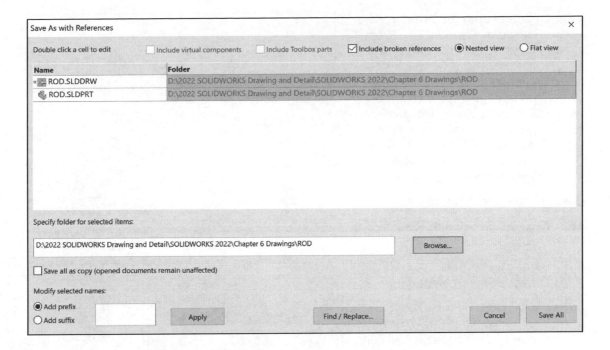

43) **Browse** to the SOLIDWORKS 2022/Chapter 6 Drawings/ROD folder.

44) Click **Select Folder**.

45) Click **Save All**. The ROD drawing and ROD is saved in the SOLIDWORKS 2022/Chapter 6 Drawings/ROD folder. Note: You can also use SOLIDWORKS Pack and Go.

A Parent view is an existing view referenced by other views. The Front view is the Parent view. The Right and Top views are Projected from the Front view. The Right and Top views are called Child views. Child views move relative to the Parent view. Retain exact positions between the views, press Shift while dragging the views.

Move the drawing views.

46) Position the **mouse pointer** on the edge of Drawing View1 (Front view) as illustrated.

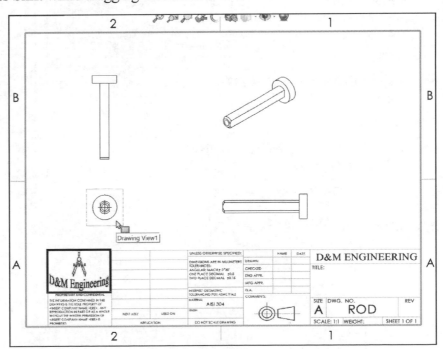

47) Click and drag the **Front view** in an upward direction. The Front view is the Parent view. The Right and Top views are Projected from the Front view. The Right and Top views are called Child views. Child views move relative to Parent views. Retain exact positions between the views, press Shift while dragging the views.

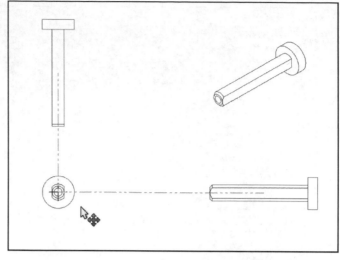

Display the Sheet1 properties.

48) Click inside **Sheet1**. Not inside of a view.

49) Right-click **Sheet1** in the ROD Drawing FeatureManager.

50) Click **Properties**. Review the Properties of the Sheet. Sheet1 Scale is 1:1. Type of Projection: Third Angle.

51) Click **Cancel** from the Sheet Properties dialog box.

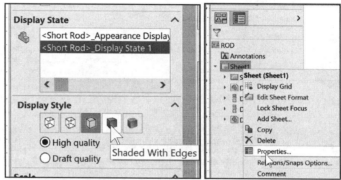

Display the Isometric view Shaded With Edges.

52) Click inside the **Isometric view**.

53) Click **Shaded With Edges** from the Drawing View4 PropertyManager. Note: You can also select Shaded With Edges from the Heads-up View toolbar.

Hide the Top view.

54) Right-click **Drawing View2** (Top view).

55) Click **Hide**.

56) Click **OK** ✔ from the Drawing View2 PropertyManager.

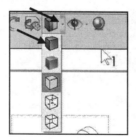

Save the ROD drawing.

57) Click **Save** 💾.

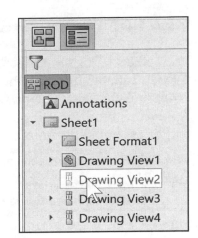

The FeatureManager icons indicate the visible and hidden views. Modify the view state quickly with the FeatureManager.

The Drawing View2 icon displays hidden views. The Drawing View1 icon displays visible Model views. The Drawing View3 icon displays visible Projected views. Utilize Show to display a hidden view. Right-click the view name in the FeatureManager. Select the Show option.

View Boundary Properties and Lock View Options

As a drawing becomes populated with views, utilize the Lock options to control annotation and sketch geometry into the view or the sheet. The Lock View Position, Lock View Focus, and the Lock Sheet Focus options provides the following:

- **Lock View Position**: Secures the view at its current position in the Sheet. Right-click in the drawing view to Lock View Position. To unlock a view position, right-click and select Unlock View Position.

- **Lock View Focus**: Adds sketch entities and annotations to the selected locked view. Double-click the view to activate Lock View Focus. To unlock a view, right-click and select Unlock View Focus or double click outside the view boundary.

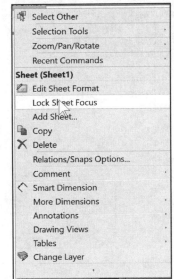

- **Lock Sheet Focus**: Adds sketch entities and annotations to the selected sheet. Double-click the sheet to activate Lock Sheet Focus. To unlock a sheet, right-click and select Unlock Sheet Focus or double click inside the sheet boundary.

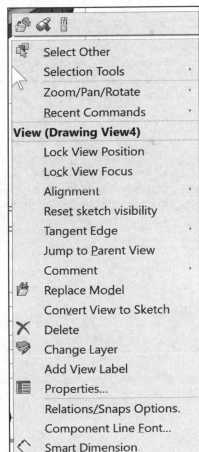

View ROD Drawing Sheet1 - Properties

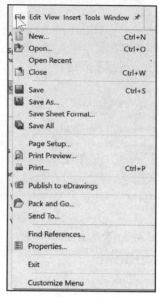

View Sheet1 Custom Properties. Add Revision and DrawnBy.
The Custom tab provides the ability to specify Custom
Properties for the active part, assembly, or drawing document.
Apply Custom Properties to specific configurations in the active
part or assembly document.

View Sheet1 Custom Properties. Add Custom Properties.

58)   Click **FIle**, **Properties** from the Main menu. The Summary
Information dialog box is displayed.

59)   Click the **Custom** tab.

60)   Select **Revision** from the drop-down menu in the third row.

61)   Click inside the Value / Text Expression box.

62)   Enter **A**.

63)   Click inside the **Evaluated
Value** box.

64)   Select **DrawnBy** from the drop-
down menu in the fourth row.

65)   Enter you initials: **DCP**.

66)   Click **OK** from the Summary
Information dialog box. We will
address additonal Custom and
Link Properties later in the book.

Save the drawing.

67)   Click **Save** 💾. View the
Custom Properties in
Sheet1. Note: The Material
comes from the ROD part
Custom properties.

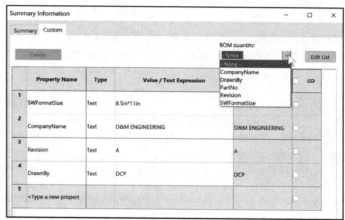

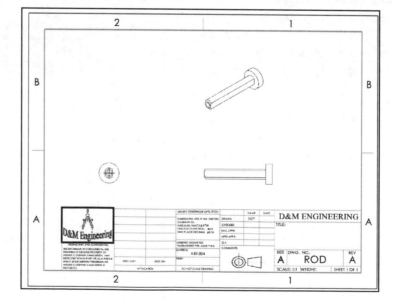

ROD Drawing: Sheet2 - Long Rod Configuration

The second sheet of the ROD drawing is Sheet2.

Rename Sheet2 tab to Sheet2-LongRod.

The Sheet2-LongRod contains the Long Rod configuration.

Copy the Front view from Sheet1 to Sheet2-LongRod.

Select the Long Rod configuration.

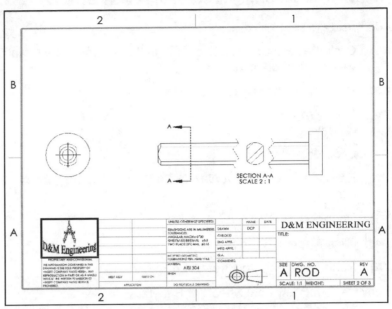

Insert a Projected Right view. Use a Sheet scale of 1:1 to display the Front view details.

The Right view is too long for the sheet using the scale of 2:1.

Insert a Break Vertical Zig Zag.

The Break Vertical Zig Zag view represents the Long Rod with a constant cross section. Modify the Zig Zag style to the Curve Cut style and gap size.

Dimensions associated with the Broken view reflect the actual model values.

Add a Revolved Section view to represent the cross section of the ROD. Position the Revolved Section between the Vertical Broken view.

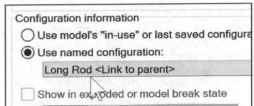

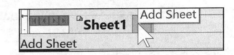

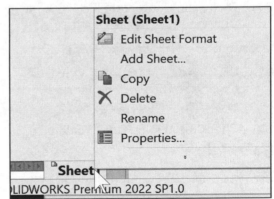

Activity: ROD Drawing-Sheet2 Projected View and Break View

Add Sheet2 to the ROD drawing.

68) Click the **Add Sheet** tab located at the bottom of the Graphics window. Sheet2 is displayed.

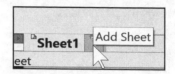

69) Right-click **Sheet2** as illustrated.

70) Click **Properties**. The Sheet Properties dialog box is displayed.

71) Click **Browse** button.

72) Browse to the **SOLIDWORKS 2022/MY-SHEETFORMATS** folder.

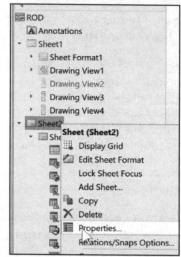

73) Double-click **CUSTOM-A MM**.

74) Click **Apply Changes**.

75) Rename **Sheet2** to **Sheet2-LongRod**.

Copy the Front view from Sheet1 to Sheet2.

76) Click the **Sheet1** tab.

77) Click inside **Drawing View1**, (Front) view.

Copy the view.

78) Click **Edit**, **Copy** from the Menu bar menu.

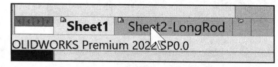

79) Click the **Sheet2-LongRod** tab.

80) Click a view **position** in the lower left corner.

Paste the Front view.

81) Click **Edit**, **Paste** from the Menu bar menu. Drawing View5 is displayed.

Modify the Scale for Drawing View5.

82) Click inside the **Drawing View5** view boundary. The Drawing View5 PropertyManager is displayed.

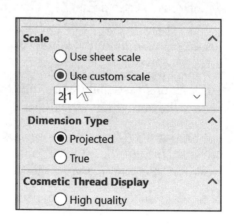

83) Check the **Use custom scale** box.

84) Enter **2:1**.

85) Click **OK** ✔ from the Drawing View5 PropertyManager.

Modify the ROD configuration. Change the configuration to Long Rod.

86) Right-click **Drawing View5** as illustrated in the ROD Drawing PropertyManager.

87) Click **Properties**. The Drawing View Properties dialog box is displayed.

88) Select **Long Rod** from the Use named configuration drop-down menu.

89) Click **OK**. Note Drawing View5 is selected.

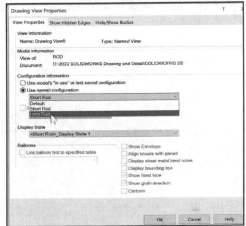

Insert a Projected view. Projected views are created by folding off an existing view in one of eight possible projections. The resulting view orientation is affected by the setting of First angle or Third angle projection as defined in the drawing sheet properties.

90) Click **Projected View** from the View Layout tab in the CommandManager. The Projected View PropertyManager is displayed.

91) **View** your options.

92) Click a **position** to the right of the Front view. DrawingView6 is displayed.

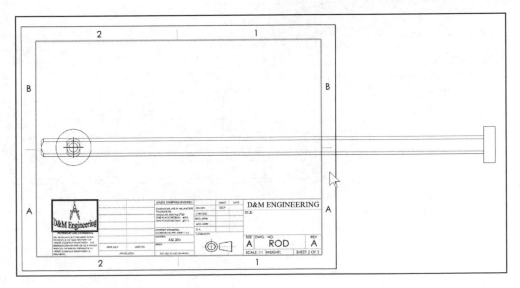

Create a Break Vertical Zig Zag Right view.

93) Click inside the **Drawing View6** boundary.

94) Click **Break** 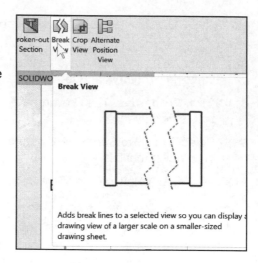 from the View Layout toolbar. The Broken View PropertyManager is displayed. Vertical is the default setting.

95) Enter **10mm** for Gap size.

96) Click a **position** as illustrated to create the left vertical break line towards the Internal Thread.

97) Click a **position** as illustrated to create the right vertical break line towards the Piston as illustrated.

98) Click **OK** ✔ from the Broken View PropertyManager.

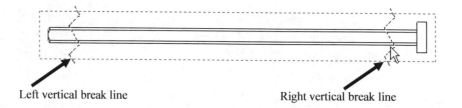

Left vertical break line   Right vertical break line

99) Right-click inside the **Drawing View6** boundary.

100) Click **Un-Break View**.

101) **View** the results.

102) Right-click inside the **Drawing View6** boundary.

103) Click **Break View**.

104) Click inside the **Drawing View6** boundary.

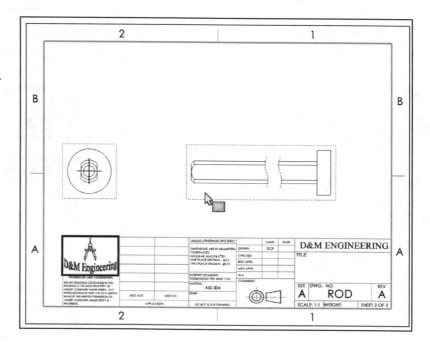

Modify the Break line style.

105) Click on the left **Break line**. The Broken View PropertyManager is displayed.

106) Select **Curve Cut** to display the curved break line.

107) Enter **20mm** for Gap.

108) Click OK ✔ from the Broken View PropertyManager.

Save the ROD drawing.

109) Click Save 💾.

Modify the Break Lines display. Right-click on the Break line. Select: *Straight Cut, Curve Cut, Zig Zag Cut,* or *Small Zig Zag Cut.*

Utilize Options, Document Properties, Line Font to modify the Break Lines Font for the drawing document.

💡 The Line Format toolbar controls: *Layer Properties, Line Color, Line Thickness, Line Style, Hide / Show Edges, Color Display Mode* for selected entities.

💡 When you right-click a component in a drawing, you can open either the part or assembly.

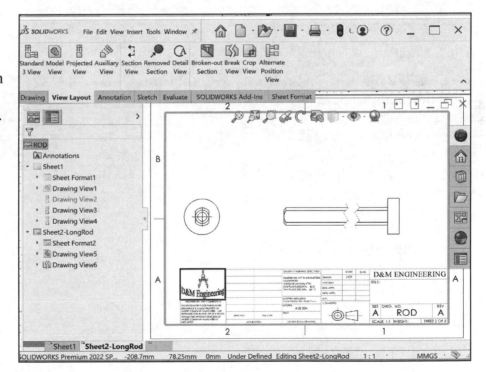

The Parent view is the original view utilized to create the Child views: *Auxiliary*, *Section* and *Detail*. Position the Child views on the same drawing sheet as the Parent view. If no space exists on the current sheet, move the Child view to a new Sheet. Label the Child view with the Parent view Sheet number. Utilize the Note tool from the Annotation toolbar, "See Sheet X" where X is the number of the Parent sheet.

Section View tool

The Section View ⤴ tool adds a section view by cutting the parent view with a section lines. Use the Section view sketch mode in conjunction with the Section tool user interface to create (Vertical, Horozontal, Auxiliary and Aligned Section views along with various Half Section views.

The Section line can also include concentric arcs. The Section view tool uses the

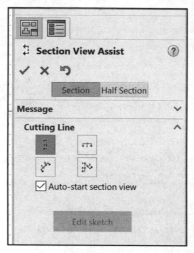

Section View PropertyManager. The Section View PropertyManager provides the ability to select either the **Section** or **Half Section** tab. Each tab provides a separate menu.

Section View tool: Section tab

The Section tab provides the following selections:

- ***Cutting Line***. The Cutting Line box provides the following selections:

    - **Vertical** Cutting line 🔲.

    - **Horizontal** Cutting line 🔲.

    - **Auxiliary** Cutting line 🔲.

    - **Aligned** Cutting line 🔲.

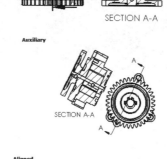

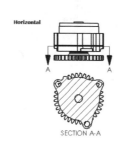

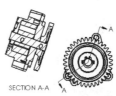

ROD Drawing - Revolved Section

A Revolved Section represents the cross section of the Rod. Utilize a Section view to create the Revolved Section between the two Break lines.

Activity: ROD Drawing-Revolved Section

Increase the default break line gap from 10mm to 25mm.

110) Click **Options** ⚙, **Document Properties** tab from the Main menu.

111) Click the **Detailing** folder under Document Properties.

112) Enter **25** in the View break lines Gap box.

113) Click **OK** from the Document Properties - Detailing dialog box.

114) Click **Save** 💾.

Create a Section View..

115) Click the **Section View** icon for the View Layout tab in the CommandManager. The Section tab and the Vertical Cutting Line is selected by default.

Uncheck the Auto-start section view box to display the Section view pop-up menu. This provides the ability to add offsets to the Section view. The options are: 1.) Select first point of arc on cutting line, then select second point of arc, 2.) Select first point of offset on cutting line, then select second point of offset, 3.) Select first point of notch on cutting line, select second point on cutting line for width of notch, then select third point for depth of notch.

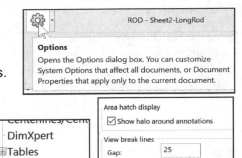
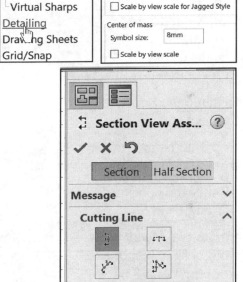

116) Click a **position** to the left of the vertical break and to the right of the internal thread feature as illustrated.

117) Click a position between the **Vertical Break lines** to place the cross section as illustrated.

118) Click **OK** ✔ from the Section View A-A PropertyManager.

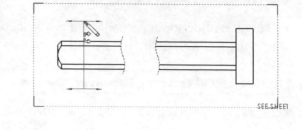

Save the ROD drawing. Sheet2 is complete.

119) Click **Save** 🖫 .

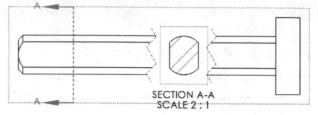

ROD Drawing: Sheet3 - Long Rod Configuration

The third sheet of the ROD drawing is Sheet2.

Rename the Sheet2 tab to Sheet3.

Copy the Isometric view from Sheet1.

Modify the configuration to Long Rod.

Create two Detail views using a sketch spline from the Long Rod Isometric view.

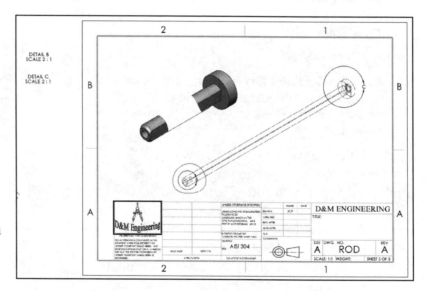

Combine two Detail views to construct the Isometric view.

Align the two Detail views with a contruction line on a layer.

ROD Drawing-Broken Isometric View

A Broken Isometric view utilizes two Detail views. Create a Front Detail view, and then a Back Detail view.

Position the two Detail views. Utilize a Sketch line to align the Front Detail view and the Back Detail view. Create the Sketch line on the Construction drawing layer.

Select the Detail views and utilize the Default Alignment option to move both views together. Create layers in a drawing document for construction geometry and dimensions.

Sketched geometry in the drawing links to the current view. Select the view and the view boundary turns blue. Sketch the geometry and the geometry moves with the view. Specify line color, thickness and line style. Add New entities to the active layer. Turn layers on/off to simplify drawings. Shut layers off when not in use.

Activity: Create Sheet3

Add a Sheet. Rename the Sheet tab name.

120) Click the **Sheet** tab.

121) Click **Add Sheet**. Sheet2 is displayed.

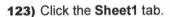

122) Rename **Sheet2** to **Sheet3**.

Copy the Isometric view from Sheet1 to Sheet3.

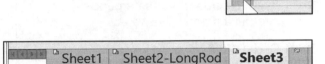

123) Click the **Sheet1** tab.

124) Click the **Isometric view**.

125) Click **Edit**, **Copy**.

126) Click the **Sheet3** tab.

127) Click a **position** in Sheet3.

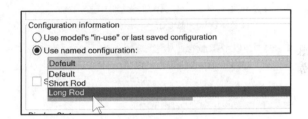

128) Click **Edit**, **Paste**.

Modify the ROD configuration.

129) Click inside the **Isometic view**.

130) Right-click **Properties**. The Drawing View Properties dialog box is displayed.

131) Click **Use named configuration**.

132) Select **Long Rod**.

133) Click **OK** from the Drawing View Properties dialog box.

134) Click and drag the **Isometric view** as illustrated.

135) Display **WireFrame** mode.

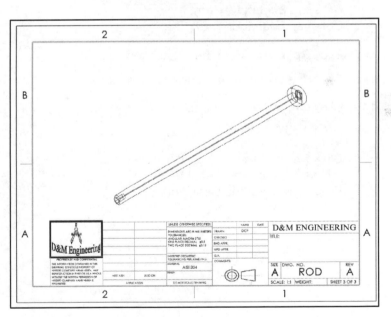

Create the first Detail view of the internal thread feature using the Sketch Spline tool.

136) Click inside the **Isometric view** area.

137) Zoom in on the internal thread feature.

138) Click the **Sketch** tab from the CommandManager.

139) Click **Spline** $\mathcal{N}$ from the Sketch toolbar.

140) Sketch a **closed** spline around the internal thread as illustrated.

141) Click **OK** ✔ from the Spline PropertyManager.

142) Click **Detail View** from the View toolbar.

143) Click a **position** in the Sheet boundary as illustrated.

144) Click **OK** ✔ from the Detail View C PropertyManager.

145) Click **Shaded With Edges** from the Heads-up View toolbar.

Create a Detail view of the Piston end feature using the sketch Spline tool.

146) Click the **Sketch** tab from the CommandManager.

147) Click **Spline** $\mathcal{N}$ from the Sketch toolbar.

148) Sketch a spline around the Piston end.

149) Click **OK** ✔ from the Spline PropertyManager.

150) Click **Detail View** $\widehat{\mathcal{A}}$ from the View Layout toolbar. The Detail View PropertyManager is displayed.

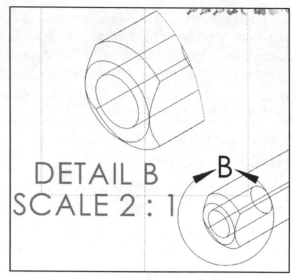

DETAIL B
SCALE 2 : 1

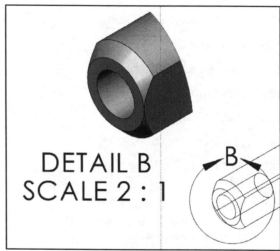

DETAIL B
SCALE 2 : 1

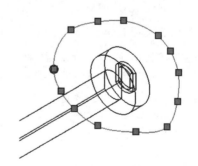

151) Click a **position** in Sheet3 as illustrated.

152) Click **Shaded With Edges** 📦 from the Heads-up View toolbar.

153) Click **OK** ✔ from the Detail View PropertyManager.

154) Move the **views and annotations** as illustrated. **View** the results.

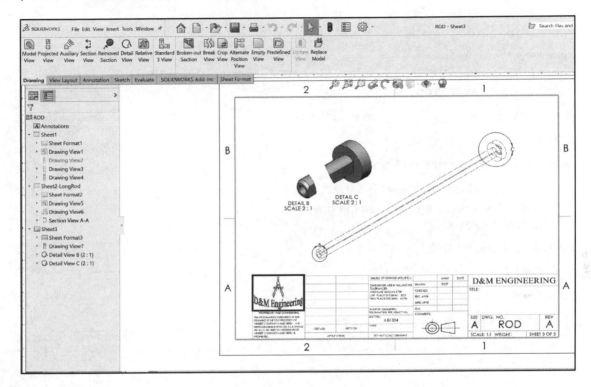

💡 Do not delete the Parent views outside the Sheet boundary. The Detail C and Detail D text is dependent on the Isometric view. Sketching Splines for Broken Isometric views requires practice.

Create layers in a SOLIDWORKS drawing document. Assign visibility, line color, line thickness, and line style for new entities (annotations and assembly components) created on each layer. New entities are automatically added to the active layer.

Layer Properties

In drawings, creates, edits, or deletes layers. Also, changes the properties and visibility of layers.

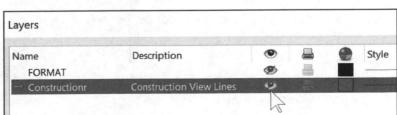

Display the Layer toolbar.

155) Click **View**, **Toolbars**, **Layer** from the Main menu. Note: You can also right-click inside the Sheet or the view and click Change Layer.

Layer Properties

In drawings, creates, edits, or deletes layers. Also, changes the properties and visibility of layers.

To hide a layer, click the open eye 👁 icon. The icon changes to a close eye ⌀ icon. All entities on that layer are hidden. To turn the layer back on, click close eye ⌀ icon.

156) Click the **Layer Properties** 📚 icon.

Display the Layers dialog box. Create a new layer.

157) Click the **New** button.

158) Enter **Construction** for Name.

159) Enter **Construction View Lines** for Description. Note: The layer is active when the open eye 👁 icon is displayed.

160) Select **Red** for Color.

161) Click **OK**.

162) Select **Dashed** for Style.

163) Click **OK** from the Layers dialog box.

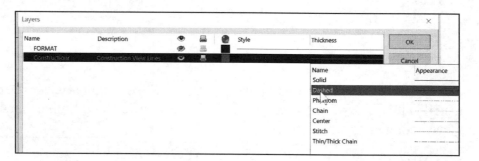

Sketch a line.

164) Click inside the **Detail B** view boundary.

165) Click **Line** ╱ from the Sketch toolbar.

166) Sketch a **line parallel** to the lower profile line on Detail C as illustrated.

Move the Detail C view.

167) Drag **Detail C** until the bottom edge is approximately aligned with the red line.

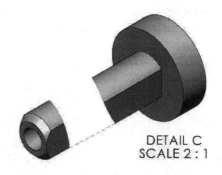

DETAIL C
SCALE 2 : 1

DETAIL B
SCALE 2 : 1

Lock View position.

168) Click inside the **Detail C** view boundary.

169) Hold the **Ctrl** key down.

170) Click inside the **Detail D** view boundary.

171) Release the **Ctrl** key.

172) Right-click **Lock View Position**.

173) Click **OK** ✓ from the Multi View PropertyManager.

Hide the red line.

174) Click the **Layer Properties**  icon.

175) Click the **Hide layer** icon to turn off the Construction layer.

176) Click **OK** from the Layers dialog box.

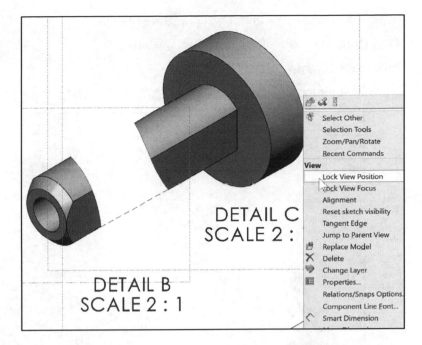

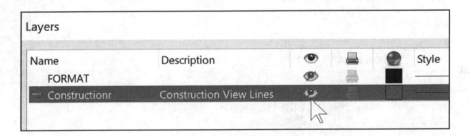

Fit the drawing to the Graphics window. Save Sheet3.

177) Drag the notes off the Sheet as illustrated.

Save the ROD drawing and ROD part.

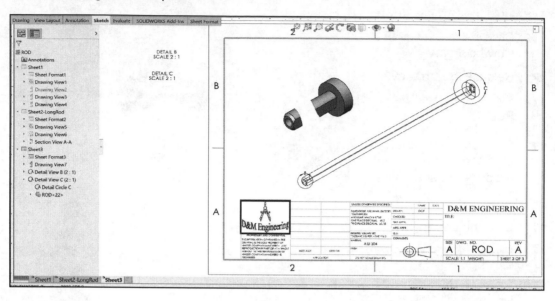

178) Click **Save** .

Close all parts and drawings.

179) Click **Windows**, **Close All** from the Main menu.

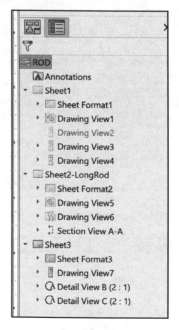

 **Review**

The ROD drawing consists of three sheets. Sheet1 contained the Front, Top, Right, and Isometric view for the Short Rod configuration.

Sheet2 was renamed to Sheet2-LongRod. The Front view from Sheet1 was copied to Sheet2-LongRod. The ROD configuration was changed. A Projected Right view was created. You applied a Sheet scale of 2:1 to display the Front view details.

The Right view was too long for the Sheet scale. A Break Vertical Zig Zag view was created. You modified the Break style and gap size.

A Revolved Section represents the cross section of the Rod. A Section view was used to create the Revolved Section between the two Break lines.

Sheet3 contained a copy of the Isometric view from Sheet1. You modified the default configuration to the Long Rod configuration. You created two Detail views using a sketch spline.

You combined two Detail views to construct the Broken Isometric view. You aligned the two Detail views with a Contruction line on a layer.

Review the TUBE Part

Perform the following recommended tasks before starting the TUBE drawing:

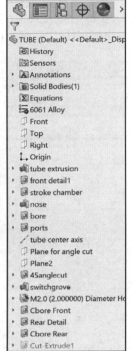

- Verify the TUBE part.

- View and move feature dimensions.

Position feature dimensions off the part before creating the drawing. Dimension schemes defined in the part require changes in the drawing. Design engineers use different dimensioning schemes than those required by manufacturing engineers.

Example 1: The design engineer references the depth dimensions 27.75mm and 32.75mm to the Front Plane for the Tube Extrusion feature. The engineer's analysis calculations also reference the Front Plane.

The manufacturing engineer requires an overall depth of 60.50mm (27.75mm + 32.75mm) referenced from the front face. Create the overall depth dimension of 60.50mm for a drawing.

Example 2: The design engineer references the depth dimensions to the Front Plane for the Stoke Chamber (Depth1 = 17.50mm and Depth2 = 17.50mm).

The manufacturing engineering requires an overall depth of 35.00mm.

Example 3: An Extruded Cut feature creates the Stroke Chamber as an internal feature. Display the Stroke Chamber dimensions in the Section view of the drawing. Reference added dimensions from the Front face in the Section view.

Activity: Review the TUBE Part

Review the TUBE part.

180) Click **Open** from the Menu bar toolbar.

181) Double-click **TUBE** from the SOLIDWORKS 2022/Chapter 6 Models folder. The TUBE FeatureManager is displayed.

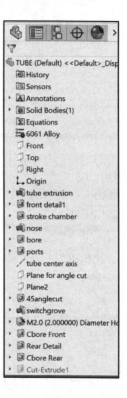

TUBE Drawing

The TUBE drawing consists of a single drawing sheet with eight views.

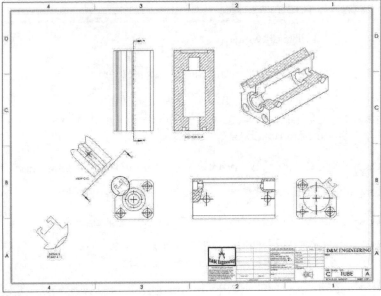

The eight views are: three Standard views, a Projected Back view, Section view, Detail view, Auxiliary view, and a Half Section Isometric (Cut away) view.

The Half Section Isometric view requires two part configurations named: Entire Part and Section Cutaway.

Utilize the A-ANSI-MM Drawing template. Insert the Front, Top, Right, and Isometric view. There is not enough space on an A-size drawing. You have two options: enlarge the sheet size or move additional views to multiple sheets. How do you increase the Sheet size? Utilize Sheet Properties.

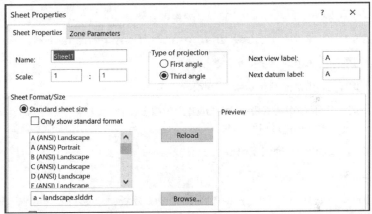

The Sheet Properties, Size option modifies an A-size drawing to a C-size drawing with a 1:1 scale. Utilize the Sheet formats which are provided.

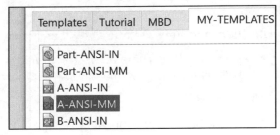

Projected views display the part or assembly by projecting an Orthographic view using the First angle or Third angle projection. Recall that Third angle projection is set in Sheet Properties in the Drawing Template. Insert a Project view to create the Back view. Provide approximately 1in. - 2in., (25mm - 50mm) between views.

Activity: TUBE Drawing

Create the TUBE drawing.

182) Click **New** ⬜ from the Menu bar toolbar.

183) Click the **MY-TEMPLATES** tab.

184) Double-click **A-ANSI-MM** from the SOLIDWORKS Document dialog box.

185) Click **Cancel** ✕ from the Model View PropertyManager.

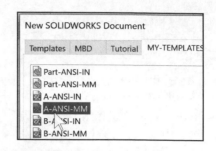

Save the TUBE drawing and TUBE part in the same folder.

186) Click **Save As** 🖫 from the Consolidated Main menu.

187) Select **SOLIDWORKS 2022/Chapter 6 Drawing/TUBE** folder for Save in folder.

188) Enter **TUBE** for File name.

189) Enter **TUBE 2A** for Description.

190) Click the **Include all referenced components** box.

191) Click the **Advanced** button.

192) Click the **Browse** button.

193) Select the **SOLIDWORKS 2022/Chapter 6 Drawing/TUBE** folder.

194) Click **Select Folder**.

195) Click **Save All**.

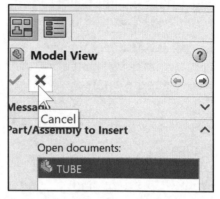

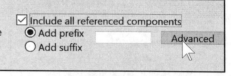

Insert the Front, Top, Right and Isometric view. Use the View Palette in the Task Pane.

196) Click the **View Palette** ⊞ icon in the Task Pane.

197) Click the Task Pane **drop-down arrow** as illustrated. This will display all open models.

198) Click **TUBE**.

199) **View** the available drawing views.

200) Click and drag the ***Front** view in the Front view location as illustrated.

201) Click **directly upward** (Top view).

202) Click **downward and to the right** of the Front view to create the Right view.

203) Click **approximately at a 45 degree** (Isometric view).

204) Click **OK** ✓ from the Projected PropertyManager.

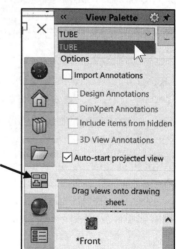

205) Click inside the **Isometric view** to align it as illustrated.

206) **View** the results.

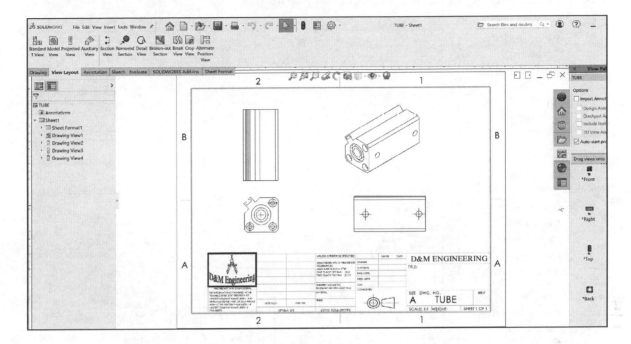

Modify Sheet1 Properties.

207) Right-click **Sheet1** in the TUBE drawing FeatureManager.

208) Click **Properties**. The Sheet Properties dialog box is displayed.

209) Select **C (ANSI) Landscape** for Sheet Format/Size.

210) Click the **Browse** button.

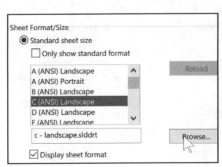

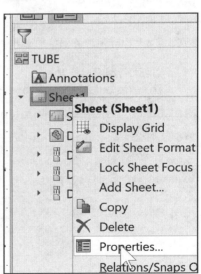

211) Double-click **C-FORMAT** from the SOLIDWORKS 2022/MY-SHEETFORMATS folder.

212) Click **OK** from the Sheet Properties dialog box.

Move the TUBE drawing views. The Sheet Scale should be 1:1.

213) Click inside the view boundary of **Drawing View1** (Front). The view boundary is displayed in blue.

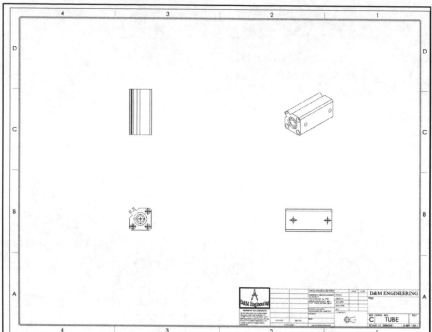

214) Position the **Front** view as illustrated. The Front view is the Parent view. The Top and Right views are the Child views.

215) Drag the **Isometric** view as illustrated.

Add a Projected Back view to the TUBE drawing.

216) Click inside the view boundary of **Drawing View3**, (Right).

217) Click **Projected View** ⊞ from the View Layout toolbar. The Projected View PropertyManager is displayed.

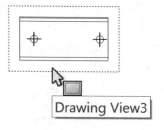

Drawing View3

218) Drag the **mouse pointer** to the right of the Right view.

219) Click a **position** for the Projected Back view. Drawing View5 is displayed.

Save the TUBE drawing.

220) Click **Save** 💾 .

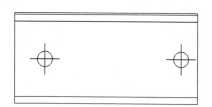

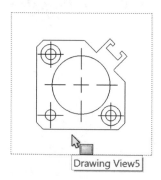

Drawing View5

TUBE Drawing-Section View and Detail View

How many views are utilized in a drawing? The number of views in a drawing depends on how many views are required to define the true shape and size of the part.

The TUBE part requires additional drawing views to display interior features and to enlarge features. Display the interior TUBE part features with a Section view.

A Section view defines a cutting plane with a sketched line in a view perpendicular to the view. Create a Full Section view by sketching a section line in the Top view.

Detail views enlarge an area of an existing view. Specify location, shape and scale. Create a Detail view from a Section view at a 4:1 scale.

Activity: TUBE Drawing-Section View and Detail View

Display the Origin. Add a Section view to the TUBE drawing.

221) Click **View, Hide/Show, Origins** from the Main menu.

222) Click inside the view boundary of **Drawing View2**, (Top).

223) Click **Section View** ↵ from the View Layout toolbar. The Section View PropertyManager is displayed.

224) Click the **Section** tab.

225) Click the **Vertical** Cutting Line button.

226) Click the **orgin**, Coincident with the Right Plane as illustrated. The line must extend past the profile lines.

227) Click a **position** to the right Drawing View2 (Top) view. The section arrows point to the right.

228) If required, click the **Flip Direction** button.

229) Click **OK** ✅ from the Section PropertyManager.

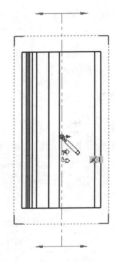

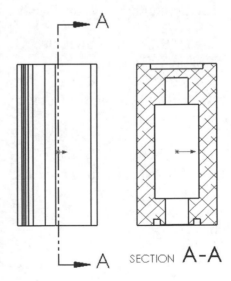

SECTION A-A

When you create a Section view, you can specific the distance of the cut, so the Section view does not create a cut of the entire drawing view. Do not display origins on the final drawing. This is for illustration purposes only.

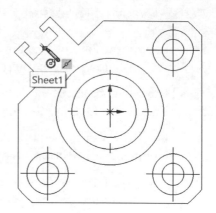

Add a Detail view to the TUBE drawing.

230) **Zoom in** on the upper left corner of Drawing View1.

231) Click **Detail View**  from the View Layout toolbar. The Circle Sketch tool is activated.

232) Click the **middle** of the switchgroove in the Front view as illustrated.

233) Drag the **mouse pointer** downwards as illustrated.

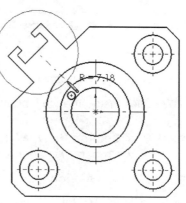

234) Click a **position** just below the large circle to create a sketched circle.

235) Click the **position** to the bottom left of DrawingView1, (Front). The Detail View name is B.

236) Click **OK** ✔ from the Detail View B PropertyManager.

237) Drag the text **B** off the profile lines.

Save the TUBE drawing.

238) Click **Save** .

To modify the size of the Detail view, position the mouse pointer on the Detail circle. The mouse pointer displays the Detail icon. Right-click and select Edit Sketch. Drag the circumference of the sketch circle. Click OK from the Circle PropertyManager.

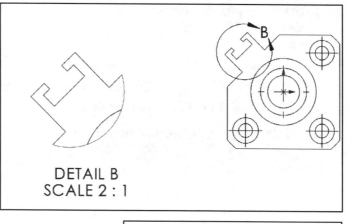

DETAIL B
SCALE 2 : 1

The Detail view profile is a circle. When a non-circular view is required, sketch the closed profile first. Then select the Detail view.

Verify view names. The A, B, & C view names increment sequentially for Section views, Detail views and Auxiliary views.

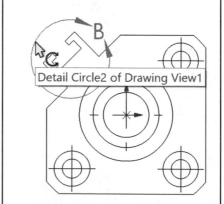

If you delete the view, the view name still increments by a letter. Modify the view name in the PropertyManager for a specific view.

TUBE Drawing-Broken-out Section View, Auxiliary View and Crop View

A Broken-out Section view removes material to a specified depth to expose the inner details of an existing view. A closed profile defines a Broken-out Section view.

An Auxiliary view displays a plane parallel to an angled plane with true dimensions. A primary Auxiliary view is hinged to one of the six principle views. Create a primary Full Auxiliary view that references the Front view.

Display the M2.0 Hole information. Create a Partial Auxiliary view from the Full Auxiliary view. Sketch a closed profile in an active Auxiliary view. Use the Crop view tool to create a Partial Auxiliary view.

Activity: TUBE Drawing-Broken-out Section View, Auxiliary View, and Crop View

Add the first Broken-out Section view to the TUBE drawing.

239) Click inside the view boundary of **Drawing View3**, (Right).

240) Click **Hidden Line Visible** ⊞ . The hidden lines do not clearly define the internal front features of the part.

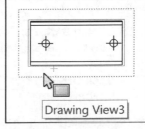

Create a Broken-out Section view with the Spline Sketch tool.

241) Click the **Sketch** tab from the CommandManager. The Sketch toolbar is displayed.

242) Click **Spline** ∿ from the Sketch toolbar.

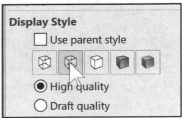

243) Sketch a **closed spline** in the top left corner. The Spline contains the Cbore Front feature.

244) Click **Broken-out Section**  from the Layout View toolbar. The Broken-out Section PropertyManager is displayed.

245) Enter **5**mm for Depth.

246) Check the **Preview** box to insure that the Cbore Front is displayed.

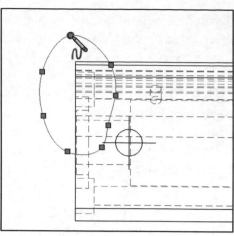

247) Click **OK** ✔ from the Broken-out Section PropertyManager.

In an assembly, you can exclude components and fasteners in a Broken-out Section view.

Add a second Broken-out Section view to the TUBE drawing.

248) Click the **Sketch** tab from the CommandManager.

249) Click **Spline** from the Sketch toolbar.

250) Sketch a **closed spline** in the top right corner of Drawing View3. The Spline contains the Cbore Rear feature.

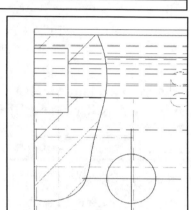

251) Click **Broken-out Section** 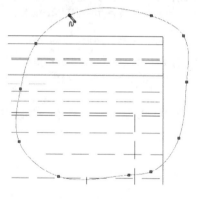 from the View Layout toolbar.

252) Enter **5**mm for Depth.

253) Check the **Preview** box.

254) Click **OK** ✔ from the Broken-out Section PropertyManager.

255) Click **inside** Drawing View3.

Display no Hidden lines.

256) Click Hidden Lines Removed ⬡ .

257) Click **OK** ✔ from the Drawing View3 PropertyManager.

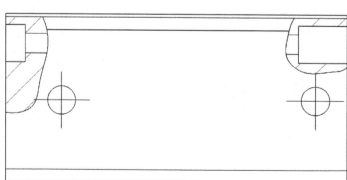

Fit the drawing to the Sheet.

258) Press the **f** key.

Deactivate the Origins.

259) Click **View, Hide / Show**; uncheck **Origins** from the Main menu.

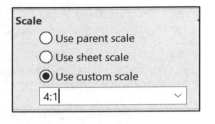

Modify the Sheet1 scale. Modify the Detail view scale. Save the TUBE drawing.

260) Right-click **Sheet1**.

261) Click **Properties**.

262) Enter **2:1** for Sheet Scale.

263) Click **Apply Changes**.

264) Click inside the **Detail view** boundary on the Sheet.

265) Enter **4:1** for Scale.

266) Click **OK** ✔ from the Detail View PropertyManager.

267) Click **Save** 💾.

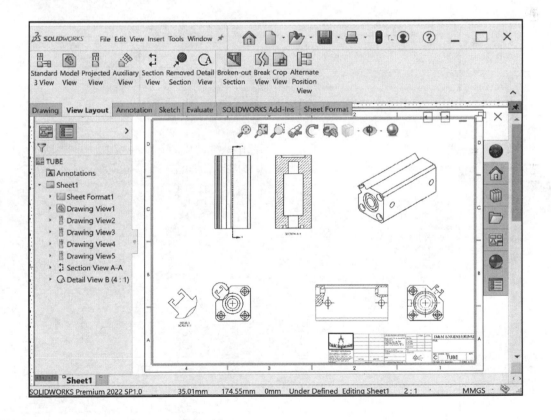

Add an Auxiliary view to the TUBE drawing.

268) Zoom in on the left top side of Drawing View1.

269) Click the **left angled edge** as illustrated.

270) Click **Auxiliary View** 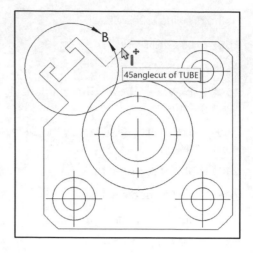 from the View Layout toolbar.

271) Click a **position** to the upper left of Drawing View1 (Front). The location selected is the center of the Full Auxiliary view. Enter **C** for the View Name.

272) Click **OK** ✔ from the Drawing View PropertyManager.

Fit the Drawing to the Sheet.

273) Press the **f** key.

Position the view arrows.

274) Click **Line C-C**.

275) Drag the **midpoint** and position it between the Auxiliary view and Front view.

276) Click each **endpoint** and drag it towards the midpoint.

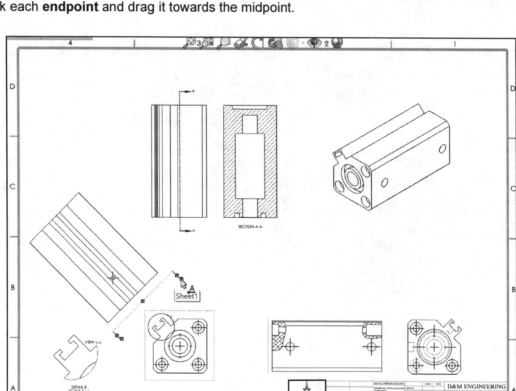

Sketch a closed profile in the active Auxiliary view using the Spline and Line Sketch tool.

277) Click the **Sketch** tab from the CommandManager.

278) Click **Spline** 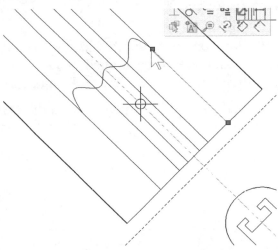 from the Sketch toolbar. The first point is Coincident with the left line of the switchgroove.

279) Sketch **7 Points** to create the closed Spline. The last point is Coincident with the right line of the switchgroove.

280) Right-click **Select**.

Sketch three lines.

281) Click **Line** from the Sketch toolbar.

282) Sketch the **first vertical line**, the mouse pointer displays Endpoint inference.

283) Sketch the **second line** Collinear with the bottom edge of the Auxiliary view. The first point and second point display Endpoint inference.

284) Sketch the **third line**. The last point must display Endpoint interference with the first point of the Spline.

Deselect the Sketch tool.

285) Right-click **Select**.

286) Window-Select the **three lines** and the **Spline**. The Properties PropertyManager is displayed. The selected entities are displayed in the Selected Entities box.

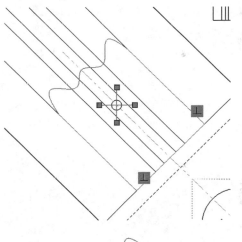

Utilize a close and continuous Sketch profile to create a Crop view. The view will not crop if the sketch is open or self-intersecting.

Crop the view.

287) Click **Crop View** from the View Layout toolbar to display the partial Auxiliary view.

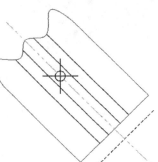

288) Click **OK** from the Properties PropertyManager.

Fit the drawing to the Sheet.

289) Press the **f** key.

Position the view.

290) Drag the **C-C view arrow** between the Auxiliary view and the Front view.

291) Drag the **VIEW C-C** text below the Auxiliary view.

292) Click **OK** ✔ from the Note PropertyManager.

Save the TUBE drawing.

293) Click **Save** 🖫.

💡 Position views in other locations on the sheet when space is limited. The Auxiliary and Section views are aligned to their Parent view. Press the Ctrl key before selecting the Auxiliary and Section view tools in order to position the views anywhere on the sheet.

The Half Section Isometric view in the TUBE drawing will be in the next section.

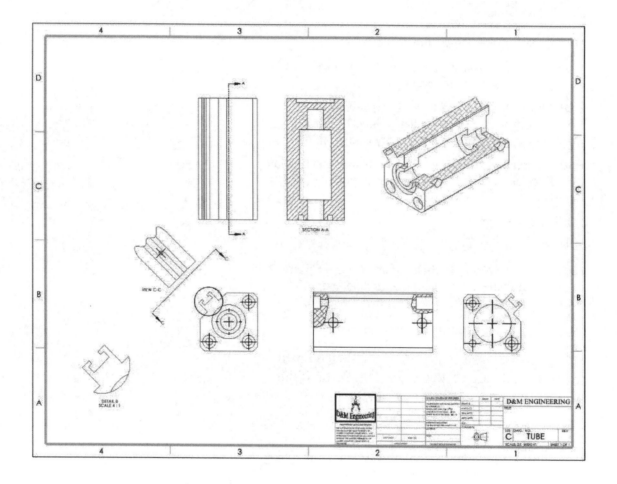

TUBE Drawing-Half Section Isometric (Cut-Away) View

A Half Section Isometric view in the TUBE drawing requires a Cut feature created in the part. The Extruded Cut feature removes ¼ of the TUBE part. Create an Extruded Cut feature. Create a Design Table to control the Suppressed State of the Extruded Cut feature.

A Design Table is an MS Excel spreadsheet that represents multiple configurations of a part. The Design Table contains configuration names, parameters to control and assigned values for each parameter.

The TUBE part consists of two configurations:

- Entire Part

- Section Cut

Add the Section Cut configuration as an Isometric view.

Insert an Area Hatch pattern in the Isometric view. A Hatch Pattern, (section lining or cross sectioning) represents an exposed cut surface based on the material.

The Hatch type, ANSI38(Aluminum) represents the TUBE material.

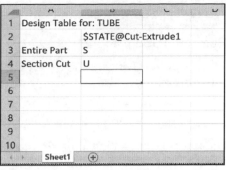

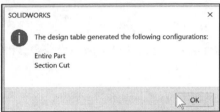

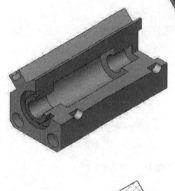

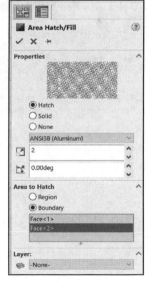

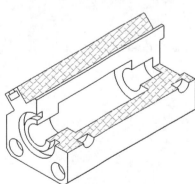

Activity: TUBE Drawing-Half Section Isometric-Cut Away View

Open the TUBE part.

294) Right-click inside the **Front view** boundary.

295) Click **Open Part**. The TUBE FeatureManager is displayed.

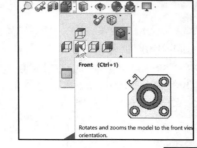
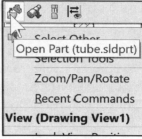

Insert a cut. Utilize the Corner Rectangle Sketch tool.

296) Click **Front view** .

297) Right-click the **front face** of the TUBE in the graphics area.

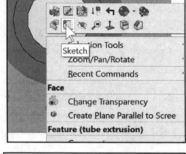

298) Click **Sketch** from the Context toolbar.

299) Click **Corner Rectangle** from the Consolidated Sketch toolbar.

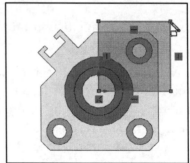

300) Sketch a **rectangle** through the Origin as illustrated.

Deselect the Sketch tool.

301) Right-click **Select** to deselect the sketch tool.

Add a Collinear relation between the top horizontal line and the top edge.

302) Click the **top horizontal** line.

303) Hold the **Ctrl** key down.

304) Click the **top edge**.

305) Release the **Ctrl** key.

306) Click the Make **Collinear** icon from the Pop-up Contect toolbar.

307) Add a **Collinear** relation between the right vertical line and the right edge.

308) Click **OK** from from the PropertyManager.

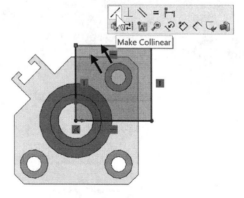

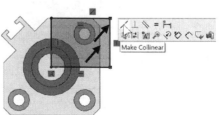

Drawing and Detailing with SOLIDWORKS

Add an Extruded Cut Feature.

309) Click the **Features** tab from the
CommandManager.

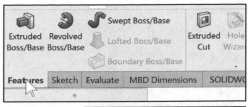

310) Click **Extruded Cut** 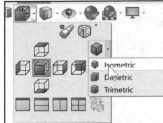 from the Feature
toolbar. The Cut-Extrude PropertyManager is
displayed.

311) Select **Through All** for End Condition in
Direction 1.

312) Click **OK** ✔ from the Cut-Extrude
PropertyManager. Cut-Extrude1 is displayed.

313) Click **Isometric** ▣ . **View** the Cut-Extrude
feature.

Suppress the Cut-Extrude1 feature.

314) Right-click **Cut-Extrude1** from the
FeatureManager.

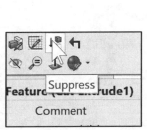

315) Click **Suppress**.

Insert a Design Table.

316) Click **Insert**, **Tables**, **Excel Design
Table** from the Menu menu.

317) Check the **Blank** box for Source.

318) Click **OK** ✔ from the Design Table
PropertyManager.

319) Click **$STATE@Cut-Extrude1** from the
Parameters box.

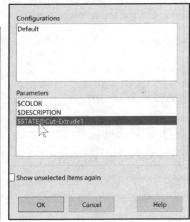

320) Click **OK** from the Add Rows and
Columns dialog box. The Design Table
for the TUBE is displayed in the upper
left corner. $STATE@Cut-Extrude1 is
displayed in Cell B2.

Rename the first configuration.

321) Rename the text **First
Instance** to **Entire Part**.

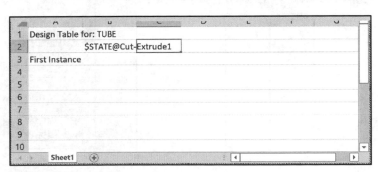

Create the second configuration.

322) Enter **Section Cut** in Cell A4.

323) Enter **S** in Cell B3.

324) Enter **U** in Cell B4.

Close the Design Table.

325) Click inside the **graphics area**.

326) Click **OK** in the SOLIDWORKS dialog box. Both TUBE configurations are created.

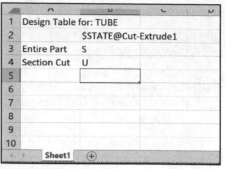

Click Edit, Design Table, Edit Table from the Menu bar menu to access an existing Design Table or Right-click the Design Table icon in the ConfigurationManager and select Edit Table.

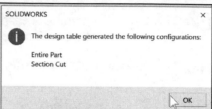

Display the TUBE part configurations.

327) Double-click **Entire Part** from the ConfigurationManager.

328) Double-click **Section Cut** from the ConfigurationManager. **View** the results.

Display the TUBE part default configuration.

329) Double-click **Default** from the ConfigurationManager.

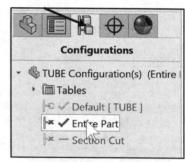

Return to the TUBE part FeatureManager.

330) Click the **Part FeatureManager** tab.

Save the TUBE part.

331) Click **Save** .

Open the TUBE drawing.

332) Right-click **Tube (Default)** from the FeatureManager.

333) Click **Open Drawing**. The TUBE drawing is displayed.

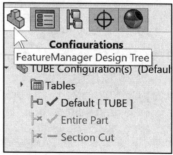

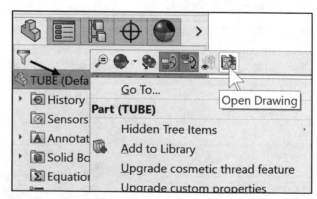

Select the TUBE configuration.

334) Right-click **Properties** in the Isometric view boundary, Drawing View4.

335) Select **Section Cut** from the Use name configuration drop-down menu.

336) Click **OK** from the Drawing View Properties dialog box. The Section Cut configuration is displayed.

Insert Area Hatch.

337) Click the **inside top face** as illustrated.

338) Hold the **Ctrl** key down.

339) Click the **inside bottom face** as illustrated.

340) Release the **Ctrl** key.

341) Click the **Annotation** tab from the CommandManager.

342) Click **Area Hatch/Fill** 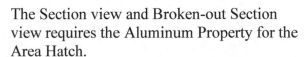 from the Annotation toolbar.

Change the Area Hatch type.

343) Select **ANSI38 (Aluminum)** from the Pattern drop-down menu.

344) Select **2** from the Hatch Pattern Scale drop-down menu.

345) Click **OK** ✓ from the Area Hatch/Fill PropertyManager.

Fit the drawing to the Sheet.

346) Press the **f** key.

Save the TUBE drawing.

347) Click **Save** 💾.

The Section view and Broken-out Section view requires the Aluminum Property for the Area Hatch.

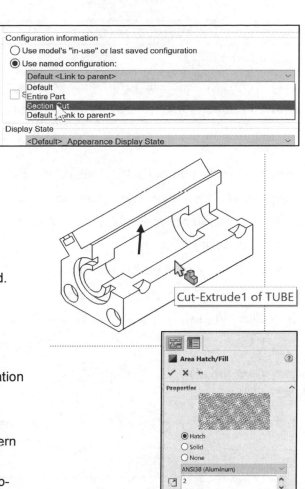

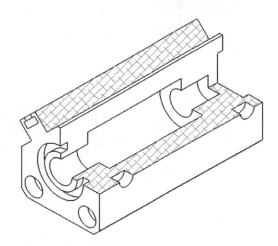

Activity: TUBE Part-Edit Material

Open the TUBE part.

348) Right-click inside the **Front view** boundary.

349) Click **Open Part**. The TUBE FeatureManager is displayed.

Set Material type.

350) Right-click **Material** in the FeatureManager.

351) Click **Edit Material**. The Material dialog box is displayed.

352) Expand Aluminum Alloys. Select **6061 Alloy**.

353) Click **Apply**.

354) Click **Close** from the Material dialog box.

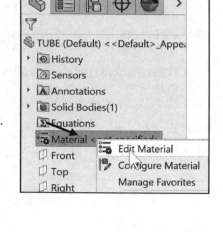

Return to the TUBE drawing. Save the drawing.

355) Click **Window**, **Tube-Sheet1** from the Main menu.

356) Rebuild the drawing to display the Aluminum hatch pattern.

357) Click **Save** .

Close all files.

358) Click **Windows**, **Close All** from the Main menu.

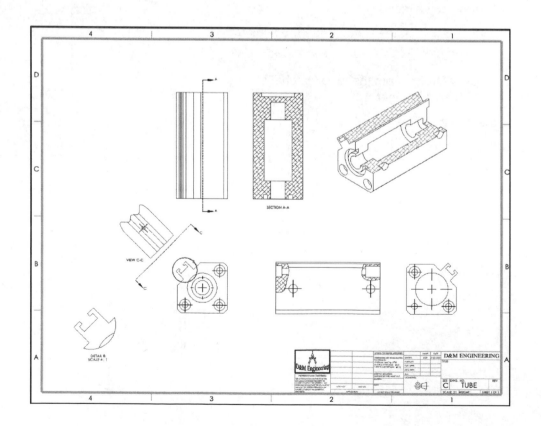

The views required for the TUBE drawing are complete. Insert dimensions and notes for the TUBE drawing in Chapter 7. Note: Utilize Detail view option to create a detail of a preexisting Detail view of a Crop view.

 **Review**

The TUBE drawing consisted of a single sheet with eight different views. Sheet Properties were utilized to modify the Sheet size from A to C. The Section view was created by sketching a vertical line in the Top view. The Detail view was created by sketching a circle in the Front view. A Partial Auxiliary view utilized the Crop view tool. The Right view was modified with the Broken-out Section tool.

The Design Table controlled the suppression state of an Extruded Cut feature in the TUBE part. The Isometric view utilized the Section Cut configuration. The Area Hatch utilized the Aluminum material in the Isometric view.

COVERPLATE Drawing

Create the COVERPLATE drawing. The COVERPLATE drawing consists of two part configurations. The first part configuration is With Nose Holes. The second configuration is Without Nose Holes.

Sheet1 contains an Offset Section view of the COVERPLATE using the With Nose Holes configuration.

Sheet2 contains an Aligned Section view of the COVERPLATE using the Without Nose Holes configuration.

The book is designed to expose the SOLIDWORKS user to many different tools, techniques and procedures. It may not always use the most direct tool or process.

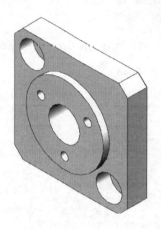

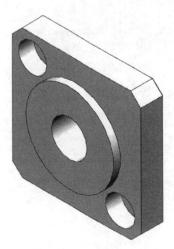

Insert a new Front view with the Model View tool. Insert an Offset Section view and a Right view. Copy the Front view from Sheet1 to Sheet2. Modify the configuration. Insert an Aligned Section view.

Activity: COVERPLATE Drawing

Open the COVERPLATE part.

359) Click **Open** from the Menu bar toolbar.

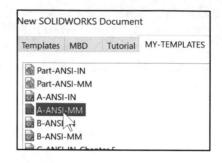

360) Double-click the **COVERPLATE** part from the SOLIDWORKS 2022/Chapter 6 Models folder. COVERPLATE should be in the default configuration.

Create the COVERPLATE drawing.

361) Click **New** from the Main menu.

362) Double-click the **A-ANSI-MM** Drawing Template from the SOLIDWORKS 2022/MY-TEMPLATES tab. COVERPLATE is the open document displayed in the Model View PropertyManager.

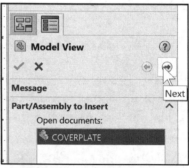

363) Click **Next** from the Model View PropertyManager.

364) Click ***Front** from the Orientation box.

365) Click a **position** in the lower left corner of the drawing.

Set the View Scale.

366) Click **Use custom scale**.

367) Enter **1.5:1**.

368) Click **OK** from the Projected View PropertyManager. Drawing View1 is displayed in the FeatureManager.

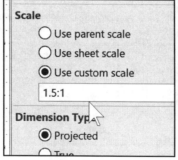

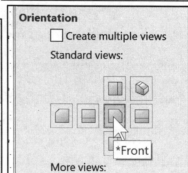

Save the COVERPLATE Drawing and part in the same folder.

369) Click **Save As** from the Main menu.

370) Select the **SOLIDWORKS 2022/Chapter 6 Drawing/COVERPLATE** folder for Save As.

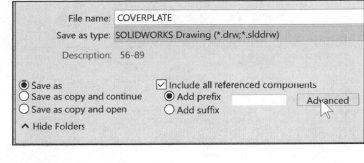

371) Enter **COVERPLATE** for File name.

372) Enter **56-89** for Description.

373) Click the **Include all referenced components** box.

374) Click the **Advanced** box.

375) Click the **Browse** button.

376) Select the **SOLIDWORKS 2022/Chapter 6 Drawing/COVERPLATE** folder.

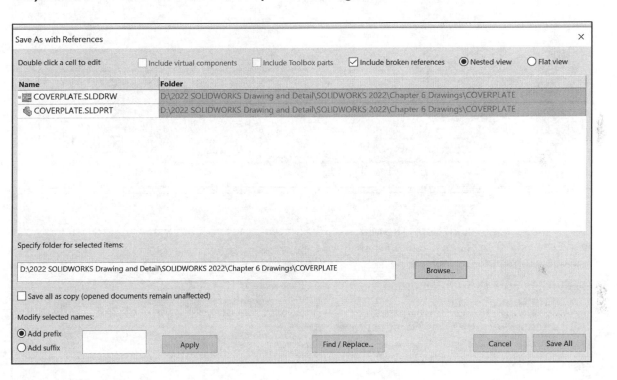

377) Click **Select Folder**.

378) Click **Save All** from the Save As dialog box.

Note: You can also use the **SOLIDWORKS Pack and Go** tool. The Pack and Go tool provides additional options to create zip files, email after packing, saving Simulation results and more in the same folder. See SOLIDWORKS Help for additional information.

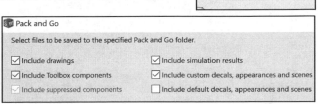

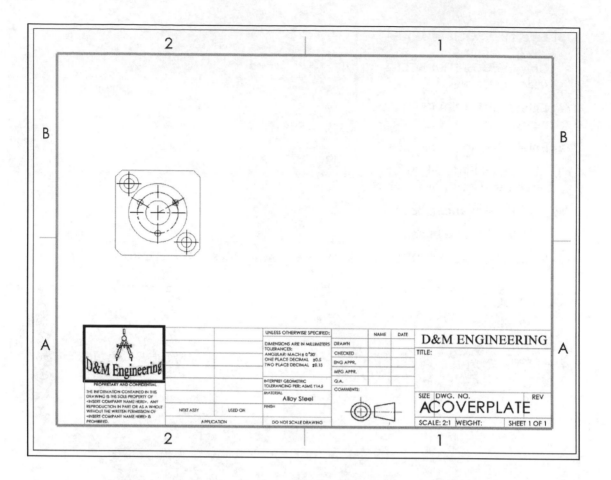

Modify the Configuration. Note: The Material in the drawing is displayed from the Part Custom Properties.

379) Right-click **Properties** inside the Front view boundary.

380) Select **Without Nose Holes** for view configuration.

381) Click **OK**.

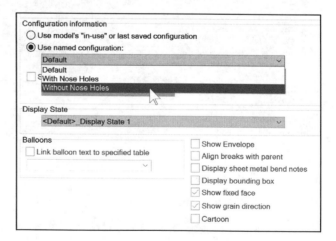

Add COVERPLATE-Sheet2.

382) Right-click the **Sheet1** tab.

383) Click **Add Sheet**. Sheet2 is displayed.

Copy the Front view from Sheet1 to Sheet2.

384) Click the **Sheet1** tab.

385) Click inside the **Front view**.

386) Click **Edit,Copy** from the Main menu.

387) Click the **Sheet2** tab.

388) Click a **position** on the left side of Sheet2.

389) Click **Edit**, **Paste** from the Main menu.

Modify the Part configuration.

390) Right-click **Properties** in the view boundary.

391) Select **With Nose Holes** from the Configuration text box.

392) Click **OK**. From the Drawing View Properties dialog box. A pattern of 3 holes is displayed.

If needed, modify the Sheet2 Properties.

393) Right-click **Sheet2** as illustrated.

394) Click **Properties**. The Sheet Properties dialog box is displayed.

395) Click the **Browse** button.

396) Double-click **CUSTOM-A** from the SOLIDWORKS 2022/MY-SHEETSFORMAT folder.

397) Click **Apply Changes** from the Sheet Properties dialog box.

398) **View** the Sheet2 results.

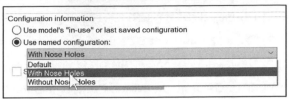
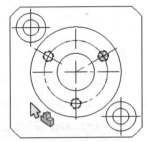
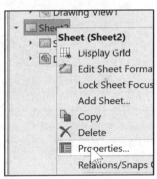
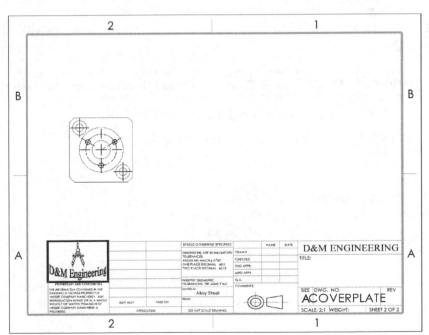

Return to the Sheet1. Modify the Drawing No. Font size.

399) Click the **Sheet1** tab.

400) Click **Edit Sheet Format** in Sheet1.

401) Double-click **COVERPLATE**.

402) Select **18** for Font Size from the Formattting toolbar.

403) **View** your options.

404) Click **OK** from the Notes PropertyManager.

405) Right-click **Edit Sheet** in Sheet1.

Save COVERPLATE drawing.

406) Click **Save** .

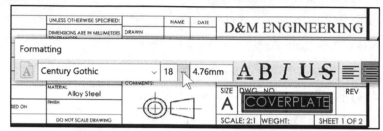

COVERPLATE Drawing-Offset Section View and Aligned Section View

Create an Offset Section view using the Single Offset option. Section A-A displays the offsets in a single plane.

In the ASME Y14.3standard, an Aligned Section occurs when features lend themselves to an angular change in the direction of the cutting plane. The bent cutting plane and features rotate into a plane perpendicular to the line of sight of the sectional view.

Create an Aligned Section view using the Aligned Cutting Line option.

Activity: COVERPLATE Drawing-Offset Section View and Aligned Section View

Create an Offset Section and Aligned Section view.

407) Click inside the **Front view** boundary.

Create the Offset Section view using the Single Offset option.

408) Click **Section View** from the View Layout CommandManager. The Section View Assist PropertyManager is displayed.

409) Click the **Section** tab.

410) **Uncheck** the Auto-start section view box.

411) Click **Horizontal** from the Cutting Line dialog box.

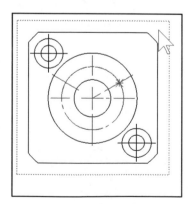

412) Click the **center point** of the top left circle.

413) Click **Single Offset** from the Section View Pop-up menu to add offsets to view.

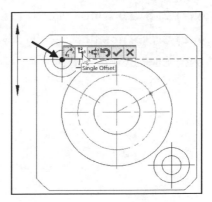

414) Click a **position** to the right as illustrated.

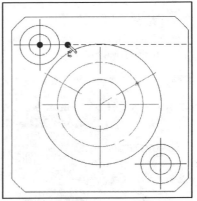

415) Click a **position** directly down as illustrated.

416) Click **Single Offset** from the from the Section View Pop-up menu.

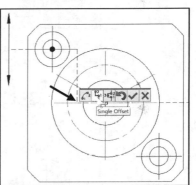

417) Click a **position** directly to the right as illustrated.

418) Click a **position** directly down as illustrated.

419) Click **Single Offset** from the Section View pop-up menu.

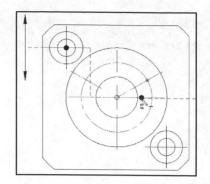

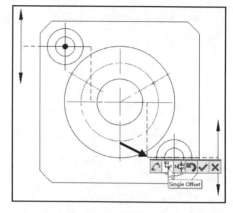

420) Click a **position** directly to the right as illustrated.

421) The section arrows point downward. If required, click **Flip direction**.

422) Click a **position** above the Front view.

423) Click **OK** ✓ from the Section View A-A PropertyManager. **View** the results.

Save the drawing.

424) Click **Save** 💾.

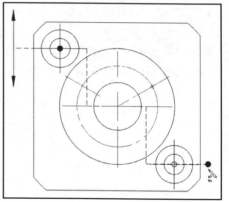

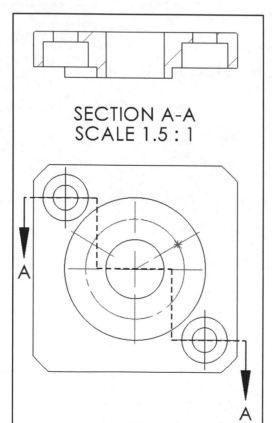

SECTION A-A
SCALE 1.5 : 1

Add a Projected Right view. Display Hidden Lines Visable.

425) Click inside the **Front view** boundary.

426) Click **Projected View** from the View Layout toolbar.

427) Click a **position** to the right of the Front view.

428) Click **Hidden Lines Visable** .

429) Click **OK** ✔ from the Projected View PropertyManager.

Save the COVERPLATE drawing.

430) Click **Save** .

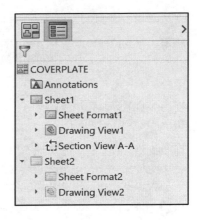

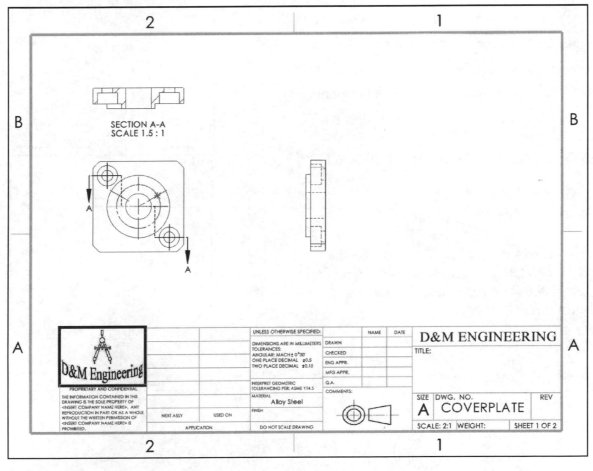

Return to COVERPLATE-Sheet2.

431) Click the **Sheet2** tab.

Create an Aligned Section view on Sheet2.

432) Click inside the **Drawing View2** view boundary. The PropertyManager is displayed.

433) Click **Section View** ⤴ from the View Layout toolbar.

434) Click the **Section** tab.

435) Click **Aligned** from the Cutting Line box. **View** the icon feedback on the pointer.

436) Click the **center of the hole** as illustrated. Note the icon feedback.

437) Click the **center point** of the top right circle.

438) Click the **center point** of the bottom circle.

Position the Aligned Section view.

439) Click a **position** to the right of the Front view.

440) Click **OK** ✔ from the Section View B-B PropertyManager.

Save and Close the COVERPLATE drawing.

441) Click **Save** .

442) Click **File**, **Close**.

💡 The book is designed to expose the SOLIDWORKS user to many different tools, techniques and procedures. It may not always use the most direct tool or process.

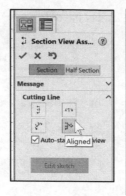
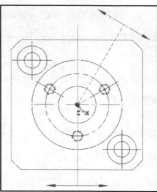
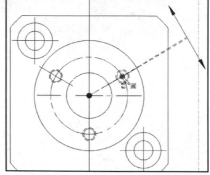
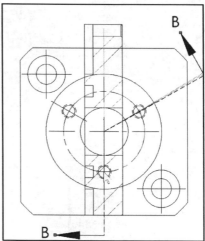
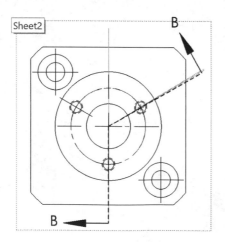
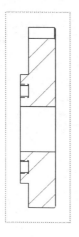

SECTION B-B
SCALE 1.5 : 1

Review

The COVERPLATE drawing consisted of two Sheets. Sheet1 utilized the Without Nose Holes Configuration. You utilized the Single Offset option to create the Offset Section view.

Sheet2 utilized the With Nose Holes Configuration. You utilized the Aligned Cutting Line option to create the Aligned Section view.

Use the Lock View Position command to prevent a view from being moved by dragging.

Use the Lock View Focus command when you need a view to remain active as you work within it. This allows you to add sketch entities to a view, even when the mouse pointer is close to another view. You can be sure that the items you are adding belong to the view you want.

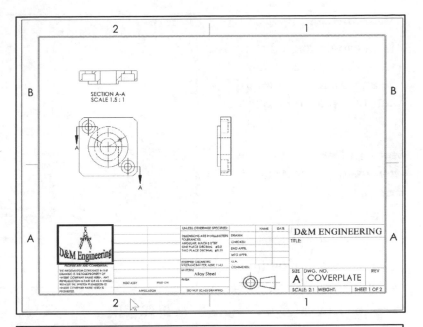

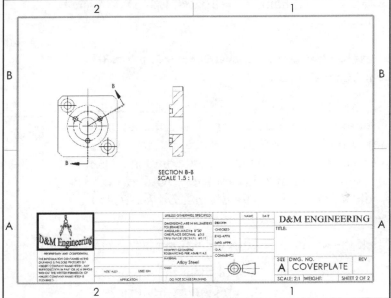

Rotate Drawing Views

Views can be rotated to fit within the sheet boundary. The angle and direction of rotation is placed below the view title.

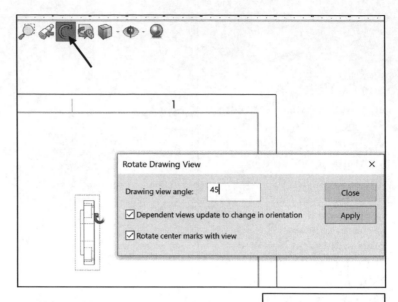

Steps to Rotate a Drawing view using the Rotate View tool

Click inside the Drawing view boundary. Click the Rotate view ↺ icon from the Heads-up View toolbar.

Enter the Drawing view angle from the Rotate Drawing View dialog box. Example: 45°. The view rotates by 45°.

Steps to Rotate a Drawing view using the 3D Drawing View tool

Use the 3D drawing view ⟳ tool to select an obscured edge for the depth. The 3D drawing view tool provides the ability to rotate a drawing view out of its plane so you can view components or edges obscured by other entities. 3D drawing view mode is not available for *Detail, Broken, Crop, or Detached views*.

Click inside the Drawing view boundary. Select the 3D Drawing view ⟳ tool from the Heads-up View toolbar. The Pop-up Context toolbar is displayed.

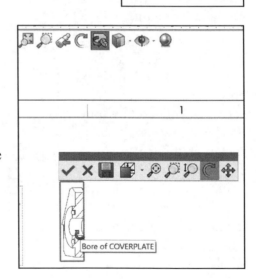

Click and rotate the selected drawing view to display the required edge, face, or vertex.

Click OK from the Pop-up Context toolbar to exit the 3D Drawing view tool.

Alternative Position View

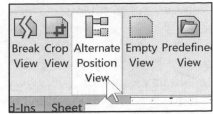

The Alternate Position View ⊞ tool provides the ability to superimpose an existing drawing view precisely on another. The alternate position is displayed with phantom lines. Use the Alternate Position View to display the range of motion of an assembly. You can dimension between the primary view and the Alternate Position View. You cannot use the Alternate Position View tool with Broken, Section, or Detail views.

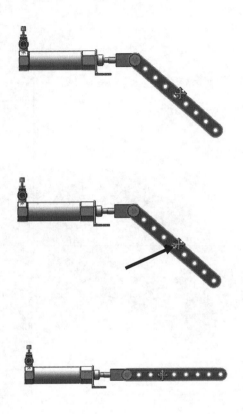

Remove Section view

The Removed Section View 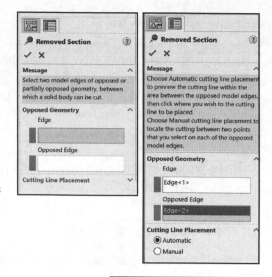 tool provides the ability to show slices of the model at selected locations along a drawing view. The Removed Section View tool uses the Removed Section PropertyManager.

Relative View

The Relative Model tool defines an Orthographic view based on two orthogonal faces or places in the model. Utilize Tile Horizontal to display the drawing and the model.

Select the drawing for the active window.

Click Relative view 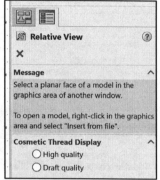 from the Drawing tab.

Click in the Part graphics area.

Select the First orientation from the model. This is the primary reference in the drawing.

Select the Second orientation from the model. This is the secondary reference in the drawing.

Click OK from the Relative View PropertyManager to return to the drawing. Position the view in the drawing. View the results.

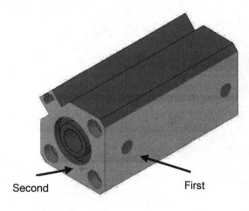

Second   First

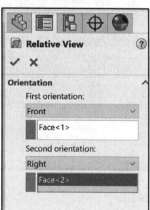

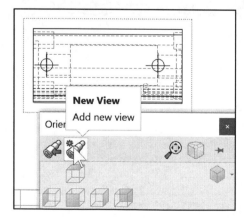

New Named View

Create a new Named view. Click in a Drawing view boundary.

Press the space bar. The Orientation dialog box is displayed.

Click Add new view.

Enter the view name. Click OK.

View the results in the Orientation box.

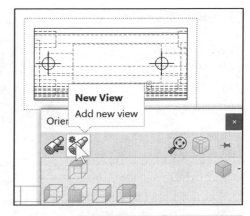

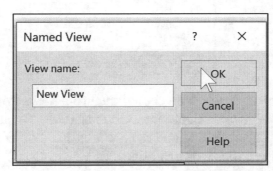

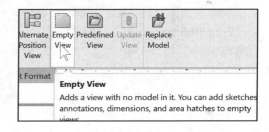

Empty View

The Empty view tool creates a blank view not tied to a part or assembly.

Insert multiple sketched entities, dimensions, relations and annotations into an Empty view. Move, Hide, and Layer Properties apply to an Empty view.

Utilize the Lock View Focus option from the Pop-up menu to link all inserted entities to the Empty view. Geometry inserted outside the view boundary maintains its relationship with the Empty view.

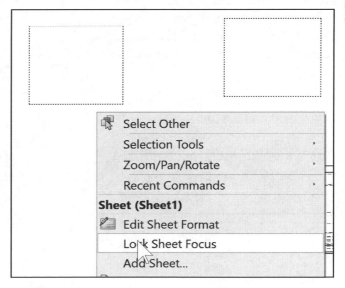

Chapter Summary

You created three drawings: ROD, TUBE, and COVERPLATE.

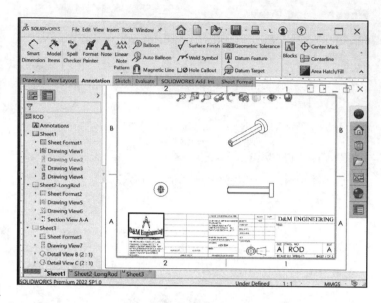

The ROD drawing contained three Sheets.

Sheet1 contained the three Standard views, (Principle views) and an Isometric view. You used the Short ROD configuration. The Top view was hidden.

Sheet2 was renamed to Sheet2-LongRod. The Sheet2-LongRod contains the Long Rod configuration. You copied the Front view from Sheet1 to Sheet2-LongRod. You inserted a Projected Right view. You inserted a Break Vertical Zig Zag and then modified the Zig Zag style and gap size. You utilized a Section view to create the Revolved Section between the two Break lines.

Sheet3 you copied the Isometric view from Sheet1. You modified the ROD configuration to Long Rod. Two Detail views were created using a Sketch spline. The two Detail views were aligned with a Contruction line. The two Detail views (Detail B-B and Detail C-C) constructed the Isometric view. A Contstruction layer was used to lock the Isometic view.

The TUBE drawing consisted of a single sheet with eight different drawing views. The eight views are: three Standard views, Projected Back view, Section view, Detail view, Auxiliary view, and a Half Section Isometric (Cut away) view.

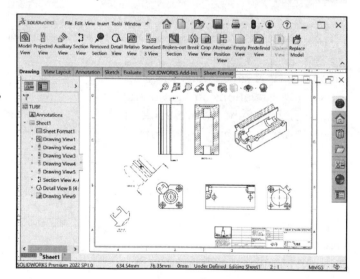

The Half Section Isometric view required two part configurations named: Entire Part and Section Cutaway. The Area Hatch utilized the Aluminum material in the Isometric view.

Sheet Properties were utilized to modify the Sheet size from A to C.

The Design Table controlled the suppression state of an Extruded Cut feature in the TUBE part.

The COVERPLATE drawing consists of two part configurations. The first part configuration was With Nose Holes. The second part configuration was Without Nose Holes. COVERPLATE Sheet1 contained an Offset Section view.

COVERPLATE Sheet2 contained an Aligned Section view with a Custom Sheet format.

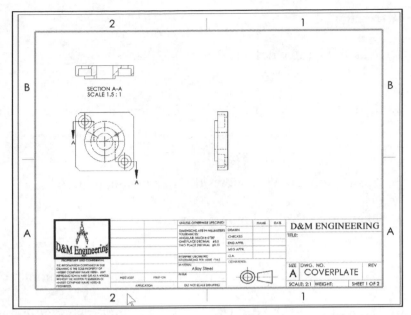

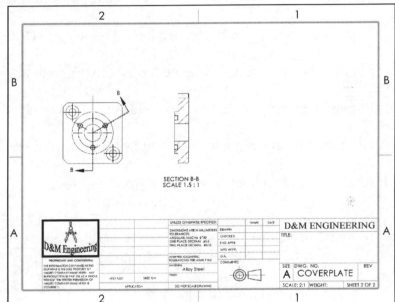

Questions:

1. Name the three default Reference Planes: _____ , _____ and _____ .

2. Identify the six principle drawing views in Orthographic Projection: _____ , _____ , _____ , _____ , _____ , _____ .

3. How many drawing views does a drawing require?

4. Name two Orthographic projection systems: _____ , _____ .

5. True or False. Delete the part when a drawing is complete.

6. True of False. All drawings contain a single part configuration.

7. Explain the procedure to create a Part (Auto-create) Design Table.

8. Explain the procedure to change the part configuration in a drawing view?

9. Explain Drawing Layers. Why would you use them in a drawing?

10. Describe the procedure to copy a drawing view from one Sheet to another Sheet.

11. Identify the procedure to rename a Drawing Sheet tab.

12. You created a drawing with 2 Sheets. The first sheet displays the Custom Sheet format. Sheet2 displays a standard SW Sheet format. Explain the procedure to modify the standard Sheet Properties to a Custom Sheet format.

13. Explain an Area Hatch in a drawing view.

14. Explain the procedure to set the Sheet Scale.

Exercises:

Exercise 6.1: FLATBAR - 9 HOLE Drawing

Note: Units are in inches.

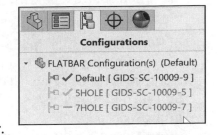

- **Create** the ANSI-IPS Third Angle Projection FLATEBAR 9 HOLE drawing. The part is located in the SOLIDWORKS 2022/Chapter 6 Homework folder. There are three configurations.

- **View** the Custom Properties of the part as shown in the Part Summary Information dialog box.

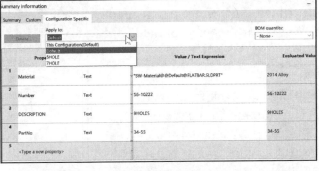

- **Create** the drawing. Use the default A (ANSI)-Landscape Sheet Format/Size. Sheet1 Scale 1:1. Third Angle Projection for Projection Type. Precision .12.

- **Create** a Front, Top, Right and Shaded Isometric view. Hide the Right view.

- **Address** display modes per the drawing views. Add all needed centerlines.

	Property Name	Type	Value / Text Expression	Evaluated Value
1	SWFormatSize	Text	8.5in*11in	8.5in*11in
2	CompanyName	Text	D&M ENGINEERING	D&M ENGINEERING
3	DrawnBy	Text	DCP	DCP
4	DrawnDate	Text	3-3-2022	3-3-2022
5	Revision	Text	A	A
6	Number	Text	334-66	334-66
7				

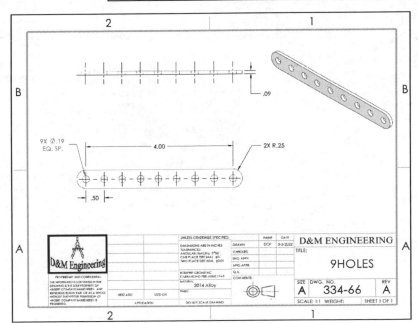

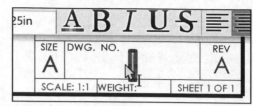

- View and address the Custom Properties of the drawing.

- In Edit Sheet Format mode, insert your school or company logo, Third Angle projection logo along with the illustrated Title box information. Use Custom Properties and Link Properties of the drawing as illustrated. Note: All needed icons are located in the SOLIDWORKS 2022/logo folder.

- Use the Link to Property command in the Notes PropertyManager to address the DWG. NO as illustrated.

- Return to the Edit Sheet mode.

- Insert all needed dimensions. Use the Model Items command in the Annotation CommandManager.

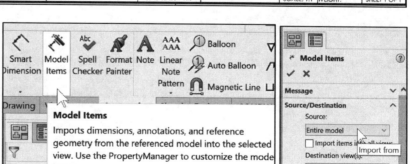

- Insert 9X - EQ. SP.

- Move the dimensions (add) as needed in the drawing views. Address dimension line gaps as illustrated.

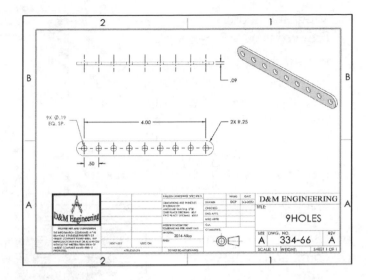

Exercise 6.2: CYLINDER Drawing

- **Create** the ANSI-IPS Third Angle Projection CYLINDER drawing. The part is located in the SOLIDWORKS 2022/Chapter 6 Homework folder.

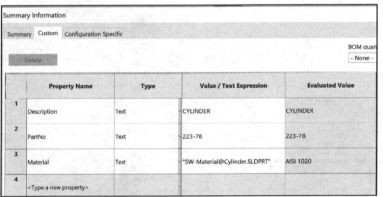

- **Create** the Custom properties of the part as shown in the Part Summary Information dialog box.

- **Create** the drawing. Use the default A (ANSI)-Landscape Sheet Format/Size. Sheet1 Scale 1:1. Third Anlge Projection for Projection Type. Precision .12.

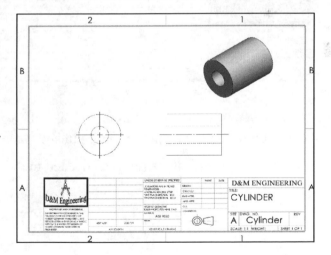

- **Create** a Front, Right and Shaded Isometric view. The model only needs two principle drawing views.

- Add all needed Annotations and display modes.

- View and address the Custom Properties of the drawing.

- In Edit Sheet Format mode, insert your school or company logo, Third Angle projection logo along with the illustrated Title box information. Use Custom Properties and Link Properties of the drawing as illustrated. Note: All needed icons are located in the SOLIDWORKS 2022/logo folder.

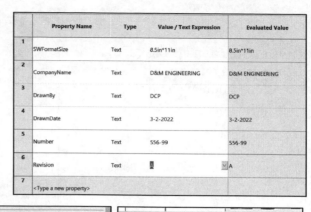

- Use the Link to Property command in the Notes PropertyManager to address the DWG. NO as illustrated.

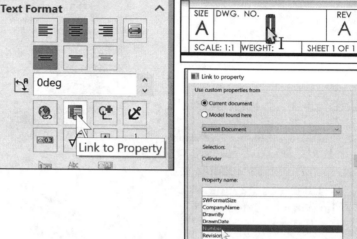

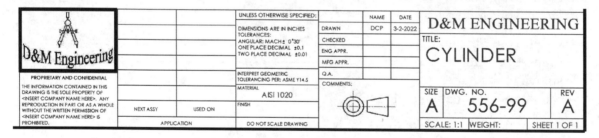

- Return to the Edit Sheet mode. Insert all needed dimensions. Use the Model Items command in the Annotation CommandManager.

- Move the dimensions (add) as needed in the drawing views. Address dimension line gaps, etc. as illustrated.

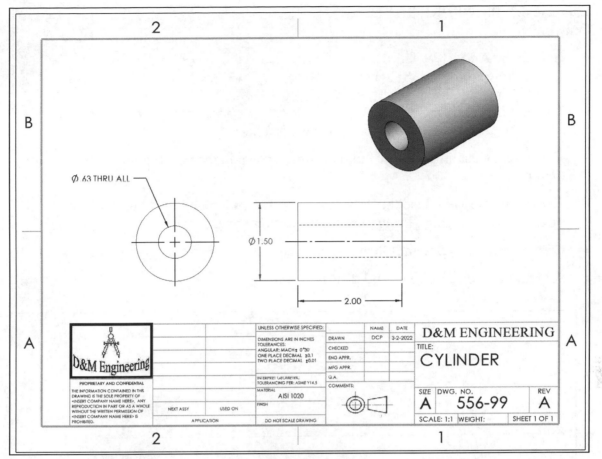

Utilize the Mass Properties tool from the Evaluate toolbar to calculate the volume and mass of the CYLINDER part. Set decimal places to 4.

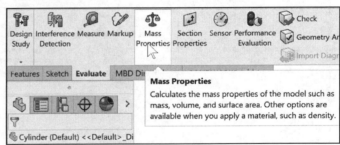

Exercise 6.3: PRESSURE PLATE
Drawing

	Property Name	Type	Value / Text Expression	Evaluated Value
1	Material	Text	"SW-Material@Pressure Plate.SLDPRT"	1060 Alloy
2	Description	Text	PRESSURE PLATE	PRESSURE PLATE
3	PartNo	Text	223-55	223-55
4	<Type a new property>			

- **Create** the ANSI-IPS Third Angle Projection PRESSURE PLATE drawing. Precision .12. The part is located in the SOLIDWORKS 2022/Chapter 6 Homework folder.

- **Create** the Custom properties of the part as shown in the Part Summary Information dialog box.

- **Create** the drawing. Use the default A (ANSI)-Landscape Sheet Format/Size. Sheet1 Scale 1:2. Third Anlge Projection for Projection Type. Precision .12. Units - inches.

- Create a Front, Right, and Shaded With Edges Isometric view.

- Add all needed centerlines and display modes.

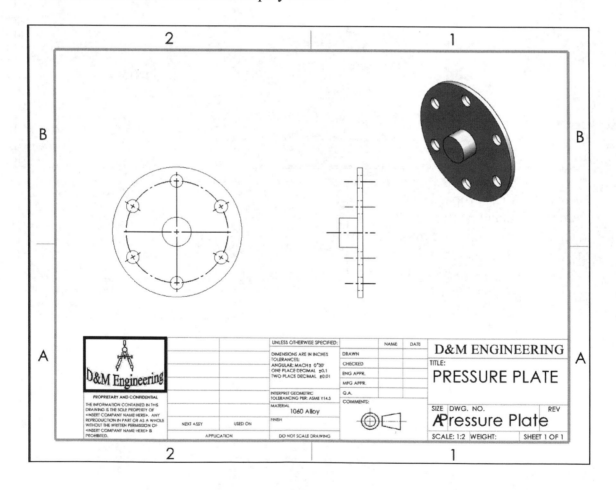

- View and address the Custom Properties of the drawing.

- In Edit Sheet Format, insert your school or company logo, Third Angle projection logo along with the illustrated Title box information. Use Custom Properties of the drawing as illustrated. Note: All needed icons are located in the SOLIDWORKS 2022/logo folder.

	Property Name	Type	Value / Text Expression	Evaluated Value
1	SWFormatSize	Text	8.5in*11in	8.5in*11in
2	CompanyName	Text	D&M ENGINEERING	D&M ENGINEERING
3	Description	Text	PLATE	PLATE
4	Number	Text	334-88	334-88
5	Revision	Text	A	A
6	DrawnBy	Text	DCP	DCP
7	DrawnDate	Text	3-3-2022	3-3-2022
8	<Type a new property>			

- Use the Link to Property command in the Notes PropertyManager to address the DWG. NO.

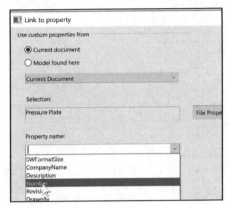

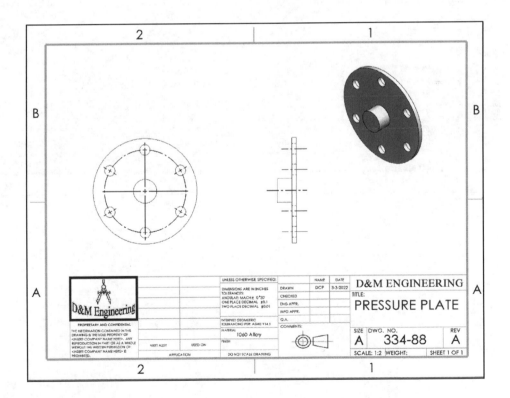

- Return to the Edit Sheet mode. Insert all needed dimensions. Use the Model Items command in the Annotation CommandManager.

- Move the dimensions (add) as needed in the drawing views. Address dimension line gaps, etc. as illustrated.

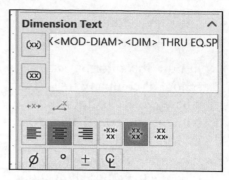

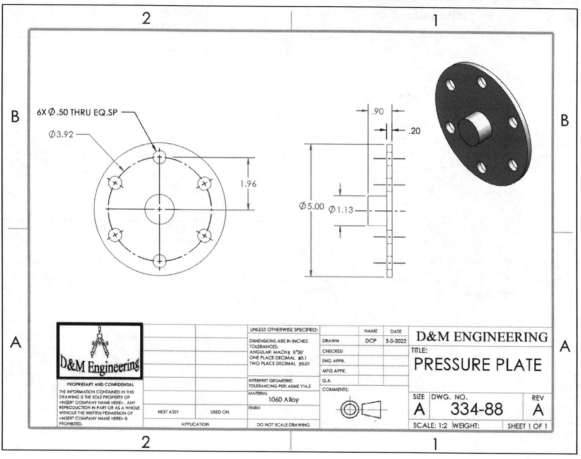

Exercise 6.4: PLATE-1 Drawing

Create the A-ANSI - MMGS - Third Angle
PLATE-1 drawing.

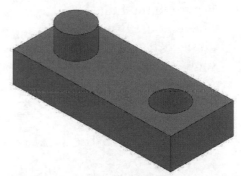

- First create the part from the drawing - then
  create the drawing. Use the default A-
  Landscape Sheet Format/Size. Precision .12.

- View the Custom Properties of the part.

- Insert the Front and Right view as
  illustrated. Insert all dimensions. Think
  about the proper views for your
  dimensions.

	Property Name	Type	Value / Text Expression	Evaluated Value
1	Description	Text	PLATE-1	PLATE-1
2	Material	Text	"SW-Material@Part.uuu1.SLDPRT"	1060 Alloy
	<Type a new property>			

- View and address the Custom
  Properties of the drawing.

- In Edit Sheet Format, insert
  your school or company logo,
  Third Angle projection logo
  along with the illustrated Title
  box information. Note: All
  needed icons are located in the
  SOLIDWORKS 2022/logo
  folder.

	Property Name	Type	Value / Text Expression	Evaluated Valu
1	Description	Text	PLATE-1	PLATE-1
2	DrawnBy	Text	DCP	DCP
3	DrawnDate	Text	3-3-2022	3-3-2022
4	CompanyName	Text	D&M ENGINEERING	D&M ENGINEERING
5	Revision	Text	A	A
6	SWFormatSize	Text	431.8mm*558.8mm	431.8mm*558.8mm
7	Number	Text	544878	544878

- Use the Link to Property
  command in the Notes
  PropertyManager to
  address the DWG. NO and
  if needed TITLE:.

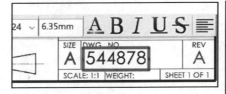

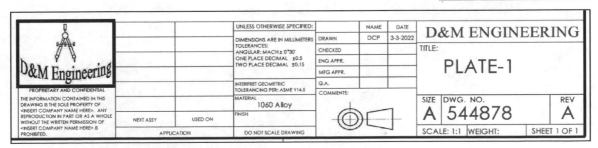

- Return to the Edit Sheet mode. Insert all needed dimensions. Use the Model Items command in the Annotation CommandManager.

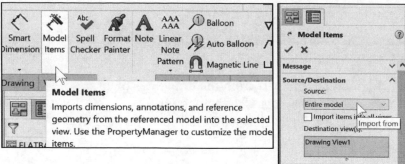

- Move the dimensions (add) as needed in the drawing views. Address dimension line gaps, etc. as illustrated. Insert needed Centerlines and Center Marks.

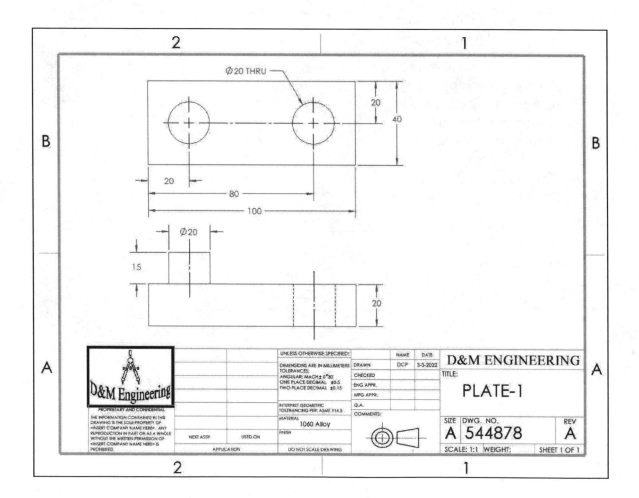

Exercise 6.5: FLATE-PLATE Drawing

Create the A-ANSI - IPS - Third Angle drawing.

- Open the FLATE PLATE part from the SOLIDWORKS 2022/Chapter 6 Homework folder. Address all needed Custom Properties as illustrated.

- Create the drawing. Use the default A-Landscape Sheet Format/Size. Scale: 1:2.

	Property Name	Type	Value / Text Expression	Evaluated Value
1	Material	Text	"SW-Material@FLAT PLATE.SLDPRT"	1060 Alloy
2	Description	Text	FLAT-PLATE	FLAT-PLATE
3	<Type a new property>			

- Insert the Front, Top, Right and Isometric view as illustrated.

- Insert dimensions. Move the dimensions (add) as needed in the drawing views.

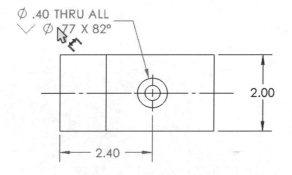

- Use the Hole Callout ⊔∅ tool as illustrated.

- Address dimension line gaps, etc. as illustrated.

- Think about the proper views for your dimensions.

	Property Name	Type	Value / Text Expression	Evaluated Value
1	DrawnBy	Text	DCP	DCP
2	DrawnDate	Text	3-3-2022	3-3-2022
3	CompanyName	Text	D&M ENGINEERING	D&M ENGINEERING
4	Revision	Text	A	A
5	SWFormatSize	Text	8.5in*11in	8.5in*11in
6	Number	Text	556-778	556-778
7	<Type a new property>			

- View and address the Custom Properties of the drawing.

- In Edit Sheet Format, insert your school or company logo, Third Angle projection logo along with the illustrated Title box information. Note: All needed icons are located in the SOLIDWORKS 2022/logo folder.

- Use the Link to Property command in the Notes PropertyManager to address the DWG. NO and if needed TITLE:.

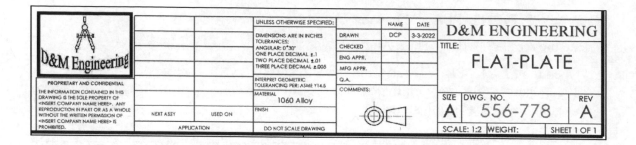

- Return to the Edit Sheet mode. View the results.

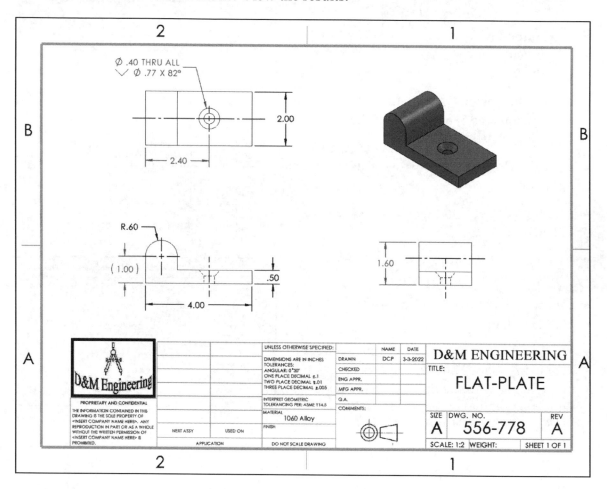

Exercise 6.6: Create a FRONT-SUPPORT Drawing with a BOM and Balloons

Create the an A-Landscape ANSI - IPS - Third Angle drawing. Sheet Scale: 1:2.

- Open the FRONT-SUPPORT assembly from the SOLIDWORKS 2022/Chapter 6 Homework folder. View the assembly and Custom Properties.

- Insert the Isometric view as illustrated.

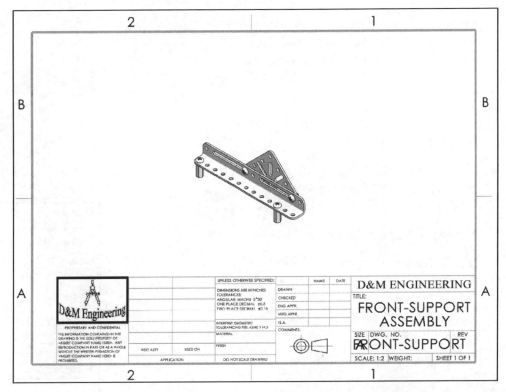

- Insert a Top Level BOM using the bom-material Table Tempate.

- Click a postion in the upper left corner of Sheet1 as illustrated. View the results.

- Open each part from the assembly to view its Linked Properties to the BOM.

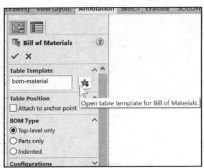

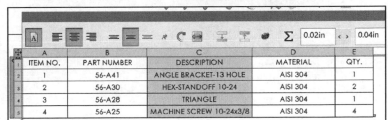

ITEM NO.	PART NUMBER	DESCRIPTION	MATERIAL	QTY.
1	56-A41	ANGLE BRACKET-13 HOLE	AISI 304	1
2	56-A30	HEX-STANDOFF 10-24	AISI 304	2
3	56-A28	TRIANGLE	AISI 304	1
4	56-A25	MACHINE SCREW 10-24x3/8	AISI 304	4

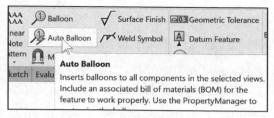

- Use the Auto Balloon tool to create balloons in the Assembly drawing.

- Move and split the balloons as illustrated.

- Open each part from the assembly to view the Linked Properties to the BOM.

- Edit Sheet Format, insert your school or company logo, Third Angle projection logo along with the illustrated Title box information. Note: All needed icons are located in the SOLIDWORKS 2022/logo folder.

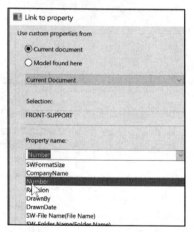

- Address all illustrated Drawing Custom Properties in the Title box.

- Use the Link to Property command in the Notes PropertyManager to address the DWG. NO:.

- Return to the Edit Sheet mode.

- View the results.

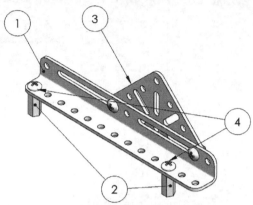

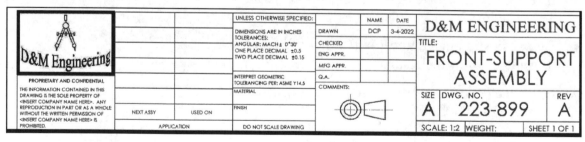

			UNLESS OTHERWISE SPECIFIED:		NAME	DATE	**D&M ENGINEERING**		
			DIMENSIONS ARE IN INCHES TOLERANCES:	DRAWN	DCP	3-4-2022			
			ANGULAR: MACH± 0°30' ONE PLACE DECIMAL ±0.5 TWO PLACE DECIMAL ±0.15	CHECKED			TITLE: FRONT-SUPPORT ASSEMBLY		
				ENG APPR.					
				MFG APPR.					
PROPRIETARY AND CONFIDENTIAL			INTERPRET GEOMETRIC TOLERANCING PER: ASME Y14.5	Q.A.					
THE INFORMATION CONTAINED IN THIS DRAWING IS THE SOLE PROPERTY OF <INSERT COMPANY NAME HERE>. ANY REPRODUCTION IN PART OR AS A WHOLE WITHOUT THE WRITTEN PERMISSION OF <INSERT COMPANY NAME HERE> IS PROHIBITED.	NEXT ASSY	USED ON	MATERIAL	COMMENTS:			SIZE	DWG. NO.	REV
			FINISH				A	223-899	A
	APPLICATION		DO NOT SCALE DRAWING				SCALE: 1:2	WEIGHT:	SHEET 1 OF 1

ITEM NO.	PART NUMBER	DESCRIPTION	MATERIAL	QTY.
1	56-A41	ANGLE BRACKET-13 HOLE	AISI 304	1
2	56-A30	HEX-STANDOFF 10-24	AISI 304	2
3	56-A28	TRIANGLE	AISI 304	1
4	56-A25	MACHINE SCREW 10-24x3/8	AISI 304	4

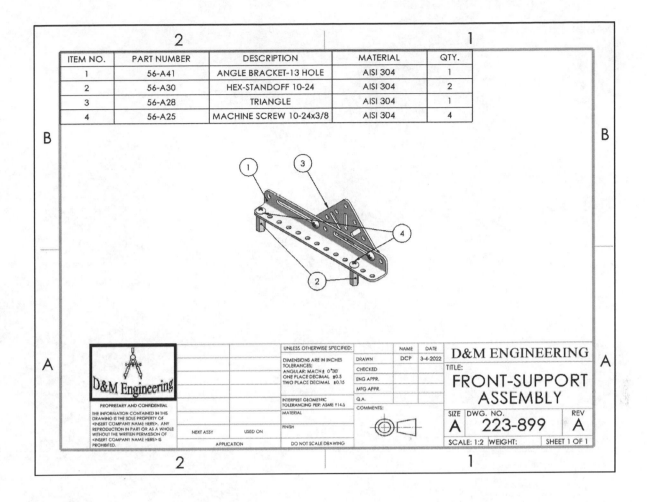

UNLESS OTHERWISE SPECIFIED:

DIMENSIONS ARE IN INCHES
TOLERANCES:
ANGULAR: MACH± 0°30'
ONE PLACE DECIMAL ±0.5
TWO PLACE DECIMAL ±0.15

INTERPRET GEOMETRIC
TOLERANCING PER: ASME Y14.5

MATERIAL

FINISH

NEXT ASSY | USED ON

APPLICATION | DO NOT SCALE DRAWING

	NAME	DATE
DRAWN	DCP	3-4-2022
CHECKED		
ENG APPR.		
MFG APPR.		
Q.A.		
COMMENTS:		

D&M ENGINEERING

TITLE:

FRONT-SUPPORT ASSEMBLY

SIZE **A** | DWG. NO. **223-899** | REV **A**

SCALE: 1:2 | WEIGHT: | SHEET 1 OF 1

D&M Engineering

Notes:

Chapter 7

Fundamentals of Detailing

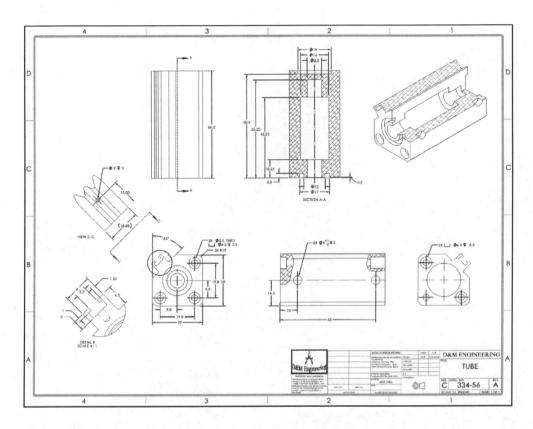

Below are the desired outcomes and usage competencies based on the completion of Chapter 7. Note: Drawing refers to the SOLIDWORKS module used to insert, add, and modify views in an engineering drawing. Detailing refers to the SOLIDWORKS module used to insert, add, and modify dimensions and notes in an engineering drawing.

Desired Outcomes:	Usage Competencies:
Two Detail drawings: • TUBE drawing with detailing and various layers. • COVERPLATE drawing with detailing and different configurations.	• Ability to insert, add and modify dimensions and annotations.
	• An understanding of adding dimensions and annotations on drawing layers.
	• Knowledge of dimensioning standards.

Notes:

Chapter 7 - Fundamentals of Detailing

Chapter Objective

Details are the drawing dimensions and notes required to document part features. Create two detailed drawings:

- TUBE

- COVERPLATE

On the completion of this chapter, you will be able to:

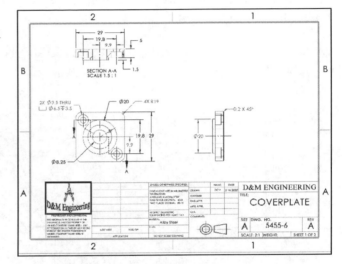

- Insert and modify drawing view dimensions on layers.

- Add Drawing Sheets with Custom Properties.

- Add and address annotations.

- Insert Hole Callouts, Center Marks, and Centerlines.

- Create over 14 different drawing views using various drawing tools and techniques.

- Use various methods to move, hide, show, suppress, and un-suppress drawing views and dimensions along with dimension lines and gaps.

- Apply the ASME Y14.5 standard for Types of Decimal Dimensions.

- Add Modifying Symbols and Hole Symbols.

Chapter Overview

You insert and add views for the TUBE, ROD, and COVERPLATE drawings in Chapter 6. In this chapter, you will insert, add, and modify dimensions and obtain an understanding of addressing annotations and Linked Properties in a drawing.

Details are the drawing dimensions and annotations required to document part features. There are two types of dimensions: Inserted dimensions and Added dimensions.

Note: Chapter 6 drawings are located in the SOLIDWORKS 2022/Chapter 7 Drawing folder. Use your own drawings, if you created them in Chapter 6.

Feature dimensions are created in the part and inserted into the drawing. Inserted dimensions are associative. Modify a dimension in the drawing and the feature dimension is modified in the part.

Added drawing dimensions are called Reference dimensions. Reference dimensions are driven by part features. You cannot edit a Driven or Reference dimension.

Add annotations such as: Notes, Hole Callouts, Centerlines, and Center Marks to the drawing document from the Annotation CommandManager.

The design intent of this chapter is to work with dimensions inserted from parts and to incorporate them into drawings. Explore methods to move, hide, and add dimensions to adhere to a drawing and drafting standard.

Work between multiple parts, drawings, and sheets. Add annotations to the drawing that reference part dimensions.

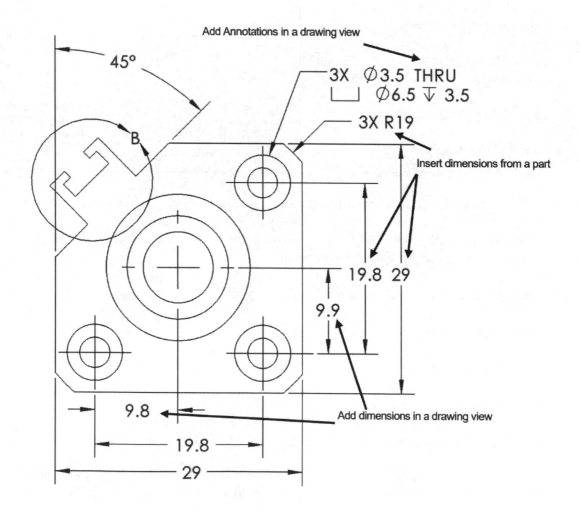

There are other solutions to the dimensioning schemes illustrated in this chapter. The TUBE, COVERPLATE, and exercise drawings are sample drawings; they are not complete. A drawing requires tolerances, materials, Revision Tables, Engineering Change Orders, and other notes prior to production and release.

You just inserted dimensions from a part into a drawing. The dimensions, extensions lines and arrows are not in the correct locations. How can you improve the position of these details? Answer: Apply an engineering drawing standard. The ASME Y14.5 standard defines an engineering drawing standard.

There are different rules for the display of decimal dimensions and tolerances based on millimeter and inch units. Review the below table.

TYPES of DECIMAL DIMENSIONS (ASME Y14.5)			
Description:	**UNITS: MM**	**Description:**	**UNITS: INCH**
Dimension is less than 1mm. Zero precedes the decimal point.	0.9 0.95	Dimension is less than 1 inch. Zero is not used before the decimal point.	.5 .56
Dimension is a whole number. Display no decimal point. Display no zero after decimal point.	19	Express dimension to the same number of decimal places as its tolerance. Add zeroes to the right of the decimal point. If the tolerance is expressed to 3 places, then the dimension contains 3 places to the right of the decimal point.	1.750
Dimension exceeds a whole number by a decimal fraction of a millimeter. Display no zero to the right of the decimal.	11.5 11.51		

TOLERANCE DISPLAY FOR METRIC AND INCH DIMENSIONS (ASME Y14.5)		
Description:	**UNITS: MM**	**UNITS: INCH**
Dimensions less than 1	0.5	.5
Unilateral Tolerance	$36^{\;0}_{-0.5}$	$1.417^{+.005}_{-.000}$
Bilateral Tolerance	$36^{+0.25}_{-0.50}$	$1.417^{+.010}_{-.020}$
Limit Tolerance	14.50 11.50	.571 .463

The Drafting
Standard used in the
book is ANSI.

Leading zeroes is set
by default to
Standard.

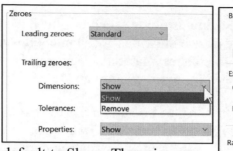

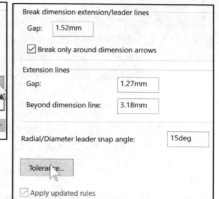

Trailing zeroes is set by default to Show. The primary
unit is millimeters in this chapter. The Standard option
trims trailing zeroes to the ASME Y14.5 standard. See the
attached ppt on Dimensioning systems.

 Click **Options**, **Document Properties** tab,

Dimensions folder, **Tolerance** [Tolerance...] button to
control tolerance type.

Click **Options**, **Document Properties**
tab, **Dimensions** folder for a Part model to
address precision.

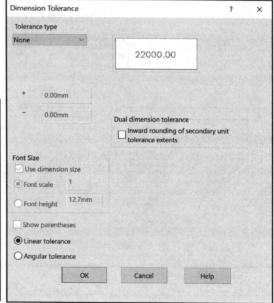

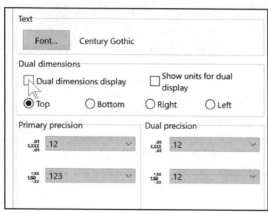

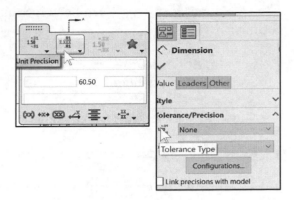

Access the Tolerance/Precision option for an active drawing document either from the Dimension PropertyManager or the Dimension Pop-up palette in the graphics area to save mouse travel to the Dimension PropertyManager.

- Example 1: Set Precision Primary Units to .12 places. The drawing dimension displays 0.55. The number of decimal places is two. No change is required.

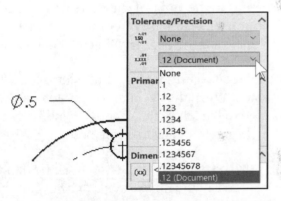

∅.55

- Example 2: The drawing dimension displays 0.50. Control individual dimension precision through the Dimension Properties Tolerance/Precision text box or the dimension Pop-up palette in the graphics area to save mouse travel to the Dimension PropertyManager.

∅.50

Modify the dimension Primary Units display to .X, (one decimal place). The drawing dimension displays 0.5.

General tolerance values apply to all dimensions on a drawing except reference dimensions and material stock sizes. Tolerance values are displayed with 1, 2 and or 3 decimal places.

∅.5

Values differ for machined parts, plastic parts, sheet metal parts, castings and other manufacturing processes.

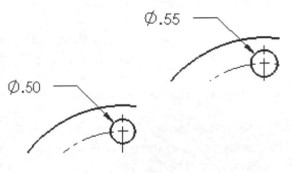

- Example: ONE PLACE is ±0.2. The dimension 0.9 has a tolerance value of ±0.2. The feature dimension range is 0.7mm - 1.1mm. The tolerance equals 1.1mm - 0.7mm = 0.4mm.

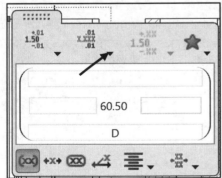

- Example: TWO PLACE is ±0.05. The dimension 0.95 has a tolerance value of ±0.05. The feature dimension range is 0.90mm - 1.00mm. The tolerance equals 1.00mm - 0.90mm = 0.10mm.

The Document Property, Leading zeroes has three options:

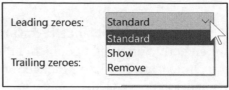

- **Standard**: Leading zeroes appear according to the overall drafting standard.

- **Show**: Zeroes before decimal points are shown.

- **Remove**: Leading zeroes do not appear.

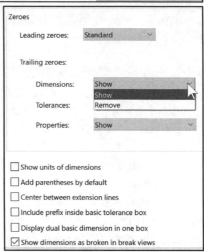

The Document Property, Trailing zeroes has three options:

- **Show**: Trailing zeroes are displayed according to the decimal places you specify for Units.

- **Remove**: Trailing zeroes do not appear.

The Show option in Trailing zeroes displays the number of zeroes equal to the number of places specified in the Units option. The Remove option displays no trailing zeroes to the right of the dimension value. The Standard option trims trailing zeroes to the ASME Y14.5 standard. See the attached ppt on Dimensioning systems.

ANSI standard for U.S. dimensioning use the decimal inch value. When the decimal inch system is used, a zero is not used to the left of the decimal point for values less than one inch, and trailing zeroes are used.

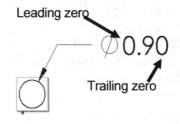

Leading zero

Trailing zero

ASME standards for the use of metric dimensioning required all the dimesnsions to be expressed in milimeters (mm). The (mm) is not needed on each dimension, but it is used when a dimension is used in a notation. No trailing zeroes should be used. The Metric or International system of units (SI) unit systems in drafting is also known as the Millimeter, Grams, Second (MMGS) unit system.

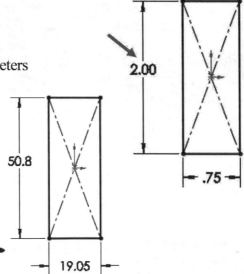

Tolerance Type

A Tolerance type is selected from the available drop-down list in the Dimension PropertyManager. The list is dynamic. A few examples of Tolerance type display are:

- **Basic**: Adds a box around the dimension text. In geometric dimensioning and tolerancing, Basic indicates the theoretically exact value of the dimension.

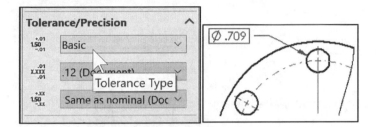

- **Bilateral**: Displays the nominal dimension followed by separate upper and lower tolerances. In $+$ and $-$, set values for the amounts over and under the nominal.

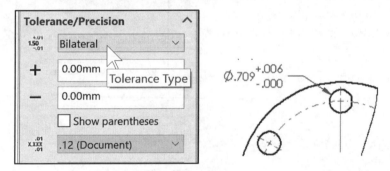

- **Limit**: Displays the upper and lower limits of the dimension. In $+$ and $-$, set values for the amounts over and under the nominal. The tolerance values are added to and subtracted from the nominal.

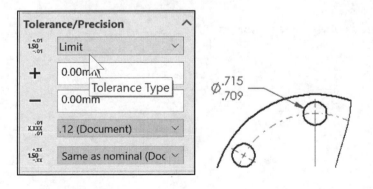

Symmetric: Displays the nominal dimension followed by the tolerance. In **+**, set the same value for the amounts over and under the nominal.

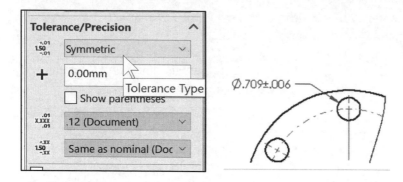

Order of Precedence of Linear Dimension Lines

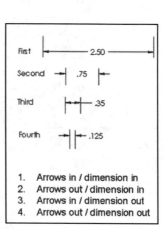

Order of Precedence of a linear dimension line. See Chapter 2 on details and ppt on Dimensioning systems. The first order of preference is that the dimensions and arrowheads are drawn between the extension line if space is available. If space is limited see illustration for second, third and fourth options per ASME Y14.5.

Example 1: Note: (MMGS) is the unit system. Precision is .12.

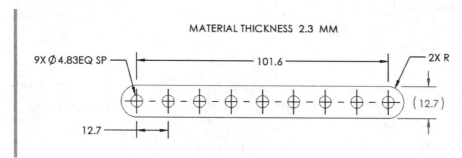

Example 2: Note: (IPS) is the unit system. Precision is .12.

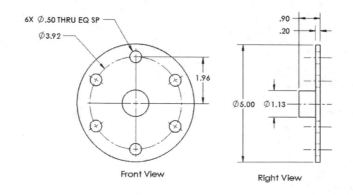

TUBE Drawing-Detailing

Detailing the TUBE drawing requires numerous steps. Example:

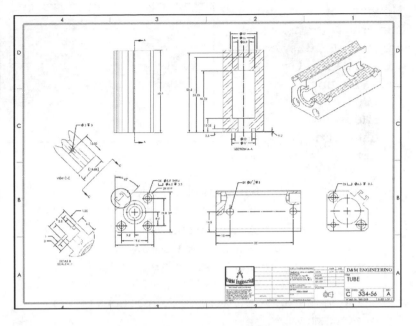

- Insert part dimensions into the Tube drawing with a Custom Drawing Template.

- Reposition dimensions to the appropriate view.

- Add reference dimensions to the drawing.

- Add annotations.

- Address various layers.

- Apply dimensions according to your company's standard.

There are two methods to import model items from the part into the drawing:

- **Entire model**: Inserts model items for the whole model.

- **Selected feature**: Inserts model items for the feature you select in the graphics area.

There are four methods to import model items from the assembly into the drawing.

- **Entire model**: Inserts model items for the whole model.

- **Selected feature**: Inserts model items for the feature you select in the graphics area.

- **Selected component**: Inserts model items for the component you select in the graphics area.

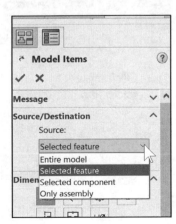

- **Only assembly**: Inserts model items for assembly features only. For example, you can insert dimensions that reside exclusively in the assembly, such as Distance and Angle mates.

How do you reposition numerous dimensions and annotations? Answer: One view at a time. Use the following tips:

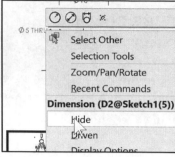

- Hide views temporarily when not in use.

- Hide dimensions that are no longer required. Utilize a layer to turn on/off dimensions. Utilize Hide / Show to control dimension display. Do not delete them. It takes less time to show a hidden dimension than to create one.

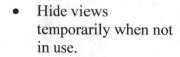

- Temporarily move views to see dimensions on top of other views.

- Deactivate the dimension parenthesis when creating baseline dimensions.

- Review each feature to determine if all feature dimensions and Geometric relations are accounted for in the appropriate view.

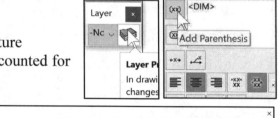

- Review each view for center marks, center lines, hole callouts and other annotations.

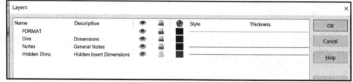

Activity: TUBE Drawing-Detailing

Open the TUBE drawing. Add a Custom Part Property (Material).

1) Click **Open** ⬚ from the Main menu. Browse to the **SOLIDWORKS 2022/Chapter 7 Drawing** folder. Double-click the **TUBE** drawing. Right-click the **Front drawing** view. Click **Open Part**.

2) Click **File**, **Properties** from the TUBE FeatureManager. Click the **Configuration Specific** tab.

3) Select **Default**. Select **Material** from the drop-down menu. Select **Material** in the Value / Text Expressions box. Click **OK**. **Save** the Part. **Return** to the TUBE drawing.

Add a few Drawing Custom Properties in the Edit Sheet Format mode.

4) Right-click **Edit Sheet Format** in Sheet1: Add the following Custom Drawing Properties: **DrawnBy**, **DrawnDate** and **Revision**.

5) Return to the drawing views. Right-click **Edit Sheet**.

Display the Layer toolbar.

6) Check **View**, **Toolbars**, **Layer** from the Main menu.

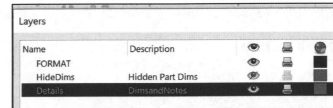

Layer Properties

In drawings, creates, edits, or deletes layers. Also, changes the properties and visibility of layers.

Create two new layers.

7) Click the **Layer Properties** icon.

8) Click the **New** button. Enter **HideDims** for Name.

9) Enter **Hidden Part Dims** for Description. Click the open **eye** icon to turn the HideDims layer off.

10) Select **Red** for color. Click the **New** button. Enter **Details** for Name.

Name	Description			
FORMAT				
HideDims	Hidden Part Dims			
Details	DimsandNotes			

11) Enter **DimsandNotes** for Description. The Layer is On when the eye icon is open. Enter **Blue** for color. Accept the default Style and Thickness. Click **OK**. Details layer is the current layer.

Insert dimensions for the entire model.

12) Click a **position** inside the sheet boundary and outside any view boundary. Note: No Drawing view boundaries are selected.

Model Items

Message

Source/Destination

Source:

Entire model

Import items into all views / Import from

Dimensions

☑ Eliminate duplicates

13) Click **Model Items** from the Annotation toolbar.

14) Select **Entire model**. Accept the defaults.

15) Click **OK** from the Model Items PropertyManager. The dimensions are displayed in blue. Your dimensions and locations maybe / will be different. Address this later in the chapter.

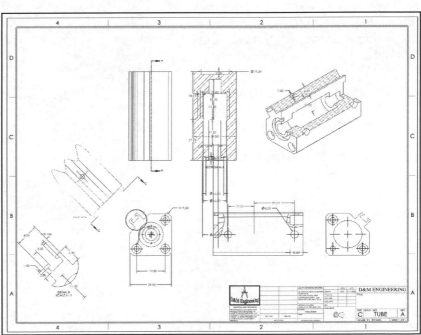

Rapid dimensioning provides the ability to enable or disable the rapid dimension manipulator. Select to enable; clear to disable. This setting persists across sessions. You can use the rapid dimension manipulator to place dimensions so they are evenly spaced and easier to read. When the rapid dimension manipulator creates dimensions on a symmetric centerline, any dimensions that might overlap are staggered for drawings in the ANSI standard. See SOLIDWORKS help for additional information.

Temporarily hide views when not in use.

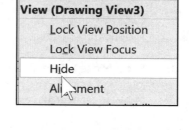

16) Right-click inside the **Right view** boundary; Drawing View3.

17) Click **Hide**.

Hide dimensions from the Half Section Isometric view.

18) Click inside the **Half Section Isometric view** boundary.

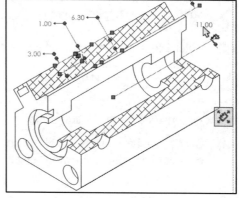

19) Drag the **view** to the right, away from the Section view dimensions.

20) Click and drag the **dimension text** until you view each dimension.

21) Hold the **Ctrl** key down.

22) Click **all of the dimension** text.

23) Release the **Ctrl** key.

24) Select the **HideDims** layer from the Dimension PropertyManager Other tab.

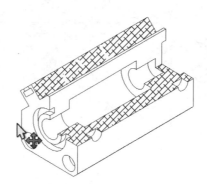

25) Click **OK** ✔ from the Dimension PropertyManager. The selected dimensions are hidden.

26) Select the **Details** layer from the Layer toolbar.

Save the TUBE drawing.

27) Click **Save** 🖫.

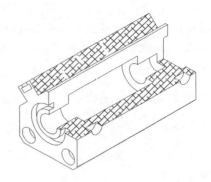

For dimensions placed on a hidden layer, hide and delete commands may not completely remove all of the graphic bits. If the dimensions are not erased completely, click Rebuild.

Hide Dimensions

What command do you select when dimensions are no longer required? Answer: There are two options: HideDims layer or the Hide command.

Number of Dimensions:	Command Sequence:
One or two dimensions	Select the dimensions. Right-click, Hide.
Many dimensions	Place the dimensions on the HideDims layer. Turn off the HideDims layer.

Hide dimensions versus delete dimensions. Use caution when deleting a dimension. You may require the dimension in the future. How do you restore the hidden dimensions? Answer: Utilize View, Hide / Show, Annotations from the Main menu.

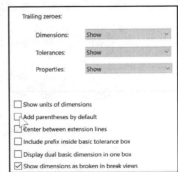

Show Dimensions

Click on the dimension text to display the Dimension PropertyManager. Dimensions placed on the HideDims layer remain turned off. To display the layer, click on the close eye 👁 icon from the Layers dialog box. The dimensions added to a drawing are called Reference dimensions. Model dimensions drive Reference dimensions.

Model dimensions are created in a part or an assembly. A Reference dimension cannot be changed. The dimensions for the overall length and Stroke Chamber are defined from the Front reference plane. The part dimension scheme was the engineer's intent. As the detailer, define the dimensions to a base line. Hide the dimensions to avoid superfluous dimensions.

Reference dimensions may be displayed with parentheses. Uncheck the Dimensions Document Property, Add parentheses by default option to conserve design time.

The DimXpertManager ⊕ tab provides the ability to insert dimensions and tolerances manually or automatically. The options are: **Auto Dimension Scheme** ⊕, **Auto Pair Tolerance** ⊞, **Basic, Location Dimension** |◁▷| , **Basic Size Dimension** ◁ , **General Profile Tolerance** ⊟, **Show Tolerance Status** ⁺◉, **Copy Scheme** ⊕, **Import Scheme** ⊕, **TolAnalyst Study** ⋅⊞ and **Datum Target** ◉.

The ASME Y14.5 standard uses parentheses to represent an Overall and an Intermediate Reference dimension. Control the dimensions that contain a parenthesis to adhere to your company's drawing standard. Select Properties on the dimension text.

Uncheck the Display with parenthesis option to control the individual Reference dimensions.

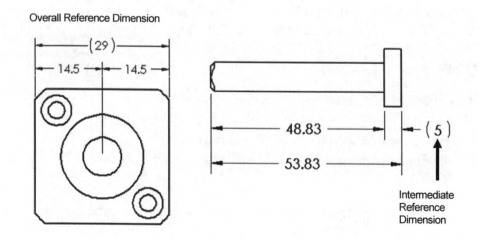

TUBE Detailing-Section View, Top View, and Detail View
===

There are numerous techniques utilized to detail a view. Start with the Section view. The Model Items tool from the Annotation tab inserted the majority of the required dimensions into the Section view.

Activity: TUBE Drawing Detailing-Section View, Top View, and Detail View

---

Temporarily move the Section view.

28) Drag the **Section view** boundary to the right.

Create the overall depth dimension.

29) Click inside the **Top view** boundary.

30) Click **Smart Dimension** from the Annotation CommandManager. The Dimension PropertyManager is displayed.

31) Click the **right vertical line** in the Top view as illustrated.

32) Position the **60.50** dimension text to the right of the Top view. A visible gap exists between the extension lines and the right vertical profile lines.

33) Select **.1** from the Primary Unit Precision text box. The 60.5 dimension text is displayed.

Precision is set to two locations in the drawing document. ASME standard states no trailing zeroes should be used. The Metric or International system of units (SI) unit systems in drafting is also known as the Millimeter, Grams, Second (MMGS) unit system.

34) Click **OK** ✔ from the Dimension PropertyManager.

35) **View** the results.

☼ Note: There are other ways to remove trailing zeroes when using the Metric or International system of units also known as the Millimeter, Grams, Second (MMGS) unit system.

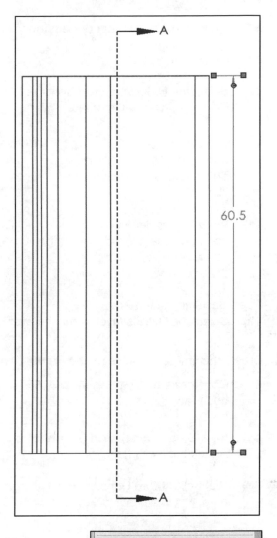

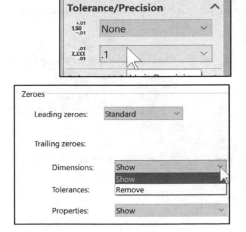

Zoom in on the Section view A-A. Hide the vertical dimensions in Section view A-A.

36)   Hold the **Ctrl** key down.

37)   Click **all of the vertical dimension** text.

38)   Release the **Ctrl** key.

39)   Select the **HideDims** layer from the Dimension PropertyManager Other tab.

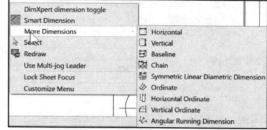

40)   Click **OK** ✔ from the Dimension PropertyManager. The selected dimensions are hidden.

41)   **View** the results. You may need to move and hide various dimensions in the drawing view.

Insert Baseline dimensions.
42)   Select the **Details** layer from the Layer toolbar.

Create the first dimensions for the Stroke Chamber.

43)   Click inside the **Section view A-A** view boundary.

44)   Click **Smart Dimension** ◇ from the Annotation CommandManager.

45)   Right-click **More Dimensions** in the graphics area. Not in a drawing view.

46)   Click **Baseline** ⊞ . The Baseline ⊞ icon is displayed.

47)   Click the **lower left horizontal line** of the stroke chamber as illustrated.

48)   Click the **left horizontal line** of the Nose as illustrated.

49)   Click the **left horizontal line** of the Tube Extrusion as illustrated.

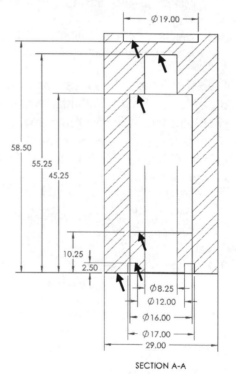

SECTION A-A

Create other dimensions.

50) Click the **left horizontal line** of the Stroke Chamber.

51) Click the **left horizontal line** of the Bore.

52) Click the **left horizontal line** of the Cbore.

53) Right-click **Smart Dimension**.

54) Click **OK** ✓ from the Dimension PropertyManager.

55) Drag the **dimension text** to the left as illustrated.

56) **Hide** any needed dimensions not shown in the illustration.

57) Drag the **dimension text** as illustrated.

58) Address **all trailing zeroes** as illustrated.

💡 All drawing views with dimensions require gaps between the visible feature line and dimension extension line. Zoom in on the dimension, click the dimension, and create the gap with the blue control points.

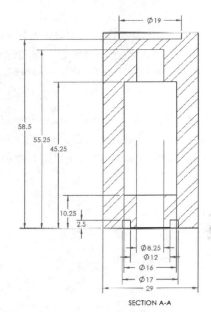

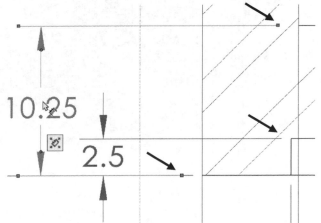

💡 Flip arrows by selecting the blue control point on the arrowhead. Arrows alternate between the outside position and the inside position.

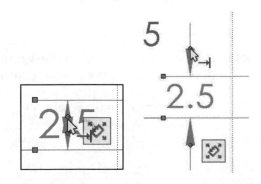

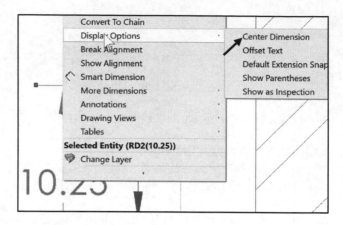

Select a line segment not a point to create a linear dimension. Fillet and Chamfer features remove points.

Center the dimension text between the extension lines.

59) Right-click on the **10.25** dimension text.

60) Click **Display Options**. Click **Center Dimension**. Click **OK** ✓ from the Dimension PropertyManager.

Baseline dimensions are aligned. Right-click Properties, Break Alignment to remove aligned dimensions. Click Show Alignment to display dimensions that are aligned. Uncheck the Center Dimension to position text along the extension lines.

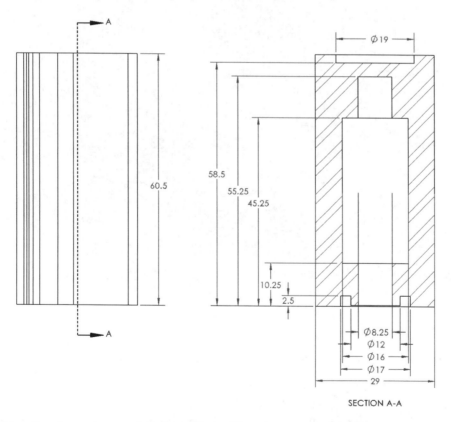

SECTION A-A

61) Review the dimensions and view positions. If required, click and drag the **Section view, dimensions** and the **extension lines** of the vertical dimensions to create needed gaps.

The vertical dimensions are equally spaced and positioned off the profiles. The Top and Section view are adequately spaced. The text and arrows are visible. There is a gap between the profile and vertical extension lines.

Move the bottom horizontal dimensions to the top in the Section view.

62) Click and drag the ⌀**8.25** bottom horizontal dimension text to the top of the Section view A-A approximately 10mm above the top horizontal profile.

63) Set Primary Unit Precision to **.1**.

64) Drag each **extension line** to the top vertex of the Bore to create a gap.

65) Click and drag the ⌀**16** text upward above the ⌀8.3 text.

66) Drag the extension lines to the **top vertex** of the Bore.

67) Repeat for the other **illustrated dimension** text.

68) **View** the results.

Align the top horizontal dimensions.

69) Hold the **Ctrl** key down.

70) Click the ⌀**8.3**, ⌀**16**, ⌀**19**, and **29** dimension text.

71) Release the **Ctrl** key.

72) Click **Tools**, **Dimensions**, **Align Parallel/Concentric** from the Main menu.

73) Click **OK** ✔ from the Dimension PropertyManager.

The Dimension Document Property, Offset distances, From last dimension option controls the spacing between parallel dimensions.

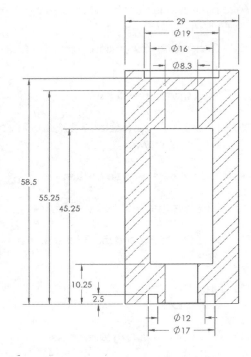

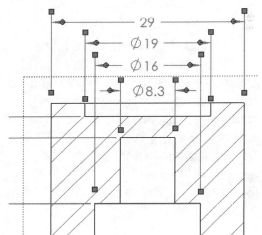

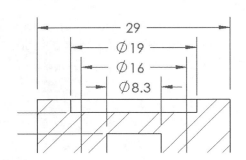

Move dimensions from the Section view A-A to the Front view.

74) Click the **29** dimension text in the Section view.

75) Hold the **Shift** key down.

76) Drag the **29** dimension text to the inside of the Front view.

77) Release the **Mouse button**.

78) Release the **Shift** key.

79) Add the **19.80** and the **3.50** dimension as illustrated.

80) Drag the **dimension text** as illustrated.

81) Address **all trailing zeroes** as illustrated.

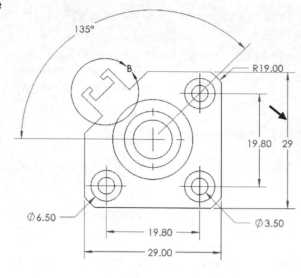

Order of Precedence of a linear dimension line. The first order of preference is that the dimensions and arrowheads are drawn between the dimension extension line if space is available. If space is limited, see illustration for second, third and fourth options per ASME Y14.5.

First	⊢—— 2.50 ——⊣	
Second	→⊣ .75 ⊢←	
Third	⊢⊣← .35	
Fourth	→⊣⊢← .125	

1. Arrows in / dimension in
2. Arrows out / dimension in
3. Arrows in / dimension out
4. Arrows out / dimension out

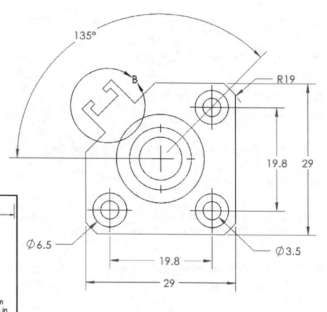

Flip arrows by selecting the blue control point on the arrowhead. Arrows alternate between the outside position and the inside position.

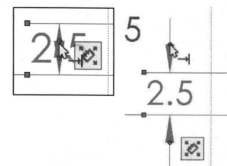

🔆 The Leaders tab in the Dimension PropertyManager provides the ability to access the Witness/Leader Display box. The

Witness/Leader Display box provides the ability to select arrow style, direction, and type. There is also a Pop-up menu with limited commands.

🔆 Selecting multiple entities becomes a challenge on a large drawing. To move, copy, or modify multiple entities, select the first entity. Hold the Ctrl key down and select the remaining entities. The first selection clears all previously selected entities.

Move the horizontal dimension text.

82) Click the Ø**12** dimension text at the bottom of the Section view.

83) Drag the Ø**12** dimension text upward to a position 10mm below the bottom horizontal profile line.

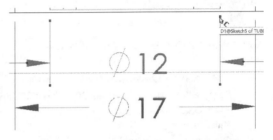

84) Drag each **extension line** off the profile. Do not use the Nose vertex. The Nose feature is too close to the bottom horizontal line of the Tube to utilize the vertex.

🔆 Use the dimension Pop-up palette in the graphics area to save mouse travel to the Dimension PropertyManager. The dimension palette appears when you insert or select a dimension so you can easily change the dimension's properties and formatting.

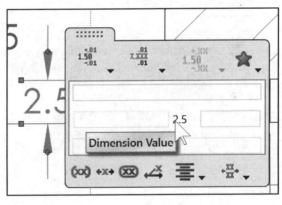

Position the Section A-A text below the bottom horizontal dimensions.

85) Center the **Section A-A** text.

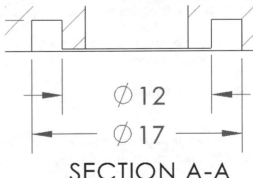

Insert a Centerline.

86) Click inside the **Section view A-A** boundary.

87) Click **Centerline** 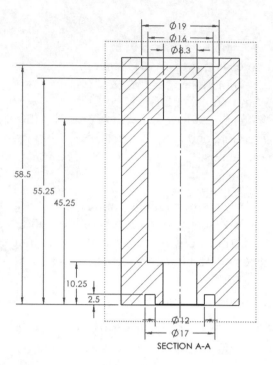 from the Annotation toolbar. Click the **Select View** box.

88) Click **OK** ✔ from the Centerline PropertyManager.

💡 Insert Centerlines quickly. Utilize the view boundary, two edges, two sketched entities (expect Splines), face or feature to manually insert a Centerline annotation. Utilize the Offset text option to position the text angled, outside the dimension arrows.

Add a vertical dimension with Offset.

89) Click **Smart Dimension** ⌄ from the Annotation tab. **Zoom in** on the horizontal line of the Nose.

90) Click the **horizontal line** of the Nose as illustrated.

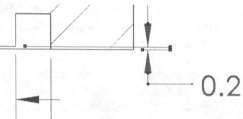

91) Click the **bottom horizontal line** of the Tube Extrusion as illustrated. Click a **position** directly to the right.

92) Modify Precision to **.1**. Drag the **dimension** to the right, off the Section view. Click **OK** ✔ from the Dimension PropertyManager.

Display offset text.

93) Click the **0.20** dimension text.

94) Click the **Value** tab in the Dimension PropertyManager

95) Click the **Offset Text** button.

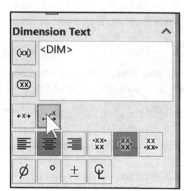

💡 To slant the dimension, position the mouse pointer at the end of the extension line. Drag the extension line to create the angled dimension.

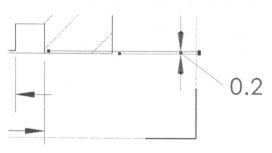

96) Click **OK** ✔ from the Dimension PropertyManager.

97) Address any **needed gaps** between the feature
lines and the extensions lines.

Save the TUBE drawing.

98) Click **Save** 💾 .

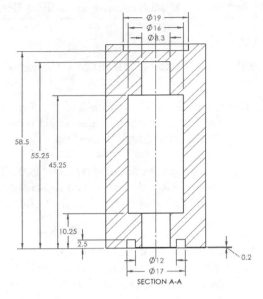

SECTION A-A

TUBE Drawing-Detailing Detail View, and Front View

Review the status of the Front view and Detail view. Dimensions are not clear or
Dimensions are on top of each other. Dimensions are too far or too close to the profile.

Hide the 11 and 135° dimensions in the Detail view or Front view with the Hide option.
Replace the 135° obtuse angle with an acute angle. Create an acute angle dimension from
a construction line Collinear with the left vertical edge in the Front view.

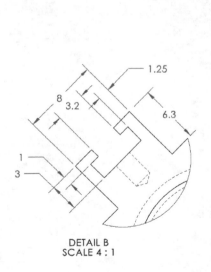

DETAIL B
SCALE 4 : 1

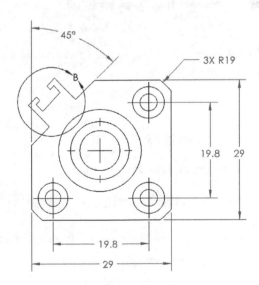

Activity: TUBE Drawing-Detailing Detail View and Front View

Hide dimensions.

99) Click inside the **Detail view** boundary.

100) Click **Hidden Lines Visible** from the Display Style box. If required, right-click the **11** dimension text. Click **Hide**.

101) Right-click the **135.0°** angle text in the Front view. Click **Hide**. Note: The location of the 11 and 135.0° dimension depends on the size of the Detail view.

102) Click inside the **Detail view** boundary. Drag the **1** dimension text approximately 10mm away from the profile. **Flip** the arrows if required.

103) Drag the **3** text to the left of the 1 text. Select the **1** dimension text. Hold the **Ctrl** key down.

104) Select the **3** dimension text. Release the **Ctrl** key.

105) Click **Tools**, **Dimensions**, **Align Parallel/Concentric** from the Menu bar menu.

106) Click **OK** ✔ from the PropertyManager.

107) Drag the **8**, **3.20** and **1.25** dimension text away from the profile.

108) Address **correct precision** for all dimensions.

A break is required when the extension lines cross the dimension lines.

Create a break.

109) Click the **3** horizontal dimension.

110) Check the **Break Lines** checkbox.

111) View the default **Use document gap** length.

112) Click **OK** ✔ from the Dimension PropertyManager.

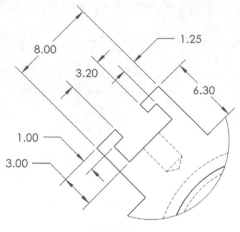

DETAIL B
SCALE 4 : 1

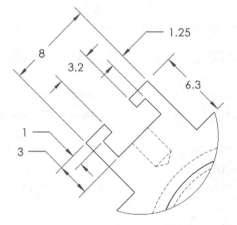

DETAIL B
SCALE 4 : 1

Align the dimensions.

113) Click the **8** dimension.

114) Hold the **Ctrl** key down.

115) Click the **3.2** and **1.25** dimension.

116) Release the **Ctrl** key.

117) Click **Tools**, **Dimensions**, **Align Parallel/Concentric** from the Menu bar menu.

118) Position the **DETAIL B** text below the profile.

Save the TUBE drawing.

119) Click **Save** 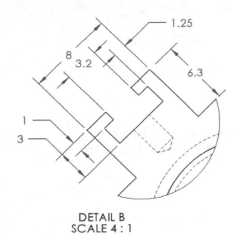.

The default Break dimension extension/leader lines Gap value is set in Tools, Options, Document Properties, Dimensions, Break dimension extension/leader lines for an active drawing document.

If the Hide option is utilized to hide an annotation, and you want to display the annotation on the sheet, select View, Hide/Show Annotations from the Menu bar menu. The hidden annotations are displayed in gray. Click the needed annotation to be displayed.

Edit Radius text. Note: The TUBE Default part configuration document needs to be active.

120) Click the **R19** text.

121) Enter **3X** in the Dimension Text box.

122) Press the **space bar**.

123) Click **OK** ✓ from the Dimension PropertyManager.

DETAIL B
SCALE 4 : 1

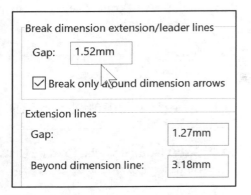

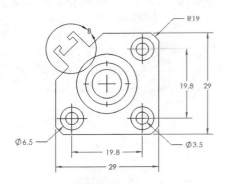

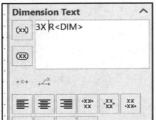

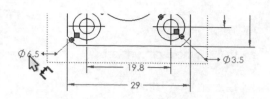

Hide dimensions.

124) Click the Ø**3.5** dimension text.

125) Hold the **Ctrl** key down.

126) Click the Ø**6.5** dimension text.

127) Release the **Ctrl** key.

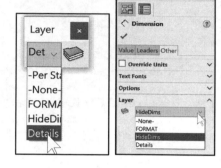

128) Select **HideDims** Layer from the Dimension
PropertyManager Other tab.

129) Click **OK** ✔ from the Dimension PropertyManager.

130) Select the **Details** layer from the Layer toolbar.

Dimension the angle cut.

131) Click **Smart Dimension** ⌐ from the
Annotation tab.

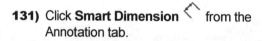

132) Click the **left vertical profile line** and
the **top angled edge**.

133) Position the **dimension** inside the
acute angle.

134) Select **None** from the Primary Units
Precision box.

135) Click **OK** ✔ from the Dimension
PropertyManager.

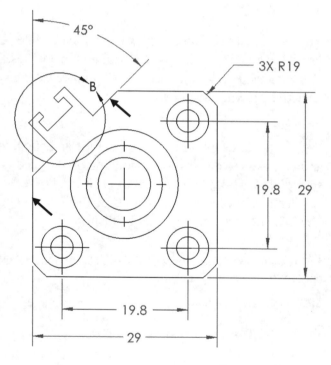

Save the TUBE drawing.

136) Click **Save** ![save icon].

Edge selection is important. Select the top angled edge, not the bottom angle edge. The bottom angle edge extension line overlaps the profile line and does not produce a gap.

TUBE Drawing-Detailing Right View, Back View, and Holes

The Right view contains a series of holes that require annotations. Display the Right view. Reposition dimensions and add annotations. The Back view requires additional annotations to detail a Counterbore.

Utilize the Dimension PropertyManager - Leaders tab to affect the display arrow options. The options are: Outside, Inside, Smart, and Directed Leader.

Utilize the Dimension PropertyManager - Leaders tab to affect Style. You can choose separate styles for each arrow when there are two arrows for a dimension. This feature supports the JIS dimensioning standard. Two lists appear in the Dimension PropertyManager only when separate styles are specified by the dimensioning standard. They are: Radius, Diameter, Linear, Foreshortened, Open Leader, One Arrow / Solid Leader, Two Arrows / Solid Leader and Two Arrows / Open Leader.

Counterbore holes in the Right view require a note. Use the Hole Callout to dimension the holes. The Hole Callout function creates additional notes required to dimension the holes. The dimension standard symbols are displayed automatically when you insert holes created with the Hole Wizard feature.

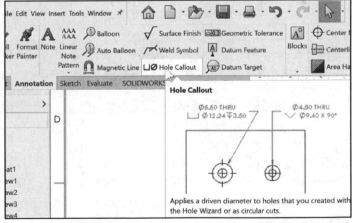

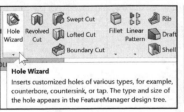

See Chapter 3 for additional information on Counterbore holes and callouts.

Fastener Hole dimension (Annotations)
Denote drilled hole information by a bent leader line as illustrated.

Example 1:

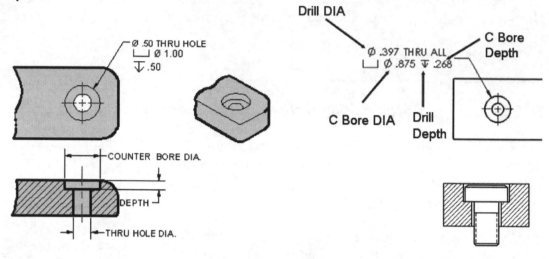

Counterbore holes are dimensioned by giving 1.) the diameter of the drill, 2.) the depth of the drill, 3.) the diameter of the counterbore, 4.) the depth of the counterbore, and 4.) the number of holes. Counterbore holes are displaced with the abbreviation C'BORE, C BORE or the symbol ⊔.

The difference between a C'BORE and a SPOTFACE is that the machining operation occurs on a curved surface.

The Countersunk hole, as illustrated, is a cone-shaped recess machined in a part to receive a cone-shaped flat head screw or bolt.

A Countersunk hole is dimensioned by giving 1.) the diameter of the hole, 2.) the depth of the hole 3.) the diameter of the Countersunk, 4.) the angle at which the hole is to be Countersunk, 5.) the Counterbore diameter, 6.) the depth of the Counterbore, and 7.) the number of holes to be Countersunk.

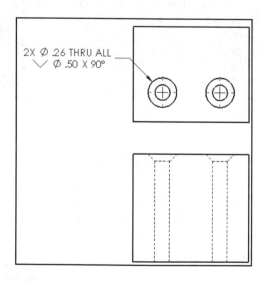

The text in brackets <>, indicates the <library name - symbol name>. Place the number of holes (3) and the multiplication sign (X) before the diameter dimension. Example: 3X<MOD-DIAM><DIM> THRU EQ SP is displayed on the drawing as: 6X Ø.50 THRU EQ SP.

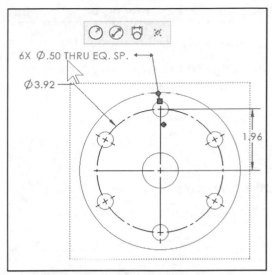

Two Extruded Cut features created the Counterbore in the Front view. The third Extruded Cut feature created the Counterbore in the Back. The Extruded Cut features did not produce the correct Counterbore Hole Callout according to a dimensioning standard. Utilize the Hole Callout tool to create the correct annotation. The mouse pointer displays the Hole Callout ⊔Ø icon, when the Hole Callout tool is active.

Create two Parametric notes to represent the Counterbore in the Front and Back view. A Parametric note contains dimensions from a part or drawing. Modify the dimension and the Parametric note to reflect the new value. Utilize the Centerline tool and Center Mark tool from the Annotation toolbar. Centerlines are composed of alternating long and short dash lines. The lines identify the center of a circle, axes, or cylindrical geometry.

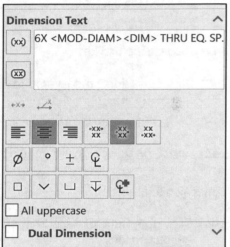

Center Marks represent two perpendicular intersecting centerlines.

Adjust adjacent extension lines after applying Center Marks.

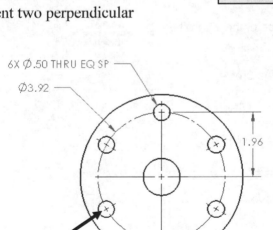

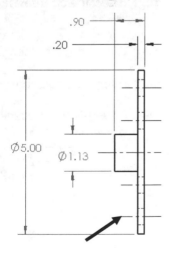

Activity: TUBE Drawing-Detailing Right View, Back View and Holes

---

Display the Right view.

137) Right-click **Drawing View3** in the
FeatureManager.

138) Click **Show**. Your drawing view
dimensions and locations may
vary.

Hide dimensions.

139) Click the Ø**5.00** dimension text.

140) Press the **Ctrl** key.

141) Click the Ø**5.00, 3.50, 8.50, 17.75**, and **27.25** dimension
text.

142) Release the **Ctrl** key.

143) Select the **HideDims** layer from the Other tab.

144) Click **OK** ✔ from the Dimension PropertyManager.

145) Select the **Details** layer from the Layer toolbar.

Dimension the Ports.

146) Click **Hole CallOut** ⊔Ø from the
Annotation toolbar.

147) Select the **circumference** of the left Port as
illustrated.

148) Click a **position** above the profile.

149) Enter **2X** before the <MOD-DIAM> text.

150) Click **Yes** to the Break Link with Model
dialog box.

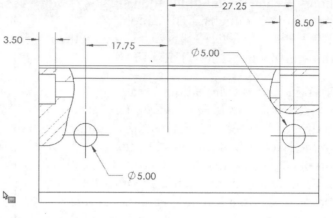

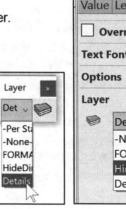

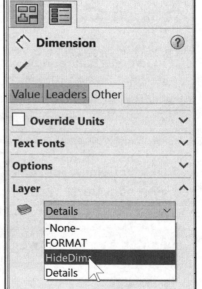

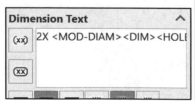

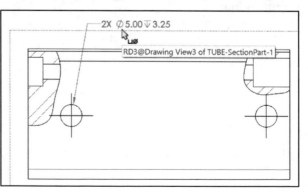

151) Press the **space** key.

152) Click **Hole CallOut** ⌴⌀ from the Annotation toolbar

153) Click **OK** ✓ from the Dimension PropertyManager.

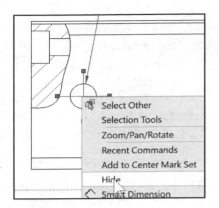

💡 Modify the part dimension from ⌀5 to ⌀6 and the drawing annotation updates. Manually edit the dimension text from ⌀5 to ⌀6 in the Hole Callout and the part dimension remains unchanged.

Add the vertical and horizontal dimensions.

154) **Hide** the two Center Marks on the Port holes.

155) Click **Smart Dimension** ✐ from the Annotation toolbar.

156) Click the **bottom horizontal edge**.

157) Click the left side of the **circumference** of the first circle.

158) Click a **position** to the left of the vertical profile line. The 14.50 dimension text is displayed.

159) Select **.1** from the Primary Unit Precision text box. The 14.5 dimension text is displayed.

160) Repeat for above procedure for the horizontal dimensions; **10** and **55**. Note: Click the lower left vertical edge to the gap.

161) Address **all trailing zeroes** and **gaps** as illustrated.

Save the TUBE drawing.

162) Click **Save** 💾.

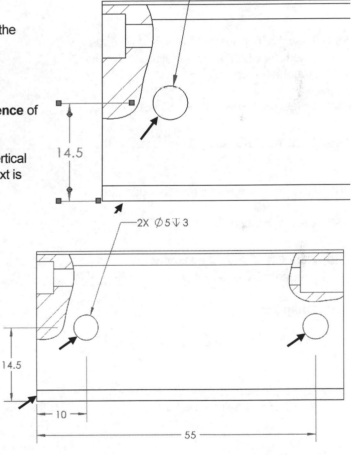

Select edges, not vertices when creating linear dimensions. Select the circumference of the circle not the Center Mark annotation when referencing the center point of circular geometry.

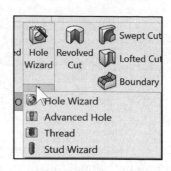

The original TUBE model was imported geometry. The Cbore features were not created using the the Hole Wizard. It used a cut feature. As a result, you cannot use the Hole Callout tool in the Annotation tab.

The Hole Callout tool adds driven diameter dimensions to holes created by the Holes Wizard feature.

View a Hole Wizard model and Hole Callout drawing.

163) Open the **Hole Callout** drawing from the SOLIDWORKS 2022/Chapter 7 Hole Callout folder.

164) View the **Top view**. This dimension was inserted using the Hole Callout tool in the Annotation tab.

165) Delete the **Hole call out dimension**.

166) Click the **Hole Callout** ⊔Ø icon in the Annotation tab.

167) Click the **circumference** as illustrated.

168) Click a position to the **top left**.

169) Click **OK** ✔ from the Dimension PropertyManager.

170) **Open** the Part.

171) View the **CSK** feature created by the Hole Wizard.

172) Close the **Part** and the **Hole Callout** drawing. The TUBE drawing is open.

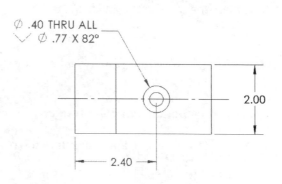

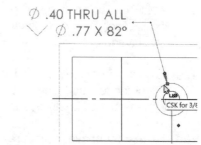

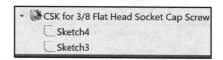

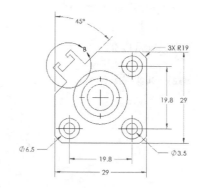

Insert a Note for the Counterbore. The Counterbore was not created with the Hole Wizard tool. It was imported geometry.

173) Click **Note** 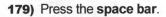 from the Annotation toolbar.

174) Click the **circumference** of the top right Counterbore in the Front view

175) Click a **position** to the top right of the view. Note: The Details layer is the active layer in the drawing.

176) Enter **3X**.

177) Press the **space bar**.

178) Click the ∅**3.5** dimension text in the Front view.

179) Press the **space bar**.

180) Enter **THRU**.

181) Press the **Enter** key.

182) Click the **Add Symbol** button in the Text Format box. **View** your options to add symbols into a drawing note.

183) Select **Hole Symbols** for Symbol library.

184) Click **Counterbore (Spotface)** ⎿⏌ .

185) Click **OK** from the Symbol Library.

186) Press the **space bar**.

187) Click the ∅**6.5** dimension text.

188) Repeat the above process for **Hole Depth** ▽ .

189) Press the **space** bar.

190) Enter **3.5**.

191) Click **OK** ✓ from the Note PropertyManager.

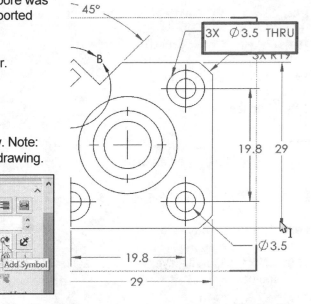

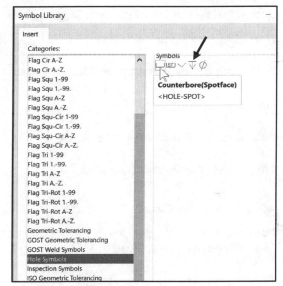

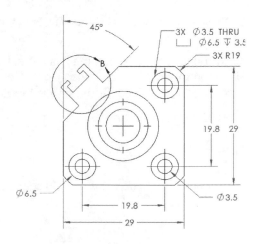

Hide the diameter dimensions.

192) Click the ∅**3.5** dimension in the Front view.

193) Hold the **Ctrl** key down.

194) Click the ∅**6.5** dimension.

195) Release the **Ctrl** key.

196) Select the **HideDims** 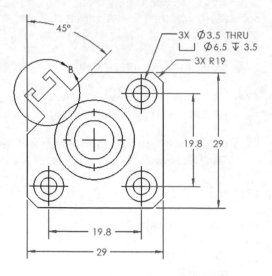 layer from the Dimension PropertyManager.

197) Click **OK** ✔ from the PropertyManager.

198) **Align** the dimension text.

199) Click the **Details** layer from the Layers toolbar.

Modify the layer in the Right view. Display HideDims.

200) Click inside the **Right view**.

201) Click the **HideDims** layer from the Layers toolbar.

202) Display **HideDims** 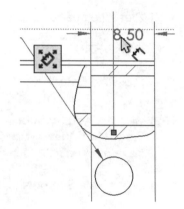.

203) Click the ∅**8.50** dimension text in the Right view.

204) Select the **Details** layer from the PropertyManager.

Add a Note to the Counterbore Rear.

205) Click **.1** for Primary Unit Precision. The 8.5 dimension is displayed.

206) Click **OK** ✔ from the Dimension PropertyManager.

207) Double-click on the **Cbore note** in the Front view.

Copy the text. At this time, there is a bug with the copy Note command. You can bypass this by creating a new note and link the ∅**6.5 dimension** in the Front view.

208) Select the **second line** of text.

209) Right-click **copy**.

210) Click **OK** ✔ from the Note PropertyManager.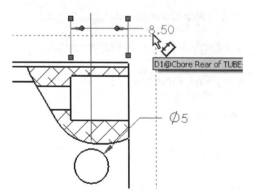

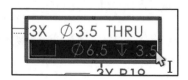

211) Click **Note** $\mathbb{A}$ from the Annotation toolbar.

212) Click the **circumference** of the top left Counterbore in the Back view.

213) Click a **position** for the Note.

Paste the Note.

214) Click-right **Paste**.

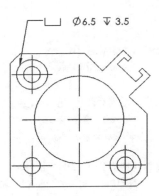

Edit the Note. Hide the 8.5 dimension in Drawing view3 (Right view).

215) Enter **2X** at the start of the line.

216) Press the **space** bar.

217) Delete the **3.5** Note text.

218) Click the **8.5** dimension text in the Right view.

219) Align the dimension text.

220) Click **OK** ✔ from the Note PropertyManager.

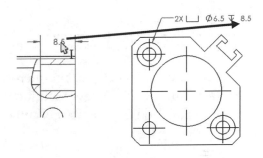

Hide the 8.5 dimension.

221) Click the **8.5** dimension text in the Right view.

222) Select the **HideDims** 🖉 layer.

223) Click **OK** ✔ from the Dimension PropertyManager.

224) Click the **Details** layer from the Layers toolbar.

💡 Delete automatically inserted Center Marks in the Right view before you investigate the next step.

Add Center Marks and a Centerline to the Right view.

225) Click **Center Mark** ⊕ from the Annotation toolbar. Note the options for Slot center marks.

226) Click the **Linear Center Mark** button.

227) Check the **Connection lines** box.

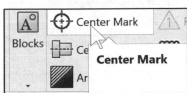

228) Click the circumference of the **left Port** in the Right view.

229) Click the circumference of the **right Port** in the Right view.

230) Click **OK** ✔ from the Center Mark PropertyManager. The two Center Marks and Centerline are displayed.

231) Drag the **centerlines** and **extension** lines off the Center Marks. Do not overlap the Center Marks.

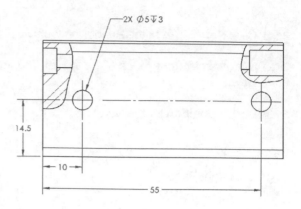

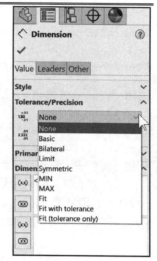

Tolerancing makes certain interchangeability in manufacturing. Parts can be manufactured by different companies in various locations while maintaining the proper functionality of the intended design.

In tolerancing, each dimension is permitted to vary within a specified amount. By assigning as large a tolerance as possible, without interfering with the functionality or intended design of a part, the production costs can be reduced and the product can be competitive. The smaller the tolerance range specified, the more expensive it is to manufacture. There is always a trade off in design.

To specify tolerance in the Hole Callout, insert the Hole Callout. Click inside the Dimension Text box and select the Tolerance type.

TUBE Drawing-Adding Dimensions

Add dimensions with the Smart Dimension tool in the drawing. The TUBE holes utilized symmetry in the initial Base sketch.

The profile contains horizontal and vertical construction lines sketched from the Origin to a midpoint. A Symmetric relationship with vertical and horizontal construction lines create a fully defined sketch. No additional dimension is required from the Origin to the center point of the hole.

Create new dimensions to locate the holes in relationship to the center of the Bore. Adjust all vertical and horizontal dimensions. Stagger and space dimension text for clarity. Create a gap between the extension lines and the Center Mark. The Auxiliary view is the last view to move and to add dimensions. Use a Hole Callout to specify size and depth. Add a dimension to locate the center of the hole. Move extension lines off the profile.

Activity: TUBE Drawing-Adding Dimensions

Create a vertical dimension in Drawing View1.

232) Click **Smart Dimension**  from the Annotations tab.

233) Click the **circumference** of the small right bottom hole.

234) Click the **circumference** of the center circle.

235) Drag the **9.90** dimension to the right of the vertical profile line.

236) Click **.1** for Primary Unit Precision. The 9.9 dimension is displayed.

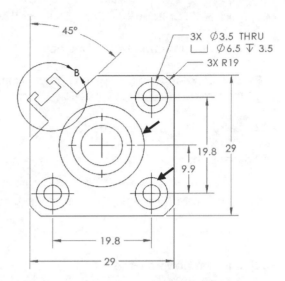

The Arc Condition option in the Dimension PropertyManager (Leaders tab) provides the ability to set the dimension between arcs or circles. The First arc condition specifies where on the arc or circle the distance is measured. The Second arc condition specifies where on the second selected item the distance is measured, when both items are arcs or circles.

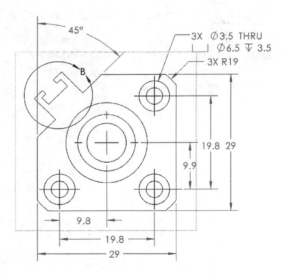

Create a horizontal dimension.

237) Click **Smart Dimension**  from the Annotations tab.

238) Click the **circumference** of the small left bottom hole.

239) Click the **circumference** of the center circle.

240) Drag the **dimension** below the horizontal profile line.

241) Click a **position**.

242) Click **.1** for Primary Unit Precision. The 9.8 dimension is displayed.

243) **Align** and **address any needed dimension** text.

244) Address any needed **gaps** between the feature line and the dimension extension line.

Add a Hole Callout to the Auxiliary view.

245) **Hide** the Center Mark in the Auxiliary view.

246) Click **Hole Callout** ⊔∅ from the Annotation toolbar.

247) Click the **circumference** of the hole.

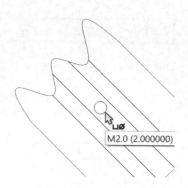

248) Click a **position** to the top left corner of the view. The depth of the Hole is calculated by the Hole Wizard.

249) Set Unit Precision to **None**.

Add dimensions.

250) Click **Smart Dimension** 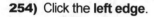 from the Annotation tab.

251) Click the **circumference** of the small hole.

252) Click the **bottom edge**.

253) Click a **position** to the right off the profile as illustrated. Set Unit Precision to **None**.

Create a Reference dimension.

254) Click the **left edge**.

255) Click the **right edge**.

256) Click a **position** below the profile.

257) Click **Add Parentheses** in the Dimension Text box.

258) Click **OK** ✔ from the Dimension PropertyManager.

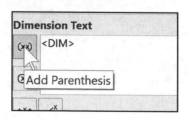

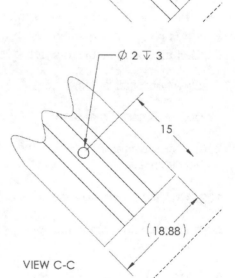

VIEW C-C

Insert a Center Mark.

259) Click **Center Mark** 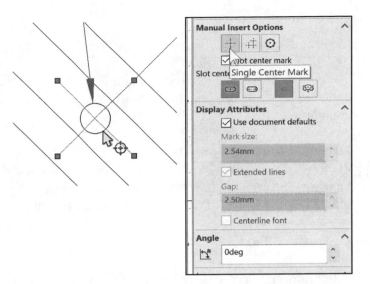 from the Annotation tab. The Center Mark PropertyManager is displayed. Single Center Mark is the default option.

260) Click the **circle** as illustrated. Click the **Single Center Mark** box.

261) Enter **0** for Angle to rotate the Center Mark. Click **OK** ✓ from the Center Mark PropertyManager.

Fit the Model to the Sheet.

262) Press the **f** key.

Save the TUBE drawing. As an exercise, insert the illustrated drawing Custom and Linked Properties in the Edit Sheet Format mode.

263) Click **Save** .

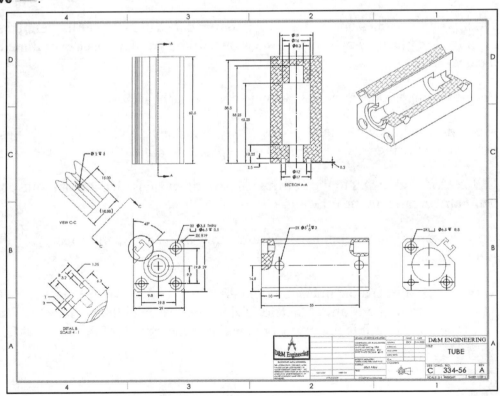

 **Review**

The TUBE drawing consisted of a single sheet with eight different views. Each view contained dimensions and annotations. You utilized layers to hide and display dimensions and annotations.

Feature dimensions were inserted from the part into the drawing. Dimensions were relocated in the view and moved to different views. Added dimensions were created in the drawing. Display options and alignment were used to modify the dimensions. Hole Callout annotations utilized symbols and dimension values to create Parametric notes.

Detailing Tips

Where do you create dimensions? Do you return to the part and change your dimension scheme to accommodate the drawing? Answer: No. Build the dimensioning scheme and design intent into the part.

Build parts with symmetric relationships. Use a line of symmetry in a sketch. Add Geometric relationships. Add reference dimensions in the drawing to detail part geometric relations such as Equal and Symmetry.

Modify part sketches and features to accommodate a drawing. Fully defined sketches are displayed in black. Drag sketch dimensions off the profiles. Insert part dimensions into the drawing.

Position dimensions in the best view to document the feature.

Move dimensions with the Shift key. Copy dimensions with the Ctrl key. Select a position inside the new view boundary to place the dimensions.

Utilize drawing layers to hide unwanted part dimensions, annotations, and construction geometry created in the drawing.

How do you display hundreds of feature dimensions for a part? Answer: Utilize the following tips:

- Organize dimension and annotation display with the FeatureManager. Select the feature from the FeatureManager. Select Insert Model Items, Selected Feature option. Repeat for multiple features from the top to the bottom of the FeatureManager.

- Utilize a two-view approach. Create a copy of the view and position the new view outside the sheet boundary. The copy of the view is called the "sloppy copy". Select the sloppy copy view boundary. Select Insert Model Items for the selected view. Utilize Ctrl-Select to choose multiple dimensions. Move the required dimensions from the sloppy copy to the original view inside the sheet boundary.

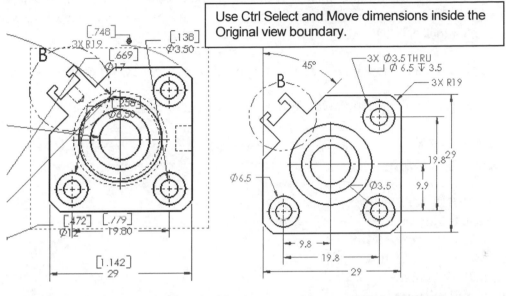

Sloppy Copy (Insert Model Items by View)   Move entities to Final view

- Create multiple part configurations with a Design Table. Configurations conserve design time and provide a record of the changes in a single part file.

Example: A Design Table controls the Suppressed/UnSuppressed State of the features. Utilize the Suppress configuration in the drawing. Replace the Fillet features with a note. To modify the note attachment point to the bent leader line, first position the note on the drawing. Select the note and then select the Attachment Leader Style

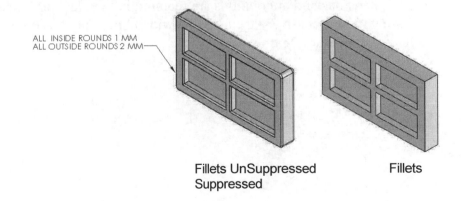

Fillets UnSuppressed   Fillets
Suppressed

- Drawings contain multiple sheets and views. The Lock Sheet Focus and the Lock View Focus options assist in complex drawings.

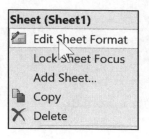

- Selecting the preferred view with the mouse is difficult when view boundaries overlap. Sketch entities belong to the view closest to the mouse pointer when you begin sketching.

- To reactivate the Dynamic drawing view activation option, right-click in the sheet boundary and select Unlock Sheet Focus, or right-click in the locked view boundary and select Unlock View Focus.

- Double-click any view boundary to activate the Dynamic drawing view activation option.

- Utilize the arrow keys to move views or notes by small increments.

COVERPLATE
Drawing-Detailing

The COVERPLATE utilizes Geometric relationships such as Symmetric to define the position of the features. The ∅8.25 dimension requires a Precision value of .12.

All of the remaining dimensions require a Precision value of .1 or None.

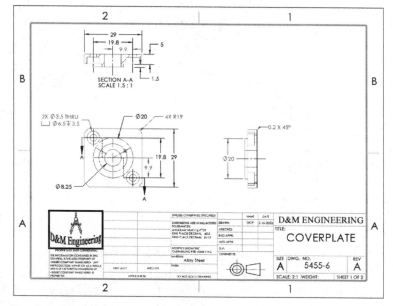

Modify the Document Properties Precision value to 1 decimal place. Review the geometric relations. What additional dimensions and annotations are required in the drawing? Answer: Locate the Counterbore with respect to the Center Hole with a linear dimension in the drawing. Add a Chamfer annotation in the drawing.

The COVERPLATE-Sheet1 Front view utilizes the Without Nose Holes configuration. Activate the part configuration to modify the dimension in the Front view. You cannot edit a dimension in the Sheet unless the configuration is active.

Activity: COVERPLATE Drawing-Detailing

Set Document Precision to .1. Set Tolerance to .12.

264) Open the COVERPLATE drawing. If you did not create the COVERPLATE drawing in Chapter 6, browse to SOLIDWORKS 2022/Chapter 7 Drawings.

265) Click the **Sheet1** tab.

266) Click **Options** ⚙ ˙, **Document Properties** tab, **Dimensions** from the Menu bar toolbar.

267) Select **.1** for Primary precision dimension value.

268) Select **.12** for Tolerance Precision.

269) Click **OK** from the Document Properties - Units dialog box.

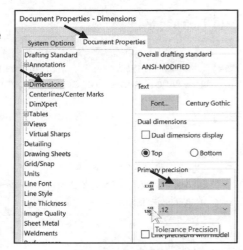

Create a Hole Callout.

270) Click **Hole Callout** ⊔⌀ from the Annotation tab. The Hole Callout PropertyManager is displayed.

271) Click the **Counterbore circumference** in Drawing View5 as illustrated.

272) Click a **position** above the profile as illustrated.

273) Enter **2X** in the Dimension Text box.

274) Click **Yes** in the Break Link with Model dialog box.

275) Click the **space** bar.

276) Click **OK** ✓ from the Dimension PropertyManager.

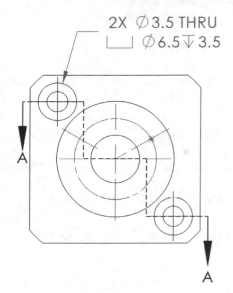

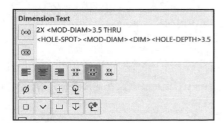

Insert the Model Item for individual features.

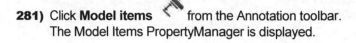
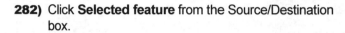

277) Click the **circumference** of the small center Bore feature in the Front view.

278) Hold the **Ctrl** key down.

279) Click the **circumference** of the large center Nose feature.

280) Release the **Ctrl** key.

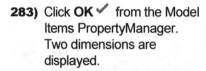
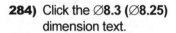

281) Click **Model items** from the Annotation toolbar. The Model Items PropertyManager is displayed.

282) Click **Selected feature** from the Source/Destination box.

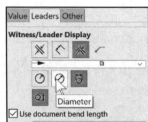

283) Click **OK** ✓ from the Model Items PropertyManager. Two dimensions are displayed.

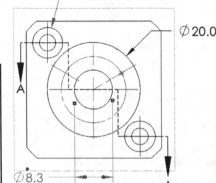

284) Click the ∅**8.3** (∅**8.25**) dimension text.

285) Click the **Leaders** tab.

286) Click **Diameter** from the Witness/Leader Display dialog box.

287) Click **OK** ✓ from the Dimension PropertyManager.

288) Move the **two dimensions** as illustrated.

289) Remove trailing zeroes from the ∅**20 dimension** text.

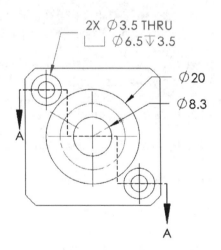

290) Click **OK** ✓ from the Dimension PropertyManager.

One of the goals in this book is to inform the SOLIDWORKS user on different ways to perform the same function.

Insert the Model Item for the Section view.

291) Click inside the **Section view** boundary.

292) Click **Model Items** from the Annotation tab. The Model Items PropertyManager is displayed.

293) Select **Entire model** from the Source/Destination box.

294) Click **OK** ✓ from the Model Items PropertyManager. The dimensions are displayed.

295) Eliminate all trailing zeroes in the Section view.

296) Hide the ∅**6.5**, ∅**3.5** and the **3.5** dimension text.

297) Drag the horizontal dimensions **29** and **19.8** 10mm away from the Profile line. A gap should exist between the extension lines and feature line.

Open the part.

298) Right-click in the **Section view A-A** boundary.

299) Click **Open Part**. The COVERPLATE is displayed in the graphics area.

🔆 The view utilizes the Without Holes Configuration.

Select the COVERPLATE Without Nose Holes Configuration.

300) Click the **ConfigurationManager** tab.

301) Double-click **Without Nose Holes**.

Return to the FeatureManager.

302) Click the **FeatureManager** tab. The active configuration is Without Nose Holes.

Return to the COVERPLATE drawing.

303) Right-click on the **COVERPLATE** name in the Part FeatureManager.

304) Click **Open Drawing**. The COVERPLATE drawing is displayed.

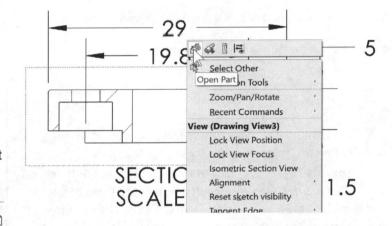

Insert Centerlines.

305) Click inside the **Section View A-A** boundary.

306) Click **Centerline** 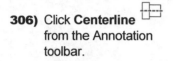 from the Annotation toolbar.

307) Click the **Select View** box. Click **OK** ✓ from the Centerline PropertyManager.

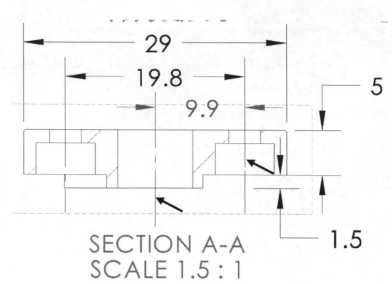

SECTION A-A
SCALE 1.5 : 1

Add a dimension.

308) Click **Smart Dimension** ◇ from the Annotation tab.

309) Click the **Centerline** of the Hole as illustrated.

310) Click the **Centerline** of the right Counterbore as illustrated.

311) Drag and click the **dimension** off the profile.

312) Click **OK** ✓ from the Dimension PropertyManager.

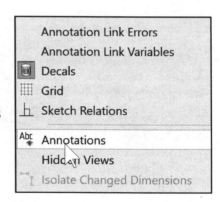

☼ To display a hidden dimension in the graphics area which is not on a layer, click **View, Hide / Show, Annotations** from the Main menu. The Hidden dimensions are displayed in the graphics area. Click the **dimension** to show in the graphics window. Click **View, Hide / Show, Annotations** from the Main menu to return to the graphics area.

Insert the remaining dimensions.

313) Click a **position** in the sheet boundary.

314) Click **Model Items** from the Annotation tab.

315) Select **Entire Model.**

316) Click **OK** ✓ from the Model Items PropertyManager.

317) Eliminate all trailing zeroes.

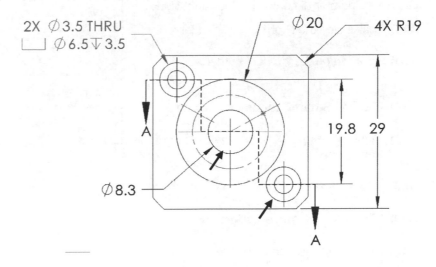

Create a vertical dimension in the Front view.

318) Click **Smart Dimension** ⌖ from the Annotation tab.

319) Click the **circumference** of the right Counterbore.

320) Click the **circumference** of the small center circle.

321) Click a **position** to the right of the profile.

322) Click **OK** ✓ from the Dimension PropertyManager.

323) Modify the ⌀8.3 dimension to ⌀8.25. Precision of .2.

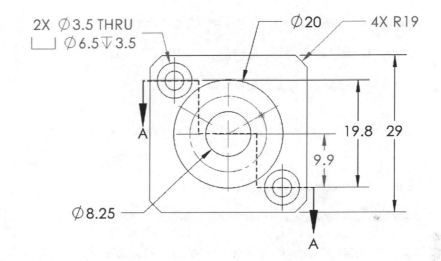

💡 If the extension line references the arc tangent, drag the endpoint of the extension line to the center point to create a center-to-center dimension.

Create a Chamfer dimension in the Right view.

324) Click inside the **Right view** boundary.

325) Zoom in on the top right corner.

326) Click the **Smart Dimension** tool.

327) Right-click **More Dimensions** from the Pop-up menu.

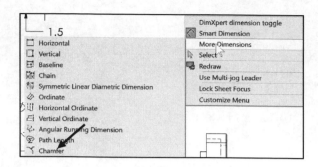

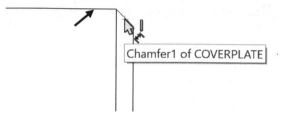

328) Click **Chamfer**.

329) Click the small **angled edge**.

330) Click the top **horizontal edge**.

331) Click a **position** to place the dimension.

332) Click **OK** ✔ from the Dimension PropertyManager.

Display Hidden Lines Visible to display the Bore feature.

333) Click inside the **Right view**.

334) Click **Hidden Lines Visible** from the View Heads-up toolbar.

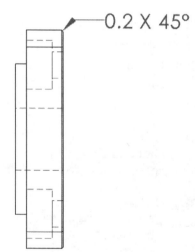

Display a Centerline. Add a dimension.

335) Click **Centerline** from the Annotation toolbar.

336) Click **OK** ✔ from the Centerline PropertyManager.

337) Add a **dimension** as illustrated.

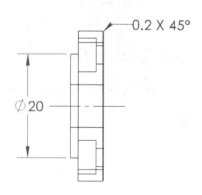

Control individual line display with the Show/Hide option. Control individual Line font. Right-click a component in the drawing. Select Component Line Font. Select the Type of edge, Line style, Line weight and Layer. Click OK.

Save the COVERPLATE drawing.

338) Click **Save** 💾 .

Insert and add dimensions and annotations, and drawing Custom and Linked Properties as an exercise to complete the COVERPLATE drawing.

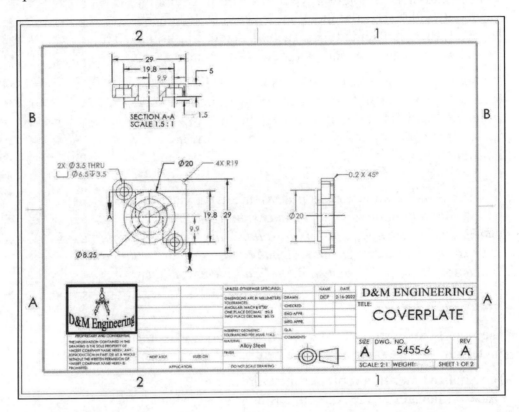

 **Review**

The COVERPLATE-Sheet1 Front view utilizes the Without Nose Holes configuration. You located the Counterbore with respect to the Center Hole with a linear dimension in the drawing. You added a Chamfer annotation in the drawing along with various display modes. Added dimensions were created in the drawing. Display options and alignment were used to modify the dimensions. Hole Callout annotations utilized symbols and dimension values to create Parametric notes.

Annotation Toolbar

Add annotations to a drawing document using the Annotation toolbar from the CommandManager.

You can add most annotation types in a part or assembly document, and then insert them into a drawing document. However, there are some types, such as Center Marks and Area Hatch that you can only add in a drawing document.

Annotations behave like dimensions in a SOLIDWORKS document. You can add dimensions in a part or assembly document, then insert the dimensions into the drawing, or create dimensions directly in the drawing. Below are a few of the Annotation tools.

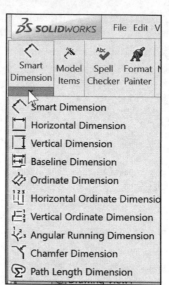

The Smart Dimension drop-down menu provides access to the following options: *Smart Dimension, Horizontal Dimension, Vertical Dimension, Baseline Dimension, Ordinate Dimension, Horizontal Ordinate Dimension, Vertical Ordinate Dimension, Chamfer Dimension, and Path Length Dimension.*

Smart Dimension tool

The Smart Dimension ✧ tool provides the ability to create a dimension for one or more selected entities in the drawing.

The Smart Dimension tool uses the Dimension PropertyManager or the Autodimension PropertyManager.

The Dimension PropertyManager provides the ability to select either the **DimXpert** or **Autodimension** tab. Each tab provides a separate menu. Note: The DimXpert tab is selected by default.

Model Items tool

The Model Items ✧ tool provides the ability to import dimensions, annotations, and reference geometry from the referenced model into the selected view of the drawing. You can insert items into a selected feature, an assembly component, an assembly feature, a drawing view or all views. When inserting items into all drawing views, dimensions and annotations are displayed in the most appropriate view. Edit the inserted locations if required.

Note tool

The Note $\mathbf{A}$ tool adds a note to the selected drawing sheet. A note can be free floating or fixed. A note can be placed with a leader pointing to an item, face, edge, or vertex in your document. A note can contain simple text, symbols, parametric text, and hyperlinks. The leader can be straight, bent or multi-jog. Use the Note tool to create a note or to edit an existing note, balloon note or a revision symbol.

Linear Note Pattern tool

The Linear Note Pattern tool adds a note to the selected drawing sheet. A note can be free floating or fixed. A note can be placed with a leader pointing to an item, face, edge, or vertex in your document.

Circular Note Pattern tool

The Circular Note Pattern tool adds a note to the selected drawing sheet. A note can be free floating or fixed. A note can be placed with a leader pointing to an item, face, edge, or vertex in your document.

Spell Checker tool

The Spell Checker tool checks for misspelled words in documents. This tool checks notes, dimensions with text, and drawing title blocks when you are in the Edit Sheet Format mode. The Spell Checker tool will not check words in a table and is only available in English using Microsoft Word 2000 or later.

Format Painter tool

The Format Painter tool provides the ability to copy visual properties from dimensions and annotations to other dimensions and annotations in the same document or another document. Format Painter is supported by parts, assemblies, and drawings. The Format tool uses the Format PropertyManager.

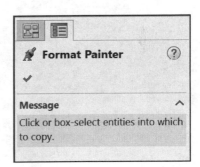

Balloon tool

The Balloon ⌖ tool provides the ability to create a single balloon or multi balloons in an assembly or drawing document. The balloons label the parts in the assembly and relate them to item numbers on the bill of materials (BOM). The Balloon tool uses the Balloon PropertyManager.

💡 You do not have to insert a BOM in order to add balloons. If your drawing does not have a BOM, the item numbers are the default values that SOLIDWORKS would use if you did have a BOM. If there is no BOM on the active sheet, but there is a BOM on another sheet, the numbers from that BOM are used.

AutoBalloon tool

The AutoBalloon ⌖ tool provides the ability to add balloons for all components in the selected view.

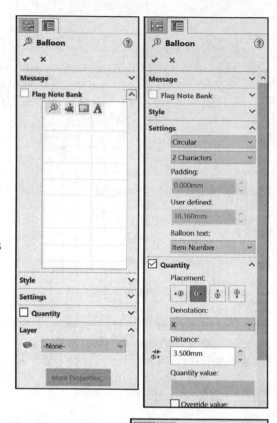

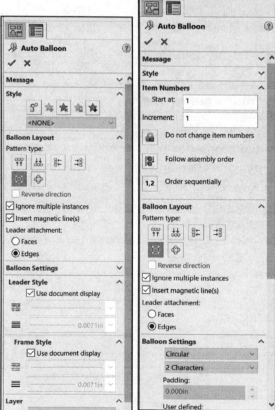

Magnetic Line tool

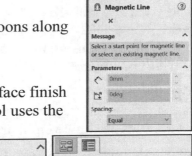

The Magnetic Line 🧲 tool provides the ability to align balloons along a line at any angle.

Surface Finish tool

The Surface Finish ✓ tool provides the ability to add a surface finish symbol to the selected drawing view. The Surface Finish tool uses the Surface Finish PropertyManager.

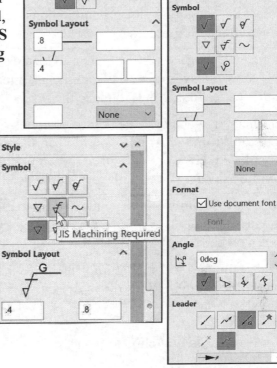

- **Symbol**. Basic and Local - selected by default. The Symbol box provides the following selections for Surface Finish symbols: **Basic**, **Machining Required**, **Machining Prohibited, JIS Basic, JIS Machining Required, JIS Machining Prohibited Local**, and **All Around**.

💡 If you select JIS Basic or JIS Machining Required, several surface textures are available.

- **Symbol Layout**. For ANSI symbols and symbols using ISO and related standards prior to 2002, specify text for the predefined locations around the symbol:
  - **Maximum Roughness, Minimum Roughness, Material Removal Allowance, Production Method/Treatment, Sampling Length, Other Roughness Values, Roughness Spacing**, and **Lay Direction**.

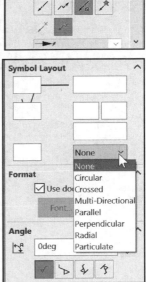

Weld Symbol tool

The Weld Symbol 〽 tool provides the ability to add a weld symbol on a selected entity, edge, face, etc. Create and apply the weld symbol by using the Properties dialog box under the ANSI Weld Symbol tab.

Weld beads use a simplified display. They are displayed as graphical representations in models. No geometry is created. The weld beads are lightweight and do not affect performance.

The dialog box is displayed for ISO, BSI, DIN, JIS and GB standards. Different dialog boxes are displayed for ANSI and GOST standards. The book addresses the ANSI dialog box. The dialog box displays numerous selections. Enter values and select the required symbols and options. A preview is displayed in the Graphics window.

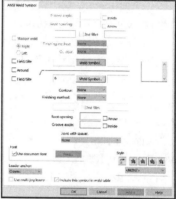

Click a face or edge where you want to locate a welded joint. If the weld symbol has a leader, click a location to place the leader first. Click to place the symbol.

If you selected a face or edge before you click the Weld Symbol tool from the Annotation toolbar, the leader is already placed; click once to place the symbol. Click as many times as necessary to place multiple weld symbols.

Construct weld symbols independently in a part, assembly, or drawing document. When you create or edit your weld symbol, you can:

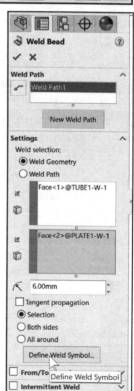

- Add secondary weld fillet information to the weld symbol for certain types of weld, example: Square or Bevel.

- Choose a Leader anchor of None.

- Choose the text font for each weld symbol.

Geometric Tolerance tool

The SOLIDWORKS software supports the ANSI Y14.5 Geometric and True Position Tolerancing guidelines. These standards represent the drawing practices used by U.S. industry. The ASME Y14 practices supersede the American National Standards Institute ANSI standards.

The ASME Y14 Engineering Drawing and Related Documentation Practices are published by The American Society of Mechanical Engineers, New York, NY. References to the current ASME Y14 standards are used with permission.

ASME Y14 Standard Name:	American National Standard Engineering Drawing and Related Documentation:	Revision of the Standard:
ASME Y14.100M-1998	Engineering Drawing Practices	DOD-STD-100
ASME Y14.1-1995	Decimal Inch Drawing Sheet Size and Format	ANSI Y14.1
ASME Y14.1M-1995	Metric Drawing Sheet Size and Format	ANSI Y14.1M
ASME Y14.24M	Types and Applications of Engineering Drawings	ANSI Y14.24M
ASME Y14.2M(Reaffirmed 1998)	Line Conventions and Lettering	ANSI Y14.2M
ASME Y14.3M-1994	Multi-view and Sectional View Drawings	ANSI Y14.3
ASME Y14.41-2003	Digital Product Definition Data Practices	N/A
ASME Y14.5M –1994 (Reaffirmed 1999)	Dimensioning and Tolerancing	ANSI Y14.5-1982 (R1988)

Datum Feature tool

The Datum Feature ⒶＴ tool adds a Datum Feature symbol. Attach a datum feature symbol to the following items:

- In an assembly or part, on a reference plane, or on a planar model surface.

- In a drawing view, on a surface that is displayed as an edge, not a silhouette or on a section view surface.

- A geometric tolerance symbol frame.

- In a note.

On a dimension, with the following exceptions:

- Chamfer dimensions.

- Angular dimensions, unless the symbols are displayed per the 1982 standard.

- Ordinate dimensions.

- Arc dimensions.

Datum Target tool

The Datum Target 🔄 tool provides the ability to attach a datum target and symbol to a model face or edge in a document. The Datum Target tool uses the Datum Target PropertyManager.

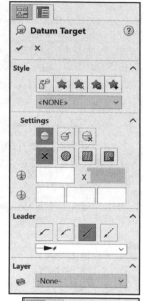

- The available Target areas are: x target area, (point), Circular target area, (applies crosshatch to the circular target area), Rectangular target area, (applies crosshatch to the rectangular target area), and Do not display target area.

- Target area size, Specify Width and Height (for rectangles) or Diameter (for X's and circles).

- Datum references Specify up to three references (balloons). The datum reference appears in the lower half of the balloon.

Hole Callout tool

The Hole Callout ⌴⌀ tool adds a Hole Callout to the selected view in your drawing. The Hole callout contains a diameter symbol and the dimension of the hole diameter. If the depth of the hole is known, the Hole Callout will also contain a depth symbol and the dimension of the depth.

The Hole Callout tool uses the information from the Hole Wizard, if the hole was created by the Hole Wizard. The Dimension PropertyManager is displayed when using the Hole Callout tool.

Revision Symbol tool

The Revision Symbol ⚠ tool provides the ability to insert a revision symbol into a drawing with a revision already in the table. Insert a revision table into a drawing to track document revisions. In addition to the functionality for all tables, you can select Revision symbol shapes or an alphabetic or numeric sequence. The latest revision is displayed under REV in the lower-right corner of a sheet format.

The Revision Symbol tool uses the Revision Symbol PropertyManager. The Revision Symbol PropertyManager uses the same conventions as the Note PropertyManager.

Revision Cloud tool

The Revision Cloud 💭 tool provides the ability to create cloud-like shapes in a drawing.

The Revision Cloud tool uses the Revision Cloud PropertyManager.

Area Hatch/Fill tool

The Area Hatch/Fill ◣ tool provides the ability to add an area hatch or fill pattern in a drawing. Apply a solid fill or a crosshatch pattern to a closed sketch profile, model face, or to a region bounded by a combination of model edges and sketch entities. You can only apply an Area Hatch in drawings. Some characteristics of Area Hatch include the following:

- If the Area Hatch is a solid fill, the default color of the fill is black.

- You can move an Area Hatch into a layer.

- You can select an Area Hatch in a Broken View only in its unbroken state.

- You cannot select an Area Hatch that crosses a break.

- Dimensions or annotations that belong to the drawing view are surrounded by a halo of space when they are on top of an area hatch or fill.

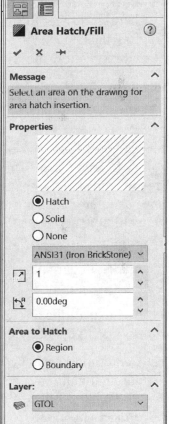

Block tool

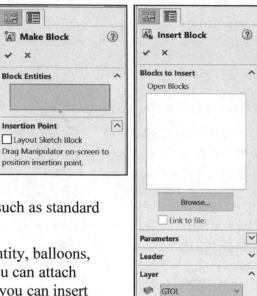

- The Block A⁰ tool from the Annotation toolbar provides the ability to either select the Make Block tool or the Insert Block tool. The Make Block tool uses the Make Block PropertyManager. The Insert Block tool uses the Insert Block PropertyManager.

- You can make, save, edit, and insert blocks for drawing items that you use often, such as standard notes, title blocks, label positions, etc.

- Blocks can include text, any type of sketch entity, balloons, imported entities and text, and area hatch. You can attach blocks to geometry or to drawing views, and you can insert them into sheet formats. You can also copy blocks between drawings and sketches, or insert blocks from the Design Library. View the Block section for additional information.

Center Mark tool

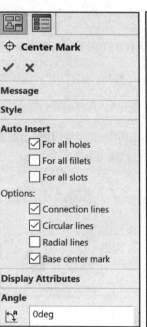
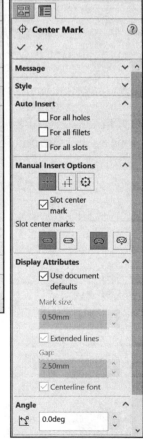

The Center Mark ⊕ tool provides the ability to locate center marks on circles or arcs in a drawing. Use the center mark lines as references for dimensioning. A few items to note about center marks are:

- Center marks are available as single marks, in Circular, Linear patterns or in a Slot center mark.

- The axis of the circle or arc must be normal to the drawing sheet.

- Center marks can be inserted automatically into new drawing views for holes or fillets if required using the option selection.

- Center marks propagate or insert automatically into patterns if the pattern is created from a feature and not a body or face.

- Center marks in Auxiliary Views are oriented to the viewing direction such that one of the lines of the center mark is parallel to the view arrow direction.

- Rotate center marks individually by specifying the rotation in degrees. Using the Rotate Drawing View dialog box.

Centerline tool

The Centerline ⊞ tool provides the ability to insert centerlines into drawing views manually. The Centerline tool uses the Centerline PropertyManager. The Centerline PropertyManager provides the following two messages: 1.) Select two edges/sketch segments or single cylindrical/conical/toroidal face for Centerline insertion; 2.) To automatically insert centerlines for entire views, select the auto insert option and then select one or more drawing views.

☀ To insert centerlines automatically into a drawing view, select **Centerlines** from the Document Properties, Detailing, Auto insert on view creation section.

Consolidated Table Toolbar

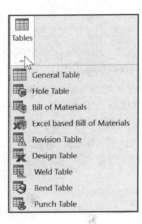

The Consolidated Table toolbar provides the ability to add a table in a drawing. The toolbar is document and function dependent. See SOLIDWORKS help for additional information.

SOLIDWORKS Detached Drawings

Detached drawings are designed so you can open and work in the drawing document without loading the model files into memory or even being present. This means you can send a Detached drawing to other SOLIDWORKS users without loading and sending the model files.

A Detached drawing provides the ability to save time when editing a drawing with complex parts or a very large assembly. A Detached drawing provides control over updating the drawing to the model. Members of the design team can work independently on the drawing, adding details and annotations, while other members edit the model.

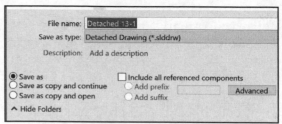

When the drawing and the model are synchronized, all the details and dimensions added to the drawing update to any geometric or topological changes in the model.

You can save a regular drawing as a Detached drawing and vice versa. A Detached drawing cannot be a Lightweight drawing. In the FeatureManager design tree, the icons for Detached drawings display a broken link:

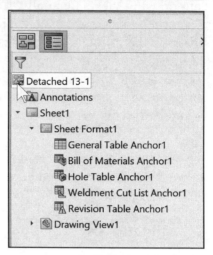

- Drawing icon for Detached drawing.

- Drawing view icon (model view) for Detached drawing with model not loaded.

If the referenced model is needed for you to complete an operation in a Detached drawing, you are prompted to load the model file. You can load the model by right-clicking a view and selecting Load Model. If the model is unavailable or fails to load, you cannot perform the selected operation. Model files are necessary when you want to: **crop drawing views**, **break drawing views**, **create section views**, **flip or change section lines**, **insert alternate position and relative views**, and **insert model items**.

Questions:

1. Explain the difference between trailing and leading zeroes using the ANSI drafting standard.

2. What does MMGS stand for in the Unit System?

3. Name three Tolerance Types and how you would address them in a part.

4. Describe the order of Precedence of Linear Dimension lines in a drawing.

5. Explain the procedure to add a layer in a drawing.

6. True or False. You can only add two layers in a drawing.

7. Describe the procedure to move a part dimension from one view to another.

8. Explain the Model Items tool. Describe a few options.

9. Name 4 different Table types that you can create in a SOLIDWORKS drawing.

10. Describe a Detached Drawing.

11. Identify 5 Surface Finish Symbols in SOLIDWORKS.

12. Define Ordinate Dimensioning.

13. Why would you use the Center Mark tool in a drawing?

14. Why would you use the Centerline tool in a drawing?

Exercises

Exercise 7.1:

Open the Rib-Model part in the SOLIDWORKS 2022/Homework 7 folder. View the model and features.

Create an A-Landscape, ANSI, IPS, Third Angle Projection drawing with a Front, Top, Right and Isometric view. Sheet1 scale: 1:3.

Use the standard SW Sheet format and Drawing Template, then add the needed Custom and Link Properties in the Part and Drawing.

Insert all need dimensions, Notes, Annotations, Center Marks, Centerlines, etc.

Address all needed extension line gaps, tangent edges, line types, display modes, etc.

Your drawing should look like the below illustration.

Address the Title Box information in the Edit Sheet Format mode.

Insert your school or work logo and name.

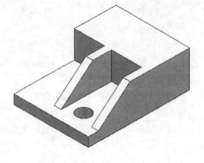

	Property Name	Type	Value / Text Expression	Evaluated Value
1	Material	Text	"SW-Material@Rib-Model.SLDPRT"	6061 Alloy
2	Description	Text	RIB	RIB
3	<Type a new property>			

	Property Name	Type	Value / Text Expression	Evaluated Value
1	CompanyName	Text	School Name	School Name
2	Revision	Text	A	A
3	DrawnBy	Text	DCP	DCP
4	DrawnDate	Text	2-2-2022	2-2-2022
5	PartNo	Text	1001	1001
6	Description	Text	Rib	Rib
7	Number	Text	1002	1002
8	SWFormatSize	Text	8.5in*11in	8.5in*11in
9				

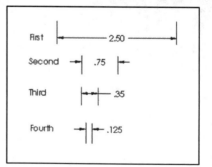

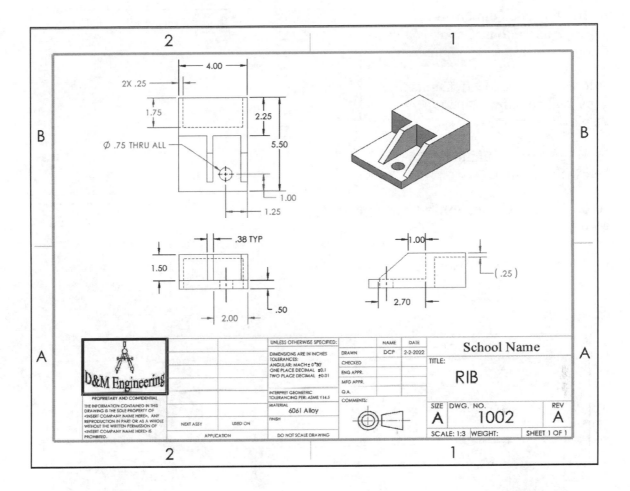

Exercise 7.2:

Open the U-Block part in the SOLIDWORKS 2022/Homework 7 folder. View the model and features.

Create an A-Landscape, ANSI, MMGS, Third Angle Projection drawing with a Front, Top, Right and Isometric view. Hide the Top view. Sheet1 scale: 1:2. Isometric view scale: 1:4.

Use the standard SW Sheet format and Drawing Template, then add the needed Custom and Link Properties in the Part and Drawing.

	Property Name	Type	Value / Text Expression	Evaluated Value
1	Description	Text	U BLOCK	U BLOCK
2	Material	Text	"SW-Material@U Block.SLDPRT"	6061 Alloy
3	<Type a new property>			

Insert all needed dimensions,
Notes, Annotations, Center Marks,
Centerlines, etc.

	Property Name	Type	Value / Text Expression	Evaluated Value
1	CompanyName	Text	School Name	School Name
2	Revision	Text	A	A
3	Description	Text	U-BLOCK	U-BLOCK
4	DrawnBy	Text	DCP	DCP
5	DrawnDate	Text	2-2-2022	2-2-2022
6	SWFormatSize	Text	215.9mm*279.4mm	215.9mm*279.4mm
7	Number	Text	223-66	223-66
8	<Type a new property>			

Address all needed extensions line
gaps, tangent edges, line types,
display modes, etc.

Your drawing should look like the
below illustration.

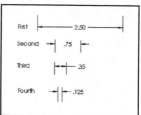

Address the Title Box information in the Edit Sheet Format
mode.

Insert your school or work logo and name.

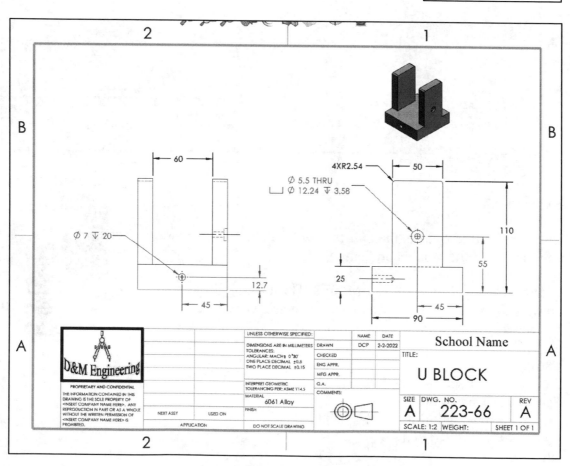

Exercise 7.3:

Open the RADIUS-ROUNDED END part in the SOLIDWORKS 2022/Homework 7 folder. Edit Sketch1. View the model.

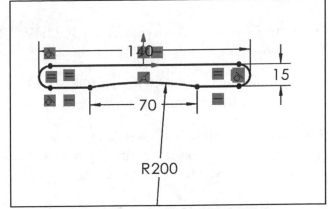

Create an A-Landscape, ANSI, MMGS, Third Angle Projection drawing with a Front view. Sheet1 scale: 1:1.

Add a Foreshorten Radius for the R200 as illustrated.

Create an overall dimension for the partially rounded ends. Modify the Radius text according to the ASME Y14.5 standard.

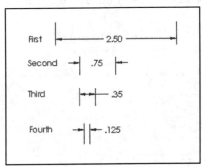

Your drawing should look like the below illustration.

Address the Title Box information in the Edit Sheet Format mode. Address all Link and Custom Properties in the part and drawing.

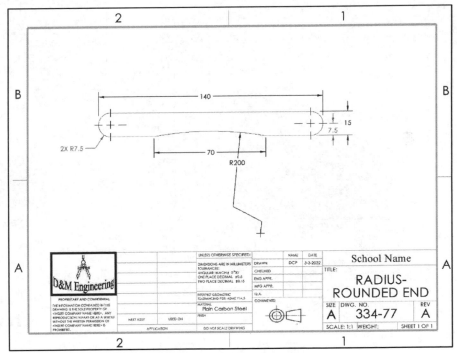

Exercise 7.4:

Open the TABLE-PLATE part in the SOLIDWORKS 2022/Homework 7 folder. View the model.

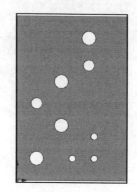

Create an A-Landscape, ANSI, MMGS, Third Angle Projection drawing with a Front view. Sheet1 scale: 1:4.

Rectangular coordinate dimensioning locates features with respect to one another, from a datum or an origin. Dimension the TABLE-PLATE with Base Line Dimensioning.

Your drawing should look like the below illustration.

Address the Title Box information in the Edit Sheet Format mode. Address all Link and Custom Properties in the part and drawing.

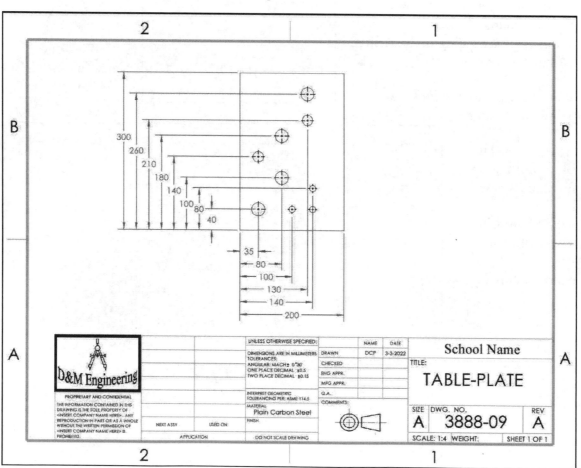

Exercise 7.5:

Open the MOUNTINGPLATE-CYLIDER part in the SOLIDWORKS 2022/Homework 7 folder. View the model.

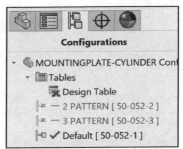

Create an A-Landscape, ANSI, MMGS, Third Angle Projection drawing with a Front view. Use the 3 PATTERN configuration on Sheet1.

Insert dimensions and Hole Callouts. Hide superfulous dimensions.

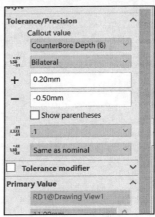

ASME Y14.5 defines a dimension for a repeating feature in the following order: number of features, an X, a space and the size of the feature. Example: 12X Ø3.5.

Modify the CounterBore Depth Callout value to include a Bilateral tolerance +0.2/-0.5. Note: At this time there is a bug with the SW software to addres the CounterBore Hole CallOut with the correct trailing zeroes.

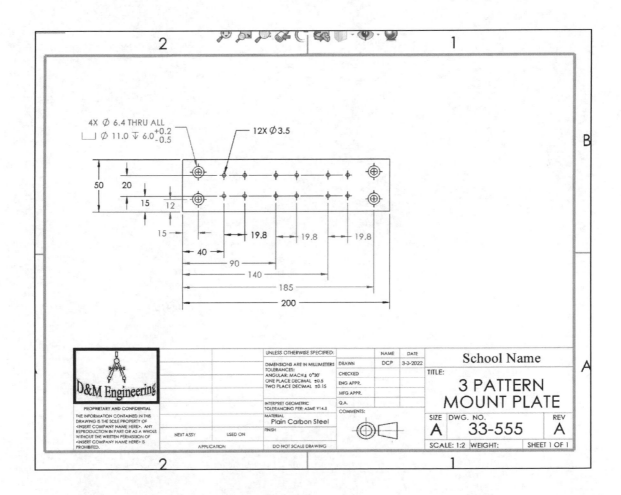

Notes:

Chapter 8

Assembly Drawings

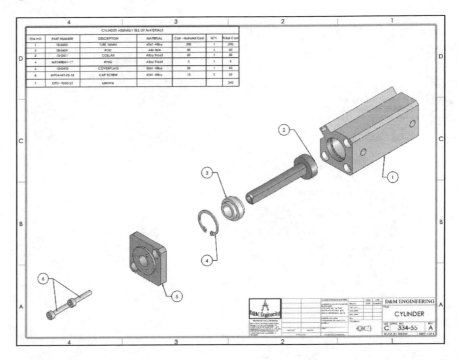

Below are the desired outcomes and usage competencies based on the completion of Chapter 8.

Desired Outcomes:	Usage Competencies:
An Assembly and Part drawing: • CYLINDER assembly with Custom Properties and a Design Table.	• Ability to create an assembly drawing with multiple Sheets and configurations.
	• An understanding of Custom Properties, Linked Properties and SOLIDWORKS Properties.
• CYLINDER assembly drawing with 3 Sheets, 5 drawing views, Custom Sheet format and Custom Drawing Properties. • COVERPLATE4 Part drawing.	• Aptitude to apply Custom Drawing Templates and Custom Sheet formats. • Apply Balloons and Sort by Cost in the Bill of Materials.
• Bill of Materials with Equations and Revision Table.	• Knowledge to develop and incorporate a Bill of Materials and Revision Tables.

Notes:

Chapter 8 - Assembly Drawings

Chapter Objective

You will create the following in this chapter:

- CYLINDER assembly with Custom Properties and a Dcsign Table.

- CYLINDER drawing with multiple sheets and linked Bill of Materials (BOM) using equations.

- COVERPLATE4 drawing with a Revision Table.

Insert an Exploded Isometric assembly view in the CYLINDER drawing. Add Custom Properties to the parts to describe: Part Number, Description, Material, Cost, and Total Cost. Insert a Design Table in the CYLINDER drawing to create five different configurations of the assembly.

Create three sheets for the CYLINDER drawing:

- Sheet1: Exploded Isometric view, Balloon labels, with a Bill of Materials using equations.

- Sheet2: Multiple configurations of the CYLINDER assembly with corresponding Bill of Materials.

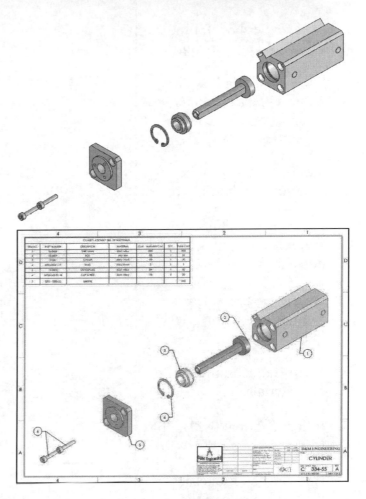

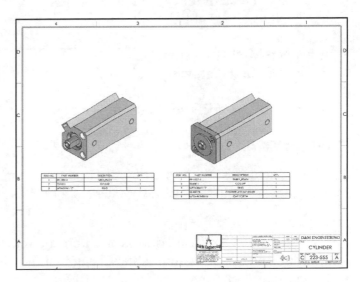

- Sheet3: Show/Hide options and configurations in drawing views.

Create a single sheet for the COVERPLATE4 drawing:

- Sheet1: Insert a Revision Table and Part Number using Link and Custom Properties.

On the completion of this chapter, you will be able to:

- Insert an assembly with multiple configurations into a drawing.

- Display an Exploded Isometric assembly view in a drawing.

- Insert Balloons and a Bill of Materials.

- Edit and format the Bill of Materials.

- Add Custom Properties to the components of the CYLINDER assembly.

- Link and Modify Custom Properties in the drawing and part.

- Modify View Properties in the drawing.

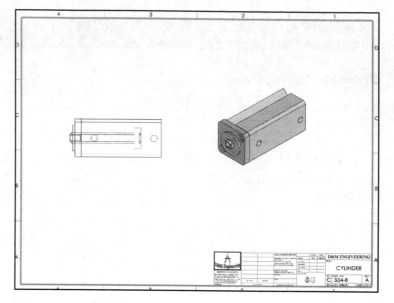

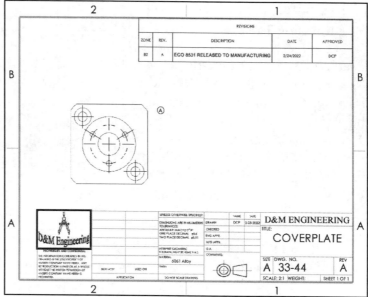

Chapter Overview

The Manufacturing and Marketing department requires a CYLINDER drawing. Manufacturing requires a Bill of Materials for the assembly configuration.

Creating a Bill of Materials is an automatic function that uses a table similar to the Hole Table and the Revision Table. Changes at the assembly level (deletions, reordering, additions and so on) are reflected in the BOM.

Create the CYLINDER
assembly with Custom and
Linked Properties and a
Design Table.

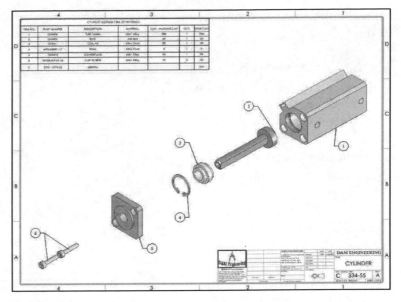

The CYLINDER drawing
consists of multiple
configurations of the
CYLINDER assembly and a
custom Bill of Materials.

Sheet1 contains an Exploded
Isometric view with a Bill of
Materials using equations.

Sheet2 contains two
CYLINDER configurations.
The COVERPLATE and
CAP-SCREWS are
suppressed in the Top Left
Isometric view.

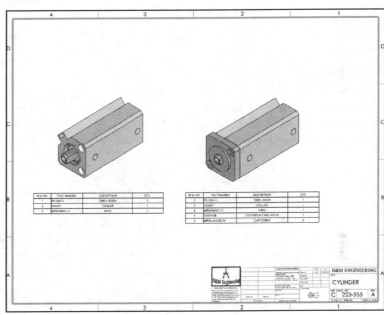

Custom Properties and
Custom Sheet formats are
used with Linked Properties.

The two parts:
COVERPLATE and CAP-
SCREWS are unsuppressed
in the Top Right Isometric
view.

The Bill of Materials reflects
the two different
configurations.

Insert Custom properties in a part; they propagate to the Design Table. Insert
Custom properties in a Design Table; they propagate to the part if the link is active.

A goal of this book is to expose the new user to various SOLIDWORKS design
tools and features. The most direct way may not be always shown.

Sheet3 contains two Front views of the COVERPLATE part.

The Left Front view displays the WithNoseHoles configuration.

The Right Front view displays the WithoutNoseHoles configuration. Custom Properties and a Custom Sheet format are used.

COVERPLATE4-Sheet1 contains the Revision Table. Use a Custom Sheet format, Custom Properties, and Linked Properties.

Add a Sheet to a drawing. If the system can't locate the Sheet format, add the Sheet format in File Location under System Options or Browse to the correct Sheet format location.

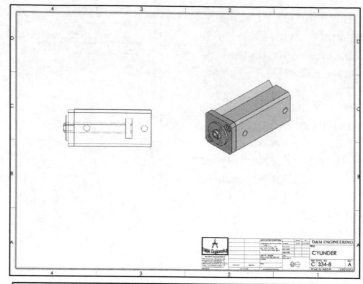

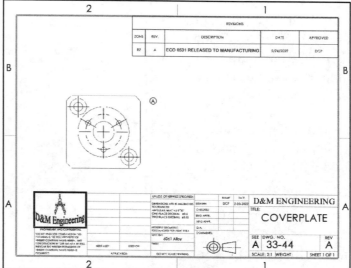

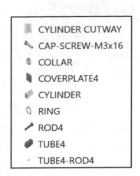

Utilize the CYLINDER assembly and other components: CAP-SCREW-M3x16, COLLAR, COVERPLATE4, RING, ROD4, TUBE4, TUBE4-ROD4, etc. located in SOLIDWORKS-2022/Chapter 8 folder.

The components contain the parts, Excel Design Tables, and Custom Properties required for the three sheets in the CYLINDER drawing. Add Drawing Linked Properties later as an exercise. Work between various different document types in this chapter: drawing views, assembly views, Design Table, Revision Table, and Bill of Materials.

SMC Corporation of America manufactures the CYLINDER assembly. The components were modified for educational purposes.

The RING and CAP-SCREW-M3x16 part were obtained from the SOLIDWORKS\toolbox and modified for the chapter.

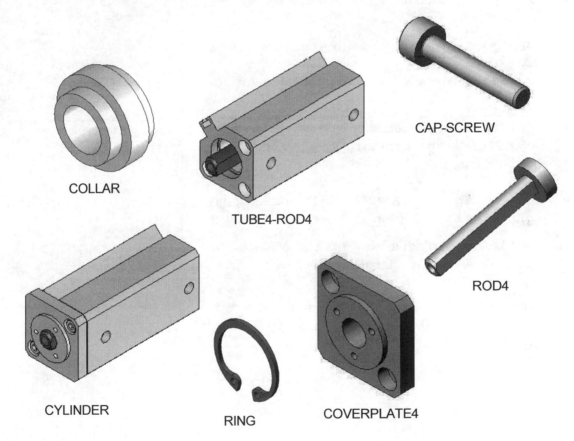

COLLAR

TUBE4-ROD4

CAP-SCREW

ROD4

CYLINDER

RING

COVERPLATE4

CYLINDER Assembly-Exploded View

The Exploded view illustrates how to assemble the components in an assembly. Create an Exploded view of the CYLINDER.

Click and drag components in the graphics area. The Manipulator icon indicates the direction to explode. Select an alternate component edge for the Explode direction. Drag the component in the graphics area or enter an exact value in the Explode distance box.

Manipulate the top-level components in the assembly. Access the Explode view option as follows:

- Right-click the configuration name in the ConfigurationManager.

- Select the Exploded View tool in the Assembly toolbar.

- Select Insert, Exploded View from the Main menu.

Access the Explode View 🧊 tool from the following locations:

- Click the **ConfigurationManager** tab. Right-click **Default**. Click **New Exploded View**. The Explode PropertyManager is displayed.

- Click the **Exploded View** 🧊 tool in the Assembly toolbar. The Explode PropertyManager is displayed.

- Click **Insert, Exploded View** from the Main menu. The Explode PropertyManager is displayed.

💡 The illustrations in this book are based on SOLIDWORKS SP1.0. The illustrations may vary slightly per your SOLIDWORKS release.

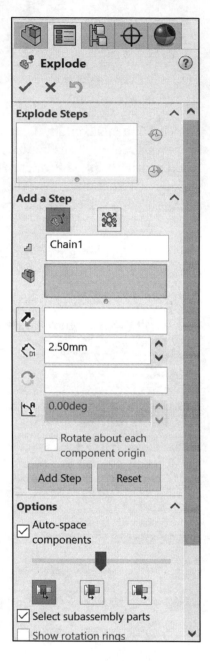

Activity: CYLINDER Assembly-Exploded View

Open the CYLINDER assembly.

1)   **Open** the CYLINDER assembly in the SOLIDWORKS 2022/Chapter 8 folder.

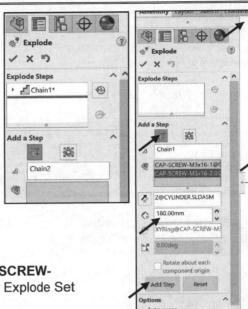

Create an Exploded view of the CYLINDER.

2)   Click **Exploded View** from the Assembly toolbar. The Explode PropertyManager is displayed.

Create Explode Step1.

3)   **Expand** the fly-out FeatureManager in the graphics window.

4)   Click **Regular Step** as illustrated.

5)   Click **CAP-SCREW-M3x16<1>** and **CAP-SCREW-M3x16<2>**. The parts are displayed in the Explode Set Components box.

6)   Enter **180**mm in the Explode distance box or use the on-screen ruler with the control points.

7)   Check the **Auto-space components** box.

8)   Click **Add Step**. Chain1 is created.

☀ Click and drag with the Manipulator icon to move the component in the assembly using the control points with the on-screen ruler.

Fit the model to the Graphics window.

9)   Press the **f** key.

Create Explode Step2.

10)   Click **COVERPLATE4<1>** from the FeatureManager.

11)   Drag the **manipulator handle** to the left approximately 100mm. Use the on-screen ruler.

12)   Click **Done**. Chain2 is created.

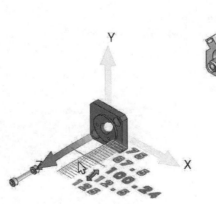

Create Explode Chain3.
13) Click **RING<1>** from the
FeatureManager.

14) Drag the **manipulator handle**
to the left approximately 50mm.

15) Click **Done**. Chain3 is created.

Create Explode Chain4.
16) Click **COLLAR<1>** from the fly-
out FeatureManager.

17) Drag the **manipulator handle**
to the left approximately 30mm.

18) Click **Done**.

Create Explode Chain5.
19) Click **Tube4<1>** from the
Graphics Window as illustrated.

20) Drag the **manipulator handle**
to the right approximately
70mm.

21) Click **Done**.

22) **View** the results.

23) Click **OK** ✅ from the Explode
PropertyManager.

Display the Exploded view steps in the
ConfigurationManager.
24) **Expand** the Default folder.

25) **Expand** the ExplView1 folder.
View the exploded steps.

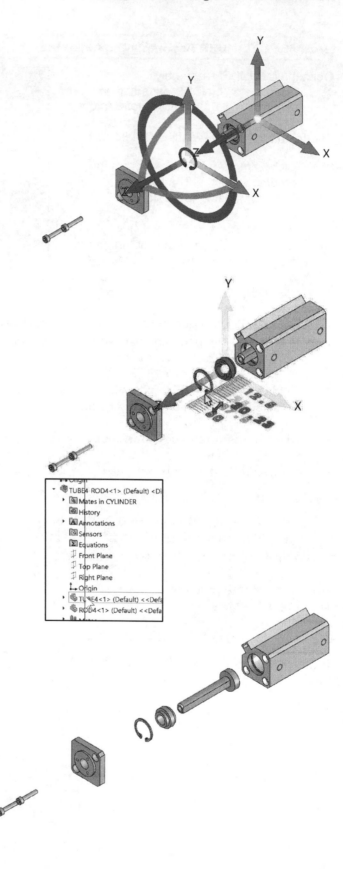

26) Right-click on **ExplView1**.

27) Click **Animate collapse**. **View** the animation.

28) Click **Close** ☒ from the Animation Controller.

Return to the CYLINDER assembly.

29) Click the **CYLINDER FeatureManager** tab.

Save the CYLINDER assembly.

30) Click **Save** .

💡 Click the **Animation1 (older SW model) tab/Motion Study1** tab at the bottom of the graphics area to perform a Motion Study on the assembly. Click the **Model** tab to return to a SOLIDWORKS graphics area.

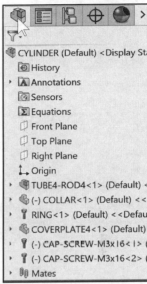

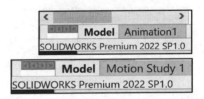

CYLINDER Assembly Drawing-Insert Balloons

The CYLINDER assembly drawing contains an Isometric Exploded view. Utilize View Properties to display the Exploded view. Use Auto Balloon annotations to label components in an assembly. The Balloon contains the Item Number listed in the Bill of Materials. A Balloon displays different end conditions based on the arrowhead geometry reference.

Drag the endpoint of the arrowhead to modify the attachment and the end condition.

- Edge/vertex: - Arrowhead.

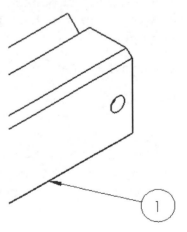

- Face/surface: - Dot.

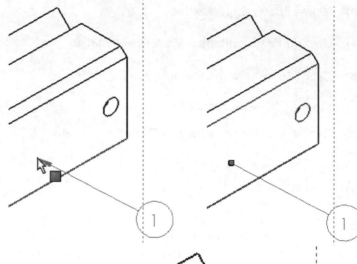

- Unattached: - Question mark.

🔆 Click the dimension, right-click the control point to select the correct arrow style.

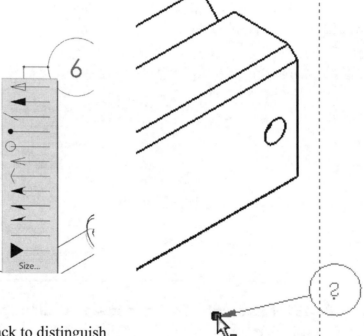

🔆 View mouse pointer feedback to distinguish between a vertex in the model and the attachment point in a Balloon. The attachment point displays the Note icon for a Balloon and the Point icon for point geometry.

🔆 Right-click an assembly in an assembly drawing, either open the part, subassembly or the assembly, (document dependent).

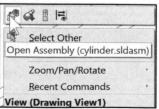

The Document Template, Drafting Standards, Balloons option defines the default arrow style and Balloons options.

The Balloons option controls: *Single balloon*, *Stacked balloons*, *Balloon text*, *Bent leaders*, and *Auto Balloon Layout* options.

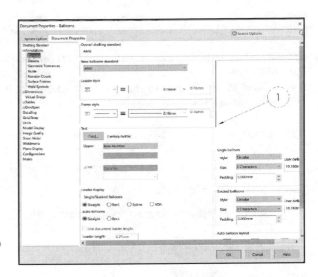

The Auto Balloon Layout option determines the display of the Balloons and the ability to use the insert magnetic lines tool. Square Layout is the default. The Top Layout displays the Balloons horizontally aligned above the model. The Left Layout displays the Balloon vertically aligned to the left of the model.

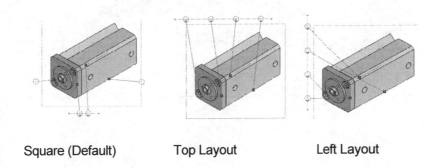

Square (Default)   Top Layout   Left Layout

Modify the selected Balloon with Balloon Properties. The Circular Split Linc Style displays the Item Number in the Upper portion of the circle and the Quantity in the Lower portion of the Circle.

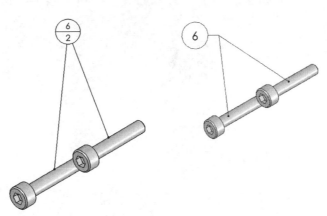

Activity: CYLINDER Assembly Drawing-Insert Balloons

Create a drawing from the assembly. Insert an Exploded Isometric view.

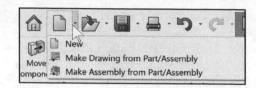

31) Click **Make Drawing from Part/Assembly** from the Main menu.

32) Double-click the **C-ANSI-MM** drawing template from the SOLIDWORKS 2022/MY-TEMPLATES folder. The CYLINDER drawing is displayed.

Part-ANSI-IN
Part-ANSI-MM
A-ANSI-IN
A-ANSI-MM
B-ANSI-IN
B-ANSI-MM
C-ANSI-IN
C-ANSI-MM-Chapter 5
C-ANSI-MM
C-SIZE-ANSI-MM-EMPTY

33) Click the **View Palette** tab from the Task Pane.

34) Click **CYLINDER** from the drop-down menu.

35) **View** the available drawing views.

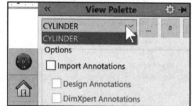
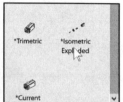

36) Drag the drop the **Isometric Exploded** view in to the upper right corner of Sheet1.

37) Click **OK** from the Drawing View1 PropertyManager. If needed, modify Sheet1 Scale to 2:1.

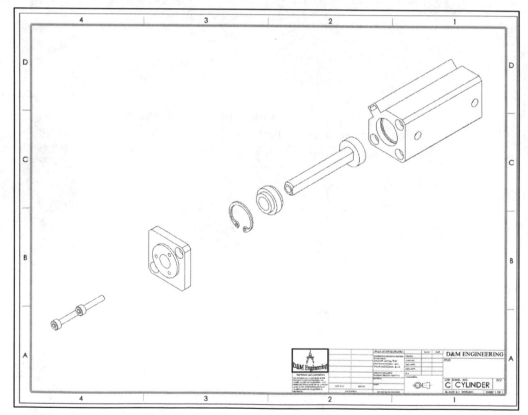

Save the CYLINDER drawing and the CYLINDER
part in the save folder.

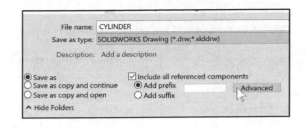

38)   Click **Save As** 🖼 from the Main menu.

39)   Enter **CYLINDER** for File name.

40)   Select the Save As folder: **SOLIDWORKS
2022/Chapter 8 Drawings**.

41)   Click the **include all referenced
components** box.

42)   Click the **Advanced button**.

43)   Click the **Browse** button.

44)   Select the **SOLIDWORKS 2022/Chapter 8 Drawings** folder.

45)   Click **Select Folder**.

46)   Click **Save All**. The CYLINDER drawing and CYLINDER are saved in the same folder.
This is a very important procedure to use for assemblies and drawings. You also can use
the SOLIDWORKS Pack and GO tool. See SOLIDWORKS Help for additional information.

Fit the Model to the Graphics window.
47)   Press the **f** key.

Insert Balloons to label each component.
48)   Click inside the **Isometric view** boundary.

49)   Click **AutoBalloon** 🎈 from the Annotation toolbar. The Auto Balloon
PropertyManager is displayed. Six balloons are displayed in the
Isometric view.

50)   Click **OK** ✔ from the Auto Balloon
PropertyManager.

Modify the Balloons.
51)   **Window-select** the six balloons in the
Graphics window. The Balloon
PropertyManager is displayed.

52)   Click the **More Properties** button. The Note
PropertyManager is displayed.

53)   **View** your options for Leader types.

54)   Click **Bent Leader** 🖉 for Leader type.

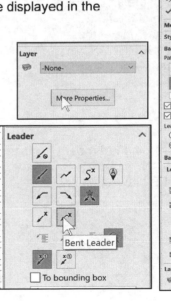

Modify the Font.

55)   Uncheck the **Use document font** box.

56)   Click the **Font** button. The Choose Font dialog box is displayed.

57)   Enter **5**mm for font Height.

58)   Click **OK**.

59)   Click **OK** ✔ from the Note PropertyManager.

Move the Balloons.

60)   Click the **arrowhead** on Balloon 1.

61)   Click and drag the **arrowhead** to the middle of the TUBE face as illustrated. The arrowhead changes shape per the Engineering Standard. The arrowhead shape is different for an edge vs. a face.

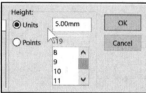

62)   Drag each **Balloon** into position. Leave space between the Balloon numbers.

Create two split leader lines.

63)   **Zoom in** on the two CAP-SCREWS.

64)   Click the **Arrowhead** on the CAP-SCREW.

65)   Hold the **Ctrl** key down.

66)   Drag and drop the **arrowhead** from the edge of the first CAP-SCREW to the edge of the second CAP-SCREW. Note: The Arrowhead type for an edge vs. a surface.

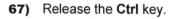

67)   Release the **Ctrl** key.

68)   Click **OK** ✔ from the PropertyManager.

Save the CYLINDER drawing.

69)   Click **Save** 🖫 .

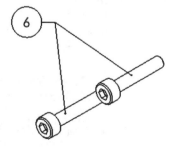

CYLINDER Assembly Drawing-Bill of Materials

The Bill of Materials (BOM) is a table that lists essential information on the components in an assembly. Insert a Bill of Materials (BOM) into the CYLINDER drawing. The BOM is linked to the Properties of the CYLINDER components. There are two options to create a BOM in the drawing:

- Bill of Materials option.

- Excel based Bill of Materials option.

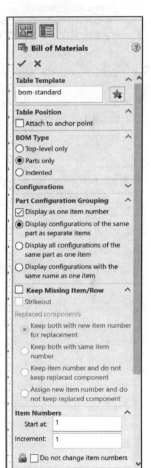

ITEM NO.	PART NUMBER	DESCRIPTION	MATERIAL	QTY.
1	TUBE4			1
2	ROD4			1
3	10-0411			1
4	MP043BM1-17	RING	Material <not specified>	1
5	10-0410	COVERPLATE	6061 Alloy	1
6	MP04-M3-05-16	CAP SCREW	Material <not specified>	2

Investigate the Bill of Materials option in this activity. The first BOM Table inserted into the CYLINDER drawing requires additional work. The information is incomplete.

Utilize the Component Properties tool to define the majority of information located in the BOM.

The foundation for the BOM is the BOM template. The bom-all.sldbomtbt contains the default column headings. A BOM template also contains User Defined Custom headings.

The User Defined Custom headings are linked to Custom Properties in the part or assembly. Define Custom Properties with the ConfigurationManager or a Design Table.

Create a Custom-BOM template. Start with a pre-defined BOM template. Insert additional headings. Right-click Save BOM template and select the SOLIDWORKS 2022/MY-TEMPLATES folder.

The BOM Table Anchor point locates the BOM at a corner of the drawing. The BOM Table moves when the Attach to anchor option is unchecked. The BOM Type contains three options:

- **Top level only**: List parts and sub-assemblies, but not sub-assembly components.

- **Parts only**: Does not list sub-assemblies. Lists sub-assembly components as individual items.

- **Indented**: Lists sub-assemblies. Indents sub-assembly components below their sub-assemblies. Select Show numbering to display item numbers for sub-assembly.

By default, component order in the assembly determines their ITEM NO. in the BOM. The occurrence of the same component in an assembly defines the value in the QTY column.

The PART NUMBER is the SOLIDWORKS File name, Example: TUBE4.

DESCRIPTION is the text entered in the Description box. The Description box is blank.

Define Description as a Custom Property in the next section. Create a Parts level only Bill of Materials with the SOLIDWORKS BOM Template, bom-material.sldbomtbt for Sheet1. Create a Top level only Bill of Materials with the bom-standard.sldbomtbt for Sheet2.

Activity: CYLINDER Assembly Drawing-Bill of Materials

Insert the default Bill of Materials.
70) Click inside the **Isometric view** boundary.

71) Click **Bill of Materials**  from the Consolidated Tables toolbar.

72) Click the **Open table template for Bill of Materials** icon as illustrated.

73) Double-click **bom-material.sldbomtbt** from the SOLIDWORKS default folder. bom-material is displayed in the Table Template box.

74) Click the **Parts only** box.

75) Click **OK** ✔ from the Bill of Materials PropertyManager. The Bill of Materials is attached to the mouse pointer.

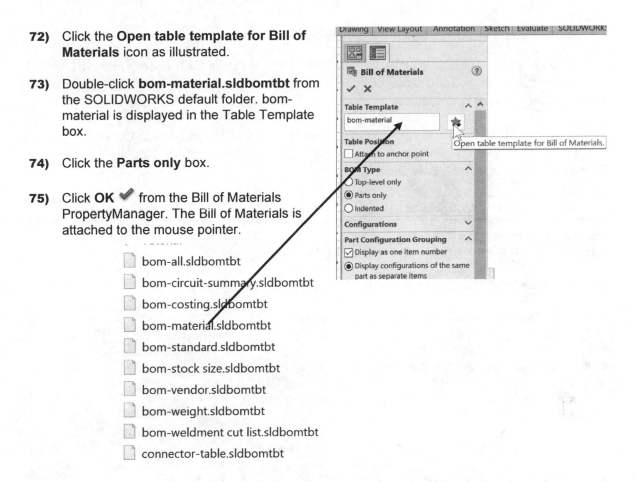

bom-all.sldbomtbt

bom-circuit-summary.sldbomtbt

bom-costing.sldbomtbt

bom-material.sldbomtbt

bom-standard.sldbomtbt

bom-stock size.sldbomtbt

bom-vendor.sldbomtbt

bom-weight.sldbomtbt

bom-weldment cut list.sldbomtbt

connector-table.sldbomtbt

76) Click a **position** in the upper left corner of Sheet1. **View** the results.

	A	B	C	D	E
	NO.	PART NUMBER	DESCRIPTION	MATERIAL	QTY.
	1	TUBE4			1
	2	ROD4			1
	3	10-0411			1
	4	MP043BM1-17	RING	Material <not specified>	1
	5	10-0410	COVERPLATE	6061 Alloy	1
	6	MP04-M3-05-16	CAP SCREW	Material <not specified>	2

77) **Zoom in** to enlarge the BOM. The RING and CAPSCREW components were taken from the SOLIDWORKS Toolbox. Note the information in the Material column. The order in your BOM may be different than the illustration.

Information in the current BOM is incomplete. The Custom Properties in the parts/components are linked to the PART NUMBER, DESCRIPTION, MATERIAL, and QTY. columns in the BOM. Create additional Custom Properties in the parts and in the BOM to complete the BOM in the drawing.

Materials Editor and Mass Properties

The BOM contains a Material column heading. The Materials Editor provides a list of predefined and user defined materials and their physical properties. Access the Materials Editor through the FeatureManager.

Select Tools, Mass Properties to calculate mass and other physical properties of the part. The physical properties of the part depend on different configuration. Review the Mass Properties for each part configuration.

Activity: Materials Editor and Mass Properties

Edit and apply material for TUBE4.

78)   **Expand** TUBE4-ROD4<1> in the Drawing FeatureManager.

79)   Right-click the **TUBE4<1>** part in the Drawing FeatureManager.

80)   Click **Open tube4.sldprt**. The TUBE4 FeatureManager is displayed

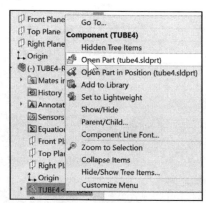

81)   Right-click **6061 Alloy** from the TUBE4 (Default) FeatureManager. Part material information in the BOM is not transferred to the drawing until you address it in the Part Custom Properties section.

82)   Click **Edit Material**. The Materials dialog box displayed.

83)   **View** the available information on the material.

84)   Click **Apply**. Click **Close** from the Materials dialog box.

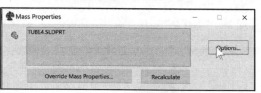

85)   Apply **Material** to Part Custom Properties.

View the Mass Properties.

86)   Click **Mass Properties** from the Evaluate tab in the CommandManager. The Mass Properties dialog box is displayed. Note: You can add a Center of Mass feature to a part or to an assembly. When you add the Center of Mass feature to the part or assembly, you can then dimension to it in a drawing.

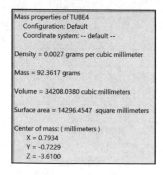

87)   Click the **Options** button. Enter **4** for Decimal Places.

88)   Click **OK**. The Mass 92.3617g is displayed. The Density 0.0027g/mm³ is determined from the assigned material.

89)   Click **Close** from the Mass Properties dialog box.

Apply Material for ROD4 in the Part FeatureManager.

90)   **Open** the ROD4 part.

91)   Right-click **Material** from the FeatureManager.

92)   Click **Edit Material**. **Expand** Steel. Select **AISI 304**. Click **Apply**. Click **Close** from the Material dialog box.

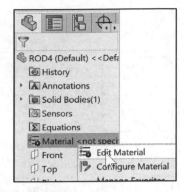

Apply Material for the ROD4 Configurations for Custom Properties. Save the changes.

93)   Click **File**, **Properties** from the Main menu. The Summary Information dialog box is displayed.

94)   Click the **Configuration Specific** tab.

95)   Click the Apply to **drop-down arrow**. **View** the various configurations.

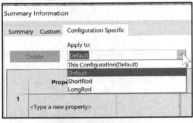

96)   Input **Material** for the Default, ShortRod, and LongRod configurations.

97)   Click **OK** from the Summary Information dialog box. Default is the active ROD4 configuration.

98)   Click **Save**.

Return to the Default configuration.

99)   Double-click **Default**.

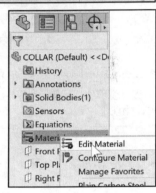

Apply Material to the COLLAR part.

100)   **Open** the COLLAR part from the SOLIDWORKS 2022/Chapter 8 folder. Right-click **Material**. Click **Edit Material**. **Expand** Steel.

101)   Select **Alloy Steel**. Click **Apply**. Click **Close** from the Material dialog box. The FeatureManager displays the material. Apply **Material** to the Part Custom Properties.

102)   Click **Save**.

103)   Repeat the above process for the **RING**. Select **Alloy Steel** for Material. Apply **Material** to the Part Custom Properties.

104)   Click **Save**.

105)   Repeat the above process for the **CAP-SCREW-M3x16**. Select **6061 Alloy** for Material. Apply **Material** to the Part Custom Properties.

106)   Click **Save**.

All of the parts are open along with the CYLINDER drawing.

ITEM NO.	PART NUMBER	DESCRIPTION	MATERIAL	QTY.
1	TUBE4		6061 Alloy	1
2	ROD4		AISI 304	1
3	10-0411		Alloy Steel	1
4	MP043BM1-17	RING	Alloy Steel	1
5	10-0410	COVERPLATE	6061 Alloy	1
6	MP04-M3-05-16	CAP SCREW	6061 Alloy	2

Custom Configuration Properties

In a previous chapter, you linked Custom Properties and
SOLIDWORKS Properties to Notes in the Sheet format. In this
chapter, cell entries in the BOM are linked to Properties created
in the part and assembly. Create Properties in the part with two
techniques: **Configuration Properties** and **Design Table**.

Access the Configuration Properties through the
ConfigurationManager. The BOM requires a part number. There
are three options utilized to display the Part number in the
BOM:

- **Document Name (file name)**. Note: Default setting.

- **Configuration Name**.

- **User Specified Name**.

Utilize two options in this section. The Document name is
TUBE4. The current BOM Part Number column displays the
Document Name. Utilize the User Specified Name to assign a
numeric value.

The Custom Properties button contains the Summary
Information, Custom Properties and Configuration Specific
options. Utilize the Configuration Specific tab to control the
Description, Material, and Cost Properties.

The Description Property links the BOM Description column heading. The TUBE 16MM value corresponds to the Cell entry in the BOM.

Link the Material Property to the value; "SW-Material@@Default@TUBE4.SLDPRT". This value corresponds to the Material assigned with the Materials Editor. The parameter is in the form:

"SW-Material@@Default@TUBE4.SLDPRT".

Property Name@@Configuration Name@Part Name

Link the Mass Property to the value; "SW-Mass@@Default@TUBE4.SLDPRT". The value corresponds to the mass calculated through the Mass Properties tool. Enter values for the Custom Property Cost. Insert the Cost column into the BOM.

The Design Table is an MS Excel spreadsheet utilized to create multiple configurations of a part or assembly.

Utilize Custom Properties in the Design Table to save time in creating multiple configurations and their properties.

Activity: Add Part Custom Configuration Properties

Add Custom Properties to TUBE4.
107) Display the TUBE4 part.

108) Click the **ConfigurationManager** tab.

109) Right-click **Properties** on the Default [TUBE4] configuration.

Add a User Specified Part number.
110) Select the **User Specified Name** from the drop-down menu.

111) Enter **10-0408** for Part number displayed when used in bill of materials option.

112) Check the **Use in bill of materials** box.

113) Enter **TUBE 16MM** for Description.

Insert Custom Properties.
114) Click the **Custom Properties** button from the Configuration Properties dialog box.

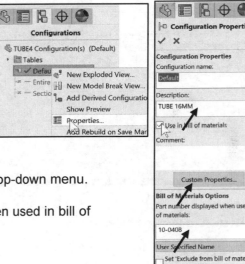

115) Click the **Configuration Specific** tab. Default is selected.

Add Material, Cost, and Mass Custom Property.
116) Select **Material** from the Property Name drop-down menu.

Summary Information		
Summary	Custom	Configuration Specific
		Apply to:
Delete		Default

117) Select **Material** from the Value / Text Expression drop-down menu.

118) Select **Cost - Material Cost** from the Property Name drop-down menu.

119) Enter **200** in the Value / Text Expression box.

120) Enter **Mass** from the Property Name drop-down menu.

121) Select **Mass** from the Value / Text Expression drop-down menu.

Add a Description Custom Property.
122) Select **Description** from the Property Name drop-down menu.

123) Enter **TUBE 16MM** in the Value / Text Expression box.

124) Click **OK** from the Summary Information dialog box.

125) Click **OK** ✔ from the Configuration Properties PropertyManager.

	Property Name	Type	Value / Text Expression	Evaluated Value
1	Material	Text	"SW-Material@@Default@TUBE4.SLDPRT"	6061 Alloy
2	Cost - Material Cost	Text	200	200
3	Description	Text	TUBE 16MM	TUBE 16MM
4	Mass	Text	"SW-Mass@@Default@TUBE4.SLDPRT"	92.3617

126) Return to the FeatureManager.

Save the TUBE4 part.
127) Click **Save** 💾.

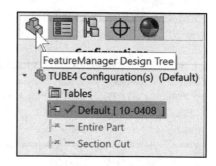

Add Custom Properties to the ROD4 (Default) part.
128) Open the ROD4 (Default) part.

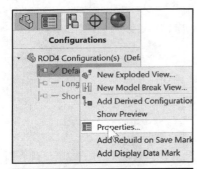

129) Click the **ConfigurationManager** tab.

130) Right-click **Properties** on the Default configuration.

Add a User Specified Part number.
131) Select the **User Specified Name** from the drop-down menu.

132) Enter **10-0409** for Part number displayed when used in bill of materials option.

133) Click the **Custom Properties** button.

Add Material, Description, Cost and Mass Properties to the Default configuration.
134) Click the **Configuration Specific** tab.

135) Select **Default** from the Apply to drop-down menu.

136) Select **Material** from the Property Name drop-down menu.

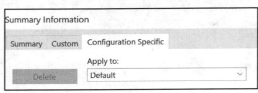

137) Select **Material** from the Value / Text Expression drop-down box.

138) Select **Description** from the Property Name drop-down menu.

139) Enter **ROD** in the Value / Text Expression box.

140) Select **Cost - Material Cost** from the Property Name drop-down menu.

141) Enter **50** in the Value / Text Expression box.

142) Enter **Mass** in the Property Name box.

143) Select **Mass** from the Value / Text Expression drop-down box.

	Property Name	Type	Value / Text Expression	Evaluated Value
1	Material	Text	"SW-Material@@Default@ROD4.SLDPRT"	AISI 304
2	Description	Text	ROD	ROD
3	Mass	Text	"SW-Mass@@Default@ROD4.SLDPRT"	23.82
4	Cost - Material Cost	Text	50	50
5				

144) Click **OK** from the Summary Information dialog box.

145) Click **OK** ✔ from the Configuration Properties PropertyManager.

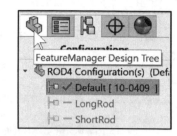

146) Click the **Part** FeatureManager icon.

Save the ROD4 part.

147) Click **Save** .

Review Custom Properties for COVERPLATE4.
148) Open COVERPLATE4 (Default).

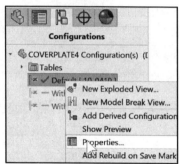

149) Click the **ConfigurationManager** tab.

150) Right-click **Properties** on the Default configuration.

151) Click the **Custom Properties** button.

152) View the Property Names and Values: Material, Mass, Description and Cost - Material Cost. Make any changes if needed.

	Property Name	Type	Value / Text Expression	Evaluated Value
1	Material	Text	"SW-Material@@Default@COVERPLATE4.SLDPRT"	6061 Alloy
2	Mass	Text	"SW-Mass@@Default@COVERPLATE4.SLDPRT"	10.8125
3	Description	Text	COVERPLATE	COVERPLATE
4	Cost - Material Cost	Text	50	50
5	<Type a new property>			

153) Click **OK** from the Summary Information dialog box.

154) Click **OK** ✔ from the Configuration Properties PropertyManager.

155) Return to the FeatureManager.

Add Custom Properties to the COLLAR part.
156) Open the COLLAR part.

157) Click the **ConfigurationManager** tab.

158) Right-click **Properties** on the Default configuration.

159) Select the **User Specified Name** from the drop-down menu.

160) Enter **10-0411**.

161) Click the **Custom Properties** button.

162) Select **Description** from the Property Name drop-down menu.

163) Enter **COLLAR** for Value / Text Expression.

Add a Cost Custom Property.
164) Enter **Cost - Material Cost** in the Property Name drop-down menu.

165) Enter **20** in the Value / Text Expression box.

166) Click **inside** the Evaluated Value box.

167) Click **OK**.

168) Click **OK** ✔ from the Configuration Properties PropertyManager.

Add Custom Properties to the RING part.

169) Open the RING part. Click the **ConfigurationManager** tab. Right-click **Properties** on the Default configuration.

170) Click the **Custom Properties** button.

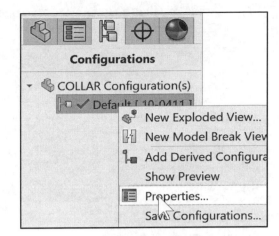

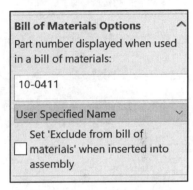

	Property Name	Type	Value / Text Expression	Evaluated Value
1	Material	Text	"SW-Material@@Default@COLLAR.SLDPRT"	Alloy Steel
2	Description	Text	COLLAR	COLLAR
3	Cost - Material Cost	Text	20	20
4				

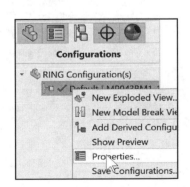

171) Address the **illustrated Custom Properties**.

	Property Name	Type	Value / Text Expression	Evaluated Va
1	Description	Text	RING	RING
2	Material	Text	"SW-Material@@Default@RING.SLDPRT"	Alloy Steel
3	Cost - Material Cost	Text	5	5
4	<Type a new property>			

172) Click **OK**.

173) Click **OK** ✔ from the Configuration Properties PropertyManager.

Design Table

A Design Table is an MS Excel spreadsheet utilized to create configurations and control parameters in a part or assembly.

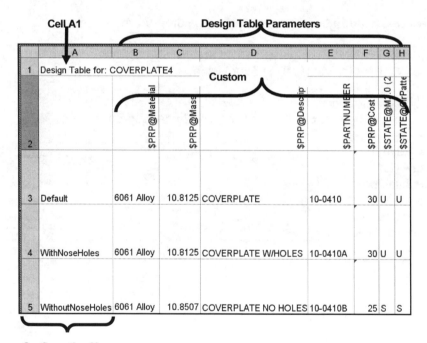

The model's name associated with the MS Excel Design Table is located in Cell A1. Define the configuration names in the first column of an Excel spreadsheet.

Enter values in the Cells that correspond to the configuration name and the parameter name.

Entering parameters into an Excel Design Table is a cumbersome task. Utilize the Auto-create option to load all configured parameters and their associated values from a part or assembly. Utilize the Excel Design Table to create multiple configurations for the ROD part and the CYLINDER assembly.

The current ROD Default Configuration contains Custom Properties: Mass, Material, Description and Cost. The Design Table with the Auto create option inserts the Custom Property parameters.

Custom Properties begin with the prefix, $PRP@. Enter user defined values for the BOM Part Number in the Excel Design Table. The Property, $PARTNUMBER displays three options in a Design Table:

- **$D Document Name (filename)**

- **$C Configuration Name**

- **User defined**

Additional part and assembly control parameters control Configuration, State, Color, Comment and Dimension. All parameters begin with a $, except Dimension.

Enter parameters carefully. The "$", "@" and "<>" symbol format needs to match exactly for the result to be correct in the BOM.

The Summary of an MS Excel Design Table Parameters is as follows:

Summary of Excel Design Table Parameters:		
Parameter Syntax (header Cell)	Legal Values (body Cell)	Default if Value is Left Blank
Parts only:		
$configuration@part_name	configuration name	not evaluated
$configuration@<feature_name>	configuration name	not evaluated
Parts and Assemblies:		
$comment	any text string	empty
$part number	any text string	configuration name
$state@feature_name	Suppressed, S Unsuppressed, U	Unsuppressed
dimension @feature	any legal decimal value for the dimension	not evaluated
$parent	parent configuration name	property is undefined
$prp@ property	any text string	property is undefined
$state@equation_number@equations	Suppressed, S Unsuppressed, U	Unsuppressed
$state@lighting_name	Suppressed, S Unsuppressed, U	Unsuppressed
$state@sketch relation@sketch name	Suppressed, S Unsuppressed, U	Unsuppressed
$sw-mass	Any legal decimal value for mass of a component.	The calculated value of mass in the Mass Properties option
$sw-coq	Any legal decimal value for the center of gravity in x, y, z.	The calculated cog in the Mass Properties option.
$user_notes	any text string	not evaluated
$color	32-bit integer specifying RGB (red, green, blue) color. See Online Help, Color for more info	zero (black)

Parameter Syntax (header Cell)	Legal Values (body Cell)	Default if Value is Left Blank
Assemblies only:		
$show@component<instance>	Yes, Y No, N	No
$state@component<instance>	Resolved, R, Suppressed, S	Resolved
$configuration@component<instance>	configuration name	Component's "in-use" or last saved configuration NOTE: If the component uses a derived configuration, and the value is left blank, the configuration used is linked to its parent.
$never_expand_in_BOM	Yes (never expand) No (allow to expand)	No

In this section, review the MS Excel Design Table for COVERPLATE4.

Activity: EXCEL Design Table

Review the COVERPLATE4 Design Table.
174) Open the COVERPLATE4 part.

175) Click the **ConfigurationManager** tab.

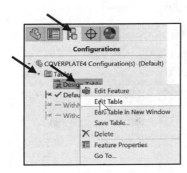

176) Right-click the **Design Table** folder as illustrated.

177) Click **Edit Table**. Review the Parameters for the Design Table. Enlarge the Design Table.

178) Drag the **lower right corner** downward.

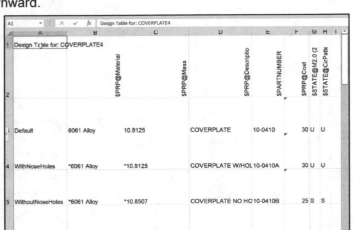

179) Click a **position** in the graphics area to close the Design Table and to return to SOLIDWORKS.

180) **Close** the part.

Bill of Materials - Part 2

The Custom Properties in the TUBE4, ROD4, and COVERPLATE4 parts produce changes to the BOM. Return to the CYLINDER Sheet1.

ITEM NO.	PART NUMBER	DESCRIPTION	MATERIAL	QTY.
Sheet1	10-0408	TUBE 16MM	6061 Alloy	1
2	10-0409	ROD	AISI 304	1
3	10-0411	COLLAR	Alloy Steel	1
4	MP043BM1-17	RING	Alloy Steel	1
5	10-0410	COVERPLATE	6061 Alloy	1
6	MP04-M3-05-16	CAP SCREW	6061 Alloy	2

Editing Cells

The BOM requires additional changes. Double-clicking a cell brings up the Context toolbar with items specific to the selected cell. The Context toolbar provides the ability to change the header, border, text and layer settings for the entire table.

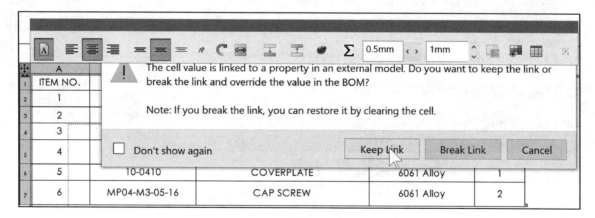

Editing Columns

Hovering over a cell displays the Editing Table icon. Click a cell to display the Context toolbar. The toolbar's buttons reflect the available options for the type of table and selections (rows, column, and cells).

To access a table's PropertyManager, click the move table icon in the upper left corner or Right-click the table, and click Properties from the Pop-up menu.

Click the vertical arrow as illustrated to insert a row. Click the Horizontal arrow to insert a column. The Insert tool provides the ability to insert a column to the right or left side of the selected column or a row, above or below the selected column or row.

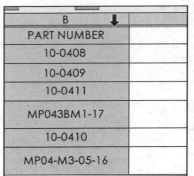

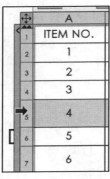

The Select tool provides the ability to select a Table, Column, or Row.

The Formatting tool provides the ability to format the width of a column, the height of a row, or the entire table.

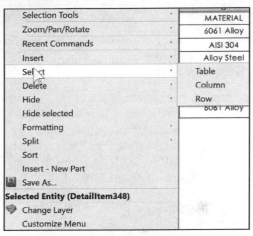

The Formatting Entire Table tool displayed the Entire Table dialog box.

The Sort tool provides the ability to sort selected items in the Bill of Materials.

The Sort tool displays the Sort dialog box.

Select the sort by item from the drop-down menu and check either ascending or descending order.

Spend time and explore the various options and tools.

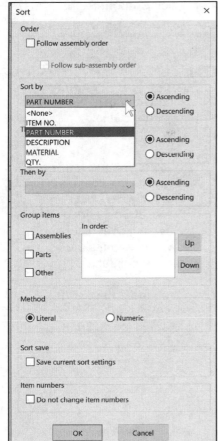

Activity: Bill of Materials-Part 2

Open the CYLINDER drawing. View the updated BOM.

181) Open the CYLINDER drawing-Sheet1. **View** the updated BOM.

ITEM NO.	PART NUMBER	DESCRIPTION	MATERIAL	QTY.
1	10-0408	TUBE 16MM	6061 Alloy	1
2	10-0409	ROD	AISI 304	1
3	10-0411	COLLAR	Alloy Steel	1
4	MP043BM1-17	RING	Alloy Steel	1
5	10-0410	COVERPLATE	6061 Alloy	1
6	MP04-M3-05-16	CAP SCREW	6061 Alloy	2

Insert a column called Cost - Material Cost.

182) Right-click inside the **MATERIAL** cell. The Pop-up toolbar is displayed.

183) Click **Insert**.

184) Click **Column Right**.

185) Select **Column Properties**.

186) Select **Cost - Material Cost** from the Custom Property drop-down menu. **Cost - Material Cost** is inserted into the Bill of Materials. Remember, you added a Custom property (Cost - Material Cost) to a few parts in the chapter.

187) Position the **mouse point** on the column line between Cost - Material Cost and QTY. Hovering over a column divider changes the mouse pointer.

188) Drag the **column divider line** to the left, to shrink the column size if needed.

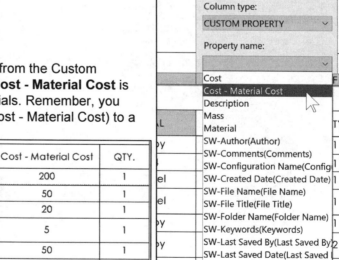

Cost - Material Cost	QTY.
200	1
50	1
20	1
5	1
50	1
	2

You can add Cost - Material Cost to other items in the BOM either from the Part Custom Properties or directly from the cell. If you click inside the BOM cell, you will see the following warning.

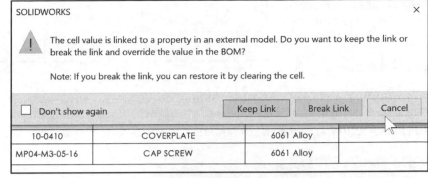

Bill of Materials - Header

Insert the BOM Title.
189) Click **inside** the ITEMS NO. cell.

190) Click the **vertical up-arrows**. The Bill of Materials header is displayed. Note: BOM Table is displayed by default.

191) Enter **CYLINDER ASSEMBLY BILL OF MATERIALS** for Title in the Header box.

192) Click **outside** of the Bill of Materials.

Insert a bulk item in the BOM.
193) Right-click inside **Cell Item No 6**.

194) Click **Insert**, **Row Below**. Row No. 7 is displayed.

195) Double-click the **Cell** to the right of Item No 7.

196) Click **Yes** to the question Continue editing the Cell?

197) Enter **DP01-1010-23** for the PART NUMBER.

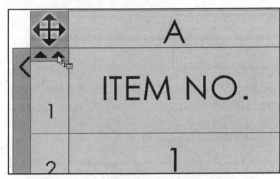

198) Double-click inside the **Cell** to the right of DP01-1010-23.

6	MP04-M3-05-16	CAP SCREW
7	DP01-1010-23	**LOCTITE**

199) Click **Yes**.

200) Enter **LOCTITE** for DESCRIPTION.

201) Click **outside** of the Bill of Materials.

Bill of Materials - Equation

Apply an equation to the Bill of Materials in a new column. The Equation tool from the Edit Tables Context toolbar displays the Equation editor.

Insert the Total Cost column.

202) Click the **Qty** cell. Right-click **Insert**, **Column Right**.

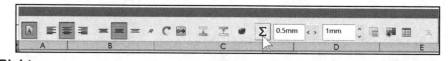

203) Enter **Total Cost** for title.

Apply the Equation tool.

204) Click the **cell** under the Total Cost header.

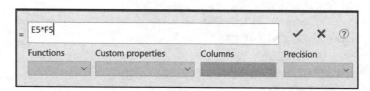

205) Click the **Equation** Σ tool from the Context toolbar. The Equation editor is displayed.

206) Click **200** in the Cost - Material Cost cell.

207) Enter the multiplication * symbol.

208) Click the **1** QTY Cost cell.

209) Click **OK** ✔.

MATERIAL	Cost - Material Cost	QTY.	Total Cost
6061 Alloy	200	1	200
AISI 304	50	1	50
Alloy Steel	20	1	20
Alloy Steel	5	1	5
6061 Alloy	50	1	50
6061 Alloy	10	2	20

210) **View** the results. 200 is displayed with an equation icon.

211) Following the above procedure, Fill in the **Cost - Material Cost** column and **Total Cost** as illustrated. Keep all links.

Calculate the Total Cost of the BOM.
212) Click inside the **bottom cell** under Total Cost.

213) Click the **Equation** Σ tool from the Context toolbar. The Equation editor is displayed.

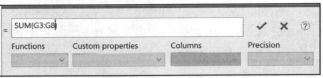

214) Select the **SUM** Function from the drop-down menu.

215) Click **Inside** cell G3. SUM(G3) is displayed.

216) Enter: as illustrated.

217) Click **inside** cell G8. SUM(G3:G8) is displayed.

218) Click **OK** ✔. **View** the results.

Fit the drawing to the Graphics window.
219) Press the **f** key.

Save the CYLINDER drawing.

220) Click **Save** 💾.

⊞ost - Material Cost	QTY.	Total Cost
200	1	200 Σ
50	1	50 Σ
20	1	20 Σ
5	1	5 Σ
50	1	50 Σ
10	2	20 Σ
		345 Σ

💡 You can double click in the PART, DESCRIPTION or Cost column to link directly back to modify the part.

	A	B	C	D	E	F	G
1			CYLINDER ASSEMBLY BILL OF MATERIALS				
2	ITEM NO.	PART NUMBER	DESCRIPTION	MATERIAL	Cost - Material Cost	QTY.	Total Cost
3	1	10-0408	TUBE 16MM	6061 Alloy	200	1	200 Σ
4	2	10-0409	ROD	AISI 304	50	1	50 Σ
5	3	10-0411	COLLAR	Alloy Steel	20	1	20 Σ
6	4	MP043BM1-17	RING	Alloy Steel	5	1	5 Σ
7	5	10-0410	COVERPLATE	6061 Alloy	50	1	50 Σ
8	6	MP04-M3-05-16	CAP SCREW	6061 Alloy	10	2	20 Σ
9	7	DP01-1010-23	**LOCTITE**				345 Σ

An Engineering Change Order is issued to modify the COLLAR from Alloy Steel to 6061 Alloy. Do you modify the BOM in the drawing? Answer: No. Return to the COLLAR part and update the Material in the Materials Editor. Investigate additional BOM options in the chapter exercises.

The CYLINDER assembly contains the default
configuration for the TUBE, ROD and COVERPLATE
parts. How do you modify the assembly to support
multiple configurations of the ROD and COVERPLATE in
a drawing? Answer: With a Design Table.

CYLINDER Assembly-Design Table

Design Tables control parameters in an assembly. Create a
Design Table in the CYLINDER assembly with four
different configurations of the COVERPLATE:

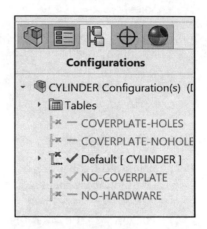

- COVERPLATE-HOLES

- COVERPLATE-NOHOLES

- NO-COVERPLATE

- NO-HARDWARE

Insert three CYLINDER assembly configurations into a
drawing. The TUBE, ROD, and COVERPLATE parts
are set to their Default configurations. Utilize the
configurations in the CYLINDER drawing views.

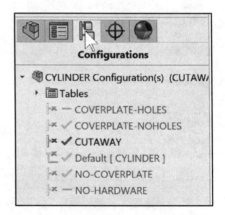

The TUBE4-ROD4 assembly contains two
configurations:

- Default

- CutAway

Activity: CYLINDER Assembly-Design Table

Create a Design Table in the CYLINDER assembly.
221) Open the CYLINDER assembly.

222) Click **Insert**, **Tables**, **Excel Design Table** from the Main menu. Accept the defaults. Note
your options in the Design Table PropertyManager.

223) Click **OK** ✔ from the Design Table PropertyManager.

224) Enter **NO-COVERPLATE** in Cell A4.

225) Enter **COVERPLATE-HOLES** in Cell A5.

226) Enter **COVERPLATE-NOHOLES** in Cell A6.

227) Enter **NO-HARDWARE** in Cell A7.

228) Drag the **column bar** between Column A and Column B to the right until the full Configuration Names are displayed.

To avoid creating a Hyperlink in EXCEL, insert a single apostrophe 'before a parameter that contains the @ symbol. The COVERPLATE4<1> parameter is the same as the FeatureManager component name. The Component Name is case sensitive. Do not interchange upper and lower case letters. Use dashes and underscores, not spaces.

Insert the COVERPLATE parameters.
229) Enter **$CONFIGURATION@COVERPLATE4<1>** in Cell B2.

230) Enter **Default** in Cell B3.

231) Enter **Default** in Cell B4.

232) Enter **WithNoseHoles** in Cell B5.

233) Enter **WithoutNoseHoles** in Cell B6.

234) Enter **Default** in Cell B7.

2		$CONFIGURATI(
3	Default	Default
4	NO-COVERPLATE	Default
5	COVERPLATE-HOLES	WithNoseHoles
6	COVERPLATE-NOHOLES	WithoutNoseHoles
7	NO-HARDWARE	Default
8		

235) Enter **$STATE@COVERPLATE4<1>** in Cell C2.

236) Enter **R** for Resolved in Cell C3, Cell C5, Cell C6 and C7.

237) Enter **S** for Suppress in Cell C4.

238) Enter **$STATE@CAP-SCREW-M3x16<*>** in Cell D2.

239) Enter **S** for Suppress in Cell D4 and Cell D7.

240) Enter **R** for Resolved in Cell D3, Cell D5 and Cell D6.

The <*> symbol indicates all instances for the CAP-SCREW-M3x16.

Display the configurations.
241) Click a **position** outside the Design Table. Four assembly CYLINDER configurations are created.

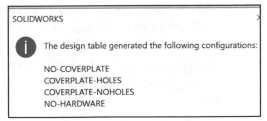

SOLIDWORKS

The design table generated the following configurations:

NO-COVERPLATE
COVERPLATE-HOLES
COVERPLATE-NOHOLES
NO-HARDWARE

242) Click **OK**.

Verify the configurations.
243) Double-click on **NO-COVERPLATE**.

244) Double-click on **COVERPLATE-HOLES**.

245) Double-click on **COVERPLATE-NOHOLES**.

246) Double-click on **NO-HARDWARE**.

Return to the default configuration.
247) Double click the **Default** configuration.

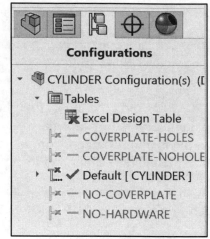

To delete a configuration, select the Configuration name in the ConfigurationManager. The Row entries are removed from the Design Table.

Save the CYLINDER assembly.
248) Click the **FeatureManager** tab.

249) Click **Save** .

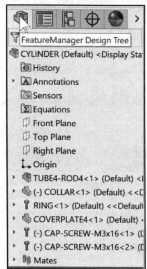

Display states let you specify different hide/show states, appearances, display modes, and transparencies for a part. Configurations let you create different versions of the part that change the physical aspects of the part. Display states are listed in the bottom section of the ConfigurationManager. When a display state is linked to a configuration, only that display state is the available when you work with the configuration. When the configuration is unlinked, you can activate other display states stored in the part when you work with the configuration.

CYLINDER Drawing-Multiple Configurations

Multiple configurations created in the CYLINDER Design Table allow you to insert various configurations into the drawing. Specify the configuration in the Properties of the current view. Modify the display options in the View Properties. Work between the three Sheets in the CYLINDER drawing.

Activity: CYLINDER Drawing-Multiple Configurations

Add Sheet2 and Sheet3.
250) Open the CYLINDER drawing. Click the **Add Sheet** icon at the bottom of the graphics area. Sheet2 is displayed.

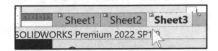

251) Click the **Add Sheet** icon. Sheet3 is displayed.

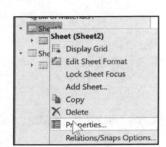

Set Custom Drawing Sheet1 Properties for Sheet2 and Sheet3.
252) Right-click **Sheet2**. Click **Properties**. The Sheet Properties dialog box is displayed.

253) Click the **Browse** button.

254) Double-click **C-FORMAT** from the SOLIDWORKS 2022/MY SHEETFORMTS folder. Sheet Scale should be 2:1. Click **Apply Changes**.

255) Click the **Sheet3** tab.

256) Perform the above procedure for a Custom Sheet format (Sheet3).

Copy the Exploded Isometric drawing view from Sheet1 to Sheet2.

257) Click the **Sheet1** tab. Click inside the **Exploded Isometric Drawing view** boundary of Sheet1.

258) Click **Edit**, **Copy** from the Main menu.

259) Click the **Sheet2** tab. Click a **position** in Sheet2.

260) Click **Edit**, **Paste** from the Main menu.

Hide the Balloons.
261) Window-select the **Balloons**. The Balloon PropertyManager is displayed.

262) Right-click **Hide**.

Default Drawing view #'s and Sheet format #'s depend on the number of views you inserted and deleted. Your entries in the FeatureManager can vary to the illustrations in the next section.

Modify View Properties.

263) Right-click **Properties** in the Isometric view boundary.

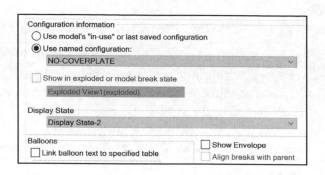

264) Click **Use named configuration**.

265) Select **NO-COVERPLATE** for the Use named configuration.

266) Uncheck **Show in exploded state or model break state**.

267) Uncheck the **Link balloon text to specified table** box.

268) Click **OK** from the dialog box.

Insert a Bill of Material.

269) Click inside the **Isometric view** boundary.

270) Click **Bill of Materials**  from the Consolidated Tables toolbar.

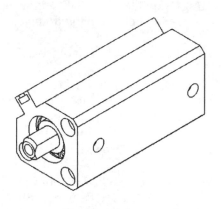

271) Select **bom-standard** for the Table Template.

272) Select **Top level only** for BOM Type.

273) Check the **Display as one item number**.

274) Click the **Display configurations of the same part as separate items**.

275) Click **OK** from the Bill of Materials PropertyManager.

276) Click a **position** below the Isometric view.

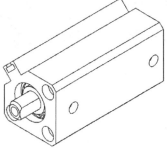

277) View the results.

ITEM NO.	PART NUMBER	DESCRIPTION	QTY.
1	99-1007-1	TUBE4_ROD4	1
2	10-0411	COLLAR	1
3	MP043BM1-17	RING	1

Copy the NO-COVERPLATE view.
278) Click inside the **NO-COVERPLATE** view boundary.

279) Click **Edit**, **Copy** from the Main menu.

280) Click a **position** to the right of the view.

281) Click **Edit**, **Paste** from the Main menu.

Modify the View Properties.
282) Right-click **Properties** in the view boundary of the new Isometric view.

283) Click **COVERPLATE-NOHOLES** for the Use named configuration.

284) Click **OK**.

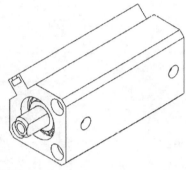

ITEM NO.	PART NUMBER	DESCRIPTION	QTY.
1	99-1007-1	TUBE4_ROD4	1
2	10-0411	COLLAR	1
3	MP043BM1-17	RING	1

Insert a Bill of Materials.
285) Click inside the new **Isometric view** boundary.

286) Click **Bill of Materials** 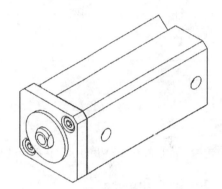 from the Consolidated Tables toolbar. The Bill of Materials PropertyManager is displayed.

287) Select **bom-standard** for the Table Template. Select **Top level only** for BOM Type.

288) Check the **Display as one item number**.

289) Click the **Display configurations of the same part as separate items**.

290) Click **OK** ✅ from the Bill of Materials PropertyManager.

291) Click a **position** below the second Isometric view. **View** the results.

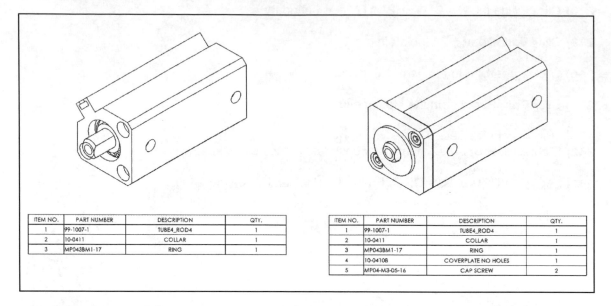

ITEM NO.	PART NUMBER	DESCRIPTION	QTY.
1	99-1007-1	TUBE4_ROD4	1
2	10-0411	COLLAR	1
3	MP043BM1-17	RING	1

ITEM NO.	PART NUMBER	DESCRIPTION	QTY.
1	99-1007-1	TUBE4_ROD4	1
2	10-0411	COLLAR	1
3	MP043BM1-17	RING	1
4	10-04108	COVERPLATE NO HOLES	1
5	MP04-M3-05-16	CAP SCREW	2

Insert views into Sheet3.

292) Click the **Sheet3** tab.

293) Click **Model View**  from the View Layout toolbar.

294) Click **Browse**.

295) Double-click the Default **CYLINDER** assembly configuration.

296) Select *****Right** from the View Orientation list.

297) Click a **position** on the upper left side of Sheet3.

298) Click **OK** ✔ from the Projected View PropertyManager.

299) Right-click **Properties** in the view boundary.

300) Click the **Show Hidden Edges** tab.

301) Expand CYLINDER in the Drawing FeatureManager.

302) Expand Sheet 3 in the drawing FeatureManager.

303) Expand DrawingView4 in the FeatureManager.

304) Expand CYLINDER in the FeatureManager.

305) Expand TUBE4-ROD4<1> default in the FeatureManager.

306) Click ROD4<1> Default in the FeatureManager.

307) Click Apply.

308) Click OK from the Drawing View Properties dialog box.

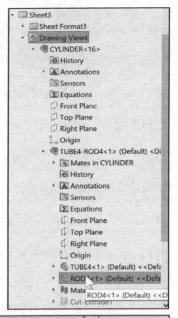

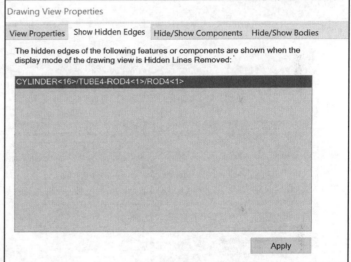

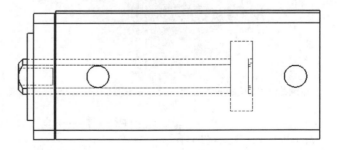

Copy the Right view.
309) Click inside the **Right** view boundary.

310) Click **Edit**, **Copy** from the Main menu.

311) Click a **position** to the right of the view.

312) Click **Copy**, **Paste** from the Main menu.

313) Click inside the **view** boundary.

314) Click ***Isometric** from the Model View PropertyManager.

315) Click **Shaded with Edges**.

316) Click **OK** ✔ from the PropertyManager.

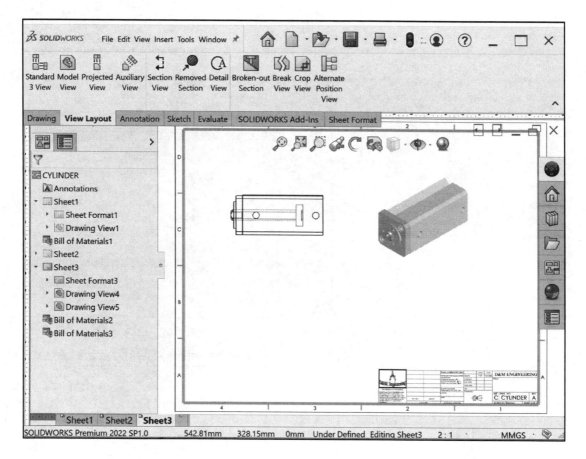

Save the Sheet1 BOM as a custom BOM Template.
317) Click the **Sheet1** tab.

318) Right-click the **BOM table** in Sheet1.

319) Click **Save as** 🖺 .

320) Select the **SOLIDWORKS 2022/MY-TEMPLATES** folder.

321) Enter **BOM-MATERIAL-COST** for file name.

322) Click **Save**.

Save the CYLINDER drawing.

323) Click **Save** 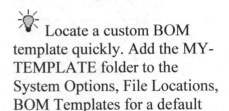.

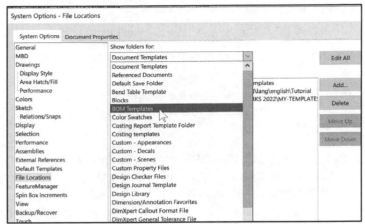

Locate a custom BOM template quickly. Add the MY-TEMPLATE folder to the System Options, File Locations, BOM Templates for a default BOM Template folder location.

Revision Table

The Revision Table lists the Engineering Change Order (ECO) in the top right section of the drawing. An ECO documents changes that occur to a component. The Engineering department maintains each ECO with a unique document number.

The Zone column utilizes the row letter and column number contained in the drawing border. Enter a Description that corresponds to the ECO number. Modify the date if required. Enter the initials/name of the engineering manager who approved the revision.

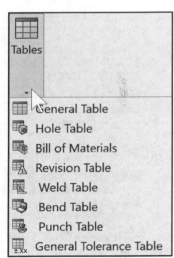

The REV. column in the Revision Table is a Sheet Property. Create a Linked Note in the Title block and utilize the Revision Sheet Property. The current Revision of the drawing corresponds to the letter in the last row of the Revision Table.

Activity: Create a new drawing with a Revision Table

Create a new drawing with a Revision table.
324) Open the **COVERPLATE4** part.

325) Click **File**, **New** from the Main menu.

326) Double-click **A-ANSI-MM** from the MY-TEMPLATES tab.

327) Click **Next** from the Model View PropertyManager.

328) Click **Front** as illustrated. Click a position to the **left** of Sheet1.

329) Click **OK**.

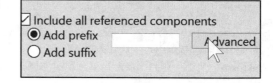

Fit the drawing to the Graphics window.
330) Press the **f** key.

Save the drawing and reference part to the same folder.

331) Click **Save As** 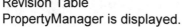 from the Main menu. Note: You can also use the SOLIDWORKS Pack and Go tool.

332) Select the **SOLIDWORKS 2022/Chapter 8 Drawings** folder. Check the **Include all referenced components**.

333) Click the **Advanced** button. Click the **Browse** button.

334) Select the **SOLIDWORKS 2022/Chapter 8 Drawings** folder. Click **Select Folder**.

335) Click **Save All**. The drawing and reference component are saved in the same folder.

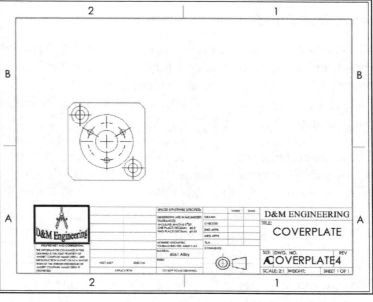

Insert a Revision Table.
336) Click **Revision Table** from the Consolidated Tables toolbar. The Revision Table PropertyManager is displayed.

337) Select the **standard revision** block Table Template

338) Click the **Circle Revision** Symbol Shape.

339) Check the **Enable symbol when adding new revision** option. Accept the default settings.

340) Click **OK** ✔ from the Revision Table PropertyManager. The Revision Table is displayed in the upper right corner.

341) Drag the **Revision Table** header downward to the inside upper right sheet boundary.

The Enable symbol when adding new revision option displays the Revision Symbol

on the mouse pointer when you execute the Add Revision command. Position the revision symbol on the drawing that corresponds to the change.

Insert the first row.
342) Right-click the **Revision Table**.

343) Click **Revisions**, **Add Revision**. The Revision letter, A and the current date are displayed in the

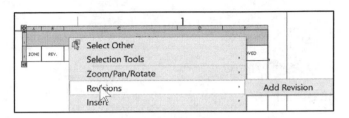

Revision Table. The Revision Symbol is displayed on the mouse pointer.

Position the Revision Symbol.
344) Click a **position** in the Front view.

345) Click **OK** from the Revision Symbol PropertyManager.

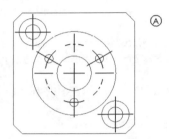

Edit the Revision Table.
346) Double-click the **text box** under the Description column.

347) Enter **ECO 8531 RELEASED TO MANUFACTURING**.

348) Click **outside** of the table. Double-click the **text box** under the APPROVED column.

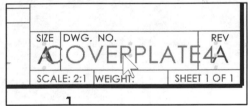

349) Enter Documentation Control Manager's Initials, Example: **DCP**.

350) Click **outside** of the table.

Edit the Sheet Format. Enter DWG. NO. in Custom Properties.
351) Right-click a **position** in the Sheet boundary.

352) Click **Edit Sheet Format**.

353) Click **File**, **Properties** from the Main menu.

354) Enter **Number**, 33-44 as illustrated.

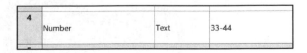

355) Click **Yes**.

356) Double-click **COVERPLATE4** as illustrated in the DWG. NO. box.

357) Delete **COVERPLATE4**.

358) Click **Link to Property** Current document is selected.

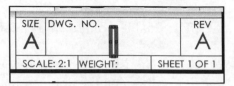

359) Click the **drop-down arrow** for Property name.

360) Select **Number** from the drop-down list.

361) Click **OK**.

362) Click **OK** ✔ from the Note PropertyManager.

Return to the drawing sheet.
363) Right-click a **position** in the sheet boundary.

364) Right-click **Edit Sheet**.

365) **View** the results.

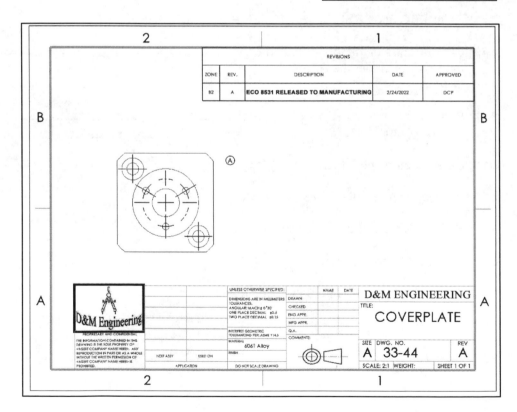

Save the COVERPLATE4 drawing. Close all open documents.

366) Click **Save** 💾 .

367) Click **Windows**, **Close All** from the Menu bar menu.

Additional Drawing Tools and Options

The following section explores additional tools and functions as they relate to assembly drawings. Explore these techniques in the chapter exercises. There are no step-by-step instructions.

Section View and Broken-out Section

The Section view and Broken-out Section view contain additional options for assemblies.

A Section view in the assembly starts similar to a Section view in the part. Click Section view from the View Layout toolbar. The Section View PropertyManager is displayed. The Section tab is displayed by default. Vertical Cutting Lines is selected by default. The dialog box displays the Section Scope option. Expand the FeatureManager that corresponds to the Sheet and Drawing View #. Select the components to exclude from the section cut. Example: COLLAR and RING.

The Auto hatching option creates alternate pattern hatching between components. The excluded components are not hatched.

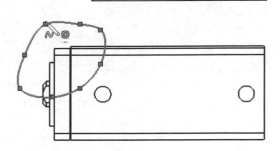

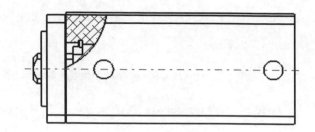

The Materials Editor determines the hatch pattern. A Broken-out Section in the assembly starts similar to a Broken-out Section View in the part. Sketch a Spline (Closed Profile) in the area of the Parent view to break away.

The Depth reference requires a value or an edge reference. The Preview checkbox displays a yellow cross arrow symbol indicating the Depth.

Hide Behind Plane

The Hide Behind Plane option hides components of an assembly drawing behind a plane. This option provides a quicker selection method than to select individual components.

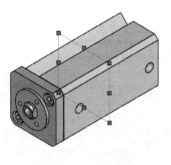

Only the components that are completely behind the plane become hidden. Example: COVERPLATE, CAP-SCREW, COLLAR and RING.

Display an Isometric view in the drawing. Select the CYLINDER Front Plane from the FeatureManager. Right-click Hide Behind Plane. Enter 25mm for Distance.

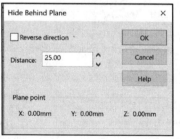

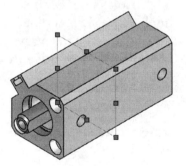

The X, Y and Z coordinates of the plane distance are shown in the Hide Behind Plane dialog box. The default offset distance is 0.

Show the hidden components. Right-click Properties in the current view. Select Hide/Show Components. Delete the component from the hidden list.

Large Assembly Drawing Performance

System Options, Drawings contains the settings for drawings that improve performance. Large assembly drawings are system memory intensive.

Check Automatically hide component on view creation. Review the available options, and uncheck any un-needed option to save system memory and time for large assembly drawings.

Set the default display style to Hidden lines removed and default display quality to Draft Quality. View SOLIDWORKS Help for additional information on opening and saving a Large Assembly and a Large Assembly drawing.

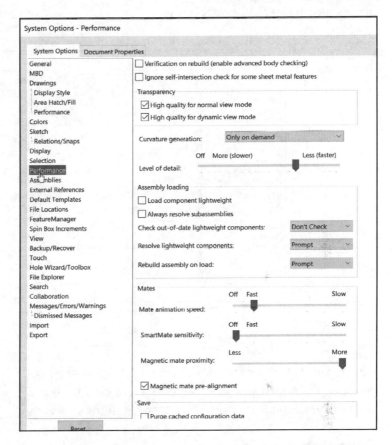

Splitting A BOM

A BOM can be split (Split options) into smaller tables by dividing horizontally or vertically. The split portion retains the column titles and can be dragged anywhere on the drawing. The Merge Table option brings a Split BOM back together.

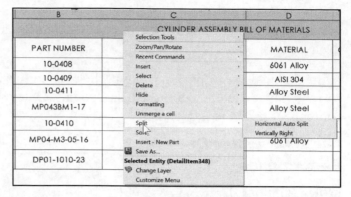

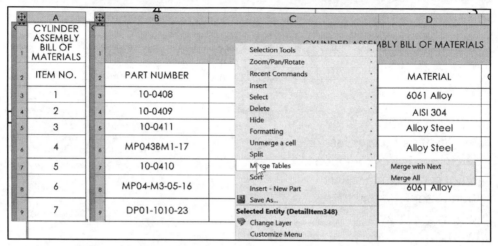

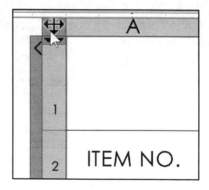

Create assembly drawings early in the assembly process. As additional components are added to the assembly, the views and BOMs update in the drawing.

Dragging A BOM

Drag the split portion of the table away from the original using the upper left handle as illustrated and "snap" it onto the upper edge of the sheet format if needed.

Tabulated Bill of Materials

A Tabulated Bill of Materials can be used when the assembly contains multiple configurations. The tabulation affects only the QTY. column. See SOLIDWORKS Help for additional information.

eDrawings

An eDrawing is a compressed document of a SOLIDWORKS part, assembly, or drawing. An eDrawing provides animation, view, measure, section, markup, etc.

In a multi sheet drawing, select the sheets to create the eDrawing. An eDrawing can be sent via email to a vendor without the corresponding part, assembly or drawing documents.

Export

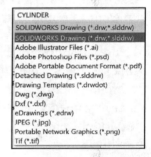

Export is the process to save a SOLIDWORKS document in another format. Exported files are used in other CAD/CAM, rapid prototyping, web, or graphics software applications.

Insert a Center of Mass Point into a Drawing

Add a center of mass (COM) point to parts, assemblies, and drawings.

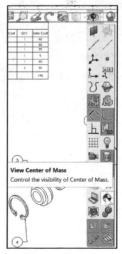

COM points added in component documents also appear in the assembly document. In a drawing document of parts or assemblies that contain a COM point, you can show and reference the COM point.

Add a COM to a part or assembly document by clicking **Center of Mass** (Reference Geometry toolbar) or **Insert, Reference Geometry, Center of Mass** ✛ or checking the **Create Center of Mass feature** box in the Mass Properties dialog box.

The center of mass of a model is displayed
on the model and in the FeatureManager
design tree just below the origin.
The position of the **COM** point ⊕ updates
when the model's center of mass changes.
The COM point can be suppressed and
unsuppressed for configurations.

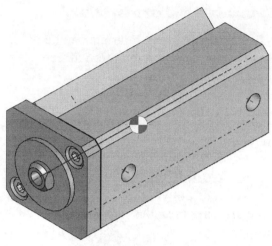

You can measure distances and add
reference dimensions between the COM
point and entities such as vertices, edges,
and faces.

🔆 If you want to display a reference
point where the CG was located at some particular point
in the FeatureManager, you can insert a Center of Mass
Reference Point. See SOLIDWORKS Help for additional
information.

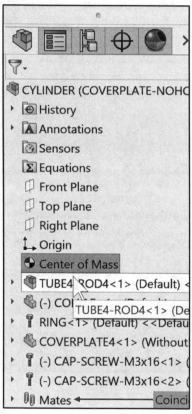

Add a center of mass (COM) point to a drawing view.
The center of mass is a selectable entity in drawings, and
you can reference it to create dimensions.

In a drawing document, click **Insert**, **Model Items**. The
Model Items PropertyManager is displayed. Under
Reference Geometry, click the **Center of Mass** icon.
Enter any needed additional information. Click **OK** from
the Model Items PropertyManager. View the results in the
drawing.

🔆 Note: The part or assembly **needs to have a COM
before** you can view the COM in the drawing. To view
the center of mass in a drawing, click **View**, **Center of
mass**.

Chapter Summary

You created two drawings in this chapter: The CYLINDER assembly drawing and the COVERPLATE4 Part drawing.

As an exercise, add the Drawing Custom Linked Properties as illustrated in the final drawings.

The CYLINDER assembly drawing contained five different configurations of the CYLINDER assembly, 3 Sheets and 5 different drawing views all using Custom Properties, Linked Properties, SOLIDWORKS Properties, and Custom Sheet formats.

Sheet1 contained the Exploded Isometric CYLINDER assembly view with Balloons and split bent leader lines.

The custom Bill of Materials used linked Properties and equations.

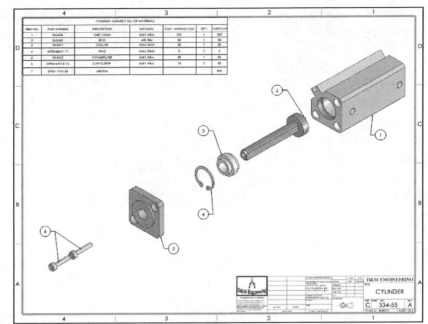

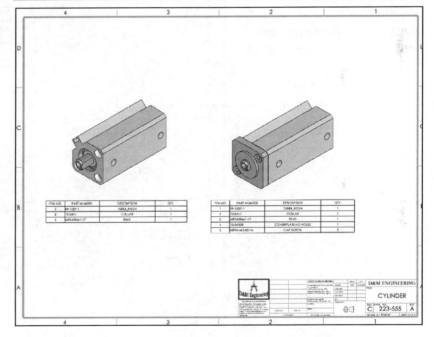

The CYLINDER assembly consisted of the TUBE4, ROD4, COLLAR, RING, COVERPLATE4, and CAP-SCREW-M3x16 parts from the Chapter 8 folder.

Sheet2 contained two drawing views with two BOMs. The two parts: COVERPLATE and CAP-SCREWS were unsuppressed in the Left and Right Isometric views.

The Bill of Materials reflects the two different configurations.

Sheet3 contained two views of the COVERPLATE part. The Left Front view displays the WithNoseHoles configuration. The Right Isometric view displays the WithoutNoseHoles configuration.

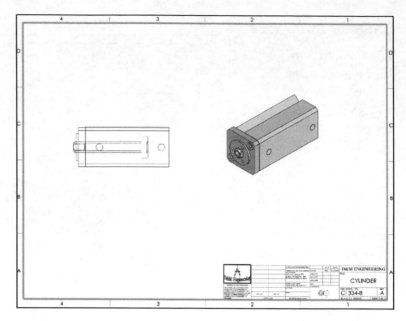

The COVERPLATE4 Part drawing contained a single Sheet with a Revision Table, Custom Properties, Linked properties, SOLIDWORKS Properties, and a Custom Sheet format.

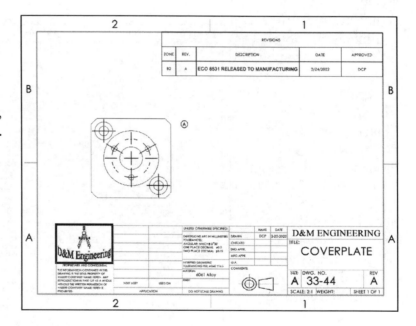

Questions:

1. True or False. Parts contained in an assembly cannot be opened from within that assembly.

2. Describe the procedure in a drawing to display an Exploded view and a Collapsed view.

3. True or False. A Design Table can be used to create multiple configurations in a part. Provide an example used in the book.

4. True or False. The Materials Editor contains a library of materials and their properties.

5. Explain a Linked Property in a drawing.

6. Identify a few parts of a Revision Table.

7. Explain the procedure to create a Parts only BOM Type.

8. Explain the differences between a Top Level, Parts only, and Indented BOM Type.

9. Describe the procedure to add a column and row to an existing BOM.

10. Describe the procedure to add the Cost Property to the part and the Bill of Materials.

11. Identify four different Balloons Settings.

12. Explain the procedure to Split Leader lines with Balloons.

13. True or False: You cannot create a BOM for an assembly document. Only for an assembly drawing.

14. Explain the differences between the Auto Balloon tool and the Balloon tool in the Annotation CommandManager.

15. Explain why you might use the Revision Cloud tool in the Annotation CommandManager.

Exercises

Exercise 8.1:

Open the LINKAGE assembly from the SOLIDWORKS 2022/Chapter 8 Homework/Example 8-1 folder.

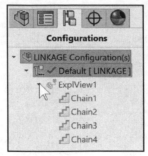

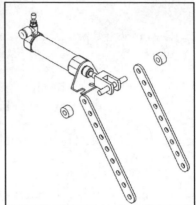

Create the Exploded Isometric LINKAGE assembly as illustrated.

Create an A-Landscape, ANSI, MMGS, Third Angle drawing. Sheet Scale: 1:2.

Insert the Exploded Isometric LINKAGE assembly into the drawing.

Insert a Bill of Materials (Top level only) table using the bom-material Table Template.

The BOM is not complete. Add all needed Custom Properties, Linked Properties and SOLIDWORKS Properties. Do not break the links in the BOM.

ITEM NO.	PART NUMBER	DESCRIPTION	MATERIAL	QTY.
1	GIDS-PC-10001	LINEAR ACTUATOR		1
2	AXLE	AXLE-ROD		1
3	FLATBAR	FLAT BAR 9-HOLE		2
4	SHAFT-COLLAR	SHAFT-COLLAR		2

ITEM NO.	PART NUMBER	DESCRIPTION	MATERIAL	QTY.
1	GIDS-PC-10001	LINEAR ACTUATOR		1
2	GIDS-SC-10017	AXLE-ROD	6061 Alloy	1
3	GIDS-SC-10001-9	FLAT BAR 9-HOLE	2014 Alloy	2
4	GIDS-SC-10012-3-16	SHAFT-COLLAR	6061 Alloy	2

Insert Balloons. Use
Circular Split Line.

Finish the Exploded
Isometric LINKAGE
assembly drawing with
Custom, Linked, and SOLIDWORKS Properties
as illustrated.

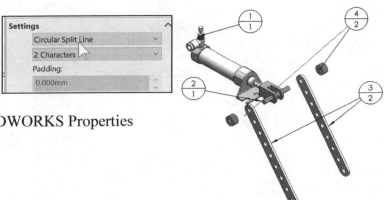

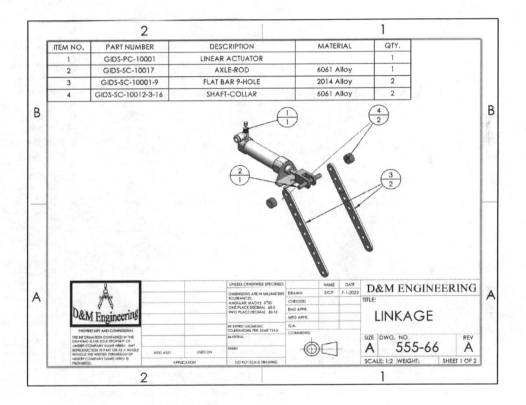

ITEM NO.	PART NUMBER	DESCRIPTION	MATERIAL	QTY.
1	GIDS-PC-10001	LINEAR ACTUATOR		1
2	GIDS-SC-10017	AXLE-ROD	6061 Alloy	1
3	GIDS-SC-10001-9	FLAT BAR 9-HOLE	2014 Alloy	2
4	GIDS-SC-10012-3-16	SHAFT-COLLAR	6061 Alloy	2

Exercise 8.2:

Open the GUIDE-ROD assembly from the SOLIDWORKS 2022/Chapter 8 Homework/Example 8-2 folder.

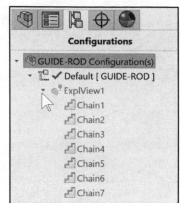

Create the Exploded Isometric GUIDE-ROD assembly as illustrated.

Create a B-Landscape, ANSI, MMGS, Third Angle drawing. Sheet Scale: 1:1.

Insert the Exploded Isometric assembly into the drawing.

Insert a Bill of Materials (Parts only) table using the bom-standard Table Template.

Add a Materials column in the BOM as illustrated.

The BOM is not complete. Add all needed Custom Properties and Linked Properties. Do not break the links in the BOM.

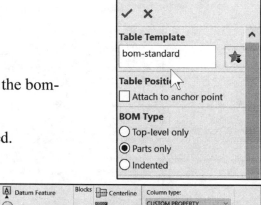

ITEM NO.	PART NUMBER	DESCRIPTION	Material	QTY.
1	56-A26	GUIDE SUPPORT		1
2	ROD	ROD		1
3	PLATE	PLATE 56MM x 22MM		1
4	M8-1.25 x 30	FLANGE BOLT M8x1.25x30	AISI 304	2
5	56-333	CAP SCREW, 4MM	AISI 304	2
6	3MMCAPSCREW	CAP SCREW, 3MM	AISI 304	6

ITEM NO.	PART NUMBER	DESCRIPTION	MATERIAL	QTY.
1	56-A26	GUIDE SUPPORT	AISI 304	1
2	56-A27	ROD	AISI 304	1
3	56-A28	PLATE 56MM x 22MM	AISI 304	1
4	M8-1.25 x 30	FLANGE BOLT M8x1.25x30	AISI 304	2
5	56-333	CAP SCREW, 4MM	AISI 304	2
6	44-4434	CAP SCREW, 3MM	AISI 304	6

Insert Balloons as illustrated. Use Circular Split Line.

Finish the Exploded Isometric GUIDE-ROD assembly drawing using Custom, Linked and SOLIDWORKS Properties. Utilize the User Specified Name to assign a numeric value.

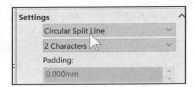

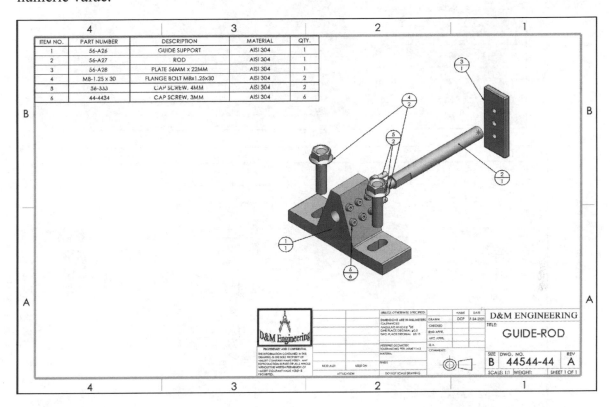

Exercise 8.3

Open the GUIDE-ROD assembly drawing from the SOLIDWORKS 2022/Chapter 8/Example 8-3 folder.

Address the Cost - Material Cost Custom Property at the part level. View the Cost - Material Cost in the final GUIDE-ROD assembly drawing BOM.

Modify the BOM to include a Cost-Material Cost column and a TOTAL MATERIAL COST column.

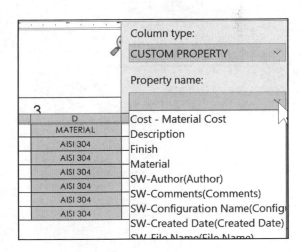

Add a new row for TOTAL COST.

Use equations for TOTAL MATERIAL COST and TOTAL COST in the BOM.

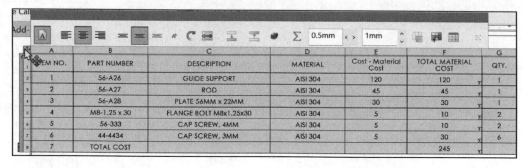

ITEM NO.	PART NUMBER	DESCRIPTION	MATERIAL	Cost - Material Cost	TOTAL MATERIAL COST	QTY.
1	56-A26	GUIDE SUPPORT	AISI 304	120	120	1
2	56-A27	ROD	AISI 304	45	45	1
3	56-A28	PLATE 56MM x 22MM	AISI 304	30	30	1
4	M8-1.25 x 30	FLANGE BOLT M8x1.25x30	AISI 304	5	10	2
5	56-333	CAP SCREW, 4MM	AISI 304	5	10	2
6	44-4434	CAP SCREW, 3MM	AISI 304	5	30	6
7	TOTAL COST				245	

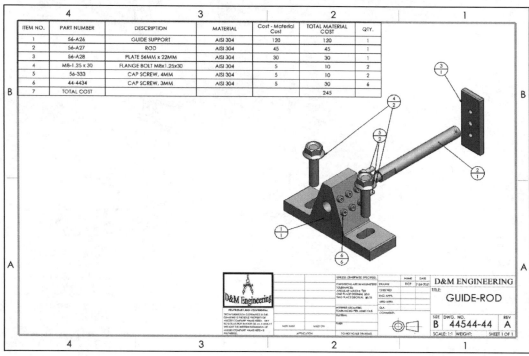

Exercise 8.4:

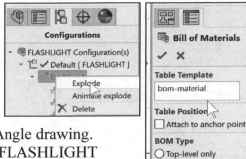

Open the FLASHLIGHT assembly from the SOLIDWORKS 2022/Chapter 8 Homework/Example 8-4 folder. View the Exploded Isometric FLASHLIGHT assembly.

Create an A-Landscape, ANSI, MMGS, Third Angle drawing. Sheet Scale: 1:1. Insert the Exploded Isometric FLASHLIGHT assembly into the drawing.

Insert a Bill of Materials (Parts only) table using the bom-material Table Template. The BOM is incomplete. Complete the BOM as illustrated in the final drawing.

Insert Balloons as illustrated.

Finish the Exploded Isometric FLASHLIGHT assembly drawing using Custom, Linked and SOLIDWORKS Properties as illustrated. Utilize the User Specified Name to assign a numeric value.

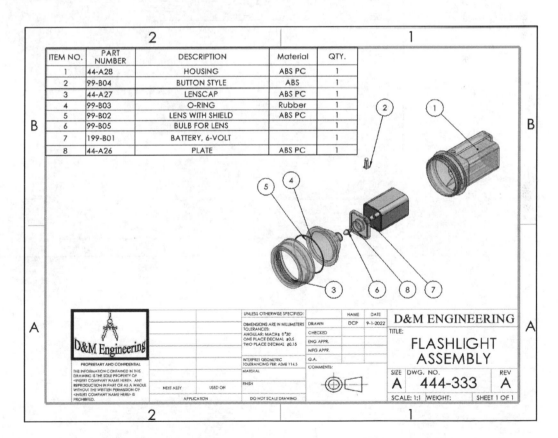

ITEM NO.	PART NUMBER	DESCRIPTION	Material	QTY.
1	44-A28	HOUSING	ABS PC	1
2	99-B04	BUTTON STYLE	ABS	1
3	44-A27	LENSCAP	ABS PC	1
4	99-B03	O-RING	Rubber	1
5	99-B02	LENS WITH SHIELD	ABS PC	1
6	99-B05	BULB FOR LENS		1
7	199-B01	BATTERY, 6-VOLT		1
8	44-A26	PLATE	ABS PC	1

D&M ENGINEERING

TITLE:

FLASHLIGHT ASSEMBLY

SIZE: A　DWG. NO. 444-333　REV: A

SCALE: 1:1　WEIGHT:　SHEET 1 OF 1

DRAWN DCP 9-1-2022

Exercise 8.5

Open the FLASHLIGHT assembly drawing from the SOLIDWORKS 2022/Chapter 8/Example 8-5 folder.

Sort by PART NUMBER in the BOM.

View the updated BOM and Balloons.

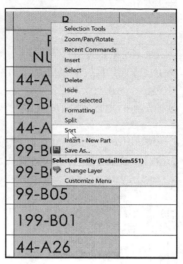

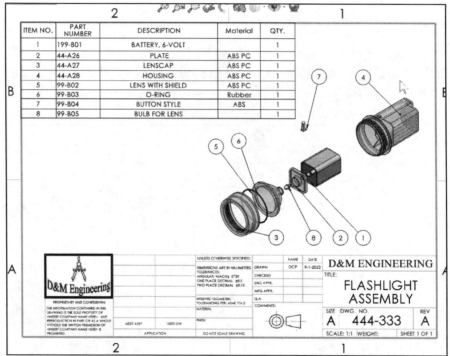

Exercise 8.6

Open the FLY WHEEL assembly drawing from the SOLIDWORKS 2022/Chapter 8/Example 8-6 folder.

Add Cost - Material Cost to the Part Custom Property.

Add a Cost - Material Cost column in the BOM.

Sort by Cost-Material Cost in the BOM (Numeric).

Column type:
CUSTOM PROPERTY ˅
Property name:
˅

D
MATERIAL
6061 Alloy
Brass
6061 Alloy
6061 Alloy
6061 Alloy
Plain Carbon Steel

Cost - Material Cost
Description
Material
SW-Author(Author)
SW-Comments(Comments)
SW-Configuration Name(Config)
SW-Created Date(Created Date)
SW-File Name(File Name)
SW-File Title(File Title)
SW-Folder Name(Folder Name)

ITEM NO.	PART NUMBER	DESCRIPTION	MATERIAL	Cost - Material Cost	QTY.
1	M14-001	BRACKET	6061 Alloy	30	1
2	P14-003	BUSHING	Brass	20	1
3	M14-002	AXLE	6061 Alloy	10	1
4	M14-005	WHEEL	6061 Alloy	120	1
5	M14-011	COLLAR	6061 Alloy	7	1
6	P14-006	2MM SET SCREW	Plain Carbon Steel	1	1

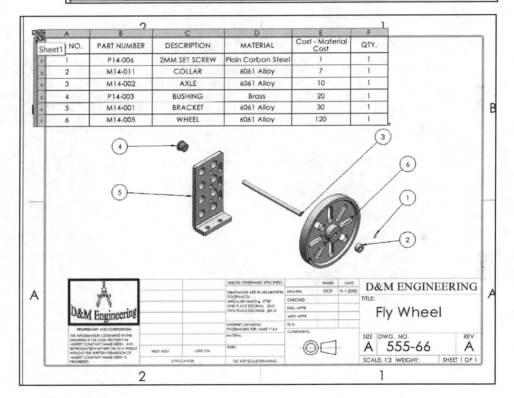

NO.	PART NUMBER	DESCRIPTION	MATERIAL	Cost - Material Cost	QTY.
1	P14-006	2MM SET SCREW	Plain Carbon Steel	1	1
2	M14-011	COLLAR	6061 Alloy	7	1
3	M14-002	AXLE	6061 Alloy	10	1
4	P14-003	BUSHING	Brass	20	1
5	M14-001	BRACKET	6061 Alloy	30	1
6	M14-005	WHEEL	6061 Alloy	120	1

D&M ENGINEERING
TITLE: Fly Wheel
SIZE A DWG. NO. 555-66 REV A
SCALE: 1:2 WEIGHT: SHEET 1 OF 1

Notes:

Chapter 9

Datums, Feature Control Frames, Geometric Tolerancing and other Drawing Symbols

Below are the desired outcomes and usage competencies based on the completion of Chapter 9.

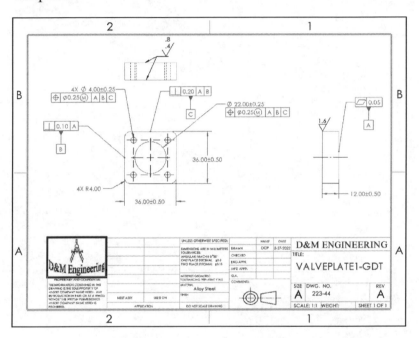

Desired Outcomes:	Usage Competencies:
• VALVEPLATE1 drawing. • VALVEPLATE1-GDT drawing. • VALVEPLATE1-GDT eDrawing. • Model Base Definition (MBD) parts. • PLATE-TUBE drawing.	• Ability to insert and edit: Dimensions, Feature Control Frames, Datums, Geometric Tolerancing, Surface Finishes and Weld Symbols using DimXpert and Model Base Definition (MBD).
	• Competence to insert and edit: Dimensions, Features Control Frames, Datums, Geometric Tolerancing, Instance count, Blocks, using Custom Templates and Part and Drawing Properties manually in a part and drawing.

Notes:

Chapter 9 - Geometric Tolerancing and other Symbols

Chapter Objective

Create four drawings: VALVEPLATE1, VALVEPLATE1-GDT, VALVEPLATE1-GDT eDrawing, PLATE-TUBE, using Custom Templates, Sheet formats, Drawing Properties, Link Properties and SOLIDWORKS Properties. Apply MBD (Model Base Definition) tools to two parts.

On the completion of this chapter, you will be able to:

- Apply DimXpert and the DimXpertManager:

  - Plus and Minus option.

  - Geometric option.

- Knowledge of the DimXpert toolbar.

- Apply MBD (Model Base Definition) tools.

- Knowledge of the View Palette and Model Items.

- Modify dimensions to contain None, Bilateral, and Limit Tolerance.

- Address Instance Counts.

- Insert Datums, Feature Control Frames, Geometric Tolerances, Surface Finishes, and Weld Symbols.

- Create multiple Leaders to the Surface Finish symbol.

- Insert a Weld Bead Assembly feature.

SOLIDWORKS MBD (Model Based Definition) lets you create models without the need for drawings giving you an integrated manufacturing solution for the SOLIDWORKS software. SOLIDWORKS MBD helps companies define, organize, and publish 3D product and manufacturing information (PMI), including 3D model data in industry standard file formats. SOLIDWORKS MBD offers 3D PMI definition capabilities using DimXpert and reference dimensions.

DimXpert speeds the process of adding reference dimensions by applying dimensions in drawings so that manufacturing features, such as patterns, slots, and pockets, are fully defined. You select a feature's edge to dimension, then DimXpert applies all associated dimensions in that drawing view for the feature.

Chapter Overview

As a designer, you work on multiple projects. Each project involves a different type of drawing.

- **VALVEPLATE1 drawing**: Open the VALVEPLATE1 part. Apply DimXpert: Plus and Minus option. Insert dimensions and Geometric tolerances. Create the VALVEPLATE1 drawing with the View Palette tool. Insert three drawing views. Hide the Top view. Insert a Centerline and Hide Tangent Edges in the Right view. Display None and Bilateral tolerance. Use a Custom Drawing Template, Drawing Properties and Link Properties.

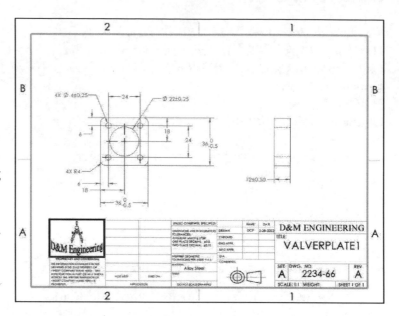

- **VALVEPLATE1-GDT drawing**: Open the VALVEPLATE1-GDT part. Apply DimXpert: Geometric option. Apply DBM Dimensions CommandManager tools. Insert Datums, Feature Control Frames, and Geometric Tolerances. Edit Feature Control Frames. Create the VALVEPLATE1-GDT drawing using the View Palette. Insert three drawing views.

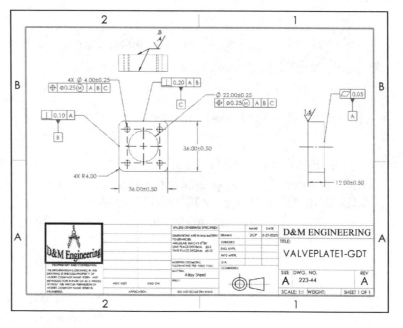

Insert the Surface Finish symbol on the Top and Right view. Create multiple leaders to the Surface Finish symbol. Insert Hide Tangent Edges in the Top and Right view.

- **VALVEPLATE1-GDT eDrawing**: Create an eDrawing. In eDrawings®, you can view and animate models and drawings and create documents convenient for sending to others. Send a SOLIDWORKS eDrawing outside to a machine shop for quotation. The VALVEPLATE1-GDT eDrawing is a compressed standalone document.

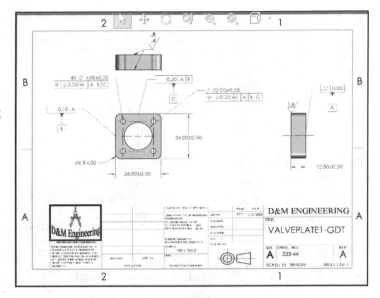

- **PLATE-TUBE drawing**: Open the PLATE-TUBE assembly. Create the PLATE-TUBE drawing. The PLATE-TUBE drawing is a conceptual customer drawing. The customer is concerned about the cosmetic appearance of a weld. Insert the Weld Bead assembly feature between the TUBE and PLATE parts in the PLATE-TUBE assembly. Use a Custom Drawing Template. Insert Custom Drawing Properties and Link Properties.

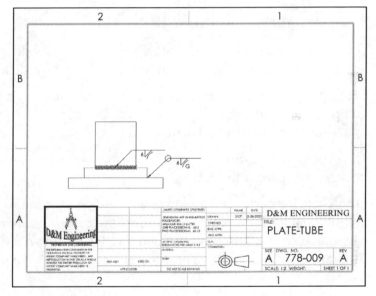

- **MBD**: Apply MBD (Model Base Definition) tools to two parts.

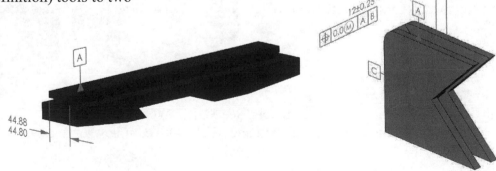

Open the VALVEPLATE1 part from the SOLIDWORKS 2022/Chapter 9 folder. View the three Extrude features, Linear Pattern feature, and the Fillet feature. Modify the Sketch plane.

Apply the DimXpert: Plus and Minus option to the part. Apply View Palette to create the VALVEPLATE1 drawing. Insert three drawing views with annotations from DimXpert. Work between the part and drawing.

The DimXpertManager ⊕ tab provides the ability to insert dimensions and tolerances manually or automatically. The options are: **Auto Dimension Scheme** ⊕, **Auto Pair Tolerance** 🔢, **Basic, Location Dimension** ⊬, **Basic Size Dimension** ⬝, **General Profile Tolerance** ⬝, **Show Tolerance Status** ±⊙, **Copy Scheme** ⊕, **Import Scheme** ⊕, **TolAnalyst Study** ⬝ and **Datum Target** ⬝.

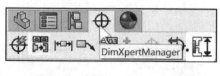

DimXpert for parts is a set of tools you use to apply dimensions and tolerances to parts according to the requirements of the ASME Y14.41 standard.

DimXpert dimensions show up in a different color to help identify them from model dims and reference dims. DimXpert dims are the dimensions that are used when calculating tolerance stack-up using TolAnalyst.

DimXpert applies dimensions in drawings so that manufacturing features (patterns, slots, pockets, etc.) are fully defined.

DimXpert for parts and drawings automatically recognize manufacturing features. What are manufacturing features? Manufacturing features are *not SOLIDWORKS features*. Manufacturing features are defined in 1.1.12 of the ASME Y14.5M Dimensioning and Tolerancing standard as "The general term applied to a physical portion of a part, such as a surface, hole or slot."

The majority of the part features reside on the top face.

Redefine the part orientation so that the top face is parallel with the Front Plane.

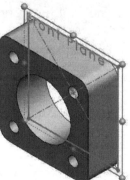

☼ Care is required to apply DimXpert correctly on complex surfaces or with some existing models. See SOLIDWORKS help for detailed information on DimXpert and MBD with complex surfaces.

Activity: VALVEPLATE1 Part - DimXpert Plus and Minus Option

Open the part and modify the plane orientation.

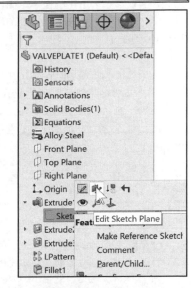

1)   Click **Open** from the Main menu.

2)   **Browse** to the SOLIDWORKS 2022/Chapter 9 folder.

3)   Double-click the **VALVEPLATE1** part. The VALVEPLATE1 FeatureManager is displayed.

Redefine the part orientation.

4)   **Expand** Extrude1 from the FeatureManager.

5)   Right-click **Sketch1**.

6)   Click **Edit Sketch Plane** from the Context toolbar. The Sketch Plane PropertyManager is displayed. Top Plane is displayed.

Modify the Sketch Plane from Top Plane to Front Plane.

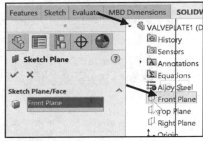

7)   **Expand** VALVEPLATE1 from the graphics area.

8)   Click **Front Plane** from the Flyout FeatureManager. Front Plane is displayed in the Sketch Plane / Face box.

9)   Click **OK** from the Sketch Plane PropertyManager. View the model in the Graphics window. The model is displayed on the Front Plane.

The DimXpertManager provides the ability to list the tolerance features defined by the DimXpert in chronological order and to display the available tools.

Apply DimXpert to the VALVEPLATE1 part.

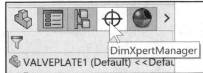

10)   Click the **DimXpertManager** tab as illustrated.

11)   Click the **Auto Dimension Scheme** tool from the DimXpertManager. The Auto Dimension PropertyManager is displayed. Prismatic, Plus and Minus, and Linear are selected by default.

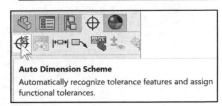

The Auto Dimension Scheme option is used to automate the process of recognizing features and adding functional tolerances. Starting with datum selection, features and planes can be added to define the scope of the scheme.

A key difference between the *Plus and Minus* option versus the *Geometric* option is how DimXpert controls the four-hole pattern, and how it applies tolerances to interrelate the datum features when in *Geometric* mode. You will apply both options in this chapter.

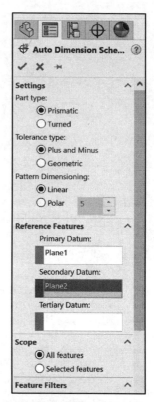

Select type of Scheme.

12) Check the **Prismatic** box.

Select the Primary Datum.

13) Click the **back face** of the model. Plane1 is displayed in the Primary Datum box. Note: Plus and Minus and Linear should be selected by default.

Select the Secondary Datum.

14) Click **inside** the Secondary Datum box.

15) Click the **left face** of the model. Plane2 is displayed in the Secondary Datum box. Two planes are selected.

16) Click **OK** ✔ from the Auto Dimension PropertyManager.

17) **View** the results.

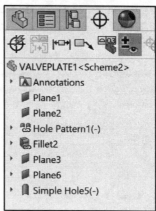

Display an Isometric view.

18) Click **Isometric view**. View the dimensions. View the features displayed in green and yellow. Green is fully constrained. Yellow is under constrained. Note: Additional dimensions are required for manufacturing. This is NOT a fully defined system at this time. Three mutually Perpendicular planes are required.

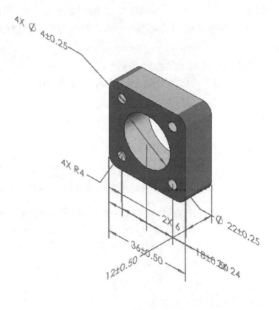

The DimXpertManager displays either *no mark*, *(+)*, or a *(-)* sign next to the Plane or Feature.

- Features with *no mark* after the name are fully constrained, as illustrated in the VALVEPLATE1 DimXpertManager and are displayed in green.

- Features with the *(+)* sign following the name are over constrained and are displayed in red in the graphics area.

- Features with the *(-)* sign following the name are under constrained and are displayed in yellow in the graphics area.

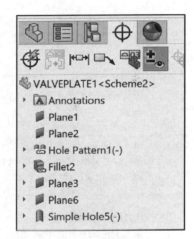

The Feature Selector is a floating, Context sensitive toolbar that you can use to distinguish between different DimXpert feature types. The available Feature Selector choices depend on the selected face and the active command.

The order of features in the Feature Selector is based on their complexity:

- Basic features like planes, cylinders, and cones are located on the left.

- Composite features like counterbore holes, notches, slots, and patterns are located in the middle.

- Compound features like compound holes and intersect points are located on the right. Compound features require additional selections.

Within DimXpert, a single face can typically define multiple manufacturing feature types that require different dimensions and tolerances.

19) Click each **Plane** and **feature** in the Show Tolerance Status FeatureManager. The selected item is displayed in blue.

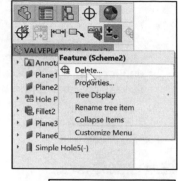

Delete the DimXpert Scheme.
20) Right-click **VALVEPLATE1** from the DimXpertManager.

21) Click **Delete**.

22) Click **Yes**.

Create a New Scheme which is fully constrained.

23) Click the **Auto Dimension Scheme** tool from the DimXpertManager. The Auto Dimension PropertyManager is displayed. Prismatic, Plus and Minus, and Linear should be selected by default.

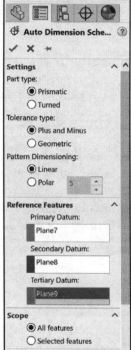

Select the Primary Datum.
24) Click the **back face** of the model. The selected plane is displayed in the Primary Datum box.

Select the Secondary Datum.
25) Click **inside** the Secondary Datum box.

26) Click the **left face** of the model. The selected plane is displayed in the Secondary Datum box.

Select the Tertiary Datum.
27) Click **inside** the Tertiary Datum box.

28) Click the **top face** of the model. The selected plane is displayed in the Tertiary Datum box.

29) Click **OK** from the Auto Dimension PropertyManager.

30) Click **Isometric view**. **View** the dimensions. All features are displayed in green.

31) Drag all dimensions off the model.

32) Right-click the **Annotations** folder. View the default settings. To display Feature Dimensions, click the Show Feature Dimensions box.

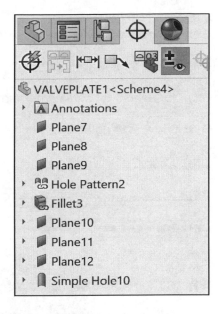

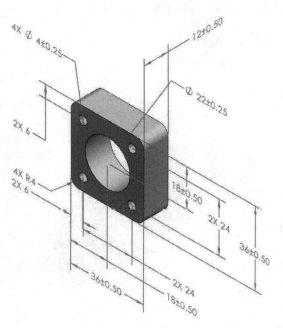

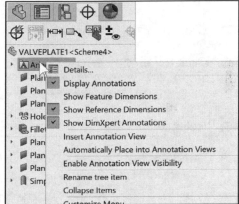

Modify tolerance and dimensions in the part.
33) Click the **36 horizontal** dimension text. The DimXpert PropertyManager is displayed.

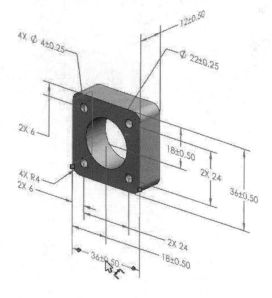

Create a Bilateral Tolerance.

34) Select **Bilateral** from the Tolerance Type drop-down menu.

35) Enter **0** for Maximum Variation.

36) Enter **-0.5** for Minimum Variation.

37) **View** your options.

38) Click **OK** ✔ from the DimXpert PropertyManager.

39) Repeat the above procedure for the **36 vertical** dimension text.

40) Click **OK** ✔ from the DimXpert PropertyManager.

Remove Instance Count from the part.

41) Click the **2X 6 vertical** dimension text.

42) Hold the **Ctrl** key down.

43) Click the **2X 6 horizontal** dimension text.

44) Click the **2X 24 vertical** dimension text.

45) Click the **2X 24 horizontal** dimension text.

46) Release the **Ctrl** key.

47) **Uncheck** the Instance Count box from the Dimension Text dialog box.

48) Click **OK** ✔ from the DimXpert PropertyManager.

49) **View** the results.

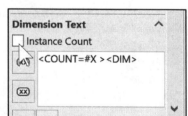

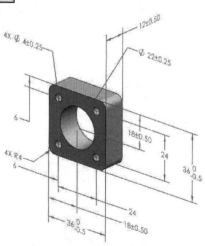

Remove a tolerance from the part.
50) Click the **18 vertical** dimension text.

51) Hold the **Ctrl** key down.

52) Click the **18 horizontal** dimension text.

53) Release the **Ctrl** key.

54) Select **None** for Tolerance Type.

55) Click **OK** ✅ from the DimXpert
PropertyManager.

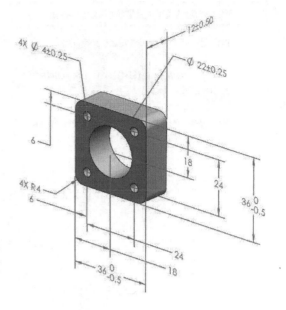

Various drawing standards display Tolerance zeros differently. The ASME Y14.5
standard states for millimeter dimensions, that there is no decimal point associated with a
unilateral tolerance on a 0 value. There is no +/- sign associated with the unilateral
tolerance on a 0 value.

A unilateral tolerance is similar to a SOLIDWORKS bilateral
tolerance with one tolerance value set to 0. The other tolerance value
contains a +/- sign. Select Bilateral Tolerance in SOLIDWORKS
when a unilateral tolerance is required.

$\phi\ 22^{+0.4}_{\quad 0}$

Decimal inch tolerance rules differ from millimeter rules.

DimXpert Annotations and Drawings

The dimensions and annotations generated when dimensions schemes are created are
considered DimXpert Annotations. These annotations, combined with the planes that
hold them, are very useful when creating drawing views. In the next section, insert
DimXpert annotations into a drawing.

Activity: VALVEPLATE1 Drawing - View Palette

56) Click the **FeatureManager** tab.

57) Right-click the **Annotations** folder from the FeatureManager.

58) **Uncheck** the Show DimXpert Annotations box. **View** the results in the Graphics area.

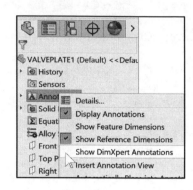

Display the DimXpert Annotations.
59) Right-click the **Annotations** folder from the FeatureManager.

60) **Check** the Show DimXpert Annotations box.

61) Click **Save**.

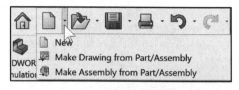

☀️ To modify the default DimXpert color, click **Options**, **Colors**. Under Color scheme settings, select **Annotations**, **DimXpert** and pick the new color.

Create a new VALVEPLATE1 drawing. Apply the DimXpert Annotations.
62) Click the **Make Drawing from Part/Assembly** from the Main menu.

63) Click the **MY-TEMPLATES** tab. Double-click the **A-ANSI-MM** drawing template.

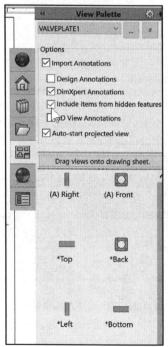

Insert three drawing views using the View Palette.
64) Click the **View Palette** [icon] tab in the Task Pane.

65) Select **VALVEPLATE1** from the drop-down menu.

66) Check the **Import Annotations** box. Check the **DimXpert Annotations** box.

67) Click the **Include items from Hidden Features** box.

68) Click and drag the **(A) Front** view into Sheet1 in the lower left corner.

69) Click a **position** directly above the Front view. Click a **position** directly to the right of the Front view. Three views are displayed.

70) Click **OK** ✔ from the Projected View PropertyManager.

Modify the Sheet Scale.
71) Right-click **Sheet1** in the Drawing PropertyManager.

72) Click **Properties**. Enter **1:1** for Scale.

73) Click **Apply Change** from the Sheet Properties dialog box.

74) **Arrange** the dimensions as illustrated.

75) Address all **trailing zeroes** in the Options, Documents, Dimension section as illustrated.

76) Address the **Top** and **Right** display view modes to Hidden Lines Visible.

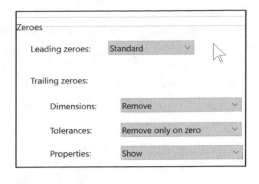

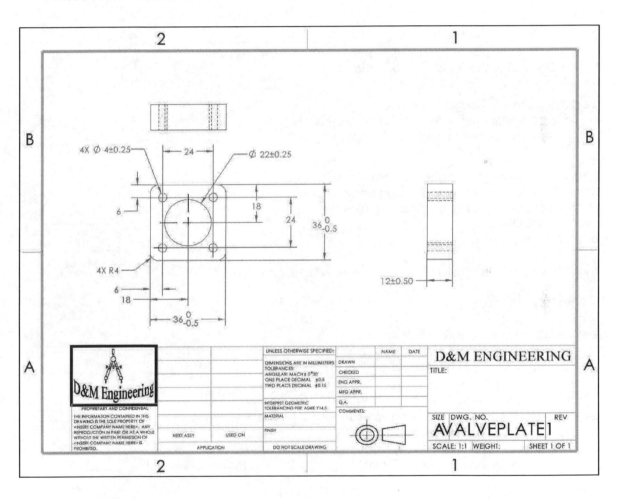

Hide the Top view.

77) Right-click **Drawing View2** in the Drawing FeatureManager.

78) Click **Hide**. Click **OK** ✔ from the Drawing View2 PropertyManager.

💡 To displayed a hidden dimension, click View, Hide/Show Annotations. The Hidden Annotations are displayed in the drawing.

Insert a Centerline in the Right view.

79) Click **Centerline** ⊞ from the Annotation toolbar.

80) Check the **Select View** box.

81) Click **inside** the Right view boundary.

82) Click **OK** ✔ from the Centerline PropertyManager. Note: The Right view is displayed with Hidden Lines Visible.

Hide small hole edges. Address Custom Properties, SOLIDWORKS Properties and Linked Properties for the final drawing. Save the Drawing. Close all open documents.

83) Hold the **Ctrl** key down.

84) Click the **four silhouette edges** as illustrated. Note the silhouette icon.

85) Right-click **Hide/Show Edges**.

86) Release the **Ctrl** key. **Hide** the Centerlines.

87) **Address** Material Custom Properties, Drawing Custom Properties, Linked Properties as illustrated in the drawing. The material comes from the part.

88) Click **Save** 💾 .

89) **Close** all open documents.

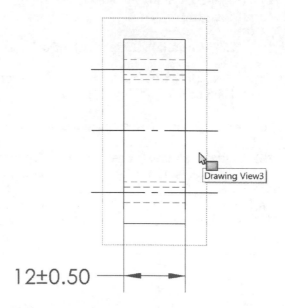

12±0.50

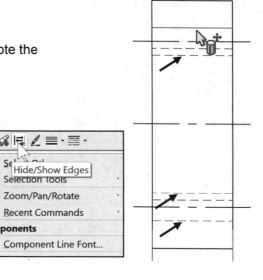

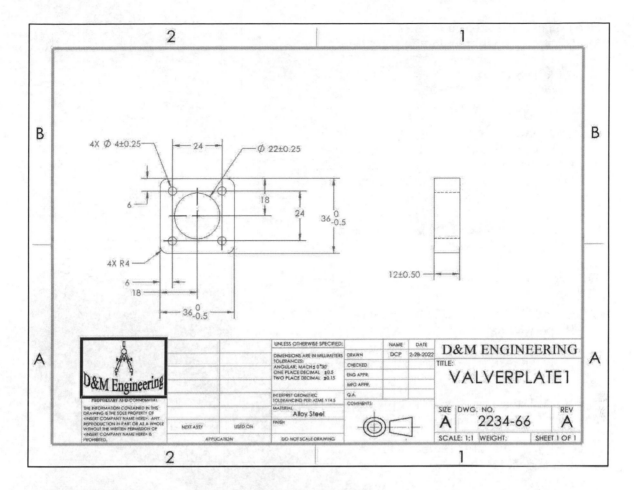

SOLIDWORKS MBD (Model Based Definition) in a Part

SOLIDWORKS MBD (Model Based Definition) lets you create models without the need for drawings giving you an integrated manufacturing solution for the SOLIDWORKS software. SOLIDWORKS MBD helps companies define, organize, and publish 3D product and manufacturing information (PMI), including 3D model data in industry standard file formats.

Activity: Vise Assembly – Model Base Definition in a Part

Open the Vise assembly. Apply the Model Base Definition method.

90) Click **Open** 📂 from the Main menu.

91) **Browse** to the SOLIDWORKS 2022/Chapter 9 folder.

92) Double-click the **Vise** assembly. The Vise FeatureManager is displayed.

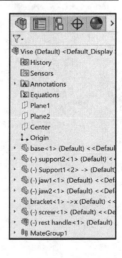

Add a Datum to the base component.

93) Right-click **base** from the FeatureManager.

94) Click **Open Part**.

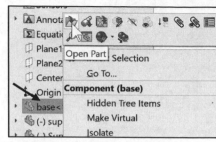

95) Click **Datum** ^{Datum} from the MBD Dimensions CommandManager. The Datum Feature PropertyManager is displayed. The default Datum label is A. The label is attached to the mouse pointer.

96) Click the **top face** of the part to located the Datum.

97) Click a **position above** the datum.

98) Click **OK** ✔ from the Datum Feature PropertyManager.

99) **View** the results.

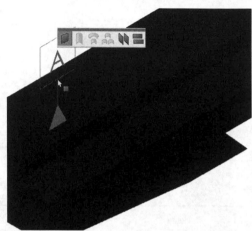

Insert a Size Dimension.

100) Click **Size Dimension**
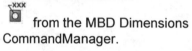 from the MBD Dimensions CommandManager.

101) Click the **right face** as illustrated.

102) Click **Create Width Feature** from the Pop-up menu.

103) Click the **opposite face** as illustrated.

104) Click **OK** ✔ from the Pop-up menu.

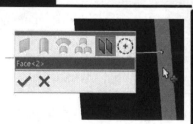

105) Place the **dimension** off the model. The DimXpert PropertyManager is displayed.

Set the Tolerance of the dimension.
106) Set Tolerance/Precision to **Limit**.

107) Enter Maximum Variation: **-0.12**mm.

108) Enter Minimum Variation: **-0.20**mm.

109) Set **Tolerance** and **Precision** as illustrated.

110) Click **OK** ✓ from the DimXpert PropertyManager.

111) **Save** and **close** the part. The Vise assembly is displayed.

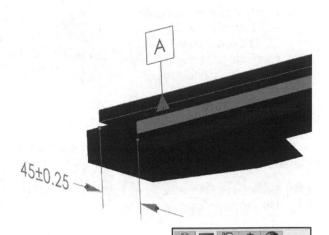

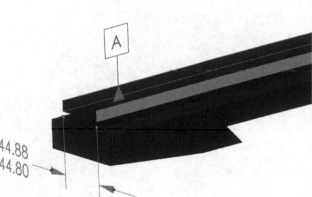

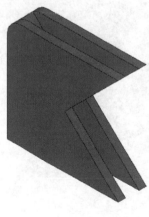

112) Open the **jaw1 part** from the vise assembly. The jaw1 FeatureManager is displayed.

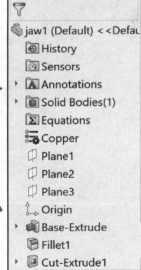

113) Insert **Datums A, B and C**
as illustrated using the
MBD Dimensions
CommandManager. Use
the same procedure as
above.

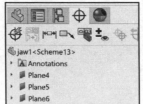

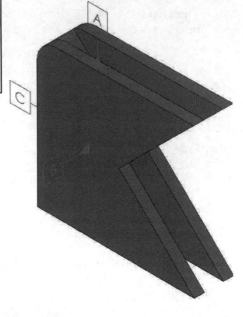

Insert a Size Dimension using the MBD Dimensions
CommandManager.

114) Click **Size Dimension** [xxx] from the MBD
Dimensions CommandManager.

115) Click the **inside right face**.

116) Click **Create Width Feature** from the Pop-up
menu.

117) Click the **inside left face.**

118) Click **OK** ✔ from the Pop-up menu.

119) **View** the results.

120) Click **OK** ✔ from the DimXpert
PropertyManager.

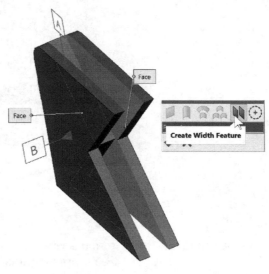

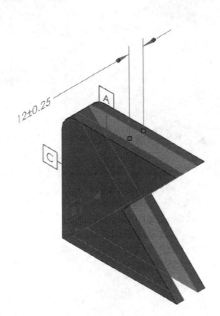

The Geometric Tolerance symbol can be added to a face or
dimension of the model. It is created in the same way as the
annotation geometric tolerance symbol in a drawing.

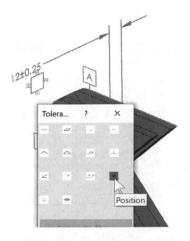

The Primary, Secondary and Tertiary datum names must
exist before adding them to the geometric tolerance symbol.

Insert Geometric Tolerance to the part.

121) Click the **Geometric Tolerance** tool from the MBD
Dimensions CommandManager.

122) Click the **Size Dimension** in the part.

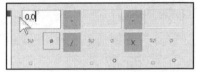

123) Click the **Symbol drop-down** arrow.

124) Click the **Position** ⊕ symbol.

125) Enter **0.0** for Tolerance 1.

126) Click **Material Condition** as illustrated.

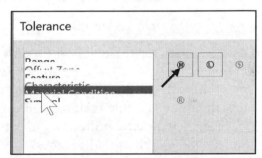

127) Click the **Max Material Condition** Ⓜ **symbol**.

128) Click **Add Datum**.

129) Enter **A**.

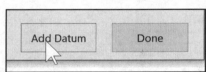

130) Click **Add New**.

131) Enter **B**.

132) Click **Done**.

133) Click **OK** ✓ from the Geometric Tolerance
PropertyManager.

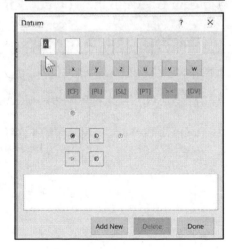

134) View the results.

135) Save and **Close** all models.

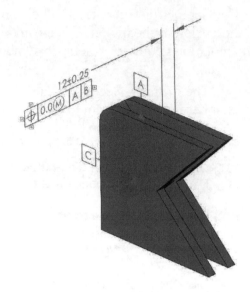

💡 Double-click the Feature Control frame as illustrated to display the Properties dialog box.

.

VALVEPLATE1-GDT Part - Datums, Feature Control Frames, Geometric Tolerances, and Surface Finish

Open the VALVEPLATE1-GDT part from the SOLIDWORKS 2022/Chapter 9 folder. View the three Extrude features, Linear Pattern feature, and Fillet feature. Apply the DimXpert: Geometric option to the part. View the inserted Datums, Feature Control Frames, and Geometric tolerances.

Edit the Feature Control Frames. Create the VALVEPLATE1-GDT drawing using the View Palette. Insert three drawing views. Insert Surface Finish on the Top and Right view. Create multiple Leaders to the Surface Finish symbol in the Top view. Insert Hide Tangent Edges in the Top and Right view.

Activity: VALVEPLATE1-GDT Part - Geometric option

Open the VALVEPLATE1-GDT part.

136) Click **Open** 📂 from the Main menu.

137) Double-click the **VALVEPLATE1-GDT** part from the SOLIDWORKS 2022/Chapter 9 folder. The Part FeatureManager is displayed.

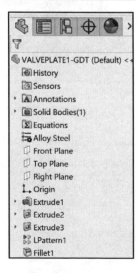

Apply DimXpert to the part.

138) Click the **DimXpertManager** ⊕ tab.

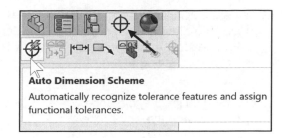

139) Click the **Auto Dimension Scheme** tool from the DimXpertManager. The Auto Dimension PropertyManager is displayed. Prismatic and Plus and Minus is selected by default. In this section, select the Geometric option.

Auto Dimension Scheme
Automatically recognize tolerance features and assign functional tolerances.

🔆 DimXpert: Geometric option provides the ability to locate axial features with position and circular run out tolerances. Pockets and surfaces are located with surface profiles.

140) Check the **Geometric** box as illustrated. Prismatic is selected by default.

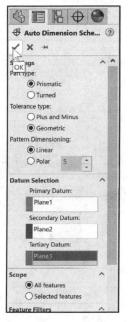

Select the three Datums.

141) Click the **back face** of the model. Plane1 is displayed in the Primary Datum box.

142) Click **inside** the Secondary Datum box.

143) Click the **left face** of the model. Plane2 is displayed in the Secondary Datum box.

144) Click **inside** the Tertiary Datum box.

145) Click the **top face** of the model. Plane3 is displayed in the Tertiary Datum box.

146) Click **OK** ✔ from the Auto Dimension PropertyManager.

147) Click **Isometric view**.

148) **View** the Datums, Feature Control Frames, and Geometric tolerances. All features are displayed in green.

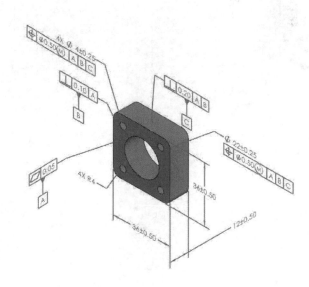

Edit a Feature Control Frame in the part.

149) Double-click the illustrated Feature Control Frame. Note the location to display the Properties dialog box.

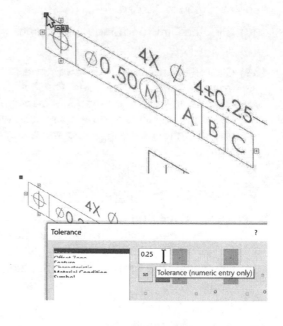

Modify the 0.50 feature tolerance.

150) Click **inside** the Tolerance 1 box.

151) Delete the existing text.

152) Enter **0.25**.

153) Click **Done**.

154) Repeat the above procedure for the second Position Feature Control Frame.

155) View the results.

156) Click **OK** ✔ from the Geometric Tolerance PropertyManager.

157) Click **Save**.

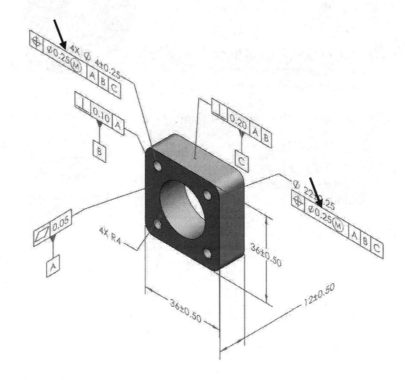

Activity: VALVEPLATE1-GDT Drawing - View Palette

Create the VALVEPLATE1-GDT drawing.

158) Click the **Make Drawing from Part/Assembly** in the Main menu.

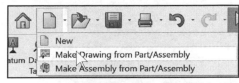

159) Click the **MY-TEMPLATES** tab.

160) Double-click the **A-ANSI-MM** drawing template.

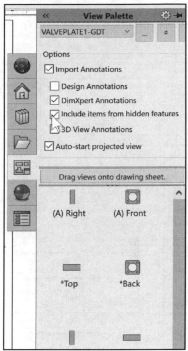

Insert three views using the View Palette tool.

161) Click the **View Palette** ⊞ tab in the Task Pane. VALVEPLATE1-GDT is displayed in the drop-down menu.

162) Check the **Import Annotations** box.

163) Check the **DimXpert Annotations** box.

164) Check the **Include items from hidden features** box. Note: The (A) next to the drawing view informs the user that DimXpert Annotations are present.

165) Click and drag the **(A) Front** view into Sheet1 in the lower left corner.

166) Click a **position** directly above the Front view.

167) Click a **position** directly to the right of the Front view. Three views are displayed.

168) Click **OK** ✔ from the Projected View PropertyManager.

Modify the Sheet Scale.

169) Right-click **Sheet1**.

170) Click **Properties**.

171) Enter **1:1** for Scale.

172) Click **OK** from the Sheet Properties dialog box.

173) **Arrange** the dimensions as illustrated.

174) Address all **trailing zeroes** in the Options, Documents, Dimension section.

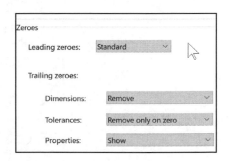

175) Address the **Top** and **Right** display view modes to Hidden Lines Visible.

Save the VALVEPLATE1-GDT drawing. Address Custom Properties, Drawing Custom Properties, Linked Properties and SOLIDWORKS Properties as illustrated. Note: The material comes from the part Custom Property.

176) Click **Save** .

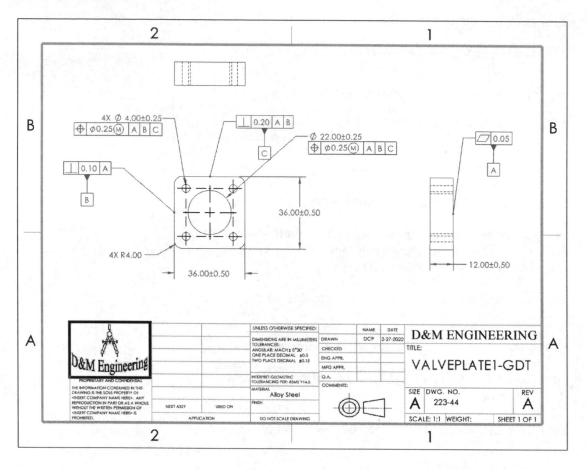

Activity: VALVEPLATE1-GDT Drawing- Surface Finish

Insert the Surface Finish symbol with a Bent Leader into the Top view.
177) Zoom in on the Top view.

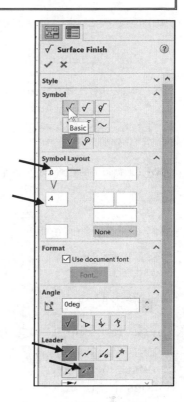

178) Click **Surface Finish** √ from the Annotation toolbar. The Surface Finish PropertyManager is displayed.

179) Click **Basic** for Symbol.

180) Enter **0.8** micrometers for Maximum Roughness.

181) Enter **0.4** micrometers for Minimum Roughness.

182) Click **Leader**.

183) Click **Bent Leader**.

184) Click the **top horizontal edge** of the Top view for the arrowhead attachment.

185) Click a **position** for the Surface Finish symbol.

186) Click **OK** ✔ from the Surface Finish PropertyManager.

Create multiple Leaders to the Surface Finish symbol.
187) Hold the **Ctrl** key down.

188) Click the tip of the **arrowhead**.

189) Drag the **arrowhead** to the bottom edge of the Top view.

190) Release the **Ctrl** key.

191) Release the mouse button.

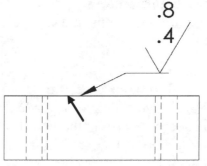

Insert Surface Finish symbol in the Right view.
192) Display **Hidden Edges Removed** in the Right view.

193) Click the **top horizontal edge** in the Right view.

194) Click **Surface Finish** √ from the Annotation toolbar. The Surface Finish PropertyManager is displayed.

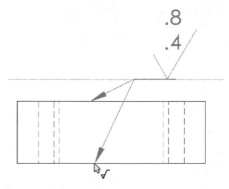

195) Select the **Machining Required** option for Symbol.

196) Enter **1.6** micrometer for Maximum Roughness.

197) Click **No Leader** .

198) Click the **top horizontal edge** of the Right view.

199) Click **OK** ✔ from the Surface Finish PropertyManager.

200) Drag the **Surface Finish Symbol** to the left of the profile line as illustrated.

201) **Insert** a Centerline ⊞ in the Right view.

Save the drawing.

202) Click **Save** 💾.

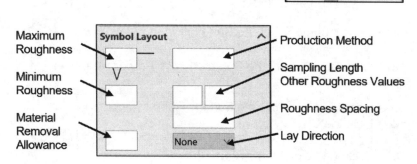

The Surface Finish PropertyManager contains additional options that refer to the machining process required to complete the part.

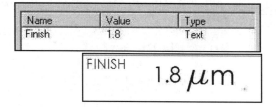

☀ To utilize a specific Finish in the Title Block, add the Custom Property, Finish in the Part. Link the Finish box in the Title Block to the Finish Property. The Greek Letter, m, is obtained from the SWGrekc Font.

Name	Value	Type
Finish	1.8	Text

FINISH   1.8 μm

eDrawing

An outside machine shop will manufacture the VALVEPLATE1-GDT. Send a
SOLIDWORKS eDrawing of the VALVEPLATE1-GDT to the machine shop for a price
quotation. Create a SOLIDWORKS eDrawing.

Activity: eDrawing

Create an eDrawing.
203) Click **File**, **Publish to eDrawings** from the Main menu.

204) Click **OK**. **View** your options.

205) **Save** the eDrawing.

206) **Close** all documents.

The Mark-up options are available in eDrawings Professional software application.

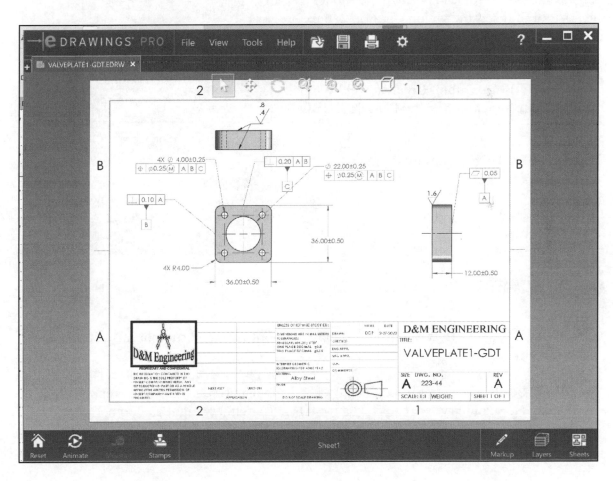

PLATE-TUBE Assembly Drawing and Weld Symbols

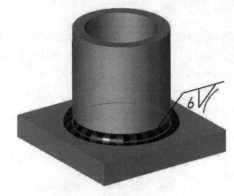

Open the PLATE-TUBE assembly from the SOLIDWORKS 2022/Chapter 9 folder. The customer requires a concept drawing of the PLATE-TUBE assembly. The TUBE part is welded to the PLATE part. Explore the procedures to create weld symbols:

- Weld Bead Assembly Feature

- Weld Symbol Annotation

Insert the Weld Bead assembly feature between the TUBE and PLATE parts in the PLATE-TUBE assembly. A weld symbol automatically attaches to the weld bead. Utilize the Model Items tool to insert the weld symbol into the Left view.

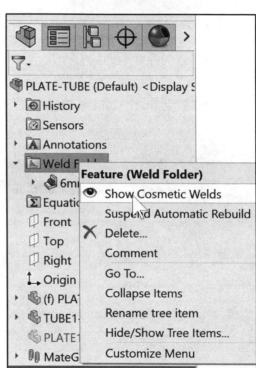

Add a second PLATE component to the PLATE-TUBE assembly. Create a weld symbol as a separate annotation in the PLATE-TUBE drawing.

The PLATE-TUBE assembly is created with three components:

- PLATE1-W<1> (Default)

- TUBE1-W<1>

- PLATE1-W<2> (Large Plate)

PLATE1-W<2> (Large Plate) is suppressed for the first portion of this activity

Weld beads use a simplified display. They are displayed as graphical representations in models. No geometry is created. The weld beads are lightweight and do not affect performance.

Activity: PLATE-TUBE Assembly Drawing and Weld Symbols

Create a Weld Bead in the PLATE-TUBE assembly.
207) Open the PLATE-TUBE assembly from the
      SOLIDWORKS 2022/Chapter 9 folder.

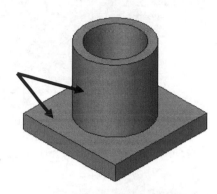

Create a Weld bead between the PLATE1-W<1> and TUBE1-
W<1> components.
208) Click **Insert**, **Assembly Feature**, **Weld Bead** from the
      Main menu. The Weld Bead PropertyManager is
      displayed.

- Weld paths are supported between two bodies. You
  cannot define a weld path among three or more bodies
  or between the faces of one body.

- Gaps between faces are supported.

- Gaps between edges are not supported. Edges must lie on
  the surface of a body.

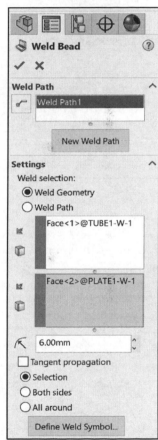

The Smart Weld Section   tool provides the ability to let
you drag the pointer over the faces where you want to apply a
weld bead.

Select the weld faces.
209) Click the **outside cylindrical face** of the TUBE1-W component.

210) Click **inside** the Weld To box.

211) Click the **top face** of the PLATE1-W<1> component.

212) Enter **6.00** for Bead size.

213) Check **Selection**.

214) Click the **Define Weld Symbol** button. The Weld dialog box is
      displayed.

215) Click the **Weld Symbol** button as
      illustrated.

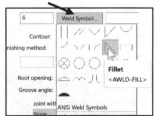

216) Select **Fillet** from the ANSI Weld
      Symbols drop-down menu.

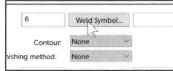

217) Select **Concave** for Contour.

218) Click **OK** from the dialog box.

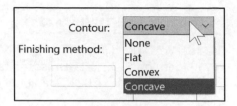

219) Click **OK** ✔ from the Weld Bead PropertyManager. View the results. A Weld Folder is displayed in the FeatureManager.

View the weld.
220) Right-click the **Weld Folder** in the FeatureManager.

221) Click **Show Cosmetic Welds**.

222) View the results in the Graphics area.

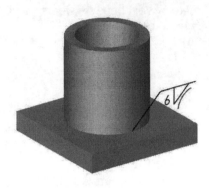

Save the PLATE-TUBE assembly.

223) Click **Save** 💾.

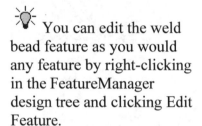 You can edit the weld bead feature as you would any feature by right-clicking in the FeatureManager design tree and clicking Edit Feature.

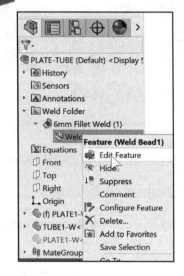

🔆 View the additional options in the Weld Bead PropertyManager to create various gaps and pitch with the bead.

Create a new PLATE-TUBE drawing.

224) Click **Make Drawing from Part/Assembly** from the Main menu.

225) Double-click **A-MM-ANSI** from the MY-TEMPLATES folder.

226) Click the **View Palette** tab.

227) Drag the ***Front** view to the left of Sheet1 as illustrated.

228) Click **OK** from the Projected View PropertyManager.

Save the PLATE-TUBE drawing.

229) Click **Save** . Accept the default name.

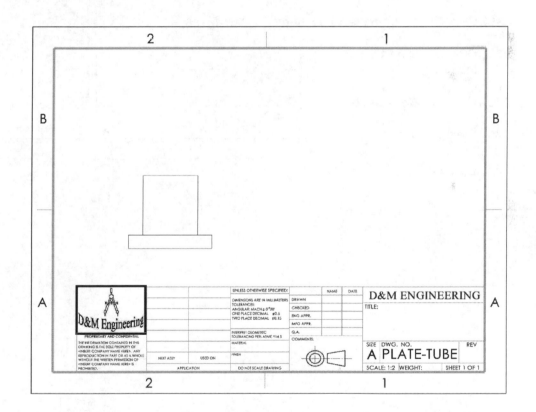

Insert the Model Items Weld Symbols.
230) Click **inside** the drawing view.

231) Click **Model Items** 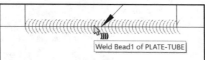 from the Annotation toolbar.

232) Select **Entire model** from the Source/Destination box.

233) Uncheck the Dimensions, Marked for Drawing option. Note: No Dimensions are inserted.

234) Deselect all options in the Annotations box.

235) Click **End Treatment** from the Annotations box.

236) Click **Weld Symbols** from the Annotations box.

237) Click the **Caterpillar** from the Annotations box. The caterpillar symbol represents the position and length of a weld bead on a drawing. The symbol comprises repeated circular or linear shapes along an edge.

238) Click **OK** ✔ from the Model Items PropertyManager.

239) Drag the **Weld Symbol** off the profile.

240) Click the **Weld Bead**.

241) View the options.

242) Click **OK** ✔.

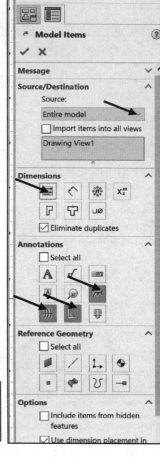

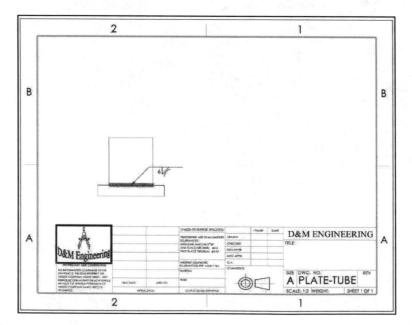

Return to the PLATE-TUBE assembly.
243) Click **Window**, **PLATE-TUBE** from the Main menu.

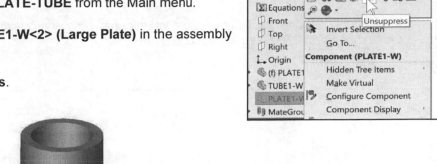

244) Right-click **PLATE1-W<2> (Large Plate)** in the assembly FeatureManager.

245) Click **Unsuppress**.

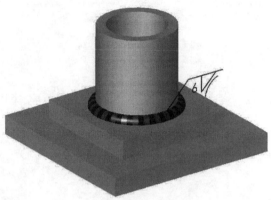

Return to the PLATE-TUBE drawing.
246) Press **Ctrl + Tab**.

247) Click the **right intersection** as illustrated.

248) Click **Weld Symbol** from the Annotation toolbar.

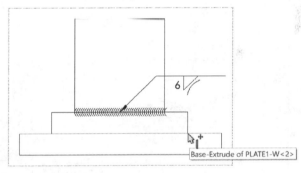

249) Click the **Around** checkbox to indicate that the weld extends completely around the joint.

250) Click the second **Weld Symbol** button.

251) Select **Fillet**.

252) Enter **6** for Bead size.

253) Select **Convex** for Contour.

254) Select **G-Grinding** for Finish Method.

255) Click **OK** from the Properties dialog box.

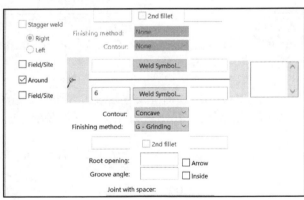

256) Drag the **Weld Symbol** off the profile line as illustrated.

Save the PLATE-TUBE drawing. Address Custom Properties, Drawing Custom Properties, Linked Properties and SOLIDWORKS Properties as illustrated.

257) Click **Save** .

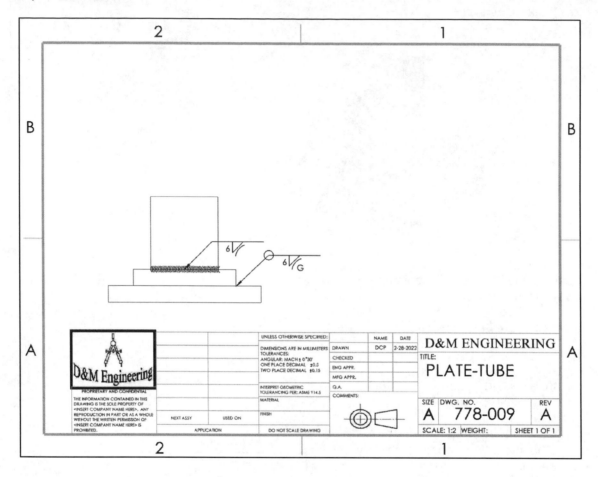

The ANSI Weld Properties dialog box contains Weld Symbols, Contour options, and Finishing method options:

- Weld Symbol options: *Square, Scarf, V Groove, Bevel, U Groove, J Groove, Flare-V, Flare-Bevel, Fillet, Seam, Flange-Edge, Flange-Corner.*

- Contour options: *None, Flat, Convex,* or *Concave.*

- Finishing method: *None, Chipping, Grinding, Hammering, Machining, Rolling,* or *Unspecified.*

Chapter Summary

You created four drawings: VALVEPLATE1, VALVEPLATE1-GDT, VALVEPLATE1-GDT eDrawing, and PLATE-TUBE. You applied MBD (Model Base Definition) tools to two parts.

VALVEPLATE1 drawing: You opened the VALVEPLATE1 part. You applied DimXpert: Plus and Minus option and inserted dimensions and Geometric tolerances. You created the VALVEPLATE1 drawing with the View Palette tool. Inserted three drawing views. Hide the Top view. Inserted a Centerline and Hide Tangent Edges in the Right view. Displayed None and Bilateral tolerance. Used a Custom Drawing Template. Inserted Custom Material and Drawing Properties.

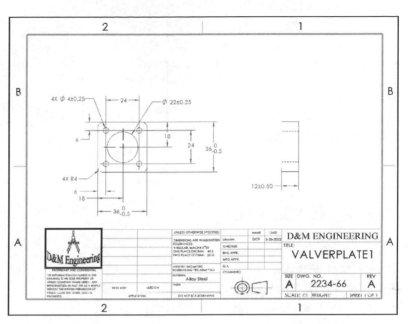

VALVEPLATE1-GDT drawing: You opened the VALVEPLATE1-GDT part. Applied DimXpert: Geometric option. Applied DBM Dimensions CommandManager tools. Inserted Datums, Feature Control Frames, and Geometric Tolerances. Edited Feature Control Frames. Created the VALVEPLATE1-GDT drawing using the View Palette tool. Inserted three drawing views. Inserted the

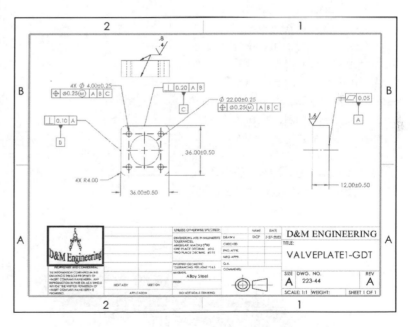

Surface Finish symbol on the Top and Right view. Created multiple Leaders to the Surface Finish symbol. Inserted Hide Tangent Edges in the Top and Right view.

VALVEPLATE1-GDT eDrawing: You created an eDrawing. In eDrawing®, you can view and animate models and drawings and create documents convenient for sending to others. Send a SOLIDWORKS eDrawing outside to a machine shop for quotation. The VALVEPLATE1-GDT eDrawing is a compressed standalone document.

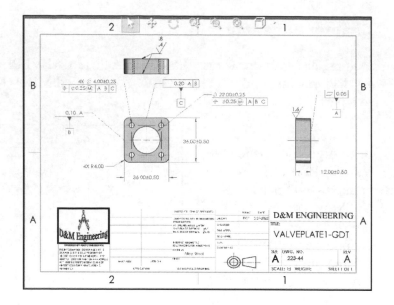

PLATE-TUBE drawing: You opened the PLATE-TUBE assembly. You created the PLATE-TUBE drawing. The PLATE-TUBE drawing is a conceptual customer drawing. The customer is concerned about the cosmetic appearance of a weld. You then inserted the Weld Bead assembly feature between the TUBE and PLATE parts in the PLATE-TUBE assembly. You used a Custom Drawing Template and inserted Custom Drawing Properties.

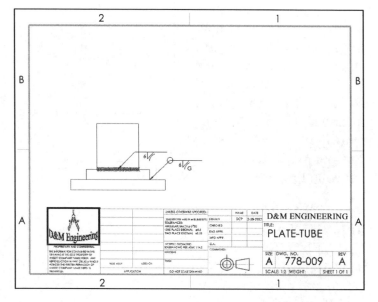

You applied MBD (Model Base Definition) tools to two parts.

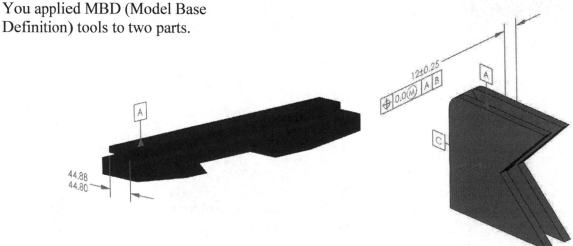

Questions:

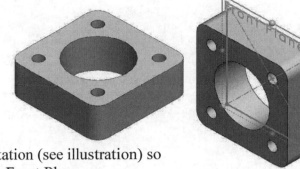

1. Datum Feature, Geometric Tolerance, Surface Finish and Weld Symbols are located in the _____ CommandManager.

2. Defined the procedure to redefine a simple part (single feature) orientation (see illustration) so that the top face is parallel with the Front Plane.

3. True or False. A SOLIDWORKS part file is a required attachment to email a SOLIDWORKS eDrawing.

4. Describe MBD. What are some of the benefits in using MBD?

5. Identify 4 tools in MBD.

6. Datum Symbols A, B and C in the VALVEPLATE1 drawing represent the _____, _____, and _____ reference planes.

7. Identify the procedure to view the Weld Bead PropertyManager.

8. True or False: Weld paths are supported between two bodies. You cannot define a weld path among three or more bodies or between the faces of one body.

9. Identify three different Finishing Methods which SOLIDWORKS supports.

10. SOLIDWORKS Design Tables use MS _____ software.

Exercises:

Exercise 9.1:

Open the ANGLE PLATE part from the SOLIDWORKS 2022/Chapter 9 Homework/Example 9-1 folder.

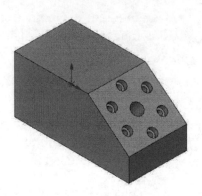

Create an A-Landscape, ANSI, MMGS, Third Angle drawing. Sheet Scale: 1:2.

Insert a Front view, Bottom view, and Auxiliary view. Use Geometric relations when constructing centerlines. The centerline drawn between the Front view and the Auxiliary view is perpendicular to the angled edge.

Insert the Feature Control Frames before applying Datum Reference Symbols as illustrated.

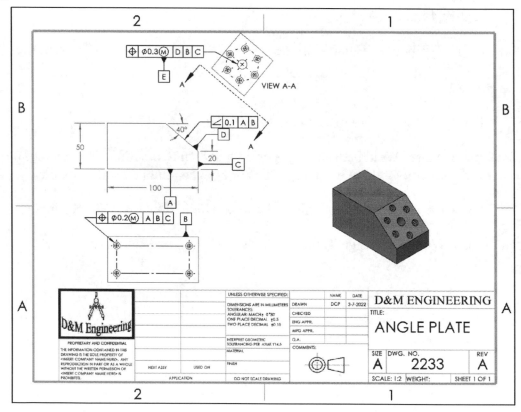

Exercise 9.2:

Investigate three different fits for a 16mm shaft and a 16mm hole using the HOLE part, SHAFT part and HOLE-SHAFT assembly configurations. See below table.

TabLE 9.1 TYPE of FIT (MILLIMETERS ASME B4.2)				
Type of Fit	**MAX/MIN**	**HOLE**	**SHAFT**	**FIT**
Close Running Fit	MAX	16.043	16.000	0.061
	MIN	16.016	15.982	0.016
Loose Running Fit	MAX	16.205	16.000	0.315
	MIN	16.095	15.890	0.095
Free Sliding Fit	MAX	16.024	16.000	0.035
	MIN	16.006	15.989	0.006

Create the HOLE part. Use the nominal dimension ∅16mm for the Hole feature and ∅16mm for the diameter of the Shaft. Set units to millimeters, 3 decimal places. Insert a Design Table for the HOLE that contains 6 different configurations.

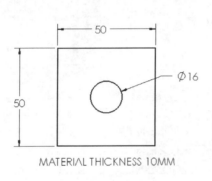

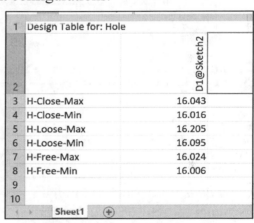

Create the SHAFT part. Insert a Design Table for the SHAFT that contains 6 different configurations as illustrated. The Min value is before the Max value. Format the columns in MS Excel to three decimal places.

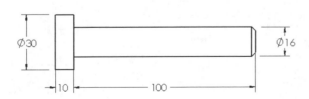

Create the HOLE-SHAFT assembly. Insert a new Design Table into the assembly that contains 6 configurations as illustrated below.

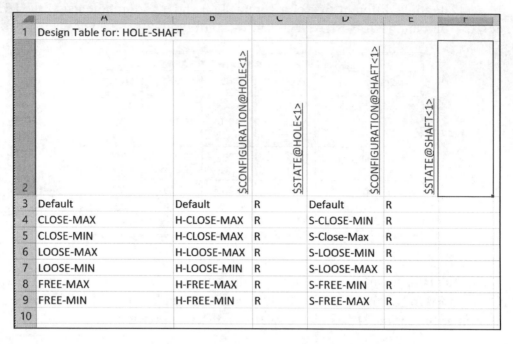

	A	B	C	D	E	F
1	Design Table for: HOLE-SHAFT					
2		$CONFIGURATION@HOLE<1>	$STATE@HOLE<1>	$CONFIGURATION@SHAFT<1>	$STATE@SHAFT<1>	
3	Default	Default	R	Default	R	
4	CLOSE-MAX	H-CLOSE-MAX	R	S-CLOSE-MIN	R	
5	CLOSE-MIN	H-CLOSE-MAX	R	S-Close-Max	R	
6	LOOSE-MAX	H-LOOSE-MAX	R	S-LOOSE-MIN	R	
7	LOOSE-MIN	H-LOOSE-MIN	R	S-LOOSE-MAX	R	
8	FREE-MAX	H-FREE-MAX	R	S-FREE-MIN	R	
9	FREE-MIN	H-FREE-MIN	R	S-FREE-MAX	R	
10						

Create an MS Excel document, HOLE-SHAFT-COMBINED.XLS.

Copy cells A3 through A8 in the Design Table HOLE-SHAFT to column A.

Copy cells B3 through B8 in the Design Table HOLE to column B.

Copy cells B3 through B8 in the Design Table SHAFT to column C.

Insert the formula =B2-C2 in column D to calculate the Fit.

	A	B	C	D
1		HOLE	SHAFT	FIT
2	CLOSE-MAX	16.043	15.982	0.061
3	CLOSE-MIN	16.016	16.000	0.016
4	LOOSE-MAX	16.205	15.890	0.315
5	LOOSE-MIN	16.095	16.000	0.095
6	FREE-MAX	16.024	15.989	0.035
7	FREE-MIN	16.006	16.000	0.006

Create a A-ANSI Landscape, MMGS, Third Angle drawing. Sheet Scale: 1:2.

Insert the HOLE-SHAFT assembly, SHAFT part and HOLE part.

Insert Balloons for the assembly. Modify the Balloon Property from Item Number to Custom. Enter H for the HOLE and S for the SHAFT.

Insert the Excel worksheet, HOLE-SHAFT-COMBINED. Click Insert, Object, Microsoft Excel. Add dimensions and Annotations. Insert all illustrated Custom Properties, Linked Properties, icons, etc.

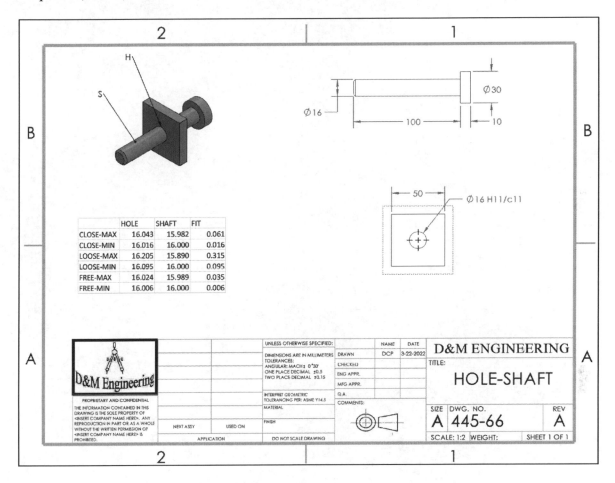

Notes:

Chapter 10

Introduction to the Certified SOLIDWORKS Associate (CSWA) Exam

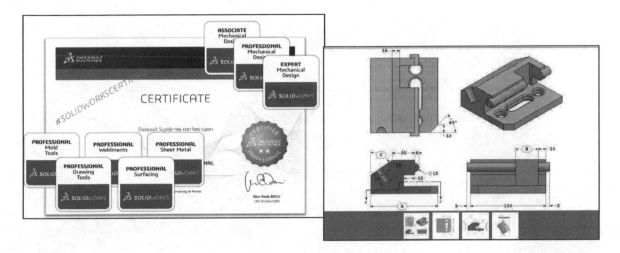

Below are the desired outcomes and usage competencies based on the completion of Chapter 10.

Desired Outcomes:	Usage Competencies:
• Procedure and process knowledge.	• Familiarity of the Certified SOLIDWORKS Associate (CSWA) exam.
• Exam categories:	• Comprehension of the skill sets to pass the Certified SOLIDWORKS Associate CSWA exam.
o Drafting Competencies.	
o Basic Part Creation and Modification.	• Awareness of the question types and exam format.
o Intermediate Part Creation and Modification.	• Capability to locate additional Certified SOLIDWORKS Associate CSWA exam information.
o Advanced Part Creation and Modification.	
o Assembly Creation and Modification.	

Notes:

Chapter 10 - Certified SOLIDWORKS Associate (CSWA) Exam

Chapter Objective

Provide a basic introduction into the curriculum and categories of the Certified SOLIDWORKS Associate (CSWA) exam. Awareness of the exam procedure, process, and required model knowledge needed to take the CSWA exam. The five exam categories are: Drafting Competencies, Basic Part Creation and Modification, Intermediate Part Creation and Modification, Advanced Part Creation and Modification, and Assembly Creation and Modification.

Introduction

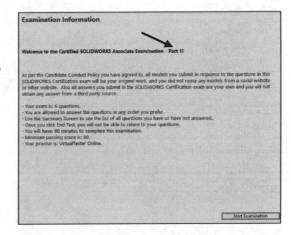

DS SOLIDWORKS Corp. offers various types of certification. Each stage represents increasing levels of expertise in 3D CAD: Certified SOLIDWORKS Associate CSWA, Certified SOLIDWORKS Professional CSWP and Certified SOLIDWORKS Expert CSWE along with specialty fields.

The CSWA Academic exam is provided either in a single 3-hour segment, or 2 - 90-minute segments.

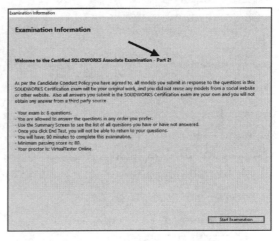

Part 1 of the CSWA Academic exam is 90 minutes, minimum passing score is 80, with 6 questions. There are two questions in the Basic Part Creation and Modification category, two questions in the Intermediate Part Creation and Modification category and two questions in the Assembly Creation and Modification category.

Part 2 of the CSWA Academic exam is 90 minutes, minimum passing score is 80 with 8 questions. There are three questions on the CSWA Academic exam in the Drafting Competencies category, three questions in the Advanced Part Creation and Modification category and two questions in the Assembly Creation and Modification category.

The CSWA exam for industry is only provided in a single 3-hour segment. The exam consists of 14 questions in five categories worth a total of 240 points.

All exams cover the same material.

CSWA Part 1:

Basic Part Creation and Modification, Intermediate Part Creation and Modification

There are **two questions** on the CSWA Academic exam in the *Basic Part Creation and Modification* category and **two questions** in the *Intermediate Part Creation and Modification* category.

The first question is in a multiple-choice single answer format. You should be within 1% of the multiple-choice answer before you move on to the modification single answer section, (fill in the blank format).

Each question is worth fifteen (15) points for a total of thirty (30) points.

You are required to build a model with six or more features and to answer a question either on the overall mass, volume, or the location of the Center of mass for the created model relative to the default part Origin location.

You are then requested to modify the part and answer a fill in the blank format question.

- *Basic Part Creation and Modification*: (Two questions - one multiple choice/one single answer - 15 points each).

  - Sketch Planes:

    - Front, Top, Right

  - 2D Sketching:

    - Geometric relations and dimensioning

    - Basic Sketch tools

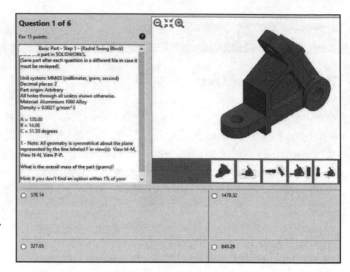

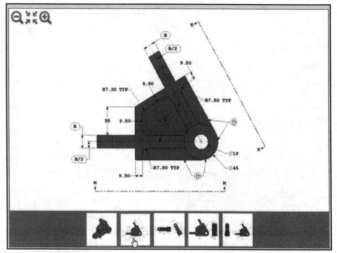

Screen shot from an exam

- Extruded Boss/Base Feature

- Extruded Cut feature

- Modification of basic part

- Mass Properties tool

In the *Basic Part Creation and Modification* category there is a dimension modification question based on the first (multiple choice) question. You should be within 1% of the multiple-choice answer before you go on to the modification single answer section.

- *Intermediate Part Creation and Modification*: (Two questions - one multiple choice/one single answer - 15 points each).

  - Sketch Planes:

    - Front, Top, Right, face, plane, etc.

  - Sketch Tools:

    - Line, Circle, Rectangle, Offset Entities, Convert Entities, etc.

  - 2D Sketching:

    - Geometric relations and dimensioning.

  - Extruded Boss/Base Feature

  - Extruded Cut Feature

  - Revolved Boss/Base Feature

  - Mirror, Chamfer, and Fillet Feature

  - Circular and Linear Pattern Feature

  - Plane Feature

  - Mass Properties and Measure tool

  - Show/Hide Axes

  - Modification of Intermediate part

You should be within 1% of the multiple choice answer before you go on to the modification single answer section.

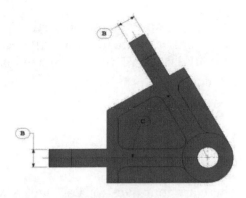

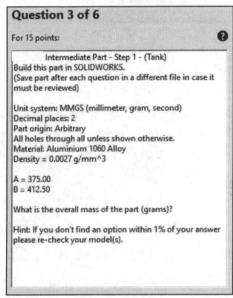

Question 3 of 6

For 15 points:

Intermediate Part - Step 1 - (Tank)
Build this part in SOLIDWORKS.
(Save part after each question in a different file in case it must be reviewed)

Unit system: MMGS (millimeter, gram, second)
Decimal places: 2
Part origin: Arbitrary
All holes through all unless shown otherwise.
Material: Aluminium 1060 Alloy
Density = 0.0027 g/mm^3

A = 375.00
B = 412.50

What is the overall mass of the part (grams)?

Hint: If you don't find an option within 1% of your answer please re-check your model(s).

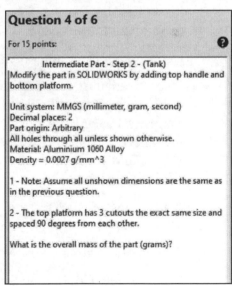

Question 4 of 6

For 15 points:

Intermediate Part - Step 2 - (Tank)
Modify the part in SOLIDWORKS by adding top handle and bottom platform.

Unit system: MMGS (millimeter, gram, second)
Decimal places: 2
Part origin: Arbitrary
All holes through all unless shown otherwise.
Material: Aluminium 1060 Alloy
Density = 0.0027 g/mm^3

1 - Note: Assume all unshown dimensions are the same as in the previous question.

2 - The top platform has 3 cutouts the exact same size and spaced 90 degrees from each other.

What is the overall mass of the part (grams)?

Screen shots from an exam.

🔆 If you do not pass the certification exam (either segment), you will need to wait 30 days until you can retake that segment of the exam.

CSWA Part 1: Cont.

Assembly Creation and Modification

There are four questions on the CSWA Academic exam (**2 questions** in Part 1, 2 questions in Part 2) in the Assembly Creation and Modification category: (2) different assemblies - (4) questions - (2) multiple choice / (2) single answer - 30 points each.

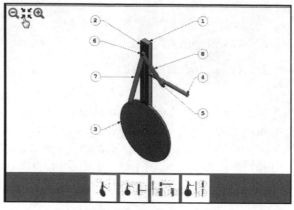

- *Assembly Creation and Modification*: (Two different assemblies - four questions - two multiple choice/two single answers - 30 points each).

  - Download Assembly zip file

  - Save zip file to a local hard drive

  - Un-zip components

  - Create a new Assembly document

  - Insert first component. Fix first component to the origin of the assembly

  - Insert all needed components

  - Insert needed mates: Coincident, Concentric, Perpendicular, Parallel, Tangent, Distance, Angle, Advanced Distance, Advanced Angle, and Aligned, Anti-Aligned option

  - Apply Mass Properties and Measure tool

  - Show/Hide Axes

  - Create a new Coordinate System

  - Modify assembly

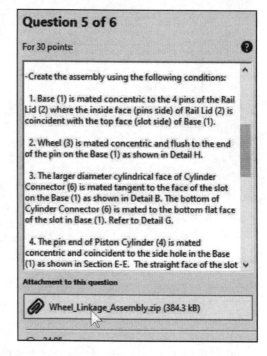

Question 5 of 6

For 30 points: ❓

-Create the assembly using the following conditions:

 1. Base (1) is mated concentric to the 4 pins of the Rail Lid (2) where the inside face (pins side) of Rail Lid (2) is coincident with the top face (slot side) of Base (1).

 2. Wheel (3) is mated concentric and flush to the end of the pin on the Base (1) as shown in Detail H.

 3. The larger diameter cylindrical face of Cylinder Connector (6) is mated tangent to the face of the slot on the Base (1) as shown in Detail B. The bottom of Cylinder Connector (6) is mated to the bottom flat face of the slot in Base (1). Refer to Detail G.

 4. The pin end of Piston Cylinder (4) is mated concentric and coincident to the side hole in the Base (1) as shown in Section E-E. The straight face of the slot ⌄

Attachment to this question

📎 Wheel_Linkage_Assembly.zip (384.3 kB)

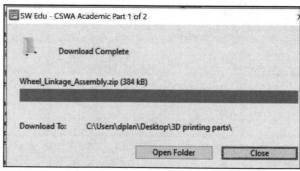

Use the view indicator to increase or decrease the active model in the view window.

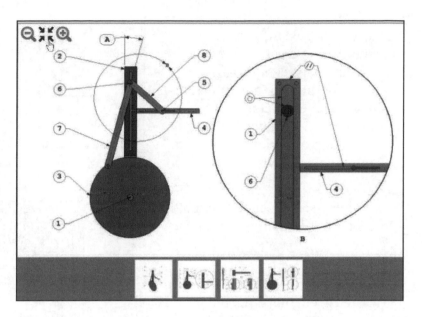

🔆 In the Assembly Creation and Modification category (Part 1 and Part 2), expect to see five to eight components. There are two-dimension modification questions based on the first (multiple choice) question. You should be within 1% of the multiple-choice answer before you go on to the modification single answer section.

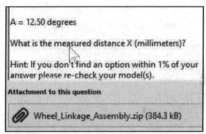

🔆 Use the Measure tool in the Assembly section. Apply correct units for measurement.

CSWA Part 2:

Introduction and Drafting Competencies

There are **three questions** on the CSWA Academic exam in the *Drafting Competencies* category. Each question is worth five (5) points.

The three questions are in a multiple-choice single answer format. You are allowed to answer the questions in any order you prefer.

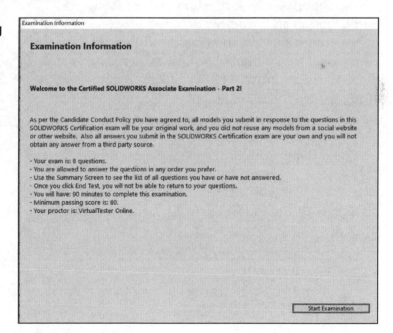

In the *Drafting Competencies* category of the exam, you are **not required** to create or perform an analysis on a part, assembly, or drawing but you are required to have general drafting/drawing knowledge and understanding of various drawing view methods.

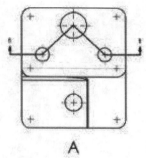

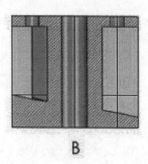

A   B

The questions are on general drawing views: Projected, Section, Break, Crop, Detail, Alternate Position, etc.

Advanced Part Creation and Modification

There are **three questions** on the CSWA Academic exam (Part 2) in the Advanced Part Creation and Modification category.

The first question is in a multiple-choice single answer format.

The other two questions (Modification of the model) are in the fill in the blank format.

The main difference between the Advanced Part Creation and Modification and the Basic Part Creation and Modification or the Intermediate Part Creation and Modification category is the complexity of the sketches and the number of dimensions and geometric relations along with an increased number of features.

Drafting Competencies - To create drawing view 'B' it is necessary to select drawing view 'A' and insert which SolidWorks view type?

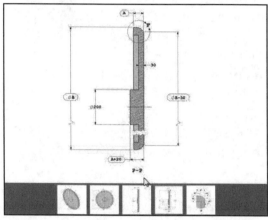

Advanced Part (Bracket) - Step 1
Build this part in SolidWorks.
(Save part after each question in a different file in case it must be reviewed)

Unit system: MMGS (millimeter, gram, second)
Decimal places: 2
Part origin: Arbitrary
All holes through all unless shown otherwise.
Material: AISI 1020 Steel
Density = 0.0079 g/mm^3

A = 64.00
B = 20.00
C = 26.50

What is the overall mass of the part (grams)?

Screen shots from the exam.

- *Advanced Part Creation and Modification:* (Three questions - one multiple choice/two single answers - 15 points each).

  - Sketch Planes:

    - Front, Top, Right, face, plane, etc.

    - 2D Sketching or 3D Sketching

  - Sketch Tools:

    - Line, Circle, Rectangle, Offset Entities, Convert Entities, etc.

  - Extruded Boss/Base Feature

  - Extruded Cut Feature

  - Revolved Boss/Base Feature

  - Mirror, Chamfer, and Fillet Feature

  - Circular and Linear Pattern Feature

  - Shell Feature

  - Plane Feature

  - Mass Properties and Measure tool

  - Show/Hide Axes

  - More difficult geometry modifications

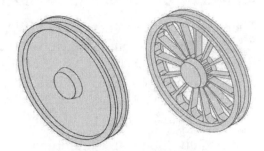

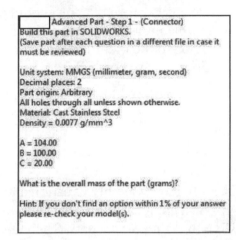

☐ Advanced Part - Step 1 - (Connector)
Build this part in SOLIDWORKS.
(Save part after each question in a different file in case it must be reviewed)

Unit system: MMGS (millimeter, gram, second)
Decimal places: 2
Part origin: Arbitrary
All holes through all unless shown otherwise.
Material: Cast Stainless Steel
Density = 0.0077 g/mm^3

A = 104.00
B = 100.00
C = 20.00

What is the overall mass of the part (grams)?

Hint: If you don't find an option within 1% of your answer please re-check your model(s).

💡 In the *Advanced Part Creation and Modification* category, there are two-dimension modification questions based on the first (multiple choice) question. You should be within 1% of the multiple-choice answer before you go on to the modification single answer section.

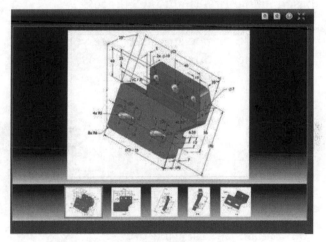

Screen shots from the exam

Each question is worth fifteen (15) points for a total of forty-five (45) points.

You are required to build a model, with six or more features and to answer a question either on the overall mass, volume, or the location of the Center of mass for the created model relative to the default part Origin location. You are then requested to modify the model and answer fill in the blank format questions.

Assembly Creation and Modification

There are four questions on the CSWA Academic exam (2 questions in part 1, **2 questions** in part 2) in the Assembly Creation and Modification category: (2) different assemblies - (4) questions - (2) multiple choice/ (2) single answer - 30 points each.

The first question is in a multiple-choice single answer format. You should be within 1% of the multiple-choice answer before you move on to the modification single answer section, (fill in the blank format).

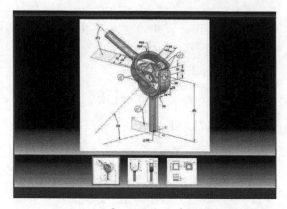

Screen shots from the exam

You are required to download the needed components from a provided zip file and insert them correctly to create the assembly.

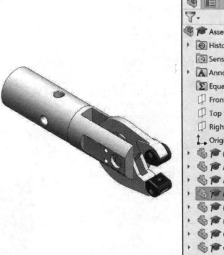

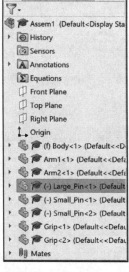

In the Assembly Creation and Modification category, expect to see five to eight components. There are two-dimension modification questions based on the first (multiple choice) question. You should be within 1% of the multiple-choice answer before you go on to the modification single answer section.

No Surfacing questions are on the CSWA exam at this time.

Know how to create and apply an Advance distance and angle mate. Use the Measure tool in the assembly on the components.

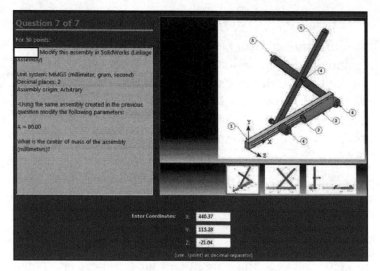

Intended Audience

The intended audience is anyone with a minimum of 3 - 6 months of SOLIDWORKS experience and basic knowledge of engineering fundamentals and practices. SOLIDWORKS recommends that you review their SOLIDWORKS Tutorials on Parts, Assemblies and Drawings as a prerequisite and have at least 45 hours of classroom time learning SOLIDWORKS or using SOLIDWORKS with basic engineering design principles and practices.

To prepare for the CSWA exam, it is recommended that you first perform the following:

- Take a CSWA exam preparation class or review a text book written for the CSWA exam.

- Visit the VirtualTester Certification site at https://3dexperience.virtualtester.com/#home. Download and open a sample CSWA exam.

- Complete the SOLIDWORKS Tutorials.

- Practice creating models from the isometric working drawings sections of any technical drawing or Engineering book.

During the Exam

During the exam, SOLIDWORKS provides the ability to click on a detail view below (as illustrated) to obtain additional details and dimensions during the exam.

During the exam, use the control keys at the bottom of the screen to:

- *Show the Previous Question.*
- *Reset the Question.*
- *Show the Summary Screen.*
- *Move to the Next Question.*

When you are finished, press the End Examination button. The tester will ask you if you want to end the test. Click Yes.

If there are any unanswered questions, the tester will provide a warning message as illustrated.

Use the clock in the tester to view the amount of time that you used and the amount of time that is left in the exam.

Use the view indicator to increase or decrease the active model in the view window.

If you do not pass the certification exam (either segment), you will need to wait 30 days until you can retake that segment of the exam.

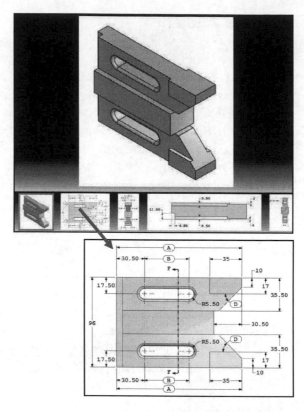

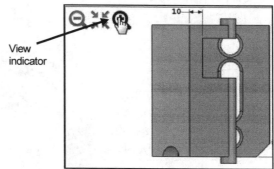

View indicator

Examples: Drafting Competencies

Drafting Competencies is one of the five categories on the CSWA exam. There are three questions - multiple choice format - 5 points each that require general knowledge and understanding of drawing view methods and basic 3D modeling techniques.

Spend no more than 10 minutes on each question in this category for the exam. Manage your time.

Sample Questions in the category

In the *Drafting Competencies* category, an exam question could read:

Question 1: Identify the view procedure. To create the following view, you need to insert a:

- A: Open Spline
- B: Closed Spline
- C: 3 Point Arc
- D: None of the above

The correct answer is B.

Question 2: Identify the illustrated view type.

- A: Crop view
- B: Section view
- C: Projected view
- D: None of the above

The correct answer is A.

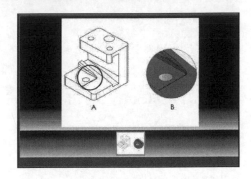

Drafting Competencies - To create drawing view 'B' it is necessary to select drawing view 'A' and insert which SolidWorks view type?

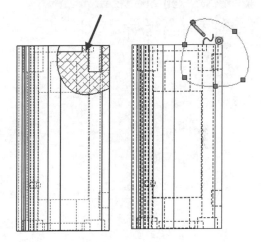

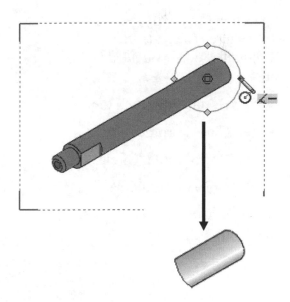

Question 3: Identify the illustrated Drawing view.

- A: Projected View
- B: Alternative Position View
- C: Extended View
- D: Aligned Section View

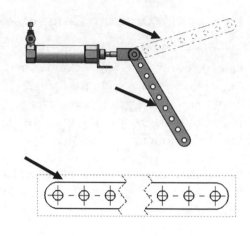

The correct answer is B.

Question 4: Identify the illustrated Drawing view.

- A: Crop View
- B: Break View
- C: Broken-out Section View
- D: Aligned Section View

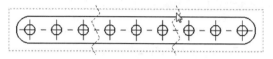

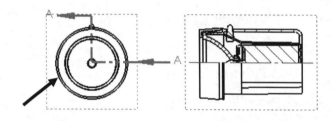

The correct answer is B.

Question 5: Identify the illustrated Drawing view.

- A: Section View
- B: Crop View
- C: Broken-out Section View
- D: Aligned Section View

The correct answer is D.

Question 6: Identify the view procedure. To create the following view, you need to insert a:

- A: Rectangle Sketch tool
- B: Closed Profile: Spline
- C: Open Profile: Circle
- D: None of the above

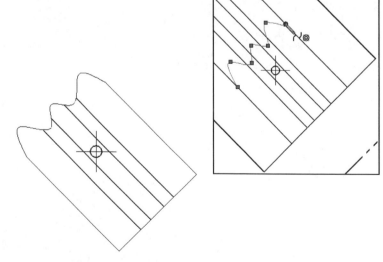

The correct answer is B.

Examples: Basic Part Creation and Modification and Intermediate Part Creation and Modification

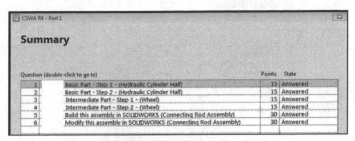

Basic Part Creation and Modification and *Intermediate Part Creation and Modification* are two of the five categories on the CSWA exam.

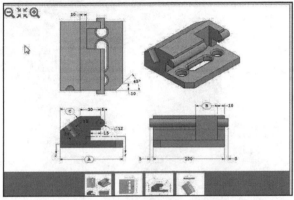

The main difference between the *Basic Part Creation and Modification* category and the *Intermediate Part Creation and Modification* or the *Advance Part Creation and Modification* category is the complexity of the sketches and the number of dimensions and geometric relations along with an increase in the number of features

There are two questions on the CSWA exam (Part 1) in the *Basic Part Creation and Modification* category and two questions in the *Intermediate Part Creation and Modification* category.

The first question is in a multiple-choice single answer format and the other question (Modification of the model) is in the fill in the blank format.

Each question is worth fifteen (15) points for a total of thirty (30) points.

You are required to build a model with six or more features and to answer a question either on the overall mass, volume, or the location of the Center of mass for the created model relative to the default part Origin location. You are then requested to modify the part and answer a fill in the blank format question.

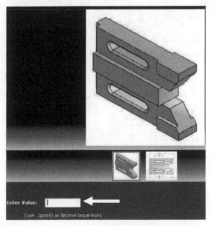

Screen shots from an exam

🔅 Spend no more than 40 minutes on the question in these categories. This is a timed exam. Manage your time.

Sample Questions in this category

Question 1:

Build the illustrated model from the provided information. Locate the Center of mass relative to the default coordinate system, Origin.

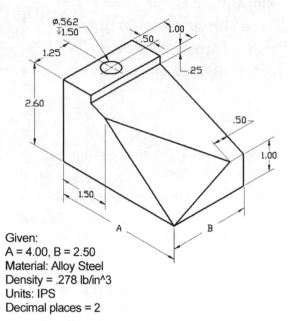

Given:
A = 4.00, B = 2.50
Material: Alloy Steel
Density = .278 lb/in^3
Units: IPS
Decimal places = 2

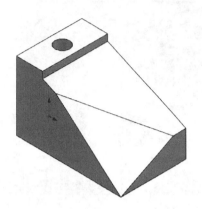

- A: X = -1.63 inches, Y = 1.48 inches, Z = -1.09 inches

- B: X = 1.63 inches, Y = 1.01 inches, Z = -0.04 inches

- C: X = 43.49 inches, Y = -0.86 inches, Z = -0.02 inches

- D: X = 1.63 inches, Y = 1.01 inches, Z = -0.04 inches

The correct answer is B.

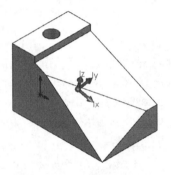

In the *Basic Part Creation and Modification* and *Intermediate Part Creation and Modification* category of the exam, you are required to read and understand an engineering document, set document properties, identify the correct Sketch planes, apply the correct Sketch and Feature tools and apply material to build a part.

Mass = 4.97 pounds

Volume = 17.86 cubic inches

Surface area = 46.77 square inches

Center of mass: (inches)
    X = 1.63
    Y = 1.01
    Z = -0.04

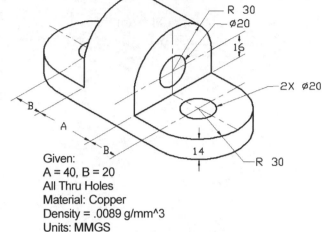

Note the Depth/Deep ⊤ symbol with a 1.50 dimension associated with the hole. The hole Ø.562 has a three decimal place precision. Hint: Insert three features to build this model: Extruded Base and two Extruded Cuts. Insert a 3D sketch for the first Extruded Cut feature. You are required to have knowledge in 3D sketching for the exam.

Given:
A = 40, B = 20
All Thru Holes
Material: Copper
Density = .0089 g/mm^3
Units: MMGS

All SOLIDWORKS models (initial and final) are provided. Download all needed folders and files: (https://www.sdcpublications.com/Downloads/978-1-63057-485-7)

Question 2:

Build the illustrated model from the provided information. Locate the Center of mass of the part.

- A: X = 0.00 millimeters, Y = 19.79 millimeters, Z = 0.00 millimeters

- B: X = 0.00 inches, Y = 19.79 inches, Z = 0.04 inches

- C: X = 19.79 millimeters, Y = 0.00 millimeters, Z = 0.00 millimeters

- D: X = 0.00 millimeters, Y = 19.49 millimeters, Z = 0.00 millimeters

- The correct answer is A.

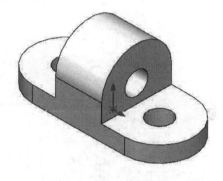

```
Mass properties of Part Modeling-Question2
      Configuration: Default
      Coordinate system: -- default --

Density = 0.01 grams per cubic millimeter

Mass = 1605.29 grams

Volume = 180369.91 cubic millimeters

Surface area = 29918.76  square millimeters

Center of mass: ( millimeters )
     X = 0.00
     Y = 19.79
     Z = 0.00
```

Question 3:

Build the illustrated model from the provided information. Locate the Center of mass of the part.

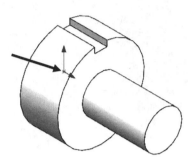

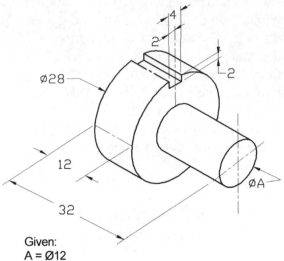

Given:
A = Ø12
Material: Cast Alloy Steel
Density = .0073 g/mm^3
Units: MMGS

- A: X = 10.00 millimeters, Y = -79.79 millimeters,
  Z: = 0.00 millimeters

- B: X = 9.79 millimeters, Y = -0.13 millimeters,
  Z = 0.00 millimeters

- C: X = 9.77 millimeters, Y = -0.10 millimeters,
  Z = -0.02 millimeters

- D: X = 10.00 millimeters, Y = 19.49 millimeters,
  Z = 0.00 millimeters

- The correct answer is B.

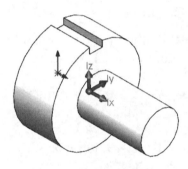

Mass properties of Part Modeling-Question3
    Configuration: Default
    Coordinate system: -- default --

Density = 0.01 grams per cubic millimeter

Mass = 69.77 grams

Volume = 9557.27 cubic millimeters

Surface area = 3069.83 square millimeters

Center of mass: (millimeters)
    X = 9.79
    Y = -0.13
    Z = 0.00

Question 4:

Build the illustrated model from the
provided information. Locate the
Center of mass of the part.

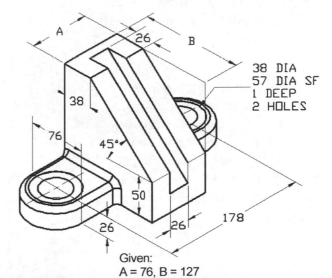

Given:
A = 76, B = 127
Material: 2014 Alloy
Density: .0028 g/mm^3
Units: MMGS
ALL ROUNDS EQUAL 6MM

There are numerous ways to build this model. Think
about the various features that create the model. Hint:
Insert seven features to build this model: Extruded
Base, Extruded Cut, Extruded Boss, Fillet, Extruded
Cut, Mirror and a second Fillet. Apply symmetry.

In the exam, create the left half of the model first, and then
apply the Mirror feature. This is a timed exam.

- A: X = 49.00 millimeters, Y = 45.79 millimeters,
  Z = 0.00 millimeters

- B: X = 0.00 millimeters, Y = 19.79 millimeters,
  Z = 0.04 millimeters

- C: X = 49.21 millimeters, Y = 46.88 millimeters,
  Z = 0.00 millimeters

- D: X = 48.00 millimeters, Y = 46.49 millimeters,
  Z = 0.00 millimeters

The correct answer is C.

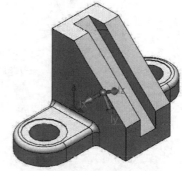

Mass = 3437.29 grams

Volume = 1227602.22 cubic millimeters

Surface area = 101091.11 square millimeters

Center of mass: (millimeters)
  X = 49.21
  Y = 46.88
  Z = 0.00

Question 5:

Build the illustrated model from the provided information. Locate the Center of mass of the part. All Thru Holes.

💡 Think about the various features that create this model. Hint: Insert five features to build this part: Extruded Base, two Extruded Bosses, Extruded Cut, and Rib. Insert a Reference plane to create the Extruded Boss feature.

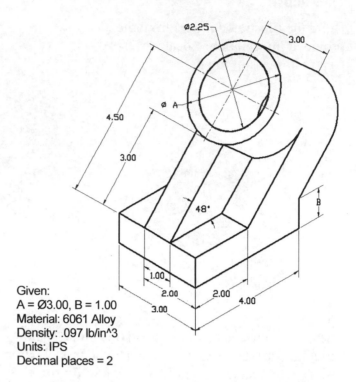

Given:
A = Ø3.00, B = 1.00
Material: 6061 Alloy
Density: .097 lb/in^3
Units: IPS
Decimal places = 2

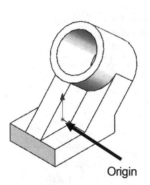

Origin

- A: X = 49.00 inches, Y = 45.79 inches, Z = 0.00 inches

- B: X = 0.00 inches, Y = 19.79 inches, Z = 0.04 inches

- C: X = 49.21 inches, Y = 46.88 inches, Z = 0.00 inches

- D: X = 0.00 inches, Y = 0.73 inches, Z = -0.86 inches

The correct answer is D.

Mass properties of Part Modeling-Question5
  Configuration: Default
  Coordinate system: -- default --

Density = 0.10 pounds per cubic inch

Mass = 2.99 pounds

Volume = 30.65 cubic inches

Surface area = 100.96 square inches

Center of mass: (inches)
  X = 0.00
  Y = 0.73
  Z = -0.86

Question 6:

Build the illustrated model from the provided information.

Calculate the overall mass and volume of the part with the provided information.

- Precision for linear dimensions = **2**.

- Material: **AISI 304**.

- Units: **MMGS**.

- All Holes ⬇ **25**mm.

- All Rounds **5**mm.

- All Holes Ø**4**mm.

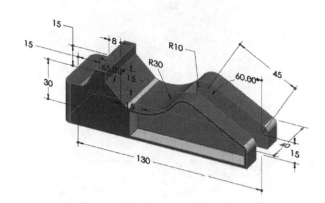

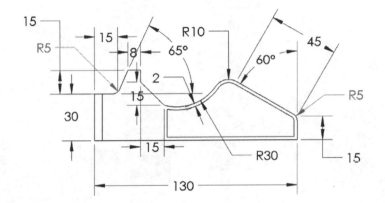

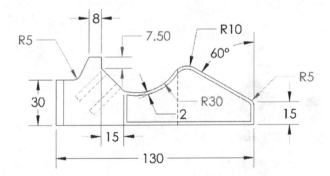

Front views

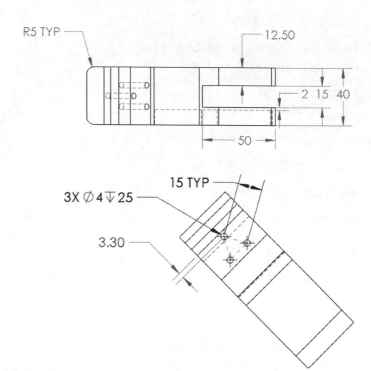

Top and Auxiliary

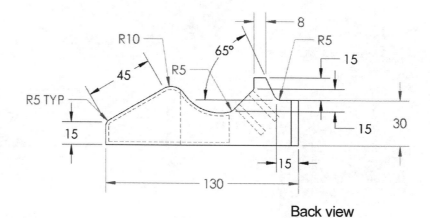

Calculate the mass:

A = 888.48grams

B = 990.50grams

C = 788.48grams

D = 820.57grams

Back view

If you don't find your answer (within 1%) in the multiple-choice single answer format section, recheck your solid model for precision and accuracy. It could be as simple as missing a few fillets.

Mass properties of Part Modeling-Question 6
　Configuration: Default
　Coordinate system: -- default --

Density = 0.01 grams per cubic millimeter

Mass = 888.48 grams

Volume = 111059.43 cubic millimeters

Surface area = 25814.97 square millimeters

Center of mass: (millimeters)
　X = -15.39
　Y = 15.93
　Z = -2.65

Calculate the volume:

A = 102259.43 cubic millimeters

B = 133359.47 cubic millimeters

C = 111059.43 cubic millimeters

D = 125059.49 cubic millimeters

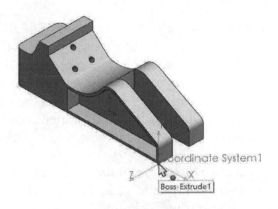

Question 6A:

Create a new coordinate system.

Center a new coordinate system with the provided illustration. The new coordinate system location is at the front right bottom point (vertex) of the model.

Enter the Center of Mass:

X = -80.39 millimeters

Y = -15.93 millimeters

Z = -22.65 millimeters

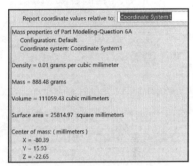

Question 6B:

Modify the illustrated model from the provided information.

Calculate the overall mass and volume of the part with the provided information.

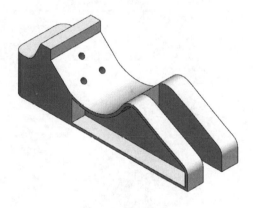

- Modify all fillets (rounds) to 7mm.

- Modify the overall length to 140mm.

- Modify material to 1060 alloy.

Enter the mass:

309.75 grams

Enter the volume:

114721.22 cubic millimeters

If you don't find your answer (within 1%) in the multiple-choice single answer format section, recheck your solid model for precision and accuracy. It could be as simple as missing a few fillets.

Examples: Advanced Part Creation and Modification

Advanced Part Creation and Modification is one of the five categories on the CSWA exam. The main difference between the *Advanced Part Creation and Modification* and the *Basic Part Creation and Modification* category and the *Intermediate Part Creation and Modification* is the complexity of the sketches and the number of dimensions and geometric relations along with an increased number of features.

There are three questions - one multiple choice/two single answers - 15 points each. The question is either on the location of the Center of mass relative to the default part Origin or to a new created coordinate system and all of the mass properties located in the Mass Properties dialog box: total overall mass, volume, etc.

Sample Questions in the Category

In the *Advanced Part Creation and Modification* category, an exam question could read:

Screen shots from the exam

Question 1:

Build the illustrated model from the provided information. Locate the Center of mass of the part.

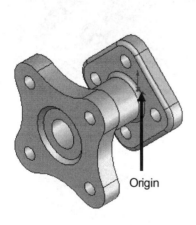

Origin

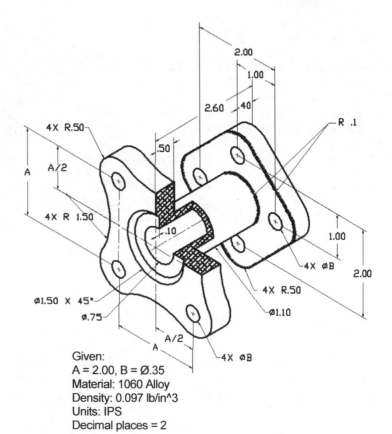

Given:
A = 2.00, B = Ø.35
Material: 1060 Alloy
Density: 0.097 lb/in^3
Units: IPS
Decimal places = 2

Think about the steps that you would take to build the illustrated part. Identify the location of the part Origin.

Start with the back base flange. Review the provided dimensions and annotations in the part illustration.

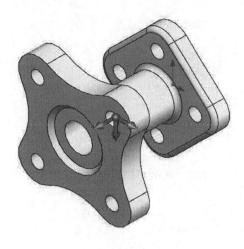

☀ The key difference between the *Advanced Part Creation and Modification* and the *Basic Part Creation and Modification* category and the *Intermediate Part Creation and Modification* is the complexity of the sketches and the number of features, dimensions, and geometric relations. You may also need to locate the Center of mass relative to a created coordinate system location.

Mass properties of Advanced Part Modeling-Question1
Configuration: Default
Coordinate system: -- default --

Density = 0.10 pounds per cubic inch

Mass = 0.59 pounds

Volume = 6.01 cubic inches

Surface area = 46.61 square inches

Center of mass: (inches)
 X = 0.00
 Y = 0.00
 Z = 1.51

- A: X = 1.00 inches, Y = 0.79 inches, Z = 0.00 inches

- B: X = 0.00 inches, Y = 0.00 inches, Z = 1.04 inches

- C: X = 0.00 inches, Y = 1.18 inches, Z = 0.00 inches

- D: X = 0.00 inches, Y = 0.00 inches, Z = 1.51 inches

The correct answer is D.

Question 2:

Build the illustrated model from the provided information. Locate the Center of mass of the part.

Hint: Create the part with eleven features and a Reference plane: Extruded Base, Plane1, two Extruded Bosses, two Extruded Cuts, Extruded Boss, Extruded Cut, Extruded-Thin, Mirror, Extruded Cut, and Extruded Boss.

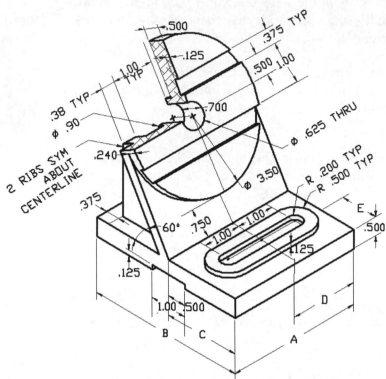

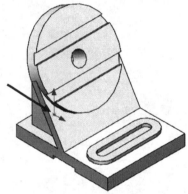

Given:
A = 3.500, B = 4.200, C = 2.000,
D =1.750, E = 1.000
Material: 6061 Alloy
Density: 0.097 lb/in^3
Units: IPS
Decimal places = 3

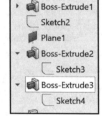

Think about the steps that you would take to build the illustrated part. Create the rectangular Base feature. Create Sketch2 for Plane1. Insert Plane1 to create Boss-Extrude2. Plane1 is the Sketch plane for Sketch3. Sketch3 is the sketch profile for Boss-Extrude2.

- A: X = 1.59 inches, Y = 1.19 inches, Z = 0.00 inches

- B: X = -1.59 inches, Y = 1.19 inches, Z = 0.04 inches

- C: X = 1.00 inches, Y = 1.18 inches, Z = 0.10 inches

- D: X = 0.00 inches, Y = 0.00 inches, Z = 1.61 inches

The correct answer is A.

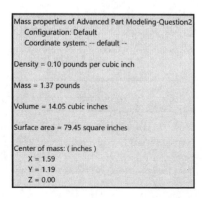

Question 3:

Build the illustrated model from the provided information. Locate the Center of mass of the part. Note the coordinate system location of the model as illustrated.

Where do you start? Build the model. Insert thirteen features: Extruded-Thin1, Fillet, two Extruded Cuts, Circular Pattern, two Extruded Cuts, Mirror, Chamfer, Extruded Cut, Mirror, Extruded Cut and Mirror.

Think about the steps that you would take to build the illustrated part. The depth of the left side is 50mm. The depth of the right side is 60mm.

Create Coordinate System1 to locate the Center of mass.

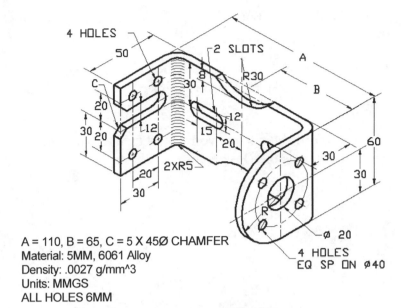

A = 110, B = 65, C = 5 X 45Ø CHAMFER
Material: 5MM, 6061 Alloy
Density: .0027 g/mm^3
Units: MMGS
ALL HOLES 6MM

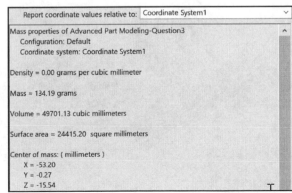

Coordinate system: +X, +Y. +Z

🔅 The SOLIDWORKS software displays positive values for (X, Y, Z) coordinates for a reference coordinate system. The CSWA exam displays either a positive or negative sign in front of the (X, Y, Z) coordinates to indicate direction as illustrated (-X, +Y, -Z).

- A: X = -53.30 millimeters, Y = -0.27 millimeters, Z = -15.54 millimeters

- B: X = 53.30 millimeters, Y = 0.27 millimeters, Z = 15.54 millimeters

- C: X = 49.21 millimeters, Y = 46.88 millimeters, Z = 0.00 millimeters

- D: X = 45.00 millimeters, Y = -46.49 millimeters, Z = 10.00 millimeters

The correct answer is A.

Report coordinate values relative to: Coordinate System1

Mass properties of Advanced Part Modeling-Question3
 Configuration: Default
 Coordinate system: Coordinate System1

Density = 0.00 grams per cubic millimeter

Mass = 134.19 grams

Volume = 49701.13 cubic millimeters

Surface area = 24415.20 square millimeters

Center of mass: (millimeters)
 X = -53.20
 Y = -0.27
 Z = -15.54

Question 4:

Build the illustrated model from the provided information. Locate the Center of mass of the part.

Hint: Insert twelve features and a Reference plane: Extruded-Thin1, two Extruded Bosses, Extruded Cut, Extruded Boss, Extruded Cut, Plane1, Mirror, and five Extruded Cuts.

Think about the steps that you would take to build the illustrated part. Create an Extrude-Thin1 feature as the Base feature.

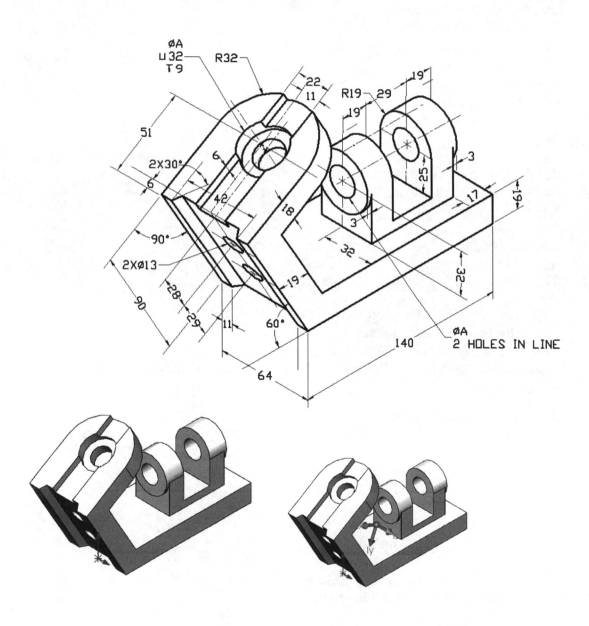

- A: X = -53.30 millimeters, Y = -0.27 millimeters, Z = -15.54 millimeters

- B: X = 53.30 millimeters, Y = 1.27 millimeters, Z = -15.54 millimeters

- C: X = 0.00 millimeters, Y = 34.97 millimeters, Z = 46.67 millimeters

- D: X = 0.00 millimeters, Y = 34.97 millimeters, Z = -46.67 millimeters

The correct answer is D.

Question 5:

Build the illustrated model from the provided information. Locate the Center of mass of the part.

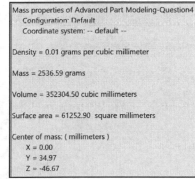

Mass properties of Advanced Part Modeling-Question4
  Configuration: Default
  Coordinate system: -- default --

Density = 0.01 grams per cubic millimeter

Mass = 2536.59 grams

Volume = 352304.50 cubic millimeters

Surface area = 61252.90 square millimeters

Center of mass: (millimeters)
  X = 0.00
  Y = 34.97
  Z = -46.67

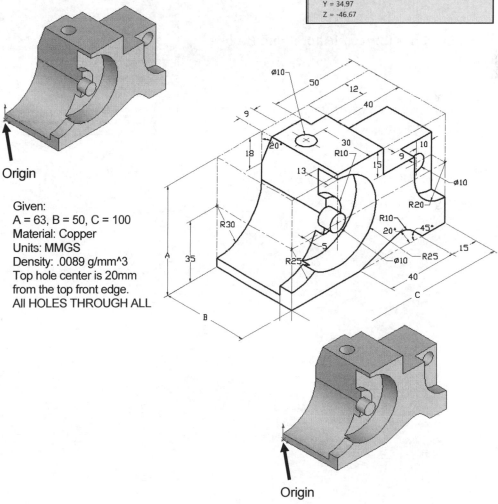

Origin

Given:
A = 63, B = 50, C = 100
Material: Copper
Units: MMGS
Density: .0089 g/mm^3
Top hole center is 20mm
from the top front edge.
All HOLES THROUGH ALL

Origin

The center point of the top hole is located 30mm from the top right edge.

Think about the steps that you would take to build the illustrated part.

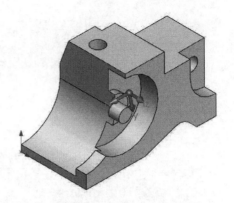

- A: X = 26.81 millimeters, Y = 25.80 millimeters, Z = -56.06 millimeters

- B: X = 43.30 millimeters, Y = 25.27 millimeters, Z = -15.54 millimeters

- C: X = 26.81 millimeters, Y = -25.75 millimeters, Z = 0.00 millimeters

- D: X = 46.00 millimeters, Y = -46.49 millimeters, Z = 10.00 millimeters

The correct answer is A.

This model has thirteen features and twelve sketches.

🔅 There are numerous ways to create the models in this chapter.

Mass properties of Advanced Part Modeling-Question5
　Configuration: Default
　Coordinate system: -- default --

Density = 0.01 grams per cubic millimeter

Mass = 1280.33 grams

Volume = 143857.58 cubic millimeters

Surface area = 26112.48 square millimeters

Center of mass: (millimeters)
　X = 26.81
　Y = 25.80
　Z = -56.06

Question 6:

Build the illustrated model from the provided information. Calculate the overall mass and volume of the part with the provided information.

- Precision for linear dimensions = **2**.

- Material: **Plain Carbon Steel**.

- Units: **MMGS**.

- The part is **not symmetrical** about the Front Plane.

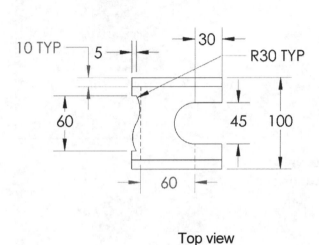

Top view

Front view

Right view

Calculate the mass:

A = 4411.05 grams

B = 4079.32 grams

C = 4234.30 grams

D = 5322.00 grams

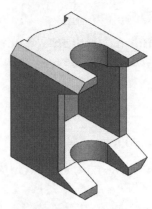

Calculate the volume:

A = 522989.22 cubic millimeters

B = 555655.11 cubic millimeters

C = 511233.34 cubic millimeters

D = 655444.00 cubic millimeters

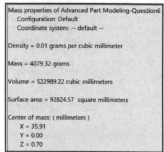

Question 6A:

Create a new coordinate system.

Center a new coordinate system with the provided illustration. The new coordinate system location is at the back right bottom point (vertex) of the model.

Enter the Center of Mass:

X = -64.09 millimeters

Y = 75.00 millimeters

Z = 40.70 millimeters

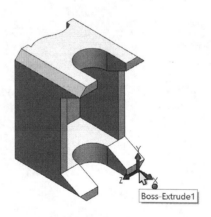

All models for this chapter are located in the CSWA model folder.

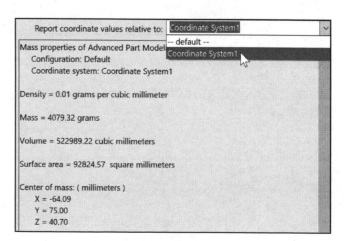

Examples: Assembly Creation and Modification

Assembly Creation and Modification is one of the five categories on the CSWA exam.

The *Assembly Creation and Modification* category addresses an assembly with numerous sub-components.

Knowledge to insert Standard and Advanced mates is required in this category.

There are four questions on the CSWA Academic exam in the Assembly Creation and Modification category: (Two different assemblies - four questions - two multiple choice/two single answers - 30 points each).

You are required to download the needed components from a zip file and insert them correctly to create the assembly.

You are then requested to modify the assembly and answer fill in the blank format questions.

Use the Measure tool in the assembly on the components. Apply correct units.

Do not use feature recognition when you open the downloaded components for the assembly in the CSWA exam. This is a timed exam. Manage your time. You do not need this information.

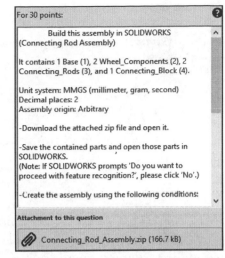

For 30 points:

Build this assembly in SOLIDWORKS (Connecting Rod Assembly)

It contains 1 Base (1), 2 Wheel_Components (2), 2 Connecting_Rods (3), and 1 Connecting_Block (4).

Unit system: MMGS (millimeter, gram, second)
Decimal places: 2
Assembly origin: Arbitrary

-Download the attached zip file and open it.

-Save the contained parts and open those parts in SOLIDWORKS.
(Note: If SOLIDWORKS prompts 'Do you want to proceed with feature recognition?', please click 'No'.)

-Create the assembly using the following conditions:

Attachment to this question

Connecting_Rod_Assembly.zip (166.7 kB)

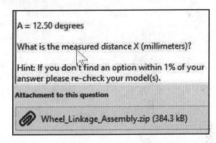

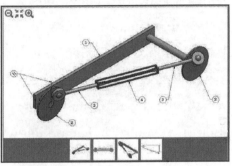

A = 12.50 degrees

What is the measured distance X (millimeters)?

Hint: If you don't find an option within 1% of your answer please re-check your model(s).

Attachment to this question

Wheel_Linkage_Assembly.zip (384.3 kB)

Sample Questions in this Category

In the *Assembly Creation and Modification* Assembly Modeling category, an exam question could read:

Build this assembly in SOLIDWORKS (Chain Link Assembly). It contains 2 long_pins (1), 3 short_pins (2), and 4 chain_links (3).

- Unit system: MMGS (millimeter, gram, second).
- Decimal places: 2.
- Assembly origin: Arbitrary.

IMPORTANT: Create the Assembly with respect to the Origin as shown in the Isometric view. This is important for calculating the proper Center of Mass. Create the assembly using the following conditions:

1. Pins are mated concentric to chain link holes (no clearance).

2. Pin end faces are coincident to chain link side faces.

A = 25 degrees, B = 125 degrees, C = 130 degrees

What is the center of mass of the assembly (millimeters)?

Hint: If you don't find an option within 1% of your answer please re-check your assembly.

A) X = 348.66, Y = -88.48, Z = -91.40

B) X = 308.53, Y = -109.89, Z = -61.40

C) X = 298.66, Y = -17.48, Z = -89.22

D) X = 448.66, Y = -208.48, Z = -34.64

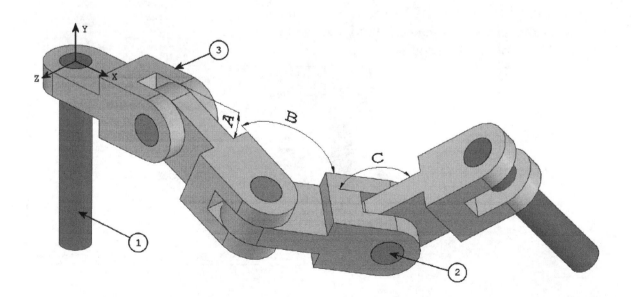

There are no step-by-step procedures in this section.

Download the needed components from the Chapter 6 CSWA Models folder.

The correct answer is:

A) X = 348.66, Y = -88.48, Z = -91.40

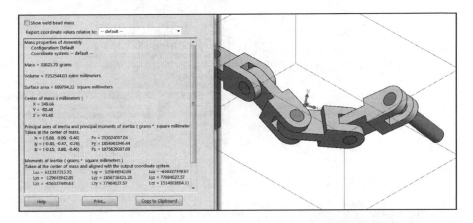

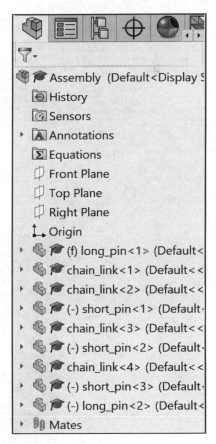

Sample screen shots from an older CSWA exam for an assembly. Click on the additional views to understand the assembly and provided information. Read each question carefully. Understand the dimensions, center of mass and units. Apply needed materials.

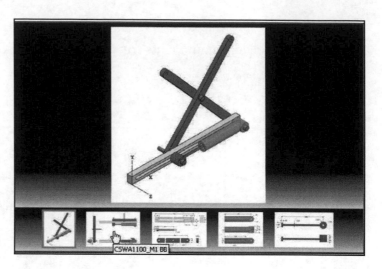

Use the Mass Properties tool to locate the new coordinate system.

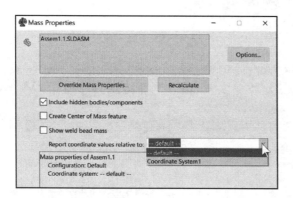

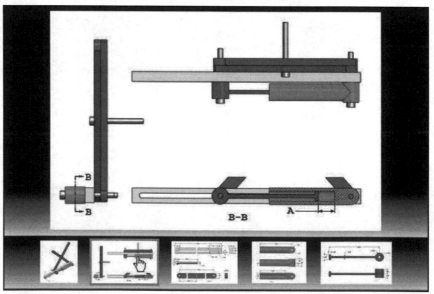

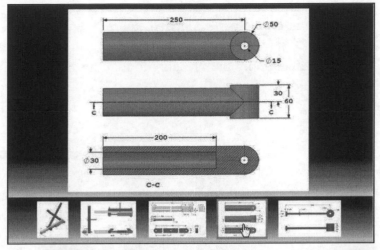

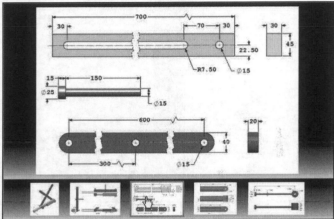

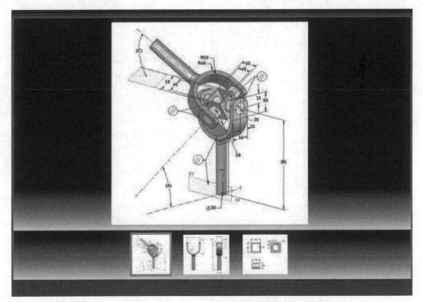

Screen shots from an exam

Zoom in on the part if needed.

 If needed, apply the Measure tool in the assembly on the components for distance or angle.

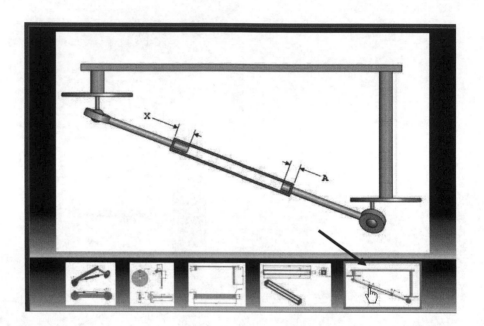

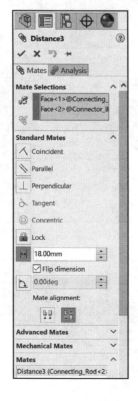

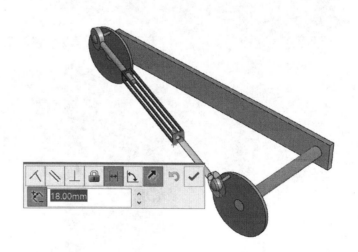

Screen shots from an exam

💡 If needed, apply the Measure tool in the assembly on the components for distance or angle.

Screen shots from an exam

Notes:

Chapter 11 Certified SOLIDWORKS Professional - Advanced Drawing Tools (CSWPA-DT)

Introduction

The Certified SOLIDWORKS Professional - Advanced Drawing tools (CSWPA-DT) exam is a test of one's knowledge of SOLIDWORKS Drawing functionality and tools. The completion of the exam proves that you have successfully demonstrated your ability to use the tools located in the SOLIDWORKS Drawing environment. This is not a test on creating dimensioned drawings that adhere to any specific standard such as ANSI or ISO standards. There are no questions on actual dimensioning processes. You need to know how to use the Measure Tool and insert dimensions.

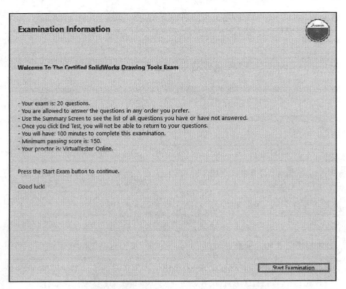

The main requirement for obtaining the certification is to take and pass the on-line 100-minute exam (**minimum of 150 out of 200 points**). The exam consists of 20 questions and you are allowed to answer the questions in any order you prefer.

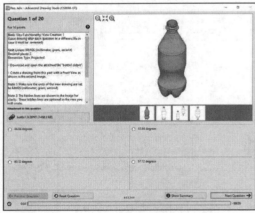

The first question in each category is in a multiple-choice single answer format. You should be within 1% of the multiple-choice answer before you move on to the next one or two modification single answer section, (fill in the blank format).

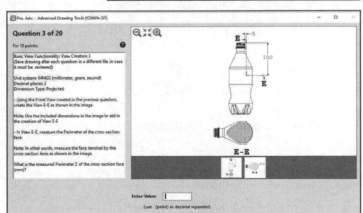

The exam is divided into six key categories. Questions on the timed exam are provided in a random manner. In order to better reflect the contents of the exam and for clarity purposes, the guidelines below may change at any time without notice.

Exam Categories

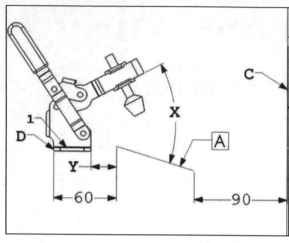

The six key categories are:

- Basic View Functionality.

- View Functionality.

- BOM Functionality.

- Linked Notes.

- Hide/Show Components.

- Advanced View Functionality.

Exam Topics

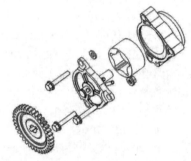

The following topics are covered in the exam:

- Basic view creation.

- Section views (Aligned Section view).

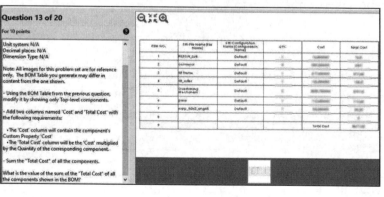

- Auxiliary views.

- Alternate Position views.

- Relative to Model view.

- Broken-out Section view.

- View focus when creating 2D geometry.

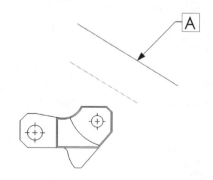

- Transferring Sketch elements to/from views.

- BOM Table creation and modification:

  o Top level.

  o Parts-only.

  o Indented.

  o Part Configuration grouping.

  o Missing Items.

  o Accessing Custom Properties in BOM.

  o Using Equations with BOM data.

- Item Numbers and their display.

- Hide/Show Components.

- Linked Notes.

- Import Model Items.

Download the needed components in a zip folder during the exam to create the drawing. Un-Zip the folder to open the models.

Use the Summary screen during the exam to view the list of all questions you have or have not answered.

The Advanced Drawing tools exam (CSWPA-DT) is a test of one's knowledge of SOLIDWORKS Drawing functionality and tools. The completion of the exam proves that you have successfully demonstrated your ability to use the tools located in the SOLIDWORKS Drawing environment.

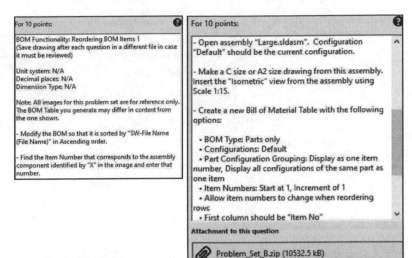

For 10 points:

BOM Functionality: Reordering BOM Items 1
(Save drawing after each question in a different file in case it must be reviewed)

Unit system: N/A
Decimal places: N/A
Dimension Type: N/A

Note: All images for this problem set are for reference only. The BOM Table you generate may differ in content from the one shown.

- Modify the BOM so that it is sorted by "SW-File Name (File Name)" in Ascending order.

- Find the Item Number that corresponds to the assembly component identified by "X" in the image and enter that number.

For 10 points:

- Open assembly "Large.sldasm". Configuration "Default" should be the current configuration.

- Make a C size or A2 size drawing from this assembly. Insert the "Isometric" view from the assembly using Scale 1:15.

- Create a new Bill of Material Table with the following options:

  • BOM Type: Parts only
  • Configurations: Default
  • Part Configuration Grouping: Display as one item number, Display all configurations of the same part as one item
  • Item Numbers: Start at 1, Increment of 1
  • Allow item numbers to change when reordering rows
  • First column should be "Item No"

Attachment to this question

📎 Problem_Set_B.zip (10532.5 kB)

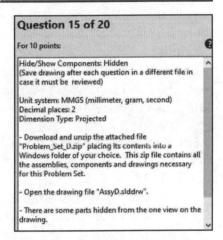

Question 15 of 20

For 10 points:

Hide/Show Components: Hidden
(Save drawing after each question in a different file in case it must be reviewed)

Unit system: MMGS (millimeter, gram, second)
Decimal places: 2
Dimension Type: Projected

- Download and unzip the attached file "Problem_Set_D.zip" placing its contents into a Windows folder of your choice. This zip file contains all the assemblies, components and drawings necessary for this Problem Set.

- Open the drawing file "AssyD.slddrw".

- There are some parts hidden from the one view on the drawing.

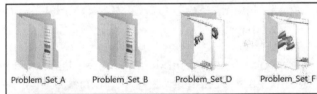

Problem_Set_A   Problem_Set_B   Problem_Set_D   Problem_Set_F

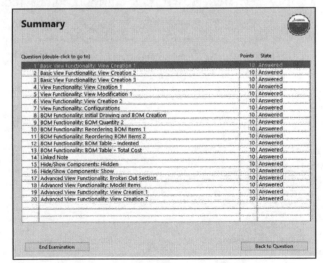

Summary

Question (double-click to go to)	Points	State
1 Basic View Functionality: View Creation 1	10	Answered
2 Basic View Functionality: View Creation 2	10	Answered
3 Basic View Functionality: View Creation 3	10	Answered
4 View Functionality: View Creation 1	10	Answered
5 View Functionality: View Modification 1	10	Answered
6 View Functionality: View Creation 2	10	Answered
7 View Functionality: Configurations	10	Answered
8 BOM Functionality: Initial Drawing and BOM Creation	10	Answered
9 BOM Functionality: BOM Quantity 2	10	Answered
10 BOM Functionality: Reordering BOM Items 1	10	Answered
11 BOM Functionality: Reordering BOM Items 2	10	Answered
12 BOM Functionality: BOM Table - Indented	10	Answered
13 BOM Functionality: BOM Table - Total Cost	10	Answered
14 Linked Note	10	Answered
15 Hide/Show Components: Hidden	10	Answered
16 Hide/Show Components: Show	10	Answered
17 Advanced View Functionality: Broken Out Section	10	Answered
18 Advanced View Functionality: Model Items	10	Answered
19 Advanced View Functionality: View Creation 1	10	Answered
20 Advanced View Functionality: View Creation 2	10	Answered

End Examination   Back to Question

During the exam, use the control keys at the bottom of the screen to:

Screen shot from the exam.

- *Show the Previous Question.*

- *Reset the Question.*

- *Show the Summary Screen.*

- *Move to the Next Question.*

Intended Audience

The intended audience for this exam is a person who has passed the CSWA and CSWP exam and who has 8 or more months of SOLIDWORKS training and usage in the drawing sector. This section is not to teach you how to use SOLIDWORKS but is written to provide exam tips, hints and information on sample questions and categories that are aligned with the exam.

To prepare for the exam, it is recommended that you first perform the following:

- Take an exam preparation class or review a textbook written for the Advanced Drawing tools exam.

- Complete the SOLIDWORKS Tutorials on the drawing sections.

- Practice creating models from the Isometric working drawings sections of any Technical Drawing or Engineering Drawing Documentation textbook.

Chapter 10 CSWA

Chapter 11 CSWPA-DT

- Complete the sample CSWPA-DT exam in a timed environment. The sample exam is located in the Chapter 11 CSWPA-DT folder.

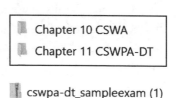

cswpa-dt_sampleexam (1)

- During the exam, SOLIDWORKS provides the ability to click on additional views to obtain additional details and dimensions.

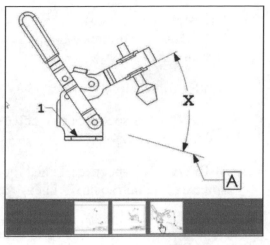

Basic View Functionality: View Creation 1

First question in the sample exam

The question setup below is similar to the sample Advanced Drawing tools exam posted by SOLIDWORKS.

Below is the needed information and steps to obtain the answer to the exam question.

Provided information:

Open "SampleDraw1.slddrw". The drawing contains one sketch line labeled "A".

Note: Do not modify the angle of Line A in any way. Doing so will compromise the answer for this question in the exam.

Unit system: MMGS (millimeter, gram, second)

Decimal places: 2

Dimension Type: True

Note: Dimensions in drawings are either:

- **True.** Accurate model values.

- **Projected.** 2D dimensions.

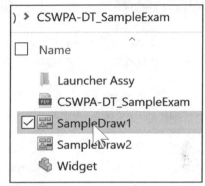

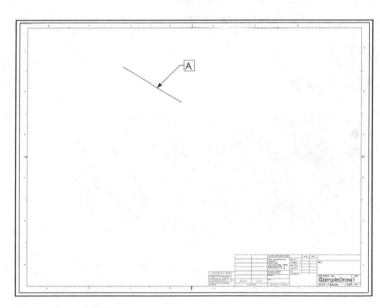

The dimension type is set when you insert a drawing view. You can view and change the dimension type in the Drawing View PropertyManager.

The rules for dimension type are:

- SOLIDWORKS specifies **Projected** type dimensions for standard and Custom orthogonal views.

- SOLIDWORKS specifies **True** type dimensions for Isometric, Diametric and Trimetric views.

Insert: Insert a "Front view" of the part "Widget" in the orientation shown. **Edge "1"** of Part1 should be horizontal with respect to the drawing. (Scale 1:1).

Create the dimension X as shown in the second image between the edge of the crank handle and line A.

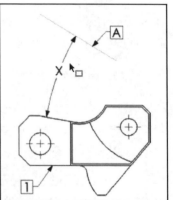

Hint: You may need to cut or copy and paste the line A to be able to create the dimension X.

What is the value of X (degrees)? This is a multiple-choice question. You should have the exact answer (within 1% of the stated value in the multiple-choice section) before you move on to the next question.

a) 23.74 degrees

b) 20.85 degrees

c) 18.79 degrees

d) 25.12 degrees

Let's begin.

1. **Create** a folder to save your documents.

2. **Open** SampleDraw1.slddrw from the Chapter 11 CSWPA-DT folder. View the location of Line A. Do not modify the angle of Line A in any way. Doing so will compromise the answer for this question in the exam.

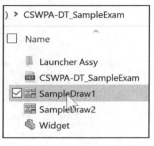

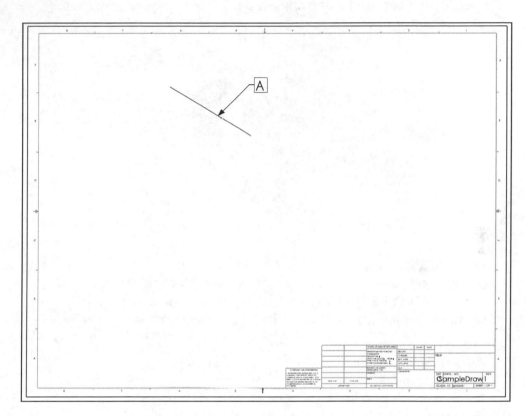

3. **Set** document properties (units and precision) for the model. **Unit system**: MMGS (millimeter, gram, second). **Decimal places**: .12. You do not need to select a drafting standard.

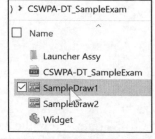

4. **Open** the Widget part from the Chapter 11 CSWPA-DT folder. Note: Click **No** to "Do you want to proceed with feature recognition?" This is a timed exam. You do not need this information. View the part in the graphics window. Re-orientate the part in the drawing per the provided information.

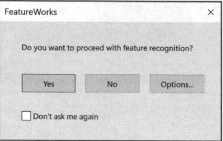

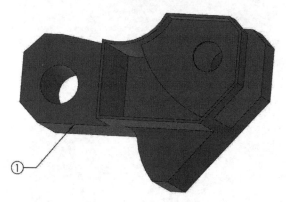

5. **Insert** a "Front view" of the part "Widget" in the orientation shown. Edge "1" of Part1 should be horizontal with respect to the drawing. (Scale 1:1). At this time, it is not in the proper orientation for the exam question.

Select True Dimension type.

6. Click **True** in the Dimension Type box - Drawing View PropertyManager.

Re-orientate the model in the Front view of the drawing per the required position. Note the location of Edge 1 relative to Line A in the provided information.

7. Click inside the **Front** view.

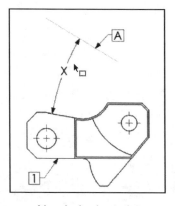

Needed orientation

8. Click **Insert, Drawing View, Relative To Model**. When you create a Relative view in a drawing, you select planar faces in a model document, and then return to the drawing document to place the view.

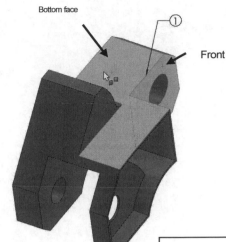

Bottom face

Front

9. Select the **Front** face and the **bottom** face of the Widget as illustrated to re-orientate the model. Use this orientation to answer the question for the exam.

10. Click **OK** ✔ in the Relative View PropertyManager.

11. Click a **location below** the Front view as illustrated. Use this view as your Front drawing view.

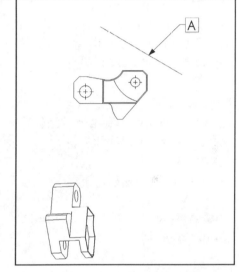

12. **Drag** the first drawing view out of the way on Sheet1.

Line A is not presently associated with the new Front view. Create a line parallel to the given Line A associated to the Front view.

13. Click inside the new **Front** view.

14. Sketch a **line** inside the new Front view. The line is associated with the Front view.

15. **Insert** a parallel relation between Line A and the new line.

16. Insert the **angle dimension** between the new line (in the new Front view and Edge "1" of Part1.) **View** the results.

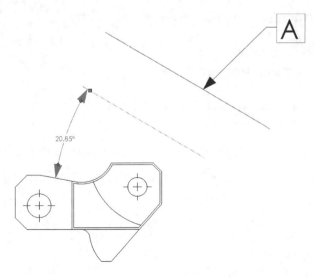

17. **Save** the drawing.

What is the value of X (degrees)?

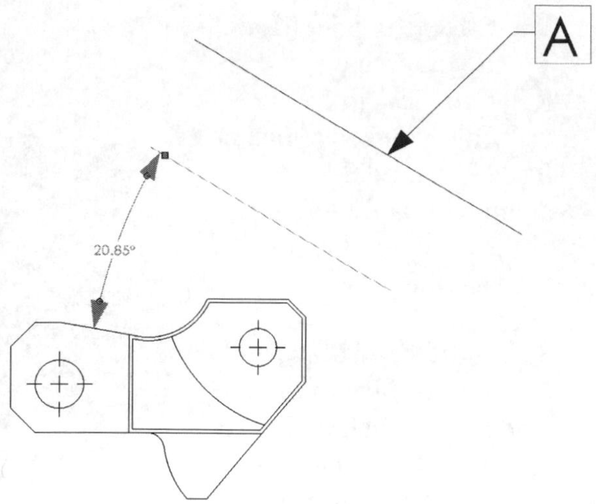

a) 23.74 degrees

b) 20.85 degrees

c) 18.79 degrees

d) 25.12 degrees

The answer is **b.) 20.85 degrees**.

This section presents a representation of the types of questions that you will see in this segment of the exam.

Second question in the sample exam - Basic View Functionality: View Creation 2

Provided information:

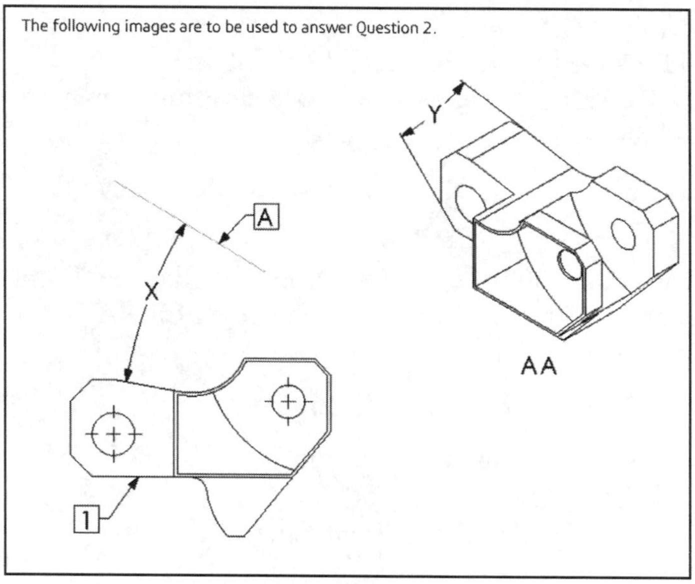

Unit system: MMGS (millimeter, gram, second)

Decimal places: 2

Dimension Type: Projected

Use the drawing and Front view as created from question 1.

Create the view AA projected from the created Front view.

Create the angled dimension Y as shown in the image.

What is the value of Y (degrees)? This is a fill in the blank question. You should have the exact answer (within 1%).

Let's begin.
Create a Projected view from the Front view.

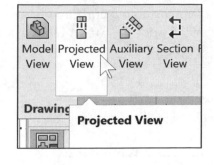

1. **Click** inside the Front view.

2. Create a **Projected view** from the Front view.

3. Select **Projected** Dimension Type.

4. Click a **position** as illustrated in Sheet1.

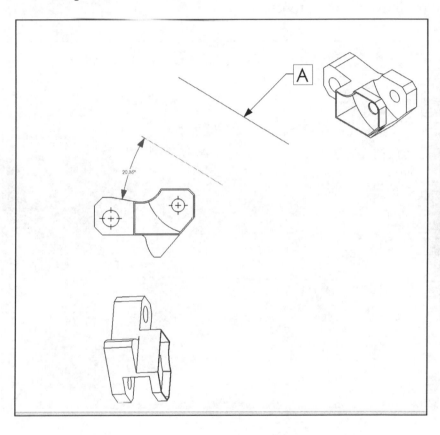

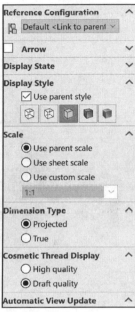

Dimension the drawing view.

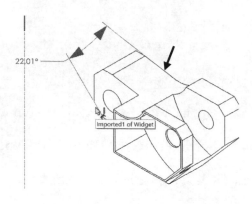

5. **Apply** the Smart Dimension tool. View the
   results.

6. **Enter** 22.01 degrees in the answer box.

7. **Save** the drawing.

8. **Save** as Sample2.

9. **View** the results of the drawing at this time.

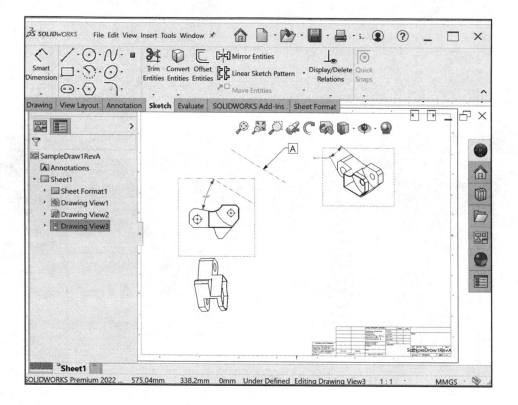

Third question in the sample exam - Basic View Functionality: View Creation 3

Provided information:

Unit system: MMGS (millimeter, gram, second)

Decimal places: .12

Dimension Type: Projected

Use the Front view created in Question 1. Create the View F-F as shown in the image.

Note: Use the included dimensions in the image to aid in the creation of View F-F.

In View F-F, measure the Perimeter of the cross-section area indicated in the second image.

What is the measured Area Y of the cross-section area selected in the second image below (mm^2)?

Let's begin.

1. **Click** inside Drawing View1.

2. **Sketch** three lines in Drawing View1. Sketch the lines as illustrated to create the profile for the Aligned section view. See Chapter 6 on using the SW Aligned Section view tool.

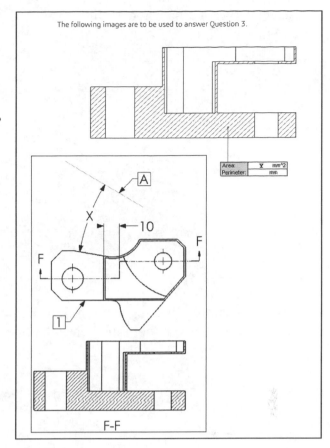

The following images are to be used to answer Question 3.

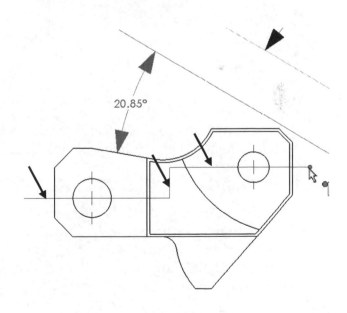

3. **Insert** a 10mm dimension as illustrated.

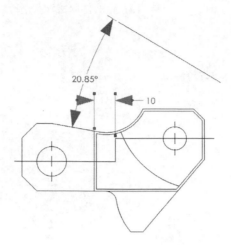

4. **Select** the cutting line segments. Select the **first horizontal** line. Hold the **Ctrl** key down. Select the **vertical line**. Select the **horizontal line**. Release the **Ctrl** key.

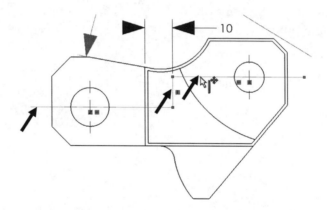

💡 There are numerous ways to create the drawings in this section. A goal is to display different design intents and techniques while utilizing commands that can be accessed using older versions of SOLIDWORKS.

Create an Aligned Section view.

5. Click **Section View** from the View Layout tab. A SOLIDWORKS dialog box is displayed.

6. Click **Create a standard section view**.

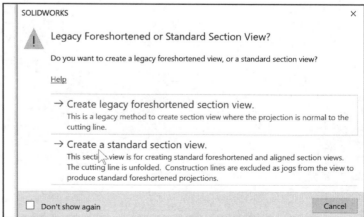

7. The Section View PropertyManager is displayed. If needed, **Flip** the arrow direction.

8. **Locate** the Aligned Section view below the Front view as illustrated.

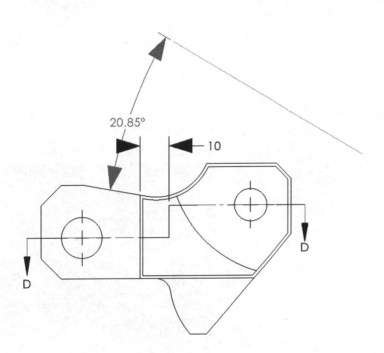

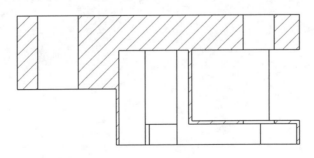

SECTION D-D

Measure the Perimeter of the cross-section area indicated in the second image. What is the measured Area Y of the cross-section area selected in the second image below (mm^2)?

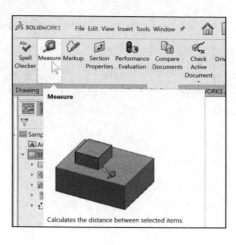

9. **Utilize** the Measure tool to provide area and perimeter of the cross-section. The cross-sectional area is 924.12 mm^2. The perimeter is 285.96mm. Be prepared to provide both area and perimeter information for the exam.

10. **Enter** 924.12.

11. **Save** the drawing.

12. Save as **Sample3**.

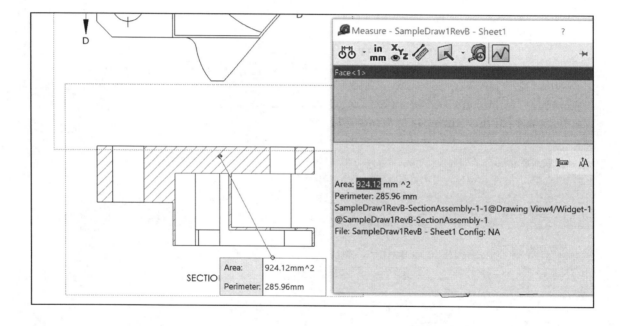

🔆 This section presents a representation of the types of questions that you will see in this segment of the exam.

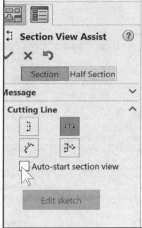

🔆 There are numerous ways to create the drawings in this section. A goal is to display different design intents and techniques while utilizing commands that can be accessed using older versions of SOLIDWORKS.

BOM Functionality: BOM Creation

Fourth question in the sample exam - BOM Creation

Provided information:

Unit system: N/A

Decimal places: N/A

Dimension Type: N/A

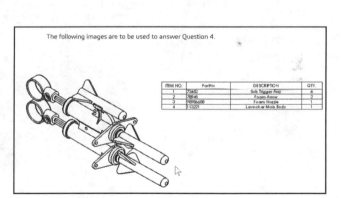

The following images are to be used to answer Question 4.

ITEM NO.	PartNo	DESCRIPTION	QTY.
1	70452	Srb Trigger Assy	6
2	78945	Foam Arrow	2
3	989Ab608	Foam Nozzle	1
4	113221	Launcher Main Body	1

Note: All images for this problem set are for reference only. The BOM Table you generate may differ in content from the one shown.

Open "SampleDraw2.slddrw".

Insert the "Isometric" view of the Default configuration of assembly "Launcher.SLDASM" using Scale 1:1.

Create a new Bill of Material Table with the following options:

• BOM Type: **Top-level only**

• Configurations: **Default**

- Part Configuration Grouping: Display as one item number, Display all configurations of the same part as one item.

- Item Numbers: Start at 1, Increment of **1**.

- Allow item numbers to change when reordering rows.

- First column should be "**Item No**".

- Second column should show the Custom Property "**PartNo**".

- Third column should show the Custom Property "**Description**".

- Fourth column should show the "**Quantity**".

Find the Quantity of "Sub Trigger Assy", Part Number 2222-32421 in the assembly and select it from the choices given:

a) Qty: 2 , b) Qty: 3 , c) Qty: 1, d) Qty: 5

Let's begin.

1. **Open** SampleDraw2.slddrw from the Chapter 11 CSWPA-DT folder. This is an empty drawing sheet.

2. **Save** as Sample4.

3. **Open** Launcher.SLDASM from the Chapter 11 CSWPA-DT folder. View the assembly in the graphics area.

4. **Insert** an Isometric view of the Launcher assembly into the drawing. (Scale 1:1).

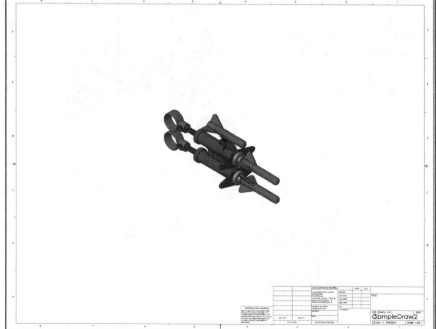

5. **Create** a new Bill of Material Table with the following options:

- BOM Type: **Top-level only**.

- Configurations: **Default**.

- Part Configuration Grouping: **Display all configurations of the same part as one item**.

- Item Numbers: **Start at 1, Increment of 1**.

- **Allow item numbers to change** when reordering rows.

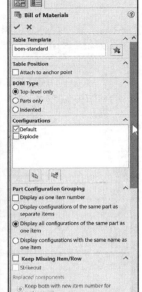

6. Click **OK** and place the Bill of Material Table into the drawing. View the results.

	A	B	C	D
1	ITEM NO.	PART NUMBER	DESCRIPTION	QTY.
2	1	SUB_trigger	Sub Trigger Assy	2
3	2	Arrow	Foam Arrow	3
4	3	Nozzle	Foam Nozzle	2
5	4	Main Body	Launcher Main Body	1

The BOM in the exam is much larger than the sample exam.

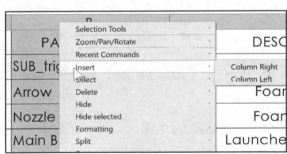

- First column should be "**Item No**".

- Second column should show the Custom Property "PartNo". **Insert** a new column to the right.

- **Insert** a new Customer Property **PartNo**.

- **View** the results.

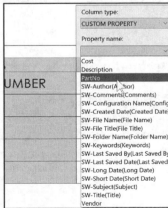

- **Delete** the PART NUMBER column.

- Third column should show the Custom Property **"Description"**.

- Fourth column should show the "Quantity". **View** the result in the drawing.

	A	B	C	D
1	ITEM NO.	PartNo	DESCRIPTION	QTY.
2	1	2222-32421	Sub Trigger Assy	2
3	2	789-224542	Foam Arrow	3
4	3	9879-9279872	Foam Nozzle	2
5	4	112234214112	Launcher Main Body	1

7. Find the Quantity of "Sub Trigger Assy", Part Number 2222-32421 in the assembly and select it from the choices given.

a) Qty: 2, b) Qty: 3, c) Qty: 1, d) Qty: 5

8. Enter **2** in the answer box.

9. **Save** the drawing (Sample4).

This section presents a representation of the types of questions that you will see in this segment of the exam.

BOM Creation - Reordering BOM Items 1

Fifth question in the sample exam - Reordering BOM Items 1
Provided information:

Unit system: N/A

Decimal places: N/A

Dimension Type: N/A

Using the BOM created in the previous question, modify the BOM so that it is sorted by Part Number in an ascending order.

Note: For example, part numbers that start with 1 are at the top of the BOM.

Find the Item Number that corresponds to the assembly component identified by "X" in the image.

Enter the number into the box on the exam.

Let's begin.

1. **Open** drawing Sample4 if needed.

2. **Save** as Sample5.

3. **Sort** the PartNo column in ascending order as illustrated.

4. **Insert** a Balloon to identify the item in the drawing. The answer is ITEM NO. 1.

5. **Enter 1** into the answer box.

6. **Save** the drawing (Sample5).

Note: To check, right-click the component in the assembly drawing, and click open part.

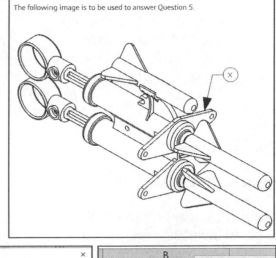

The following image is to be used to answer Question 5.

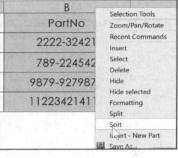

B	
PartNo	
2222-32421	
789-224542	
9879-927987	
1123421411	

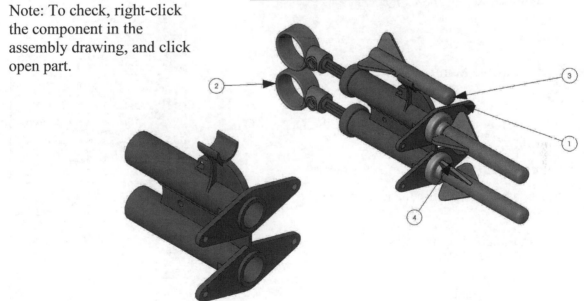

Sixth question in the sample exam - BOM Table - Total Cost

Provided information:

Unit system: N/A

Decimal places: N/A

Dimension Type: N/A

The following image is to be used to answer Question 6.

ITEM NO.	PartNo	DESCRIPTION	QTY.	Total Cost
1	112234214112	Housing	1	10.25
2	2222-32421	Sub Trigger Assy	2	4.59
3	7345643534	Ring	3	3.75
4	98734563345	Nipple	2	5.12
5			Total Cost	23.71

Note: All images for this problem set are for reference only. The BOM Table you generate may differ in content from the one shown.

Add one column named 'Total Cost' with the following requirement:

- The 'Total Cost' column will be the 'Cost' multiplied by the Quantity of the corresponding component.

- Sum the "Total Cost" of all the components.

What is the value of the sum of the "Total Cost" of all the components shown in the BOM?

Let's begin.

1. **Open** drawing Sample5 if needed.

2. **Save** as Sample6.

3. Insert a **new column** to the right of the Default/QTY. column.

4. Select **Cost** for Link Custom Property.

5. **Insert** a new column to the right of the Cost column.

6. **Insert** the column name as TOTAL COST.

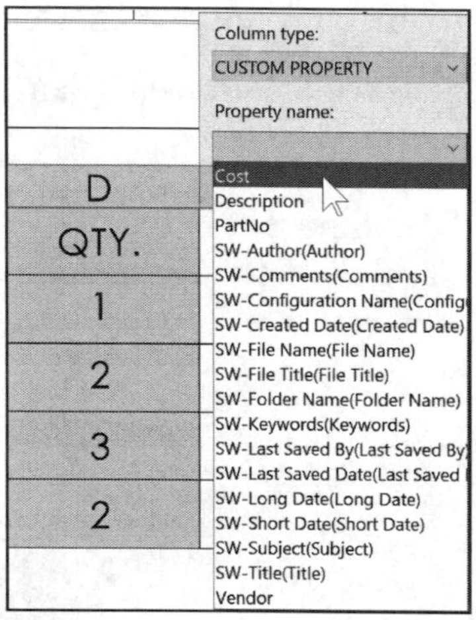

Column type:

CUSTOM PROPERTY

Property name:

D	
QTY.	
1	
2	
3	
2	

Cost
Description
PartNo
SW-Author(Author)
SW-Comments(Comments)
SW-Configuration Name(Config
SW-Created Date(Created Date)
SW-File Name(File Name)
SW-File Title(File Title)
SW-Folder Name(Folder Name)
SW-Keywords(Keywords)
SW-Last Saved By(Last Saved By
SW-Last Saved Date(Last Saved
SW-Long Date(Long Date)
SW-Short Date(Short Date)
SW-Subject(Subject)
SW-Title(Title)
Vendor

D	E	F
QTY.	Cost	TOTAL COST
1	9.99	
2	6.50	
3	1.25	
2	3.45	

7. **Create** an equation for each cell. Default / QTY * Cost as illustrated.

8. **Insert** a new row below Item No. 4 to calculate total cost.

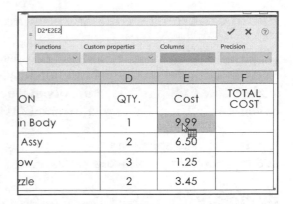

	D	E	F
ON	QTY.	Cost	TOTAL COST
n Body	1	9.99	
Assy	2	6.50	
ow	3	1.25	
zzle	2	3.45	

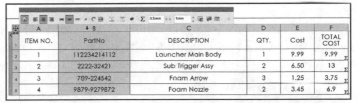

	ITEM NO.	PartNo	DESCRIPTION	QTY.	Cost	TOTAL COST
1	1	112234214112	Launcher Main Body	1	9.99	9.99
2	2	2222-32421	Sub Trigger Assy	2	6.50	13
3	3	789-224542	Foam Arrow	3	1.25	3.75
4	4	9879-9279872	Foam Nozzle	2	3.45	6.9

9. **Create** an equation to summarize the Total Cost column.

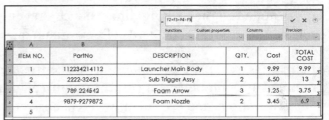

ITEM NO.	PartNo	DESCRIPTION	QTY.	Cost	TOTAL COST
1	112234214112	Launcher Main Body	1	9.99	9.99
2	2222-32421	Sub Trigger Assy	2	6.50	13
3	789-224542	Foam Arrow	3	1.25	3.75
4	9879-9279872	Foam Nozzle	2	3.45	6.9
5					

ITEM NO.	PartNo	DESCRIPTION	QTY.	Cost	TOTAL COST
1	112234214112	Launcher Main Body	1	9.99	9.99
2	2222-32421	Sub Trigger Assy	2	6.50	13
3	789-224542	Foam Arrow	3	1.25	3.75
4	9879-9279872	Foam Nozzle	2	3.45	6.9
5					33.64

What is the value of the sum of the "Total Cost" of all the components shown in the BOM?

10. Enter **33.64** into the answer box.

11. **Save** the drawing (Sample6).

💡 This section presents a representation of the types of questions that you will see in this segment of the exam.

💡 There are numerous ways to create the drawings in this section. A goal is to display different design intents and techniques while utilizing commands that can be accessed using older versions of SOLIDWORKS.

Exam Categories that the sample exam does not cover

There are six key categories in the Advanced Drawing tools exam (CSWPA-DT): **Basic View Functionality, View Functionality, BOM Functionality, Linked Notes, Hide/Show Components**, and **Advanced view Functionality**. The sample exam only covers Basic View Functionality and BOM Functionality.

Use the other chapters in this book to view the needed material on the exam categories and topics (example: Linked Notes, Hide / Show components, etc.).

Summary

The Advanced Drawing tools exam (CSWPA-DT) is a test of one's knowledge of SOLIDWORKS Drawing functionality and tools. The completion of the exam proves that you have successfully demonstrated your ability to use the tools located in the SOLIDWORKS Drawing environment.

This is not a test on creating dimensioned drawings that adhere to any specific standard such as ANSI or ISO standards. There are no questions on actual dimensioning processes.

The main requirement for obtaining the certification is to take and pass the on-line proctored 100 minute exam (**minimum of 150 out of 200 points**). The exam consists of twenty questions and you are allowed to answer the questions in any order you prefer.

The exam is divided into six key categories. Questions on the timed exam are provided in a random manner.

To obtain additional information on the Certified SOLIDWORKS Professional - Advanced Drawing tools (CSWPA-DT) exam visit
https://www.solidworks.com/certifications/drawing-tools-cswpa-dt

Appendix

SOLIDWORKS Keyboard Shortcuts

Below are some of the pre-defined keyboard shortcuts in SOLIDWORKS:

Action:	Key Combination:
Model Views	
Rotate the model horizontally or vertically	**Arrow** keys
Rotate the model horizontally or vertically 90 degrees	**Shift** + **Arrow** keys
Rotate the model clockwise or counterclockwise	**Alt** + left of right **Arrow** keys
Pan the model	**Ctrl** + **Arrow** keys
Magnifying glass	**g**
Zoom in	**Shift** + **z**
Zoom out	**z**
Zoom to fit	**f**
Previous view	**Ctrl** + **Shift** + **z**
View Orientation	
View Orientation menu	**Spacebar**
Front view	**Ctrl** + **1**
Back view	**Ctrl** + **2**
Left view	**Ctrl** + **3**
Right view	**Ctrl** + **4**
Top view	**Ctrl** + **5**
Bottom view	**Ctrl** + **6**
Isometric view	**Ctrl** + **7**
NormalTo view	**Ctrl** + **8**
Selection Filters	
Filter edges	**e**
Filter vertices	**v**
Filter faces	**x**
Toggle Selection Filter toolbar	**F5**
Toggle selection filters on/off	**F6**
File menu items	
New SOLIDWORKS document	**Ctrl** + **n**
Open document	**Ctrl** + **o**
Open From Web Folder	**Ctrl** + **w**
Make Drawing from Part	**Ctrl** + **d**
Make Assembly from Part	**Ctrl** + **a**
Save	**Ctrl** + **s**
Print	**Ctrl** + **p**
Additional items	
Access online help inside of PropertyManager or dialog box	**F1**
Rename an item in the FeatureManager design tree	**F2**

Action:	Key Combination:
Rebuild the model	**Ctrl + b**
Force rebuild - Rebuild the model and all its features	**Ctrl + q**
Redraw the screen	**Ctrl + r**
Cycle between open SOLIDWORKS document	**Ctrl + Tab**
Line to arc/arc to line in the Sketch	**a**
Undo	**Ctrl + z**
Redo	**Ctrl + y**
Cut	**Ctrl + x**
Copy	**Ctrl + c**
Paste	**Ctrl + v**
Delete	**Delete**
Next window	**Ctrl + F6**
Close window	**Ctrl + F4**
View previous tools	**s**
Selects all text inside an Annotations text box	**Ctrl + a**

In a sketch, the **Esc** key un-selects geometry items currently selected in the Properties box and Add Relations box.

In the model, the **Esc** key closes the PropertyManager and cancels the selections.

Use the **g** key to activate the Magnifying glass tool. Use the Magnifying glass tool to inspect a model and make selections without changing the overall view.

Use the **s** key to view/access previous command tools in the Graphics window.

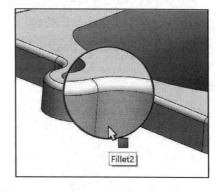

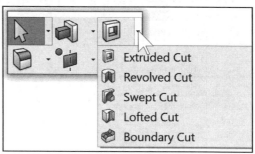

Modeling - Best Practices

Best practices are simply ways of bringing about better results in easier, more reliable ways. The Modeling - Best Practice list is a set of rules helpful for new users and users who are trying to experiment with the limits of the software.

These rules are not inflexible, but conservative starting places; they are concepts that you can default to, but that can be broken if you have good reason. The following is a list of suggested best practices:

- Create a folder structure (parts, drawings, assemblies, simulations, etc.). Organize into project or file folders.

- Construct sound document templates. The document template provides the foundation that all models are built on. This is especially important if working with other SOLIDWORKS users on the same project; it will ensure consistency across the project.

- Generate unique part filenames. SOLIDWORKS assemblies and drawings may pick up incorrect references if you use parts with identical names.

- Apply Custom Properties. Custom Properties is a great way to enter text-based information into the SOLIDWORKS parts. Users can view this information from outside the file by using applications such as Windows Explorer, SOLIDWORKS Explorer, and Product Data Management (PDM) applications.

- Understand part orientation. When you create a new part or assembly, the three default Planes (Front, Right and Top) are aligned with specific views. The plane you select for the Base sketch determines the orientation.

- Learn to sketch using automatic relations.

- Limit your usage of the Fixed constraint.

- Add geometric relations, then dimensions in a 2D sketch. This keeps the part from having too many unnecessary dimensions. This also helps to show the design intent of the model. Dimension what geometry you intend to modify or adjust.

- Fully define all sketches in the model. However, there are times when this is not practical, generally when using the Spline tool to create a freeform shape.

- When possible, make relations to sketches or stable reference geometry; such as the Origin or standard planes, instead of edges or faces. Sketches are far more stable than faces, edges, or model vertices, which change their internal ID at the slightest change and may disappear entirely with fillets, chamfers, split lines, and so on.

- Do not dimension to edges created by fillets or other cosmetic or temporary features.

- Apply names to sketches, features, dimensions, and mates that help to make their function clear.

- When possible, use feature fillets and feature patterns rather than sketch fillets and sketch patterns.

- Apply the Shell feature before the Fillet feature, and the inside corners remain perpendicular.

- Apply cosmetic fillets and chamfers last in the modeling procedure.

- Combine fillets into as few fillet features as possible. This enables you to control fillets that need to be controlled separately, such as fillets to be removed and simplified configurations.

- Create a simplified configuration when building very complex parts or working with large assemblies.

- Use symmetry during the modeling process. Utilize feature patterns and mirroring when possible. Think End Conditions.

- Use global variables and equations to control commonly applied dimensions (design intent).

- Add comments to equations to document your design intent. Place a single quote (') at the end of the equation, then enter the comment. Anything after the single quote is ignored when the equation is evaluated.

- Avoid redundant mates. Although SOLIDWORKS allows some redundant mates (all except distance and angle), these mates take longer to solve and make the mating scheme harder to understand and diagnose if problems occur.

- Fix modeling errors in the part or assembly when they occur. Errors cause rebuild time to increase, and if you wait until additional errors exist, troubleshooting will be more difficult.

- Create a Library of Standardized notes and parts.

- Utilize the Rollback bar. Troubleshoot feature and sketch errors from the top of the design tree.

- Determine the static and dynamic behavior of mates in each sub-assembly before creating the top-level assembly.

- Plan the assembly and sub-assemblies in an assembly layout diagram. Group components together to form smaller sub-assemblies.

- When you create an assembly document, the base component should be fixed, fully defined or mated to an axis about the assembly origin.

- In an assembly, group fasteners into a folder at the bottom of the FeatureManager. Suppress fasteners and their assembly patterns to save rebuild time and file size.

- When comparing mass, volume and other properties with assembly visualization, utilize similar units.

- Use limit mates sparingly because they take longer to solve and whenever possible, mate all components to one or two fixed components or references. Long chains of components take longer to solve and are more prone to mate errors.

Helpful On-line Information

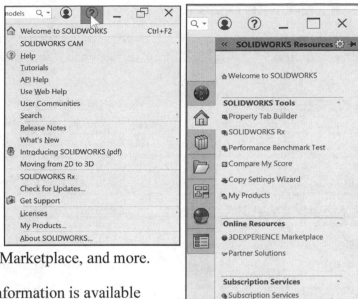

The SOLIDWORKS URL:
http://www.SOLIDWORKS.com
contains information on Local
Resellers, Solution Partners,
Certifications, SOLIDWORKS
users groups and more.

Use the SOLIDWORKS
Resources tab in the Task Pane
to obtain access to Customer
Portals, User Groups,
Manufacturers, Solution
Partners, Labs, 3DEXPERIENCE Marketplace, and more.

Helpful on-line SOLIDWORKS information is available
from the following URLs:

- http://www.swugn.org/

List of all SOLIDWORKS User groups.

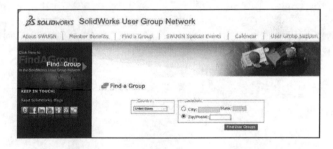

- https://www.solidworks.com/sw/edu
cation/certification-programs-cad-
students.htm

The SOLIDWORKS Academic
Certification Programs.

- http://www.solidworks.com/sw/in
dustries/education/engineering-
education-software.htm

The SOLIDWORKS Education
Program:

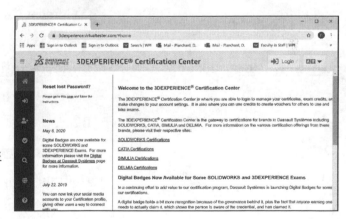

- To obtain additional
SOLIDWORKS Certification
exam information, visit
https://3dexperience.virtualtester.c
om/#home

On-line tutorials are for educational
purposes only. Tutorials are
copyrighted by their respective
owners.

SOLIDWORKS Document Types

SOLIDWORKS has three main document file types: Part, Assembly and Drawing, but there are many additional supporting types that you may want to know. Below is a brief list of these supporting file types:

Design Documents	**Description**
.sldprt	SOLIDWORKS Part document
.slddrw	SOLIDWORKS Drawing document
.sldasm	SOLIDWORKS Assembly document

Templates and Formats	**Description**
.asmdot	Assembly Template
.asmprp	Assembly Template Custom Properties tab
.drwdot	Drawing Template
.drwprp	Drawing Template Custom Properties tab
.prtdot	Part Template
.prtprp	Part Template Custom Properties tab
.sldtbt	General Table Template
.slddrt	Drawing Sheet Template
.sldbombt	Bill of Materials Template (Table-based)
.sldholtbt	Hole Table Template
.sldrevbt	Revision Table Template
.sldwldbt	Weldment Cutlist Template
.xls	Bill of Materials Template (Excel-based)

Library Files	**Description**
.sldlfp	Library Part file
.sldblk	Blocks

Other	**Description**
.sldstd	Drafting standard
.sldmat	Material Database
.sldclr	Color Palette File
.xls	Sheet metal gauge table

GLOSSARY

Alphabet of Lines: Each line on a technical drawing has a definite meaning and is drawn in a certain way. The line conventions recommended by the American National Standards Institute (ANSI) are presented in this text.

Alternate Position View: A drawing view superimposed in phantom lines on the original view. Utilized to show range of motion of an assembly.

Anchor Point: The origin of the Bill of Material in a sheet format.

Annotation: An annotation is a text note or a symbol that adds specific information and design intent to a part, assembly, or drawing. Annotations in a drawing include specific note, hole callout, surface finish symbol, datum feature symbol, datum target, geometric tolerance symbol, weld symbol, balloon, and stacked balloon, center mark, centerline marks, area hatch and block.

ANSI: American National Standards Institute.

Area Hatch: Apply a crosshatch pattern or solid fill to a model face, to a closed sketch profile, or to a region bounded by a combination of model edges and sketch entities. Area hatch can be applied only in drawings.

ASME: American Society of Mechanical Engineering, publisher of ASME Y14 Engineering Drawing and Documentation Practices that controls drawing, dimensioning and tolerancing.

Assembly: An assembly is a document in which parts, features and other assemblies (sub-assemblies) are put together. A part in an assembly is called a component. Adding a component to an assembly creates a link between the assembly and the component. When SOLIDWORKS opens the assembly, it finds the component file to show it in the assembly. Changes in the component are automatically reflected in the assembly. The filename extension for a SOLIDWORKS assembly file name is *.sldasm.

Attachment Point: An attachment point is the end of a leader that attaches to an edge, vertex, or face in a drawing sheet.

AutoDimension: The Autodimension tool provides the ability to insert reference dimensions into drawing views such as baseline, chain, and ordinate dimensions.

Auxiliary View: An Auxiliary View is similar to a Projected View, but it is unfolded normal to a reference edge in an existing view.

AWS: American Welding Society, publisher of AWS A2.4, Standard Location of Elements of a Welding Symbol.

Axonometric Projection: A type of parallel projection, more specifically a type of orthographic projection, used to create a pictorial drawing of an object, where the object is rotated along one or more of its axes relative to the plane of projection.

Balloon: A balloon labels the parts in the assembly and relates them to item numbers on the bill of materials (BOM) added in the drawing. The balloon item number corresponds to the order in the Feature Tree. The order controls the initial BOM Item Number.

Baseline Dimensions: Dimensions referenced from the same edge or vertex in a drawing view.

Bill of Materials: A table inserted into a drawing to keep a record of the parts and materials used in an assembly.

Block: A symbol in the drawing that combines geometry into a single entity.

BOM: Abbreviation for Bill of Materials.

Broken-out Section: A broken-out section exposes inner details of a drawing view by removing material from a closed profile. In an assembly, the Broken-out Section displays multiple components.

CAD: The use of computer technology for the design of objects, real or virtual. CAD often involves more than just shapes.

Cartesian Coordinate System: Specifies each point uniquely in a plane by a pair of numerical coordinates, which are the signed distances from the point to two fixed perpendicular directed lines, measured in the same unit of length. Each reference line is called a coordinate axis or just axis of the system, and the point where they meet is its origin.

Cell: Area to enter a value in an EXCEL spreadsheet, identified by a Row and Column.

Center Mark: A cross that marks the center of a circle or arc.

Centerline: An axis of symmetry in a sketch or drawing displayed in a phantom font.

CommandManager: The CommandManager is a Context-sensitive toolbar that dynamically updates based on the toolbar you want to access. By default, it has toolbars embedded in it based on the document type. When you click a tab below the Command Manager, it updates to display that toolbar. For example, if you click the Sketch tab, the Sketch toolbar is displayed.

Component: A part or sub-assembly within an assembly.

ConfigurationManager: The ConfigurationManager is located on the left side of the SOLIDWORKS window and provides the means to create, select and view multiple configurations of parts and assemblies in an active document. You can split the

ConfigurationManager and either display two ConfigurationManager instances, or combine the ConfigurationManager with the FeatureManager design tree, PropertyManager or third party applications that use the panel.

Configurations: Variations of a part or assembly that control dimensions, display and state of a model.

Coordinate System: SOLIDWORKS uses a coordinate system with origins. A part document contains an original origin. Whenever you select a plane or face and open a sketch, an origin is created in alignment with the plane or face. An origin can be used as an anchor for the sketch entities, and it helps orient perspective of the axes. A three-dimensional reference triad orients you to the X, Y, and Z directions in part and assembly documents.

Copy and Paste: Utilize copy/paste to copy views from one sheet to another sheet in a drawing or between different drawings.

Cosmetic Thread: An annotation that represents threads.

Crosshatch: A pattern (or fill) applied to drawing views such as section views and broken-out sections.

Cursor Feedback: The system feedback symbol indicates what you are selecting or what the system is expecting you to select. As you move the mouse pointer across your model, system feedback is provided.

Datum Feature: An annotation that represents the primary, secondary and other reference planes of a model utilized in manufacturing.

Depth: The horizontal (front to back) distance between two features in frontal planes. Depth is often identified in the shop as the thickness of a part or feature.

Design Table: An Excel spreadsheet that is used to create multiple configurations in a part or assembly document.

Detail View: A portion of a larger view, usually at a larger scale than the original view. Create a detail view in a drawing to display a portion of a view, usually at an enlarged scale. This detail may be of an orthographic view, a non-planar (isometric) view, a section view, a crop view, an exploded assembly view or another detail view.

Detailing: Detailing refers to the SOLIDWORKS module used to insert, add and modify dimensions and notes in an engineering drawing.

Dimension Line: A line that references dimension text to extension lines indicating the feature being measured.

Dimension Tolerance: Controls the dimension tolerance values and the display of non-integer dimensions. The tolerance types are *None, Basic, Bilateral, Limit, Symmetric, MIN, MAX, Fit, Fit with tolerance* or *Fit (tolerance only)*.

Dimension: A value indicating the size of the 2D sketch entity or 3D feature. Dimensions in a SOLIDWORKS drawing are associated with the model, and changes in the model are reflected in the drawing, if you DO NOT USE DimXpert.

Dimensioning Standard - Metric: - ASME standards for the use of metric dimensioning required all the dimensions to be expressed in millimeters (mm). The (mm) is not needed on each dimension, but it is used when a dimension is used in a notation. No trailing zeroes are used. The Metric or International System of Units (S.I.) unit system in drafting is also known as the Millimeter, Gram Second (MMGS) unit system.

Dimensioning Standard - U.S: - ASME standard for U.S. dimensioning use the decimal inch value. When the decimal inch system is used, a zero is not used to the left of the decimal point for values less than one inch, and trailing zeroes are used. The U.S. unit system is also known as the Inch, Pound, Second (IPS) unit system.

DimXpert for Parts: A set of tools that applies dimensions and tolerances to parts according to the requirements of the ASME Y.14.41-2009 standard.

DimXpertManager: The DimXpertManager lists the tolerance features defined by DimXpert for a part. It also displays DimXpert tools that you use to insert dimensions and tolerances into a part. You can import these dimensions and tolerances into drawings. DimXpert is not associative.

Document: In SOLIDWORKS, each part, assembly, and drawing is referred to as a document, and each document is displayed in a separate window.

Drawing Sheet: A page in a drawing document.

Drawing Template: A document that is the foundation of a new drawing. The drawing template contains document properties and user-defined parameters such as sheet format. The extension for the drawing template filename is .DRWDOT.

Drawing: A 2D representation of a 3D part or assembly. The extension for a SOLIDWORKS drawing file name is .SLDDRW. Drawing refers to the SOLIDWORKS module used to insert, add, and modify views in an engineering drawing.

Edit Sheet Format: The drawing sheet contains two modes. Utilize the Edit Sheet Format command to add or modify notes and Title block information. Edit in the Edit Sheet Format mode.

Edit Sheet: The drawing sheet contains two modes. Utilize the Edit Sheet command to insert views and dimensions.

eDrawing: A compressed document that does not require the referenced part or assembly. eDrawings are animated to display multiple views in a drawing.

Empty View: An Empty View creates a blank view not tied to a part or assembly document.

Engineering Graphics: Translates ideas from design layouts, specifications, rough sketches, and calculations of engineers & architects into working drawings, maps, plans and illustrations which are used in making products.

Equation: Creates a mathematical relation between sketch dimensions, using dimension names as variables, or between feature parameters, such as the depth of an extruded feature or the instance count in a pattern.

Exploded view: A configuration in an assembly that displays its components separated from one another.

Export: The process to save a SOLIDWORKS document in another format for use in other CAD/CAM, rapid prototyping, web or graphics software applications.

Extension Line: The line extending from the profile line indicating the point from which a dimension is measured.

Extruded Cut Feature: Projects a sketch perpendicular to a Sketch plane to remove material from a part.

Face: A selectable area (planar or otherwise) of a model or surface with boundaries that help define the shape of the model or surface. For example, a rectangular solid has six faces.

Family Cell: A named empty cell in a Design Table that indicates the start of the evaluated parameters and configuration names. Locate Comments in a Design Table to the left or above the Family Cell.

Fasteners: Includes Bolts and nuts (threaded), Set screws (threaded), Washers, Keys, and Pins to name a few. Fasteners are not a permanent means of assembly such as welding or adhesives.

Feature: Features are geometry building blocks. Features add or remove material. Features are created from 2D or 3D sketched profiles or from edges and faces of existing geometry.

FeatureManager: The FeatureManager design tree located on the left side of the SOLIDWORKS window provides an outline view of the active part, assembly, or drawing. This makes it easy to see how the model or assembly was constructed or to examine the various sheets and views in a drawing. The FeatureManager and the Graphics window are dynamically linked. You can select features, sketches, drawing views and construction geometry in either pane.

First Angle Projection: In First Angle Projection the Top view is looking at the bottom of the part. First Angle Projection is used in Europe and most of the world. However, America and Australia use a method known as Third Angle Projection.

Fully defined: A sketch where all lines and curves in the sketch, and their positions, are described by dimensions or relations, or both, and cannot be moved. Fully defined sketch entities are shown in black.

Foreshortened radius: Helpful when the centerpoint of a radius is outside of the drawing or interferes with another drawing view: Broken Leader.

Foreshortening: The way things appear to get smaller in both height and depth as they recede into the distance.

French curve: A template made out of plastic, metal or wood composed of many different curves. It is used in manual drafting to draw smooth curves of varying radii.

Fully Defined: A sketch where all lines and curves in the sketch, and their positions, are described by dimensions or relations, or both, and cannot be moved. Fully defined sketch entities are displayed in black.

Geometric Tolerance: A set of standard symbols that specify the geometric characteristics and dimensional requirements of a feature.

Glass Box method: A traditional method of placing an object in an *imaginary glass box* to view the six principal views.

Global Coordinate System: Directional input refers by default to the Global coordinate system (X-, Y- and Z-), which is based on Plane1 with its origin located at the origin of the part or assembly.

Graphics Window: The area in the SOLIDWORKS window where the part, assembly, or drawing is displayed.

Grid: A system of fixed horizontal and vertical divisions.

Handle: An arrow, square or circle that you drag to adjust the size or position of an entity such as a view or dimension.

Heads-up View Toolbar: A transparent toolbar located at the top of the Graphic window.

Height: The vertical distance between two or more lines or surfaces (features) which are in horizontal planes.

Hidden Lines Removed (HLR): A view mode. All edges of the model that are not visible from the current view angle are removed from the display.

Hidden Lines Visible (HLV): A view mode. All edges of the model that are not visible from the current view angle are shown gray or dashed.

Hole Callouts: Hole callouts are available in drawings. If you modify a hole dimension in the model, the callout updates automatically in the drawing if you did not use DimXpert.

Hole Table: A table in a drawing document that displays the positions of selected holes from a specified origin datum. The tool labels each hole with a tag. The tag corresponds to a row in the table.

Import: The ability to open files from other software applications into a SOLIDWORKS document. The A-size sheet format was created as an AutoCAD file and imported into SOLIDWORKS.

Isometric Projection: A form of graphical projection, more specifically, a form of axonometric projection. It is a method of visually representing three-dimensional objects in two dimensions, in which the three coordinate axes appear equally foreshortened and the angles between any two of them are 120º.

Layers: Simplifies a drawing by combining dimensions, annotations, geometry and components. Properties such as display, line style and thickness are assigned to a named layer.

Leader: A solid line created from an annotation to the referenced feature.

Line Format: A series of tools that controls Line Thickness, Line Style, Color, Layer and other properties.

Local (Reference) Coordinate System: Coordinate system other than the Global coordinate system. You can specify restraints and loads in any desired direction.

Lock Sheet Focus: Adds sketch entities and annotations to the selected sheet. Double-click the sheet to activate Lock Sheet Focus. To unlock a sheet, right-click and select Unlock Sheet Focus or double click inside the sheet boundary.

Lock View Position: Secures the view at its current position in the sheet. Right-click in the drawing view to Lock View Position. To unlock a view position, right-click and select Unlock View Position.

Mass Properties: The physical properties of a model based upon geometry and material.

Menus: Menus provide access to the commands that the SOLIDWORKS software offers. Menus are Context-sensitive and can be customized through a dialog box.

Model Item: Provides the ability to insert dimensions, annotations, and reference geometry from a model document (part or assembly) into a drawing.

Model View: A specific view of a part or assembly. Standard named views are listed in the view orientation dialog box such as isometric or front. Named views can be user-defined names for a specific view.

Model: 3D solid geometry in a part or assembly document. If a part or assembly document contains multiple configurations, each configuration is a separate model.

Motion Studies: Graphical simulations of motion and visual properties with assembly models. Analogous to a configuration, they do not actually change the original assembly model or its properties. They display the model as it changes based on simulation elements you add.

Mouse Buttons: The left, middle, and right mouse buttons have distinct meanings in SOLIDWORKS. Use the middle mouse button to rotate and Zoom in/out on the part or assembly document.

Oblique Projection: A simple type of graphical projection used for producing pictorial, two-dimensional images of three-dimensional objects.

OLE (Object Linking and Embedding): A Windows file format. A company logo or EXCEL spreadsheet placed inside a SOLIDWORKS document are examples of OLE files.

Ordinate Dimensions: Chain of dimensions referenced from a zero ordinate in a drawing or sketch.

Origin: The model origin is displayed in blue and represents the (0,0,0) coordinate of the model. When a sketch is active, a sketch origin is displayed in red and represents the (0,0,0) coordinate of the sketch. Dimensions and relations can be added to the model origin but not to a sketch origin.

Orthographic Projection: A means of representing a three-dimensional object in two dimensions. It is a form of parallel projection, where the view direction is orthogonal to the projection plane, resulting in every plane of the scene appearing in affine transformation on the viewing surface.

Parametric Note: A Note annotation that links text to a feature dimension or property value.

Parent View: A Parent view is an existing view on which other views are dependent.

Part Dimension: Used in creating a part, they are sometimes called construction dimensions.

Part: A 3D object that consist of one or more features. A part inserted into an assembly is called a component. Insert part views, feature dimensions and annotations into 2D drawing. The extension for a SOLIDWORKS part filename is .SLDPRT.

Perspective Projection: The two most characteristic features of perspective are that objects are drawn smaller as their distance from the observer increases, and foreshortened: the size of an object's dimensions along the line of sight are relatively shorter than dimensions across the line of sight.

Plane: To create a sketch, choose a plane. Planes are flat and infinite. Planes are represented on the screen with visible edges.

Precedence of Line Types: When obtaining orthographic views, it is common for one type of line to overlap another type. When this occurs, drawing conventions have established an order of precedence.

Precision: Controls the number of decimal places displayed in a dimension.

Projected View: Projected views are created for Orthogonal views using one of the following tools: Standard 3 View, Model View or the Projected View tool from the View Layout toolbar.

Properties: Variables shared between documents through linked notes.

PropertyManager: Most sketch, feature, and drawing tools in SOLIDWORKS open a PropertyManager located on the left side of the SOLIDWORKS window. The PropertyManager displays the properties of the entity or feature so you specify the properties without a dialog box covering the Graphics window.

RealView: Provides a simplified way to display models in a photo-realistic setting using a library of appearances and scenes. RealView requires graphics card support and is memory intensive.

Rebuild: A tool that updates (or regenerates) the document with any changes made since the last time the model was rebuilt. Rebuild is typically used after changing a model dimension.

Reference Dimension: Dimensions added to a drawing document are called Reference dimensions and are driven; you cannot edit the value of reference dimensions to modify the model. However, the values of reference dimensions change when the model dimensions change.

Relation: A relation is a geometric constraint between sketch entities or between a sketch entity and a plane, axis, edge or vertex.

Relative view: The Relative View defines an Orthographic view based on two orthogonal faces or places in the model.

Revision Table: The Revision Table lists the Engineering Change Orders (ECO), in a table form, issued over the life of the model and the drawing. The current Revision letter or number is placed in the Title block of the Drawing.

Right-Hand Rule: Is a common mnemonic for understanding notation conventions for vectors in 3 dimensions.

Rollback: Suppresses all items below the rollback bar.

Scale: A relative term meaning "size" in relationship to some system of measurement.

Section Line: A line or centerline sketched in a drawing view to create a section view.

Section Scope: Specifies the components to be left uncut when you create an assembly drawing section view.

Section View: You create a section view in a drawing by cutting the parent view with a cutting, or section line. The section view can be a straight cut section or an offset section defined by a stepped section line. The section line can also include concentric arcs. Create a Section View in a drawing by cutting the Parent view with a section line.

Sheet Format: A document that contains the following: page size and orientation, standard text, borders, logos, and Title block information. Customize the Sheet format to save time. The extension for the Sheet format filename is .SLDDRT.

Sheet Properties: Sheet Properties display properties of the selected sheet. Sheet Properties define the following: Name of the Sheet, Sheet Scale, Type of Projection (First angle or Third angle), Sheet Format, Sheet Size, View label, and Datum label.

Sheet: A page in a drawing document.

Silhouette Edge: A curve representing the extent of a cylindrical or curved face when viewed from the side.

Sketch: The name to describe a 2D profile is called a sketch. 2D sketches are created on flat faces and planes within the model. Typical geometry types are lines, arcs, corner rectangles, circles, polygons, and ellipses.

Spline: A sketched 2D or 3D curve defined by a set of control points.

Stacked Balloon: A group of balloons with only one leader. The balloons can be stacked vertically (up or down) or horizontally (left or right).

Standard views: The three orthographic projection views, Front, Top and Right positioned on the drawing according to First angle or Third angle projection.

Suppress: Removes an entity from the display and from any calculations in which it is involved. You can suppress features, assembly components, and so on. Suppressing an entity does not delete the entity; you can unsuppress the entity to restore it.

Surface Finish: An annotation that represents the texture of a part.

System Feedback: Feedback is provided by a symbol attached to the cursor arrow indicating your selection. As the cursor floats across the model, feedback is provided in the form of symbols riding next to the cursor.

System Options: System Options are stored in the registry of the computer. System Options are not part of the document. Changes to the System Options affect all current and future documents. There are hundreds of Systems Options.

Tangent Edge: The transition edge between rounded or filleted faces in hidden lines visible or hidden lines removed modes in drawings.

Task Pane: The Task Pane is displayed when you open the SOLIDWORKS software. It contains the following tabs: SOLIDWORKS Resources, Design Library, File Explorer, Search, View Palette, Document Recovery and RealView/PhotoWorks.

Templates: Templates are part, drawing and assembly documents that include user-defined parameters and are the basis for new documents.

Third Angle Projection: In Third angle projection the Top View is looking at the Top of the part. First Angle Projection is used in Europe and most of the world. America and Australia use the Third Angle Projection method.

Thread Class or Fit: Classes of fit are tolerance standards; they set a plus or minus figure that is applied to the pitch diameter of bolts or nuts. The classes of fit used with almost all bolts sized in inches are specified by the ANSI/ASME Unified Screw Thread standards (which differ from the previous American National standards).

Thread Lead: The distance advanced parallel to the axis when the screw is turned one revolution. For a single thread, lead is equal to the pitch; for a double thread, lead is twice the pitch.

Tolerance: The permissible range of variation in a dimension of an object. Tolerance may be specified as a factor or percentage of the nominal value, a maximum deviation from a nominal value, an explicit range of allowed values, be specified by a note or published standard with this information, or be implied by the numeric accuracy of the nominal value.

Toolbars: The toolbar menus provide shortcuts enabling you to access the most frequently used commands. Toolbars are Context-sensitive and can be customized through a dialog box.

T-Square: A technical drawing instrument, primarily a guide for drawing horizontal lines on a drafting table. It is used to guide the triangle that draws vertical lines. Its name comes from the general shape of the instrument where the horizontal member of the T slides on the side of the drafting table. Common lengths are 18", 24", 30", 36" and 42".

Under-defined: A sketch is under defined when there are not enough dimensions and relations to prevent entities from moving or changing size.

Units: Used in the measurement of physical quantities. Decimal inch dimensioning and Millimeter dimensioning are the two types of common units specified for engineering parts and drawings.

Vertex: A point at which two or more lines or edges intersect. Vertices can be selected for sketching, dimensioning, and many other operations.

View Palette: Use the View Palette, located in the Task Pane, to insert drawing views. It contains images of standard views, annotation views, section views, and flat patterns (sheet metal parts) of the selected model. You can drag views onto the drawing sheet to create a drawing view.

Weld Bead: An assembly feature that represents a weld between multiple parts.

Weld Finish: A weld symbol representing the parameters you specify.

Weld Symbol: An annotation in the part or drawing that represents the parameters of the weld.

Width: The horizontal distance between surfaces in profile planes. In the machine shop, the terms length and width are used interchangeably.

Zebra Stripes: Simulate the reflection of long strips of light on a very shiny surface. They allow you to see small changes in a surface that may be hard to see with a standard display.

INDEX